THE BOYS ON THE TRACKS

THE BOYS ON THE TRACKS

DEATH, DENIAL, AND A MOTHER'S CRUSADE TO BRING HER SON'S KILLERS TO JUSTICE

MARA LEVERITT

ST. MARTIN'S PRESS
NEW YORK

FOR LSB

THOMAS DUNNE BOOKS.
An imprint of St. Martin's Press.

THE BOYS ON THE TRACKS: DEATH, DENIAL, AND A MOTHER'S CRUSADE TO BRING HER SON'S KILLERS TO JUSTICE.

BOOK DESIGN BY JENNIFER ANN DADDIO
MAP COURTESY OF LORRI DAVIS

Library of Congress Cataloging-in-Publication Data

Leveritt, Mara.
The boys on the tracks : death, denial, and a mother's crusade to bring her son's killers to justice /
Mara Leveritt. — 1st ed.
p. cm.
ISBN 0-312-19841-8
1. Murder—Arkansas—Saline County—Investigation Case studies. 2. Political corruption—Arkansas—Saline County Case studies. 3. Drug traffic—Arkansas—Saline County Case studies. 4. Ives, Linda. 5. Ives, Larry Kevin. 6. Henry, Don George. 7. Political corruption—United States—History—20th century. 8. Clinton, Bill, 1946– —Friends and associates. I. Title.
HV6533.A8 L48 1999
364.15'23'0976772—dc21 99-21877
CIP

First Edition: November 1999

1 3 5 7 9

CONTENTS

ACKNOWLEDGMENTS

I thank Linda Bessette first of all. Her love, encouragement, and countless readings were crucial to this book.

I also thank, in particular, Helen Bennett, Ph.D., for editing the book; Celeste Phillips for scrutinizing it; my agent, Sandra Dijkstra, for her early faith in it; and Thomas Dunne of St. Martin's Press, for bringing it into being. I thank U.S. Rep. Vic Snyder of Arkansas for his help in eliciting some information from an unwilling FBI. I thank all the reporters who have worked to uncover elements of this story—many of whom are quoted here—and the papers that have published them.

I am more grateful than I can express to my family: my mother, my brothers, and my children—and their spouses and children. Their love has been a constant support. So has been that of many friends, particularly, Catherine Nesbit, Lorri Davis, and Jane Mendel.

Every reporter owes a debt to those who take time to talk. I thank all who granted me an interview—or, in some cases, many interviews—or who provided me with records. Chief among these are Curtis and Marvelle Henry, whose lives were upended by this tragedy; Jean Duffey and her brothers, Mark and David Keesee, whose commitment to justice is matched by their faith in an informed public; and Larry Ives, whose quiet support of his family has anchored these events. Most of all I thank Linda Ives, who gave me her time, her records, and her trust—and who keeps this story alive.

AUTHOR'S NOTE

Unlike in fictional mysteries, there will be no tidy wrap-up here. This book does not purport to answer the deepest questions that arise in it. Rather, it offers what is known about a strange period in Arkansas's—and in this nation's—history in the hope that readers will not accept official silence as the end. There is still information to be released. There is official conduct to be examined.

What happened here could happen to anyone. A middle-class woman finds her life upended by a bizarre form of violence. In her attempts to understand the crime, she trusts first in local authorities, then in state and, finally, in federal officials. Inevitably, their investigations lead nowhere. The conclusions offered only obscure her tragedy. The more she presses for answers, the more she finds herself blocked.

Refusing to go home and be quiet, she finds herself drawn into a web of mysteries on the edge of a dark and complex world: a world of big money and petty criminals, of drug smugglers and a crooked prosecutor, of the White House and the CIA. The deeper she walks into this world of crime and shunned explanations, the more hostility she encounters.

Some elements of this story have been reported in the mainstream press. Other parts have been co-opted and used as propaganda. Many accounts have been exaggerated. This book is an attempt to relate the story, as experienced by the woman at its center, based on the direct experience of those involved and extensive documentation. The book's purpose is no greater than its subject's: to report what happened and how officials reacted, and to keep the story alive.

The stakes are high. The explanations this mother is seeking are owed, not just to her, but to the nation as a whole. It is the writer's hope that, by joining in the demand for answers, readers may help bring about the conclusion this story has too long deserved.

THE BOYS ON THE TRACKS

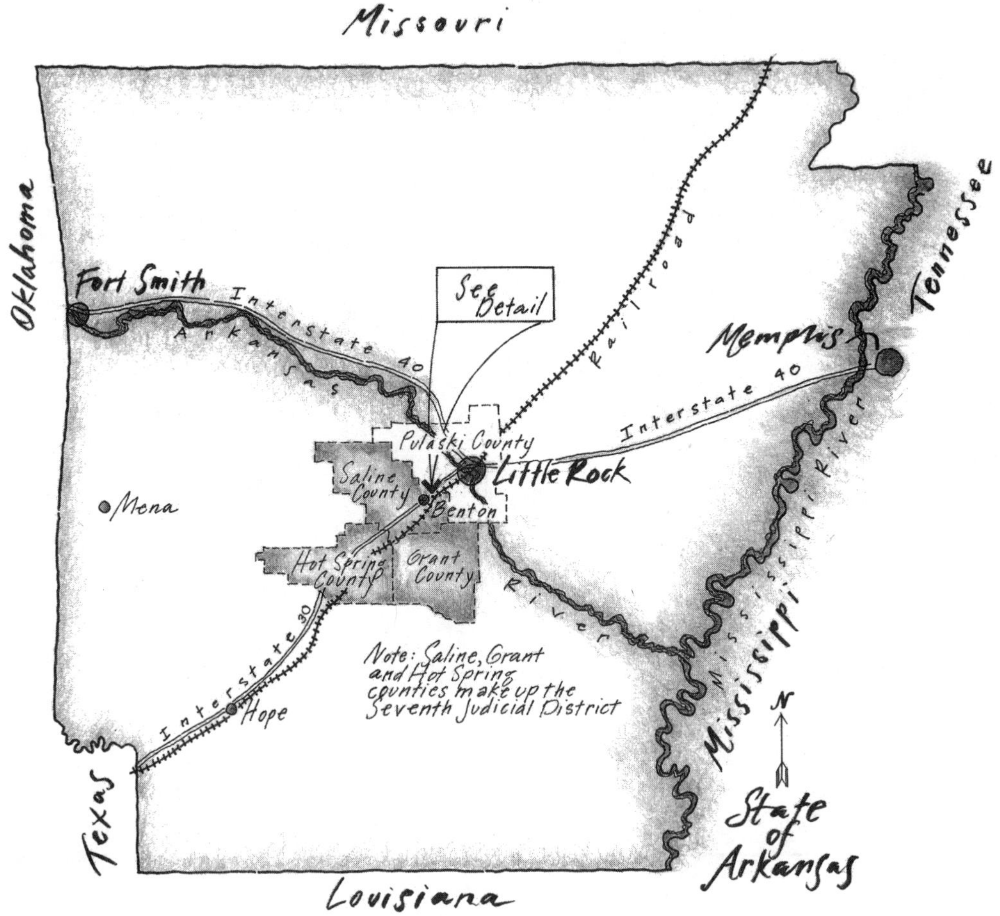

Missouri
Oklahoma
Fort Smith
Interstate 40
Arkansas
See Detail
Railroad
Memphis
Tennessee
Interstate 40
Pulaski County
Little Rock
Saline County
Benton
Mena
Hot Spring County
Grant County
River
Mississippi River
Interstate 30
Note: Saline, Grant and Hot Spring counties make up the Seventh Judicial District
Hope
Mississippi
N
Texas
State of Arkansas
Louisiana

To Benton
Interstate 30
Pulaski County
Saline County
Creek
Bryant
Site where bodies were found
Shobe Road
Alexander Human Development Center
Railroad
Crooked
N
Detail of Saline County
0
1/2
1
1 1/2
2
scale of miles

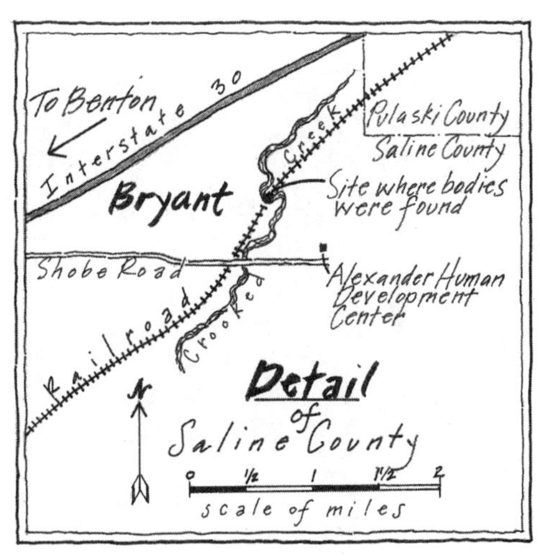

ONE

THE TRACKS

AUGUST 23, 1987

By all accounts, the engineer did a masterful job of bringing his train to a stop. It had taken a screaming, screeching half mile. By the time the engine shuddered to a standstill, Conductor Jerry Tomlin was on the radio notifying an approaching train on a parallel track to stop because some boys had been run over. He also called the dispatcher. "Have you got injuries?" the dispatcher asked. "No," Tomlin said. "We've got death. I'm sure we've got death. They passed under us. It has to be death."[1]

THE BODIES

The three men in the Union Pacific locomotive, all railroad veterans, were holding themselves together, trying to cope with a sudden nightmare at the end of a routine run. It was a little after 4:00 A.M. on Sunday morning, August 23, 1987. They were coming north from Texarkana, pulling a rattling mile of freight and empty cars. The trip toward Little Rock was uneventful, the weather mild, the temperature about eighty degrees. Later, each would remember the night as having been particularly dark.

For miles they'd felt the landscape rise beneath them as the engines hauled the train up from south Arkansas's tree-farm flatness into the rolling countryside surrounding the capital. At the slumbering town of Alexander, about twenty-five miles south of Little Rock, the train topped a moderate hill known locally as Bryant Hill, then descended quickly into bottomland, a low-lying stretch of topography prone to flooding in heavy rains. But high water was no problem tonight. All that Engineer Stephen Shroyer had to worry about on his descent from Bryant Hill was keeping his train in check and making sure it stayed within the federal speed limit of fifty-five miles per hour.

He was still braking the train hard as it approached the Shobe Road crossing. Shroyer sounded his horn as required. There was not a car, not a person, in his sight.

From his place in the lead engine's right-hand seat, Shroyer concentrated on controlling his speed. Beside him on the left, Danny DeLamar, the brakeman, helped. Behind DeLamar, Conductor Jerry Tomlin completed paperwork for the trip. By now their train had traveled about a half mile past the crossing at Shobe Road. They were approaching a small trestle over a trickle called Crooked Creek. It was not even a trickle on this dry August night.

"Our headlight was on the 'bright' position," DeLamar later recalled, "and I noticed down the rail in front of me, some ten or fifteen cars away, there was a dark spot on the rail. I looked hard at it, and towards the last, I stood up to see what it was." Shroyer also stood up. So did Conductor Tomlin.

The men knew from experience that when a bush or other debris is picked up by the light, the spot on the rail will often appear dark. Any obstruction is a concern. The men peered intently ahead. In the same, heart-stopping instant, they realized what they were seeing.

"When we were approximately one hundred feet away from this dark spot, Engineer Shroyer yelled out, 'Oh, my God!' He hit the whistle and the emergency brakes at the same time," DeLamar recalled. "We could tell there were two young men lying between the rails just north of the bridge, and we also saw there was a gun beyond the boy who was lying to the north. There was something covering these boys from their waist to just below their knees, and I'm not sure what this object was. They were both in between the rails, heads up against the west rail, and their feet were over the east rail. Both were right beside each other and their arms and hands were to their sides, heads facing straight up. I never noticed any movement at all."[2]

At fifty-five miles per hour the crew had fewer than five seconds to respond. Reflexively Shroyer shoved the brake forward to its emergency position. The move is a desperate one, producing such sudden jerking and slacking that the engineer risks losing control. Steel wheels scream on steel tracks. If the braking continues long enough, the wheels will be ground flat on the bottom. For at least four seconds the train resisted Shroyer's efforts, banging and screeching, wailing its violent approach to the motionless figures ahead. The brakes exhaled a gasping whoosh of air. The cars vibrated. The tracks vibrated. The horn never went silent. And still, to the crewmen's mounting horror, the boys did not jerk, did not open an eye, did not move a muscle.

Tomlin dropped his paperwork and lurched forward between Shroyer and DeLamar to get a better look. "When we recognized that it was two people," he recalled, "I hollered, 'Big hole!' which means for the engineer to set the brake in emergency. I saw two boys lying side by side, like soldiers at attention.

There was a dark-headed boy to the south—that was the one we were going to hit first—and the second boy had lighter hair. They were covered up to around the waistline with a pale green tarp, something like a boat cover. They looked like they had laid down there and pulled this cover up on them like a blanket, but part of it was off. I noticed they never moved. Here we were, bearing down on them, and there was no movement of their heads. They made no attempt to rise.

"And there was that rifle. It was lying flat on the ground, the barrel part near the boy's head, the stock under the cover."

That was all there was to see. Then the sight was gone, vanished beneath the train. "We could hear them hit," Tomlin continued. "You can hear it even when you hit a dog. It's mostly a thud and then you hear some rocks flying because, if what you hit is still under the train, you're scooting it along."[3]

With his hands on the controls, Shroyer felt the impact like a body blow, one from which he'd never quite recover. "I was standing and continued to blow the horn until we had impact," Shroyer recalled. "There were the two boys and then the weapon, all very one-two-three. And there was a piece of green material, very light, very faded. It looked well worn, laying out on the boys, and it looked like it had been blown back, partly exposing them. The first boy had on a shirt, blue in color. The second boy did not have a shirt on. From my observation, they were both in a totally relaxed position. There was never any movement. There was no flinching, even with the whistle, and the train bearing down on them. Their feet were on my side of the engine, extending across the rail, and I remember noticing their feet were in a totally relaxed position. That's the thing that caught my thoughts, was how completely relaxed they were. And the thing that caused me so much problem afterward was the fact that they didn't flinch, didn't jerk, didn't move at all—either one of them—with all of it happening, all that noise, all of it coming down on them."

Shroyer's attention was riveted on the boys. "I never took my eyes off them," he said. "What had caught my attention at first was a big brilliant flash. Apparently that was my headlight striking the barrel of the gun. The next thing I was totally aware of was the chest and the head of that second boy, the one without the shirt. And from then on, I never took my thoughts off of him. What I focused on were his chest and his head—and how relaxed he looked. To me he looked as relaxed as a boy sunbathing on a beach."

The image of two boys appearing so calm as death was about to roll over them was almost more than the men could absorb. Yet the one thing more certain than the boys' immobility was the impossibility of stopping the train. Shroyer recognized the onrushing inevitability in a nauseating wave of despair.

"Your immediate thought is, My God, please get out of the way! And you can't stop," he said. "You can't stop a train that fast, and it's a hopeless feeling."

Shroyer was enough of a veteran to realize that he, like his train, was verging out of control. "When we hit them, they rolled with us," he said. "They stayed with the engines for a while. My immediate reaction was that I was traumatized. My thoughts, and everything else, you know—my God, you know—I was holding on. I was thinking, Please, this is not really happening.

"I allowed my engines to lock up and felt my train operation just going to hell. When that happened, I immediately realized I had to get back to the business at hand. I had to get my train under control again. And I did. But when it happened, there was nothing we could do. I just know that, without a doubt, if willpower could have had anything to do with it, that train would have stopped. We would not have run over those boys."

When a train hits an object on the tracks, one of two things usually happens. Either the scoop on the front of the engine, commonly called the cowcatcher, will toss the object violently aside, or the object will be sucked up under the engines, tumbled a while, and tossed out. By the time it's ejected, the struck object has picked up the speed of the train.

As their train slowed to a stop, the crew could imagine the destruction their locomotives had wrought on the human flesh beneath them. The boys' legs, which had been draped across the rail, would have been severed immediately, sliced off by the first right wheel, somewhere between the knees and the ankles. Because the heads and torsos were between the rails, the train had most likely cleared them, resulting in the bodies being rolled, which fit with what the men had heard—and felt. After that, pieces of bodies would have been spit out from beneath the engines, probably in all directions.

Once the train had stopped, the crewmen wasted no time. Shroyer would stay with the radio to keep in touch with railroad officials. Tomlin and DeLamar would walk back to confront the mayhem. "If you start to get sick, go right ahead," Tomlin told DeLamar as the two picked up their flashlights and climbed out of the engine.

About thirty-five cars back they located the first pieces of body, a trio of dismembered toes. Over the course of the next hour or so, they found evidence of the carnage scattered along a quarter mile of track. The single biggest body part they found was the chest and head of the second boy, the one without a shirt. The body of the first boy was considerably more chopped up.

In those eerie first few minutes before the police arrived, while the crewmen struggled to control their emotions, a disturbing half thought lurked at the edge of their minds. It was a barely formed thought, one almost too troublesome to admit. But here it was: the boys had not moved or flinched. And now, though neither man spoke of it, they noticed something else. The scene was a bloody mess, but there was something wrong with the blood.

Like many Arkansans, Tomlin had hunted since childhood. He'd seen many a fresh-killed deer, field-dressed dozens of them. He knew how animals bleed, especially when they've just been killed; he knew how fresh blood flows.

But this blood wasn't like that. As a matter of fact, "There was very little blood," Tomlin later recalled. "Even with all those wounds, with everything cut up. We had reached the bodies within ten minutes after impact. You would think that if the heart had been pumping when we ran over the boys, then the blood would have naturally flowed out. But it wasn't flowing. There was hardly any blood spilled at all. And the color of it bothered me, too. It was night, and we couldn't tell for sure, but the blood we saw was not red—not as red as you would think blood would be on a fresh kill like that. It was dark, more of a purplish color."

For Tomlin, the blood suggested something odd. "Out there that night," he said, "I kind of smelled a rat."[4]

IMMEDIATE DENIAL

The site in Saline County where the train had stopped and where police and railroad officials converged lies at the geographical center of Arkansas. Benton, the county seat, was named after Thomas Hart Benton, a Missouri politician, newspaper editor, and lawyer who had had extensive dealings in Arkansas during the nineteenth century and who was the grand uncle of the painter who later bore his name. During World War II and through most of the years that followed, the county made most of its income from the strip-mining of bauxite or aluminum ore. In 1987 the county was still mostly rural, though for several years the population on its northern edge had been growing rapidly as bedroom communities sprung up, housing workers who commuted to Little Rock. Castle Grande Estates, the development that would later prove troublesome to First Lady Hillary Rodham Clinton as an offshoot of the Whitewater investigation, was but one of several subdivisions created to accommodate the population spurt brought on by families fearing crime and uncertainties about desegregation in the state's capital city.

But this burst in settlement was recent. Throughout its history Saline County's most important feature had been its positioning in the center of the state, on the south edge of Little Rock, and smack on the Southwest Trail. In the early 1800s thousands of frontier folk plodded the trail from the East, toward the snaky Red River, which they crossed into the wilds of Texas. When the railroad came, it, too, followed the Southwest Trail, grateful for the easy terrain, cutting across Arkansas diagonally, skirting the Ouachita Mountains to the west. In this century the designers of Interstate 30 also appreciated the route's advantages. For most of the 315 miles connecting Little Rock with Dallas, the highway traces the old Southwest Trail. A little farther down Interstate 30, southwest of where it passes through Saline County and thirty miles from the Arkansas-Texas border, is the famous "place called Hope," the birthplace of President Bill Clinton.

While Clinton was governor of Arkansas and for many years before, this particular route across the state had been recognized by police as important. For decades they had been aware that some of their biggest concerns—first bootleg whiskey and later drugs—were flowing along the trail. By the mid-1980s cocaine was their biggest problem. It was taking the state by storm, having blown into the country from Central America and into Arkansas via the freeways that connected to Miami, Los Angeles, and Dallas. Police knew that tons of the drug traveled along Interstate 30 and that from there it was dispersed to cities as big as Little Rock—and to communities as small as the ones that dotted Saline County.

What police were only beginning to suspect, however, by that summer of 1987, was that all forms of transportation were suspect. Just a few months earlier police in Benton had received word from local informants that cocaine was being dropped from trains at locations along the tracks. Officers had contacted the railroad, asking train crews to watch. So far, nothing unusual had been reported.

There were also reports that airplanes might be using Saline County as a drop site, a convenient unloading area on the outskirts of Little Rock, the urban center of Arkansas. Half the state's population resides within sixty miles of the capital—an hour by car in any direction. In the past few months, Benton police had staked out the local airport, where residents had reported unusual activity—planes landing briefly without shutting off their engines, then taking off again, frequently at night and often without benefit of lights. After patrol cars had begun parking at the airport and after a few planes had aborted their approach upon spotting the cars, the unusual activity had ceased. Detectives were aware that, however it was getting in, cocaine was flowing through the county at a rate disproportionate to its population of fewer than sixty thousand.[5]

The site where the bodies lay scattered that exceptionally dark August morning was in a rural, unincorporated area under the jurisdiction of the Saline County Sheriff's Office. Deputies responded to the dispatcher's call. By 4:40 A.M., thirteen minutes after the crew reported the collision, Deputy Chuck Tallent and Lt. Ray Richmond, head of the department's criminal investigation division, arrived at the span of tracks just past the trestle alongside some woods. Tallent set to work diagramming the scene, mapping out the locations of various body parts and other pieces of evidence as they were discovered. Soon an Arkansas State Police trooper arrived, then officials from the railroad, then an ambulance.

The investigators' arrival did little to calm the crew. The train men had hoped to make their reports, then leave the matter to the authorities. Instead, as they spoke to the police they found their misgivings heightened.

The crew did not realize it at first—no one did—but hope for an accurate reconstruction of the scene ended within minutes of the deputies' arrival. In diagramming the site, Tallent made an immediate and crucial mistake. He chose as his reference point the corner of one of the train cars and mapped everything in relation to that. Hours later, when the train was allowed to move forward after most of the evidence had been bagged and removed, that reference point was lost forever. The diagram of where each piece of evidence was found became instantly worthless. It was a costly mistake, one that, when it came to light several months later, undercut public confidence in the deputies' investigation and exposed the sheriff's office to ridicule. So did the decision, made soon after the deaths, to let the train that had been waiting pass, further disturbing the scene.

To the even greater astonishment of the crew, Tallent and Richmond appeared to be treating the deaths as an accident despite the railroad men's urgent accounts of having seen the boys lying side by side, unmoving, as the train approached. The deaths did not look like an accident to the crew. As Tomlin blandly observed, "One boy not moving—maybe. But two? I have some trouble with that."

Still, the crew had to acknowledge that accidents involving trains did happen, and so did suicides. They all knew there had been at least two suicides by train in Saline County within the past eight years.[6] Such things happened. The crew let the police do their job.

But the treatment of the deaths as suicides, or an accident, was unsettling to others as well. Hours earlier, Trooper Wayne Lainhart of the Arkansas State Police had investigated a report of two shots having been fired in the area. His look-around had turned up nothing. Now, though the deputies had jurisdiction, he also responded to the scene and heard the train crew's statements. (Ordinarily, sheriffs have jurisdiction in unincorporated areas of their counties, while local police operate in the cities. State police officers like Lainhart usually patrol the highways and assist in local investigations when their help is requested by either sheriffs or local chiefs of police.)

Lainhart's assessment, as he later recalled, was that aspects of the situation didn't seem quite "kosher." Part of what bothered him was the deputies' apparent disinterest in the possibility of murder. According to Lainhart's training, any unnatural death should be investigated first as a possible homicide so that evidence can be preserved and the most serious possibilities eliminated before less serious ones are considered. The practice is standard police procedure. But not all police, especially in small, rural sheriffs' offices, receive the training offered state troopers. Lainhart let the deputies handle their investigation. Still, it disturbed him to see such a basic rule so quickly abandoned, and in such a strange case.

Lainhart mentioned his misgivings to the deputies, noting that he doubted the deaths were an accident, but he did not press the issue. Nor did the two emergency medical technicians who arrived on the scene a couple of minutes later and who immediately found causes of their own for alarm. One of those EMTs was Billy Heath, who later talked to a state police detective. "Mr. Heath stated the bodies looked more like mannequins, that there was very little blood at the scene, and that the blood at the impact site was very dark," the investigator noted. "Mr. Heath stated the blood was just too dark for him to consider normal. Mr. Heath stated he did not see any bright blood and that, in his opinion, there should have been some fresh blood at the scene."[7]

The other attendant, Shirley Raper, reached the same conclusion. "We grabbed our paramedics' equipment and took off down the tracks," she later told the state police. "Billy reached the first body, and he told me to stop and not to come any closer. I just observed the one body and it occurred to me right off that it was strange, because of the lack of blood and the color of the body parts and the color of the blood. The body parts had a pale color to them, like someone that had been dead for some time."

In an unusual move, and one they knew could be controversial, the two paramedics attached what they titled a "note of interest" to their official report on the incident, a report prepared within hours after leaving the scene. The note read, "Blood from the bodies and on the body parts we observed was a dark color in nature. Due to our training, this would indicate a lack of oxygen present in the blood and could pose a question as to how long the victims had been dead."

While the train crew, the state police trooper, and the two paramedics all expressed misgivings, Tallent and Richmond proceeded to treat the deaths as a probable accident or a double suicide. Only one officer vigorously objected. Deputy Cathy Carty surveyed the scene, listened to the train crew's account, and heard the paramedics' misgivings. She then confronted her superior officers, protesting their disregard of the possibility that the boys had been murdered. She was infuriated when Richmond ordered her and other deputies to treat the case "like a traffic fatality." Later Carty recalled, "I told the coroner, 'We either have two of the damnedest suicides I've ever seen here or we have a double homicide.' "[8] But Carty's objections were to no avail. The scene was investigated in the manner of a traffic accident, and the bodies were sent to a funeral home, since traffic accidents did not require an autopsy in Arkansas.

Within hours, however, Tallent changed his mind and redirected the bodies to the state crime lab where they would undergo autopsies.

That came as good news to the train crew. But their long night was not over. By the time the sun was rising and the investigation, such as it was, was winding down, they were to be unsettled by yet another peculiar aspect of this sickening morning. A disagreement arose over the piece of faded green tarp that Shroyer, Tomlin, and DeLamar had seen on top of the boys. For reasons that none of the crew could fathom, the police appeared reluctant, if not actively resistant, to accept their unanimous reports that such a covering had existed. The crew could not imagine why their statements on such a neutral piece of information would be met with disbelief.

Tomlin was especially unnerved by the reaction. He had walked the tracks with his flashlight, looking for that tarp, and had found it. Having apparently blown off the boys upon impact, it had landed at the base of the trestle. Shining his flashlight on the tarp, he had pointed it out to Deputy Tallent.

"He denied that later," Tomlin recalled. "He said I didn't tell him about finding the tarp, but I did. And I told him where part of it was, at the bridge bulkhead, I remember it as well as I remember him. I'm pretty observant. I catch most stuff. I remember seeing that tarp as well as I remember how Tallent was dressed that morning. He had on a navy blue or a black ball cap that said SALINE COUNTY DEPUTY. He was wearing cowboy boots and blue jeans. He had on a belt buckle that also said SALINE COUNTY SHERIFF'S OFFICE. He had a package of cigarettes rolled up in his shirtsleeves, like a sailor going on leave. And he had his pistol, an automatic, stuck in the back of his pants, like Magnum, P. I."

Inexplicably, Tomlin felt that much of what the train crew had reported was being dismissed. The reaction perplexed and angered him. "We all saw the tarp," he said. "They were definitely covered up from their waist down to their feet with it. But he told us it must have been an optical illusion. Just like the gun. When he first arrived and we told him there'd been a gun, he acted like he didn't know what we were talking about. Then when we were walking along the tracks the deputies asked me where this 'alleged gun' was. We had to take them and show them where it was. We'd already found that, too."[9]

DeLamar later testified that he remembered Tomlin having said that he had located the tarp.[10] Shroyer reported the same thing. As the engineer told an investigator, "I was standing with DeLamar and the special agent for the railroad down there in front of the engine. Lieutenant Richmond was there, and Chuck Tallent was there with his T-shirt and a stainless steel pistol stuck in the back of his pants. And I never said anything, but I remember Chuck Tallent asking Jerry Tomlin about that piece of material. And I remember Jerry telling Chuck, 'The last time I saw it was right back off the bridge abutment, right back there at the scene.' " However, no tarp was ever recovered.

A shattered .22-caliber rifle, without bullets, was collected as evidence along with a long-handled flashlight. For years the trainmen would bridle at the deputies' position that night that what they had seen was "an optical illusion." They felt the assessment contradicted their experience and insulted them as professionals.

Residents of Alexander and the slightly larger community of Bryant, unaware of the nightmare that had occurred while they slept, were preparing for early church services by the time the police, the coroner, and the train crew finally left the scene. Throughout the nearly four hours of the initial investigation, Saline County Sheriff James Steed never came to the tracks, even though by sunup dozens of people had gathered at the Shobe Road crossing, attracted by the cluster of police cars. As word of the deaths and the circumstances surrounding them spread, many in the county found Steed's absence from the scene of such a double fatality peculiar. The son of a longtime sheriff, Steed, now in his fifth two-year term, was a prominent law officer himself; the youngest sheriff ever elected in the county, he had already served as president of the Arkansas Sheriffs Association. He had built his reputation as an active, hands-on sheriff. But where was he now? As the Sunday morning wore on, the sheriff's whereabouts became one more oddity in a situation that was already shaping up as bizarre.

The cool and minimalistic police approach contrasted sharply with the out-of-control and gruesome quality of the scene, and that sense of dissonance that had left so many unsettled on Sunday returned with a vengeance the following day. On Monday, after an account of the deaths made the television news and the papers, relatives and curiosity seekers flocked to the tracks. There one of them discovered a severed foot lying in the gravel. To the train crew, still stung by the attack on their professionalism, such carelessness by the deputies seemed unconscionably unprofessional.

"I'm just an old country boy," Jerry Tomlin later complained. "I was born at night, but I wasn't born last night. And I can tell you, I didn't think too much of the investigation. The deputies' attitude was more like 'Let's get this cleaned up and get back to the coffee shop.' I don't know. People don't realize what a mess it was. Maybe they were in shock. Maybe they had weak stomachs. Maybe they just didn't want to face it. Whatever it was, I sensed all along that they were not out there looking for clues."

For Shroyer the night would leave a permanent scar. "I was rattled," the engineer later told an investigator. "There's no question, I was rattled. I was sick of everything that there was about the whole situation. But I maintained my professional stance. When my superintendent arrived, I halfheartedly apologized for being shaken. I told him I didn't understand why it was affecting me so deeply, except for the fact that it was kids. And the situation was just not right. And it disturbs me to this day. It really does. The thought of it, of what happened to those kids, why they were there, what was going on . . . I've lived with it. I've looked at it. And it does not add up."[11]

The deputies admitted to being somewhat bewildered by the events. Two days after the deaths, Chief Deputy Rick Elmendorf told the local newspaper, "We are trying to come up with any feasible reason for something like this to happen." And he added, "We haven't ruled out anything except foul play."

Shroyer's dark sense that explanations did not "add up" would afflict him and others for many years. The train crew's suspicion that something ugly and unspoken had hovered in the air in the early hours of the investigation—that their observations had been ignored and common sense assaulted—would come to be widely shared. Instead of leaving the scene confident that the grotesque discovery at the tracks would be properly investigated, the men walked away feeling insulted as well as emotionally injured. Why had no one taken seriously Tomlin's and the medics' concerns about the condition of the blood? Why had deputies been so quick to doubt the crew—referring to the weapon they had reported seeing as "the alleged gun" until it was pointed out to them? And most disturbing of all, why had police dismissed the crew's unanimous reports of the tarp, insisting instead that they must have seen "an optical illusion"? Why, the men began to wonder, were they encountering such doubt?

TWO

"SOMETHING'S WRONG"

AUGUST–SEPTEMBER 1987

The house that Sunday morning was quiet. Linda Ives was home alone, her children and husband gone. Kevin had spent the night with his high school buddy, Don. Alicia had just gone back to Fayetteville, in the northwestern corner of Arkansas, for her sophomore year in college. Larry, an engineer for Union Pacific, had left earlier in the morning on his run up through the northeastern part of the state to Poplar Bluff, Missouri. He wouldn't be back until tomorrow.

The phone rang at about 10:00 A.M.

"Hello?" Her voice sounded comfortable, accommodating, like the interior of her ranch-style house. The country motif of the kitchen where she stood was more than a decorating touch. It was a way of making the place deliberately informal, cozy. That impulse to soften edges could be heard in her voice on the phone.

It was Don's father, Curtis Henry, on the other end. "Linda," he said, "are Kevin and Don with you?"

"No, Curtis," Linda said, her voice straining. "I thought they were with you."

THE CALL

Six hours earlier, about 4:00 A.M., in a mobile home park adjoining the tracks about a mile from where the train had struck the boys, Curtis Henry had awakened, listening for his son Don. Curtis got up and checked the house. The boy was not at home.

At daylight, a little before five, Curtis shook his wife, Marvelle. "Don should be back by now," he told her. "Something's wrong."

Curtis put on his cap, a camouflage duckbill featuring the logo of Little Rock Electric Company, his employer. He'd given Don a cap just like it. Outside, Don's Firebird and Kevin's Camaro were both still parked in the driveway. Curtis had told the boys to be in by midnight and they had been, or at least they had arrived by twelve-fifteen. Close enough. But then Don had asked permission to go out again, to do a little nighttime hunting. Don had promised that he and Kevin would stay in the woods near the tracks, woods he had hunted with his father since childhood. It was beside the point that what Don was asking—to go "spotlighting"—was illegal, just as it was beside the point that deer weren't in season. Curtis accepted it as a fact of life that traditions and game laws didn't always coincide and that when they didn't, he sided with tradition. He'd given the boys permission. Now he got into his own car to go out hunting for them.

Already, with the sun barely at the horizon, the quiet Sunday morning was growing warm. As Curtis Henry pulled onto Shobe Road, near where it crossed the tracks, he passed a deputy sheriff. Curtis slowed and stuck his head out the window. "You haven't seen two teenagers running around down here, have you?" he asked. The officer seemed surprised by the question. He asked Curtis who he was looking for. Curtis grew wary. He did not know what was going on, but he decided to shut up. He thanked the officer and drove across the tracks, heading east toward Bryant Hill. Curtis was proud of Don's ability in the woods. The boy could hunt better than most adults. Curtis couldn't imagine him getting caught, couldn't imagine anyone being able to sneak up on him in the woods. And Don wasn't stupid. He knew that trains had radios, and that an engineer noticing illegal hunters could report their whereabouts to authorities. Don was too smart to get spotted. Still, it was obvious that something was up. When asked later why he hadn't searched for the boys on foot, in the area where he knew they'd been hunting, Curtis could not explain. "Maybe it just wasn't intended," was the best he had to offer.[1] Nor could he guess why the deputy, knowing that two boys had just died on the tracks, had not mentioned that.

For several hours, by his account, Curtis drove around the streets and back roads of northern Saline County looking for the boys. At 10:00 A.M., he returned home to call Linda Ives. He explained that the boys had been home by midnight and that he'd let them go back out to go hunting. On top of her worry, the news was annoying. Linda did not hunt, but her husband, Larry, did, and Larry abided by the game laws. Linda could not imagine a parent letting boys go out after midnight to do something he knew was illegal, but she said nothing and Curtis Henry filled the void with assurances. "Don't worry," he said. "They're okay. Don knows his way around those woods."

"Did they take guns?" Linda finally asked.

"Of course they took guns," Curtis said. "You don't go hunting without guns."

He hung up, saying that he was going to check with Don's older sister, Gayla, and look around some more. He told Linda he would keep her posted.

Linda paced through the too still house. So help me, God, she thought, I'm going to kill Kevin Ives when I see him. This is the last time that boy spends the night at that house. Fighting panic, she went to the clothes dryer and removed the new underwear she'd washed for Kevin. For her, it was the last of those back-to-school rituals. Kevin would be starting his senior year tomorrow. Linda folded the warm underwear to calm down. This wasn't like Kevin at all.

Kevin is too responsible to be pulling this kind of stunt, she thought. Until a month ago, he had worked as a sacker at the Bryant Safeway store so he could afford to take care of his car, a 1981 Camaro, pale blue inside and out. Just a month ago, he had left that job to work as a carpenter's helper. The change had suited him. Kevin liked the physicality of the work. He liked being outside. Linda thought of all those mornings he had gotten up so early, showering and leaving the house by five-thirty to take advantage of the morning cool. She hated to think of him working in the heat, especially as the Arkansas summer progressed, but when she'd mentioned her concern, Kevin had just laughed and told her he loved it.

He's so funny, she thought. He always looked proud leaving the house, a strapping boy of seventeen, wearing the leather tool belt his father had bought him. It wasn't that he was particularly big. Kevin only stood about five feet ten. But he had played football all his life and loved to work out with weights, so he had broad shoulders and muscular arms. Folding a T-shirt, Linda thought of her two young nieces hanging on to Kevin and begging him to show them his muscles. He'd act annoyed for as long as he could, then grin and roll up his sleeves.

What could have gotten into him? Linda fumed. He knew that she'd be worried. It wasn't like Kevin to do this—especially after what had happened last time. What had she been thinking? Kevin had known Don for only about six months. And she barely knew Don's family at all. Until last year, she and Larry had known all of Kevin's friends. Most were neighbors. In the pine-shaded development where they lived, the Iveses not only knew the other kids and their parents, they knew the other parents' rules as well. Linda liked that, but she was even more comfortable when the kids hung out at her house where she could keep an eye on them herself. There was a pool table in a room off the kitchen and a swimming pool in the backyard. There was a ski boat in the garage that the family took on weekends to Lake Ouachita, trips on which neighbors often went along. Some of the neighbors' children she knew so well they almost seemed like her own.

But kids grow. Mike, who lived three streets down, had been Kevin's best friend since the two were little. The boys had been like brothers until last year, when they had parted over a girl. Mike had liked her first, then she'd started dating Kevin. The boys' lifelong friendship had cooled. Kevin had taken up with new friends. Don Henry had become his closest.

It bothered Linda that she didn't know Don very well. Last month, when Kevin had asked if he could spend the night with him, she had objected. Pleading, he'd reminded her that he was, after all, seventeen. He'd be graduating in less than a year. He was right, of course. And she'd relented. But the weekend had been a fiasco.

Thinking about it, Linda moved to Kevin's bedroom and began rearranging his clothes, growing more agitated and self-reproachful as she did. What could she have been thinking! That experience had wound up just like this morning. That time, too, Curtis Henry had ended up calling the house, asking Linda if the boys were with her. But on that morning, Larry had not yet left for his run. Larry had canceled the trip and the couple had spent a few anxious hours until, late in the morning, Kevin had sauntered into the kitchen, surprised to find his parents upset. As though it were the most natural thing in the world, he had explained that Don and his dad had had an argument. Kevin had driven Don to a friend's house where they both had spent the night. That was all. No big deal. He couldn't understand what the fuss was about.

So his parents had angrily explained: Linda, that she had been worried to death; Larry, that he would be forfeiting some pay because of the work he'd missed. They had given Kevin a pretty hard time. He had apologized. Don had returned home to his father a few days later. The incident was forgotten.

But now this. When Kevin had called home at about nine last night to ask if he could spend the night again with Don, Linda's immediate response had been adamant and negative. He'd been calling from a pay phone on Geyer Springs Road, a strip of restaurants and stores in southwest Little Rock that was a popular cruise scene for teenagers from the city and north Saline County.

"Not on your life," Linda had told Kevin. "I don't like that idea at all."

"Mom," he'd argued, "everything's okay. Don and his dad are fine. We're just up here on Geyer messing around and talking to people."

"I just don't like this," she'd told him. "I don't want another repeat of what happened last time."

"Oh, Mom, get a grip."

"Okay," she'd relented. "But I'm going to call Don's dad. And, Kevin, this had better not be anything like last time." He had assured her that she had nothing to fear. Linda had called Curtis Henry. He'd also reassured her, telling her that he'd have the boys in by twelve-thirty, and that he'd call her if they were not. That was all barely twelve hours ago, but now all the assurances had vanished. Fear was all Linda felt. Staring around Kevin's room, she told herself to stay calm. It'll be like last time, she told herself. Kevin will come walking in any minute. She sat on his bed trying to convince herself of that, while with another part of her brain she thought of calling the police.

The phone rang again at about noon. Curtis's voice edged on hysteria. "Get over here quick," he said. "They've been shot and tied to the railroad tracks and run over by a train."

Linda struggled to comprehend the words, while experiencing an odd sense of relief. The absurdity of what she was hearing struck her as almost consoling. The fears she had been fighting back were that the boys had been hurt in a car wreck or in a hunting accident. But this? Shot and tied to the tracks? Run over by a train? Curtis had taken leave of his senses. He obviously had lost his mind. What Don's father was telling her was so bizarre, so inconceivable, that she did not think for a moment it could possibly be true. Still, however ridiculous the story, she had to acknowledge the troubling thought that the boys still had not been found.

Curtis tried to give her directions to his house. Linda found she could not write. She told him she would call back in a minute. She called her neighbor, L. A. Washam. In seconds Washam was dashing over the path between their houses. Shoving the paper with Henry's phone number into L.A.'s hand, Linda said, "Call this man and get directions to his house."

Washam's wife, Gayle, was close behind him. Linda asked Gayle to call her sister, while Linda hustled L.A. toward the car.

"Why are we going over there, Linda?" he asked.

"I have to go straighten out something about Kevin," she said.

"What's wrong with Kevin?"

"Curtis Henry said he's been shot and tied to the railroad tracks."

Gayle Washam collapsed and started to cry. Linda, dry-eyed and rigid, left in the car with L.A., reminding Gayle to call her sister. A friend seeing Linda at that moment would hardly have recognized her. Yes, there was the slightly plump figure, the casual clothes Linda preferred, the blond hair also casually styled. But gone was the buoyant cheerfulness that seemed like a physical characteristic. She was never one to wear much makeup, and her face now looked like a mask, its flesh so tightly controlled as to appear almost contorted.

They followed Curtis Henry's directions to a cluster of house trailers near the tracks. Linda did not know which house was Curtis's, but she spotted Kevin's car at the end of one driveway. Again a wave of relief surged over her.

The car meant that Kevin was back. The boys had not been killed in a wreck. Oh, thank God, she thought.

But as Washam parked the car, an officer with the Saline County Sheriff's Office walked out of the house to meet them.

"Where are Kevin and Don?" she asked.

"Why don't you come inside, Mrs. Ives," Deputy Tallent said gently.

"Curtis said they'd been shot and tied to the railroad tracks."

The officer turned and looked at her. "We don't have any indication that they were shot or tied."

The earth began to tremble.

Inside the house, Marvelle Henry, Don's stepmother, remained quietly in the background. A registered nurse at Saline County Memorial Hospital, she was fond of Don. She had found the boy easy to like. He did well in school, had never been in trouble with the law, and he couldn't get enough of her biscuits. To Marvelle, their family was like any other. Sure, Curtis and Don had their ups and downs, but in ways, they were exceptionally close. Until this summer, when Don had started hanging out with Kevin, Curtis and Don had spent most of their weekends together, hunting and fishing, either in the vast deer woods of southern Arkansas or, more often, in the woods around their home. Just this summer, Don had gone to work with Curtis. Don was thinking of becoming an electrician after he graduated from high school, so Curtis, a general superintendent at Little Rock Electric, had tried to give him a taste of the work, helping him to get hired on as a gofer. All summer long the two had gone off to work together wearing their identical caps.

Now, suddenly, Don's cap was telling them something unbearable. First there had been the phone calls from Tallent—two of them—in the late morning before Curtis had returned. Then when Curtis had arrived, he burst in with the news that a neighbor had said that two boys had been found dead. They'd been shot and tied to the tracks. When Tallent had arrived at the house, just minutes before Linda and her neighbor, Curtis had asked the officer about the rumor. Told that two boys had indeed been found run over by a train, Curtis Henry drew in a breath. "Was one of them wearing a cap like this?"

Presumably the cap also had been the deputies' first clue as to who the dead boys might be. Now Tallent turned to Linda. He asked what Kevin had been wearing. She heard the question, but it crashed over her like a wave. She listened and somehow spoke. Inside, part of her screamed. Another part curled up and lay dead.

The officer was saying that the police had not positively identified the boys, that a definite ID would have to wait for dental work from the state crime lab. Again he asked what Kevin had been wearing. Linda described the T-shirt Kevin had been wearing, his jeans, his high-top Nikes and Nike socks, the gold chain around his neck. Tallent nodded. That fit the description—that and the camouflage cap from Little Rock Electric Co.

WAITING FOR LARRY

Shock descended like an avalanche. The deputies were officious. The bodies were at the crime lab. No, she could not go there. No, there was nothing to be seen at the tracks. They told L.A. that it would be best if he took Linda home. Linda listened in a daze. She climbed into the car feeling separated from herself, detached, like an observer. She felt immunized from the calamity bearing down on her as though she were hovering safely above it. As word of what had happened spread and friends gathered at the house, she watched herself moving through them, not crying, absorbed in her role as hostess. She watched herself go into her bedroom and call the railroad, telling the dispatcher that something had come up, asking someone to have Larry call home. To those around her she looked supernaturally controlled, but at the honest core of her being she knew she was hanging on by threads. When Larry called, she discovered she could not speak. She could not form the words to relate the unspeakable. Larry kept asking her questions.

"Linda, has something happened to your mom? Is it one of the kids? Is it Alicia?"

"No, no, no," she said.

"Is it Kevin? Did something happen to Kevin?"

It took all the strength in her body to speak the words she felt more as a scream.

"Larry, I think he's dead."

There was no point in groping for details. "I'll be home as soon as I can."

At best, that would be four or five hours. Linda resolved to survive until he arrived. When Larry gets here, she thought, I'll know what to do. Then we'll be able to handle this. Meanwhile she listened from somewhere outside herself as friends persuaded her to let them arrange to fly Alicia home. She watched, not calm but not crying, while her life flew apart at the seams. She had only to hold on to what she could until Larry could get home. Then, she kept telling herself, I'll know what to do.

The day crept on. By midafternoon the house around Linda was full. Family and friends huddled and murmured, all awaiting yet fearing the expected call that would confirm the boys' identities. So long as the call did *not* come, there was still a strand of hope. Maybe it was some other boy. Kevin might still walk in. But as the hot afternoon faded to evening with no call from the officials—but no sign of Kevin—even that frail hope disappeared.

As the sky began to darken, a group of men left the house to pick up Larry, who had hopped an express train back. Linda, her shield of shock wearing thin, stood waiting for him in the garage. There was so much to do, so much to try to think about. Alicia had arrived, and some friends had brought her home from the airport. But now people began mentioning funeral arrangements, talking about questions to ask the police. She could barely hear what they were saying, let alone make sense of it. Over and over she told them, "We'll decide that when Larry gets here." In the crush of her fear and confusion, she clung to her confidence in Larry and the strength he brought to their marriage. "When Larry gets here," she told her comforters, "we'll know what to do."

When the car finally pulled into the drive, two men opened the door and helped her husband out. She saw him stagger. The hope she had been relying on could barely walk. The men assisted him, like a wounded comrade, into the couple's bedroom. Linda watched the procession dumbstruck. Larry was in a state of collapse, worse off than she. She followed, fear closing around her. Larry and Kevin were close. Now Larry looked as though part of his own body had been severed. He seemed to have been cut in two by pain. Her pillar of strength was broken. Linda saw her family in agony and afraid. If she didn't know what to do and Larry didn't either, and Alicia was in a daze, and Kevin was gone and maybe dead, and none of it made any sense, then how could she—how could any of them—go on?

Alicia followed her parents into the bedroom. The other men left. Linda closed the door behind them. "What are we going to do?" Larry sobbed when the three of them were alone. "What are we going to do?"

She stroked him like a baby. "I don't know, Larry," Linda said. "But we'll get through this somehow. We can do it." She only wanted to calm him. She did not believe a word that she was saying.

That night Larry paced the bedroom floor, wringing his hands. He cried for Kevin. He curled up in pain. "I need some help," he sobbed. "I need some help."

"What do you want me to do, Larry?" she asked. She suggested calling a doctor, a minister, other friends. "No, no," Larry said to each offer. Yet, he kept pacing and crying and repeating, "I need some help." But in the face of Kevin's sudden, monstrous, and inexplicable death, all of them were helpless. Linda sat hopelessly on the bed. She had seen her husband cry only once before, when his mother had died. Now all the softness she had brought to the house, all the coziness in which she had tried to wrap her family—none of it could buffer any of them from this horror invading their lives. Something had happened against which she had no defense, no way of protecting her children, her husband, or herself. She lay back, alone and struggling, reaching for some strategy, some way not to let death win.

"WHAT MORTUARY, MA'AM?"

The medical examiner's office never called. By Monday the Iveses and the Henrys had begun to accept the impossible: that their sons had not come home, that they would not be coming home, that they were the boys on the tracks. Around noon a deputy called. His announcement was indirect. "The crime lab needs to know where you want the body sent."

It took Linda a second to respond. She was so used to thinking of Kevin as alive. "The body?" she asked dumbly. She thought of water-skiing with the kids at Lake Ouachita and of watching Kevin rise up on skis behind the boat, his strong young body glistening in the sun.

"What mortuary, ma'am?" the deputy coaxed. "Where should they send the body?"

The dental records had proven conclusive.

A rote formality takes over, even in cases of the most awful deaths. It's another form of protection. A million questions pressed like a headache on Linda's mind. How? How? How? How could Kevin, an engineer's son, have let himself be run over by a train? How could all the elements of such a nightmare have come together? But such questions would have to wait. Linda had been taking care of Kevin all his life, and now, despite all that had been lost, there was still his body to be cared for. Kevin's funeral was arranged for the next day, with Don's to follow on Wednesday. Everything was happening fast. One minute Linda would be walking down the hall in her house glancing into Kevin's bedroom and reflexively thinking about what he still needed for the start of school. The next minute there would be the jolting reminder that someone was waiting for a decision about some aspect of his funeral. She and Larry felt like ghosts wandering in their own home. They went through motions that felt new and strange, while looking, almost accidentally, on remnants of the life they had had.

The casket was cherry wood with a blue satin interior like the interior of Kevin's Camaro. How does one pick a coffin for one's son? It's not like picking out clothes, or a bedspread. The choice was as close to logic as Linda could come. Kevin's old friend Mike asked on behalf of his friends and classmates if, at some point in the service, they could play a recording of one of Kevin's favorite songs, a piece called "Stairway to Heaven." Linda didn't know the song, but she liked the title. She told Mike that sounded fine. Only much later in the day, when she thought everything had been arranged, did she remember that she had not brought any of Kevin's clothes to the mortuary. She called and said she'd run some over. There was silence on the other end of the line. Finally the funeral director replied, "Linda, we don't need any clothes."

She felt herself being torn apart anew. Until that moment Linda had not thought—had not allowed herself to think—of the trauma her son's body had suffered; the body she had bathed as a baby and dressed for his first day at school, the body whose new underwear she had been folding just the day before. Now the reality she had been struggling to hold at bay rushed in with a vengeance. There was not enough of her son left to dress. Kevin had grown into a handsome young man, and now, after an accident no one could yet explain, his beautiful body lay in pieces.

She hung up the phone and stared at her house, which was filling with flowers and plants. This was not how she had ever imagined it. The house was to have been their refuge. The peacefulness of the neighborhood, the tranquillity of the little town of Bryant, were why she and Larry had moved here in the first place, when Kevin and Alicia were young. Both she and Larry had grown up on the southwest edge of Little Rock. The city was okay, but cities were unpredictable.

Not that Linda was much of a worrier. Her family had not been rich, her father working most of his life as a used-car salesman, but she had been a happy child, content to go with the flow. At fifteen she had met Larry, four and a half years older than she. He was a senior, having missed several years of school due to polio. He came from a large family that was extremely close. In his senior year Larry had gotten a job as a school bus driver, and it was on the bus that their courtship had begun. After Larry's father, a machinist for the railroad, had helped him get hired on as a fireman, Larry had joined the union, and in April 1967 he and Linda were married. She was two months shy of her high school graduation, and three months pregnant with Alicia. Kevin came three years later.

At first the couple had rented a mobile home and then houses in Little Rock, but as Larry's career became more secure, they had begun to dream of a home outside the city. Eventually they had built on a three-acre lot on the western edge of Bryant, on the very northern edge of Saline County. Here, in their spacious stone-and-cedar home, they had felt comfortable, watching their children grow. And now, for no reason anyone could offer, an undertaker was on the telephone, the house was filling with plants, and Kevin's room was empty.

The funeral home, too, was filled with flowers. Brother Ed, a longtime friend of the family, offered a short and simple eulogy. He talked to the family about their grief. He addressed Kevin's friends and classmates. Then someone pressed a button on a tape player. Led Zeppelin filled the chapel. Older relatives looked around in surprise. Kevin's classmates, recognizing "Stairway to Heaven" as Kevin's favorite song, began hugging each other and crying. The service was at once comforting and draining.

When the red-eyed mourners left the chapel, they walked into a phalanx of media. Linda looked blankly at the assembled cameras. She could not comprehend such callousness. Her anger rose and hardened. Could these people not, she thought, respect her family's privacy?

Don Henry's service was held the following day. As newspapers and television stations reported on the two bizarre deaths in Saline County, one station in particular, KARK-TV, Channel 4, kept rerunning segments of film that one of its photographers had shot early in the morning, while the bodies were still at the tracks. The clips showed deputies loading bags into the back of a pickup truck—bags containing the remains. But that was not the worst the families were to see. In one frame a sheriff's deputy who was standing in the back of the truck momentarily stepped on one of the body bags while helping load in the other. By the day of the funerals, another clip had become a symbol of the story: a solitary tennis shoe lying between the tracks. For the families, who had avoided going to the tracks, the scene felt like another assault.

But the story had captivated the state. It was at once so horrible and so odd. And the theories offered by police seemed to fall so short. Officially, deputies were describing the deaths as an apparent accident, though they hastened to add that an official ruling as to the cause and manner of death would have to come from the state medical examiner, Dr. Fahmy Malak. Unofficially, when they spoke with the families, they suggested that suicide was the more likely explanation.

All four parents rebelled at the idea. Everything they knew of their sons contradicted it. Others who knew the boys agreed. Both boys had reputations as being happy-go-lucky. But the deputies said there was evidence that the boys had been using drugs: a small amount of marijuana, about 1.9 grams, had been found in the pocket of Kevin's pants. The Iveses hadn't thought that Kevin smoked—at least, not since a summer incident a couple of years ago when Kevin had been caught with a friend using marijuana. Larry and Linda had come down hard on him, and so far as they had known, that had been the end of it.[2] School had resumed, and sports with it, and life had returned to normal. Surprised as they were at the deputies' news, they still could not believe Kevin would have killed himself, even under the influence of marijuana. Nor could Curtis and Marvelle Henry believe that Don would have done such a thing. None of them had ever heard of marijuana inducing such tragic behavior. Nor had the boys' friends and classmates. As one young friend of Kevin's confided to Linda after the rumor got out: "Mrs. Ives, Kevin and Don did smoke a little dope. A lot of us did. But you don't kill yourself when you get high."

In the weeks after the funerals, two other problems with the deputies' theories that the deaths were an accident or suicides gnawed at Curtis Henry. From the moment he'd heard of the deaths, he told friends, he had had a feeling that something had gone wrong, something, perhaps, that the police were not seeing—or perhaps that they had seen but were failing to mention. On the Sunday morning when the bodies were found, after Deputy Tallent had left the Henrys' house, Curtis had called his old friend T. U. Daniel, a longtime hunting buddy, and asked him to go down the tracks just to look around. It was a big favor to ask of a friend. T.U. had been raised in the woods. He knew that when you shoot something—or, in this case, when you dismember it—there's going to be an abundance of blood. To go to the site of his friend's son's death, and under such unusual circumstances, called not just for loyalty, but also a strong stomach. T.U. had set off looking grim. When he'd returned a couple of hours later, his countenance had been even more disturbed. "Let's go out in the backyard and talk," he'd said. When they had seated themselves under a tree, T.U. had lowered his voice. "Curtis, there's not any blood down there to speak of. . . . "

That was one of the thoughts that kept troubling Curtis. The other was what the deputies had told him about Don's gun. They'd said that when the train hit, the gun had been lying between the tracks in the gravel. Who had put it there? Curtis felt certain it had not been Don. Don had worshiped his guns. He'd owned six and cleaned them all religiously. Don Henry wouldn't lay one of his guns down on grass, much less on gravel. No, Curtis thought, that boy wouldn't have committed suicide. And he would never have laid his gun down on gravel.

At the Iveses' house a few miles to the west, Larry and Linda grappled with similar doubts. The train crew had come to Kevin's funeral, but there had been little anyone could say. Larry understood how helpless the men in the engine had been. He felt their anguish, not only at having run over the boys, but also that one of the victims had been the son of someone they knew. At the time Larry had not known about the lack of blood at the scene, as reported by the EMTs, the train crew, and later by Curtis Henry's friend. So he'd seen no point in pressing the crew for information—details that would have been painful for them all. Yet even in the void of information, everyone sensed that there was something very strange about these deaths—something that defied comprehension.

On one hand, there was the realization that, but for a providential turn of fate, the horror might have been compounded. For years Larry Ives had been the engineer on the very route where the boys were killed, the run from Texarkana to Little Rock. He had been switched to a different route—the one to Poplar Bluff, Missouri—only two months before the deaths. Stephen Shroyer, the engineer at the controls when the boys were run over, had taken over the route as Larry Ives's replacement. The realization was chilling. Had it not been for that change, it would almost certainly have been Larry at the controls of the train that ran over his son. Even years later, after therapy to cope with his shock, Larry would contemplate that possibility. "I don't know," he would quietly admit, "if I could have took that or not."

But for many who knew the Ives family, the deaths held an even more disturbing aspect. A friend put the worry into words. "I'm a dentist," he told Larry and Linda. "So what do I teach my children? Over and over again I tell them they've got to take care of their teeth." He shook his head, disturbed by the implication of what he was saying. But he continued, as gently as possible, making his point. "So I think, what is an engineer going to teach his kids? From the time they're little, I think, he's going to teach them to watch out for trains."

THREE

"THC INTOXICATION"

SEPTEMBER 1987–FEBRUARY 1988

There was nothing to do but wait for the autopsy reports. In the meantime, deputies let the families know that the unofficial word was that traces of THC, the active ingredient in marijuana, had been found in the blood of both boys. The deputies said the medical examiner was conducting further tests to screen for alcohol and other drugs.

THE AUTOPSIES

The news hit Larry and Linda hard. Kevin's body was barely in the ground and she was having to listen to deputies portray him as a drug-using, suicidal kid. That was not Kevin. His friends told her and Larry that that was not the Kevin they knew, either. At first, when the shock was fresh, she had expected that she would understand more as time passed. Her mind would clear. The police would investigate. There would be explanations. They might be horrible, but at least they would make sense.

Yet none of that was happening. Every day, it seemed, there was *more* to these deaths—not *less*—that Linda could not understand. Drugs? She knew almost nothing about them and had not wanted to know. But now, as police talked about the presence of marijuana in the boys' blood, suggesting that that discovery somehow explained their deaths, friends were telling Linda and Larry about rumors that were circulating around Saline County. There apparently was a story going around that, contrary to what the police were saying, the boys' deaths had had nothing to do with marijuana—but everything to do with cocaine. Linda felt herself verging on a realm about which she knew only enough to fear.

Naive as she had been, even in the idyllic days before Kevin's death, Linda had at least known that drugs were available even in a small school like Bryant High. But apart from the incident with marijuana when Kevin was fourteen, drugs had seemed a faraway problem. Both children were involved in football, Kevin on the field and Alicia on the drill team, and the demands of school, work, and sports dominated the family's routine. During the school year Linda would come home from her job at the Alcoa credit union, feed the kids, and get them to practice or to games. Weekends were even more hectic. During the summer Alicia and Kevin had part-time jobs and the family went to the lake whenever everyone could get away.

But now, if the rumors were to be believed, some darkness from the world of drugs had reached out and taken Kevin. Linda paced through the house, sleeping little at night, unable to rest in the day. Part of her longed to bury her own doubts and so she struggled to accept what the deputies were saying: that if the deaths were not suicides, they were accidental; that Kevin and Don had smoked too much marijuana, fallen asleep on the tracks, and been run over by the train. But try as she might to accept it, the scenario troubled her. Could marijuana do that? Could both boys have fallen asleep together? And on the tracks, no less?

Dragging into bed at night, desperate with confusion, she told herself to wait, that the answers must lie with the bodies. When the medical examiner reported his findings, she consoled herself, she and Larry finally would understand how this tragedy had come about. His findings would be scientific, no matter how difficult to hear. Linda told herself that she could accept anything—whatever truth emerged—if only she could understand. Then she would have a chance to work toward some peace. Turning off the light, she tried not to let herself think about Kevin's body in the morgue at the crime lab. When she thought of the autopsy itself—of the cold steel table, the saws, the probes, the labels—she had to remind herself that the pieces of flesh assembled there had once been, but were not now, Kevin. She prayed that in those precious, torn-up remains, the doctors would find the clues that would reveal the truth that would put her own heart to rest. With so many questions swirling through her mind and through the community, she closed her eyes, whispered good night to her son, and rested her hopes on the autopsy findings.

MEETING DR. MALAK

A week after the funerals, Linda and Larry Ives drove the twenty miles to Little Rock, to the pine-shaded office park on the west side of town that held the headquarters of the Arkansas State Police. In the parking lot they met Don's parents and deputies Elmendorf and Tallent. As they approached the building a state police investigator joined them. Introducing himself as Lt. Frank Mitchell, he said that he was assigned to work in Saline County and, naturally, was interested in the case. This came as good news to the parents. Since the boys' deaths, they had begged the Saline County Sheriff's Office to request assistance from the state police, but that was never done. Larry told Mitchell that in the trunk of his car he had a large piece of cardboard that he and some other men had found near the site where the boys had died. The piece was big enough that it could have been used to drag two bodies, and on it was a stain that looked like it might be blood. Larry wanted to have it analyzed, but he knew that the sheriff's office lacked facilities for that, so he was bringing it to Malak. When Mitchell assured Larry that he would take the piece to the crime lab to have the stain examined, Larry opened the trunk of his car and handed the piece of cardboard to the investigator. Curtis, in turn, handed over parts of what appeared to be a gun that he and some of his friends had found in the same vicinity. That was the last they would hear of the items, until, months later, when they inquired at the crime lab. The families learned that the cardboard had never been examined. The pieces of gun had disappeared.

But at the moment of the transfer, there in the parking lot, the parents felt hopeful. Entering the building, they took an elevator to the top floor, which was devoted entirely to the crime lab. Also on the floor were the offices of Dr. Fahmy Malak, the Arkansas medical examiner. Pushing open the door, Linda did not know what to expect. She had tried to prepare for this meeting, but she could not imagine how a mother could brace to hear her son's autopsy discussed. She knew Larry was struggling, too.

The two of them had always had an easy, amicable marriage. Now, for the first time, Linda was angry and Larry was withdrawn. They knew the Henrys were going through a hell of their own. Curtis told them he was still upset about his meeting a few days earlier with Elmendorf and Tallent, when the deputies had told him that Malak was "leaning" toward a ruling of suicide. There was no way, Curtis responded hotly, that they were going to cram that down his throat. Those two boys did not get into a suicidal state together, he said. And he added that if that was the best explanation they could come up with, they needed to regroup. Where the official opinion stood now, no one in the room yet knew. The parents were emotional wrecks, battered and confused. Privately, all sat summoning what strength they could for the coming ordeal. Beneath the table, Larry reached over and clasped Linda's hand.

Malak entered the room. He wore thick glasses beneath dark, bushy eyebrows. His manner was dramatic and authoritative. The medical examiner greeted the parents politely in a voice still bearing a heavy accent from his native Egypt. Linda and the others realized quickly that they had to listen closely. Malak's accent and his sometimes unusual phraseology required extra attention. Moreover, they were somewhat taken aback by Malak's first demand, which was to take everybody's picture. The couples looked at each other quizzically but quickly arranged themselves where Malak directed. He shot Polaroid photos of each person in the room, then circulated forms for them to sign acknowledging their attendance at the meeting. That done, he laid several large envelopes on the table.

"What we have here," he said, without further delay, "are two accidental deaths due to THC intoxication." The parents listened, stunned. As if through a fog, Linda could see Malak passing out copies of his official ruling. The statement read: "At 4:25 A.M. on August 23, 1987, Larry Kevin Ives (17) and Don George Henry (16) were unconscious and in deep sleep on the railroad tracks, under the psychedelic influence of THC (marijuana), when a train passed over them causing their accidental death."

Whatever she had been braced to hear, it had not been this. "The psychedelic influence of THC?" She and Larry looked at each other blankly. They had been forewarned that "traces" of marijuana had been found in the boys' blood. But this sounded as though the amounts must have been significant. How much marijuana would it have taken, they wondered, to lead the boys to their deaths? Unfamiliar as they were with marijuana, Larry and Linda had never heard of it blamed for such a death. They had never heard of it leading to unconsciousness. And could this be right, what Malak had written, about its "psychedelic influence"?

Malak sat confidently at the head of the table. The parents looked at him, uncertain where to begin. At last Linda broke the silence. "THC intoxication," she began. "Dr. Malak, what exactly does that mean?"

"The level of marijuana in the children's blood was very, very high," Malak replied. It seemed he expected no further questions. But the parents, incredulous, persisted. "How high?"

Malak looked perturbed. He turned to the blackboard and drew a vertical line. Near the bottom of the line he scribbled "5." At the top end he wrote "100." Turning to the parents, he explained that a person whose blood registered five was considered to be under the influence of marijuana. Then, jabbing the chalk at the blackboard, indicating with an insistent tapping the one hundred mark, he announced, "Your children's levels were here. *This* is how stoned they were."

The Iveses and the Henrys were confounded, silenced. Linda's mind raced. "What kind of measurement is that?" she finally asked, pointing to the board.

"Units," Malak replied impatiently. He spoke as if she should be satisfied.

The response seemed vague, but then, what did Linda know? She had no medical background. Marvelle Henry was a nurse, but when Linda looked at her, Marvelle, too, shook her head, indicating that she had no idea of what Malak was talking about. The parents did not know how THC was measured, how it accumulated, or how long it might remain active. Reaching for some explanation that a lay person might understand, they asked how many marijuana cigarettes the boys would have had to smoke and over how long a period of time, to reach a state of such intoxication.

Malak launched into a lengthy response, but he never answered the questions to their satisfaction. The parents repeated them, and again Malak responded at length, saying much about marijuana as a hallucinogen, but never offering even a ballpark estimate of how many cigarettes the boys must have smoked. As the tension in the room rose, Malak picked up the envelopes on the table before him. "You want to know?" he said. "Here are the autopsy photos." He reached inside the envelopes, threatening to extract their contents, insisting that in the photos the parents would find "the proof" of what he was saying. They recoiled in horror.

No, they insisted. They did not want to see the photos. And besides, how could seeing the photos answer the questions they were asking, which centered on toxicology reports on the blood? They steered their questions in other directions, backing off from those that seemed to antagonize Malak, but whatever they asked, Malak's answers came back vague and increasingly hostile. The more the parents pressed, the more insistently Malak reached for the envelopes. Finally Elmendorf stood up.

"They don't want to look at these," he told Malak. With that, Elmendorf reached over and removed the envelopes from the table. In the years ahead, Linda would come to distrust Rick Elmendorf but she would always appreciate what he had done for her and the other parents at that moment in Malak's office. As Elmendorf resumed his seat, he leaned over to Linda and whispered, "He told me twenty, Linda. They would have had to smoke about twenty joints."

"Who told you twenty?" she asked.

"Malak," Elmendorf replied.

It was an answer, but a problematical one, and one that, later, Malak would deny having offered. Ultimately, the number came to symbolize the meeting's ambiguities and the parents' state of confusion. As she sat there in Malak's office, believing Malak had said that the boys had smoked twenty joints before they died, Linda's mind raced back to the days after the boys' bodies were found. Elmendorf and Tallent had told her and Larry that they had tracked the boys' whereabouts on the night before they died, and that one of the stops they had made was to buy a ten-dollar bag of marijuana. The officers said that they thought they knew who had supplied the marijuana, though they did not reveal the source to the parents. Now, with Malak repeating the words "THC intoxication," the parents struggled to imagine how much marijuana one could buy for ten dollars and whether it was enough to make twenty cigarettes; and if it was, how long it would have taken the boys to smoke that many.

Finally Curtis Henry asked, "Well, Dr. Malak, we know that they were lying in identical positions, soldier style, on the tracks. If they were so stoned, so intoxicated and in a psychedelic stupor, how could they have done that?"

"I've seen stranger things in my career," Malak replied, and once again he launched into a lengthy dissertation, this one about the effects of hashish on camels.[1]

MALAK'S RULING STUNS ARKANSAS

It was classic Malak, as the parents were to learn. By the time of this meeting in 1987, Malak had been Arkansas's medical examiner for nine years, his appointment having been approved by the governor during Bill Clinton's first term in that office. Malak boasted that he was one of the few in the state who could see the governor on fifteen minutes' notice. The claim struck reporters covering state government as odd, considering the exceptionally high level of controversy that had dogged Malak throughout his term in office. Malak, who frequently had to fend off charges of incompetence or worse, had become something of an anomaly in the administration of a governor who, even by the mid 1980s, was attracting national attention as a gifted politician and able leader.

Malak received his medical training at Cairo University. He came to the United States in 1970 and performed a residency in pathology at South Bend, Indiana. He received his training in forensic pathology on the job while working in Pittsburgh as an assistant coroner. From that position Malak moved to Arkansas in 1978. A year later, after taking a job at the state crime lab, he was promoted to the powerful position of chief medical examiner.

From the start, Malak's tenure was fraught with controversy. At one point his chief field investigator publicly charged that Malak had kept outdated crime lab stationery. According to the allegations, he sometimes used the out-of-date stationery to falsify findings in autopsy reports as certain insurance or criminal cases were about to go to court.[2] Turnover in his office was high. Malak blamed the problem on low state wages, but several departing employees cited as their reasons for leaving Malak's "bizarre behavior" and "paranoia." Law enforcement officers familiar with the crime lab, including FBI agents and sheriff's deputies, underlined that charge, complaining about Malak's insistence on photographing all visitors to his office. This included not only families, but police officers as well.[3]

Now Malak's ruling in the deaths of Don Henry and Kevin Ives had catapulted him to a level of controversy and notoriety remarkable even for him. As newspapers and television stations reported his death-by-locomotive-and-marijuana ruling, reactions ranged from skepticism to outright ridicule. Only the Saline County Sheriff's Office appeared to be content with the medical examiner's findings. "We are satisfied with the ruling," Elmendorf told the *Benton Courier.* "We don't question it."

CONFRONTING THE EMT

But questions persisted—questions that Malak had not addressed. A major one concerned, not the level of marijuana in the boys' blood, but the state of the blood itself. Shortly after the deaths, Linda and Larry had begun hearing the rumors that the paramedics at the tracks were troubled by the blood's appearance. One day, in the weeks after their meeting with Malak, Linda saw an opportunity to question one of the paramedics in person.

Linda had a friend who worked at Saline Memorial Hospital, the facility that had dispatched the ambulance to the tracks. The friend related that the word around the hospital was that the EMTs who had gone to the tracks doubted that the train had killed the boys. Noting that ambulance workers frequently met with the families of accident victims, the friend said she would arrange such a meeting for Linda. At first, to the friend's surprise, the paramedics refused. Then a few nights later, one of them—Billy Heath—agreed to meet.

Linda drove straight to the hospital. It was dark when she arrived, well past visiting hours. The place was settling down for the night. She and her friend walked through the quiet corridors toward the EMTs' office near the emergency room. They found Heath, a man about Linda's age, standing in the hall. Around him stood three Saline County deputies. Heath told the women that he had changed his mind. He had decided not to talk.

Heath was shaking, but Linda was not about to let the opportunity pass. Addressing him calmly, she pleaded with him to step into a nearby office, to talk with her for just a minute. Heath hesitated, then agreed.

"Billy, we've been hearing rumors about the appearance of the blood."

"I can't talk to you, Mrs. Ives," he stammered. "Just get my report. I spent five hours writing that report. I knew I would need to have total recall about the events of that day. It's all in my report." His voice was shaking like his body.

Linda pressed. "Billy, have the deputies intimidated you?"

"No, ma'am," he said. "They haven't."

Exasperated, Linda gave up. Leaving Heath and the deputies, she and her friend walked down the hall in silence. "You know," the friend observed, "we never see three deputies in this hospital at once. And after nine at night? Why, usually there aren't even four deputies on duty this time of night." She checked with a group of co-workers. "Nothing," she said, shaking her head. "No shootings. No wrecks. There's nothing going on."

As the women neared the door of the hospital, Heath came running up behind them. Catching his breath, he said, "Mrs. Ives, I just wanted to know one thing. I referred to the boys in my report as 'large boy' and 'small boy' because I didn't know one from the other." Unsure of what he meant, Linda guessed that Heath did not want her to think he had been callous, referring to the victims with such dispassion. She told Heath it was okay. He rushed away.

In the next few weeks, as school resumed and the shock of missing Kevin gradually turned to numbness, Linda groped for what information she could get. A sudden death is hard enough to accept when the facts are clear and the wound they produce is a clean one, but here there were jagged edges. Linda thought she could smooth those edges, close the wound, and let some healing begin if only she could grasp what had happened.

But how could that be done when the deputies were treating the case as closed? And when Malak had issued his pronouncement certifying the deaths as accidents? Lacking confidence in the police investigation, confounded by Malak's ruling, and knowing that time was critical, Linda and Larry discussed the situation with Curtis and Marvelle. Grasping at straws, the couples decided to hire a private investigator, a man who had done some work for the company where Curtis worked. First off, the investigator suggested, the parents should obtain a court order for whatever records existed in the case. He wanted to see Malak's reports, the case file from the sheriff's office, and the hospital's EMT records. The parents complied, but when the order was obtained and the investigator presented it at the hospital, the clerk told him that no EMT reports existed from the night at the tracks. No patient care had been rendered, the clerk explained, so no report had been written. He added, "That's why the families were not billed."

In the face of the rumors of the EMTs' concerns and Heath's statement that he had spent five hours writing a report, the hospital's insistance that they did not have the reports was another affront. Frustrated and furious, the Iveses and Henrys felt they could not relent. Convinced that Heath's report did exist, they instructed the private investigator to press their demand. Finally the hospital delivered a record, but it was not what they had expected. In October 1987, two months after the deaths, Saline Memorial Hospital released to the families one paramedic's report on the ambulance call to the tracks. It was short. And it had not been written by Heath, but by Shirley Raper. The hospital insisted that it was the *only* report that had ever been written. The words "large boy" and "small boy" did not appear anywhere in it. Still, there in writing was Shirley Raper's observation about the color of the blood. It looked like it lacked oxygen, she wrote, adding that the color had led the EMTs to question "how long the boys had been dead."

OPTICAL ILLUSIONS

The parents struggled on. When they pressed the deputies for more information, Elmendorf and Tallent explained that the boys could not have been covered with a tarp because the crime lab had conducted tests on their clothing. If there had been a tarp, the deputies explained, microscopic fibers from it would have been found embedded in the boys' clothing, and even in their bodies. But no such fibers were found. The deputies reiterated what they had told the train crew—information that Larry's friends on the railroad had passed on to him: that the tarp had been an optical illusion.

Larry protested. He knew the crew. They were neither blind nor idiotic. As an engineer himself, he had driven that same route hundreds of times. He had never seen an optical illusion. How, he demanded, could three men in a locomotive, all sitting in different places, have experienced the same illusion? The police offered no explanation.

Linda felt that not only Kevin's young body, but the truth of his death, had been mutilated. She and Larry drove themselves to look deeper, however hard that would be. Feeling isolated but determined, they and the Henrys decided to seek a second pathologist's opinion. Local physicians recommended Dr. J. T. Francisco, a forensic pathologist in Memphis, Tennessee.

Noting that his fee was two hundred dollars an hour, Francisco told Curtis how the samples of blood and urine were to be preserved and shipped. An official at the crime lab agreed to send the samples, though he explained that no urine could be sent for Don because his bladder had been completely destroyed. The other samples were sent, however. The boys had been dead a little more than three weeks. Linda waited anxiously for the results.

Several weeks later, in a conference call with the parents, Francisco reported, "I am able to confirm Dr. Malak's ruling." The parents asked Francisco to send them his results in writing. They hung up feeling discouraged. Days later Curtis received the letter from Francisco outlining his results. "The testing in Arkansas was on blood of both," Francisco wrote, "and our test was on urine of [Kevin]. Our results support the results that were obtained in Arkansas." Francisco then quoted the same levels of THC that Malak had reported: 97 micrograms per milliliter for Kevin and 122 for Don.[4]

Reading the letter, the parents realized for the first time that *Francisco had not tested the blood*. He had tested only urine—and only Kevin's urine at that, since no urine from Don was available. Larry and Linda, Curtis and Marvelle, looked at each other in disbelief. How could Francisco confirm Malak's *blood* levels of THC for both the boys when he had tested the *urine* of only one? Baffled, they placed another call to Memphis. In a tense conversation, Francisco admitted that he had not retested the blood. When pressed as to how, then, he could "confirm" Malak's ruling on the THC levels in the blood, he acknowledged that he could not. He said he was able to confirm Malak's findings "by inference" because he "knew that the tests by the Arkansas crime lab followed standard procedures," and that being the case, his "confirmation of one finding gave added weight of confidence that the other findings were true."[5] Asked if he had spoken with Malak before calculating his "results," Francisco acknowledged that he had. He never sent the families a bill.

By now, the couples felt that they were confronting cronyism among professionals and that the circle of illusion around this case was widening.

Larry tried to console Linda. "This can't be some great conspiracy. Not everyone can be against us."

"Then tell me what's going on," she snapped. "Tell me what all this means."

Tips, mostly unsolicited and from anonymous callers, continued to come to the house. One they heard repeatedly concerned a man in camouflage clothing who was reportedly sighted near the tracks on the morning of the deaths. The report was of particular interest. The deputies acknowledged that one morning before dawn, a week before the deaths, a man dressed in camouflage had shot out the blue light of a deputy's car as he was driving near Shobe Road. The man ran and was never apprehended. Linda took notes of all such calls and reported them to Elmendorf and Tallent. But the deputies' interest in the case had never seemed hot, and by Thanksgiving it was decidedly cool. With Malak's ruling, the case was closed, and, though the deputies promised to follow up any new leads that arose, it was clear to Larry and Linda that the investigation was as dead as the boys. Christmas was a holiday to endure.

With the start of 1988, she and Larry, Curtis and Marvelle, dug in again. They sent copies of Malak's ruling and autopsy reports to two pathologists noted for their work with marijuana. They also contacted the crime lab directly, requesting samples of the boys' remains so that they could have them reexamined. Malak resisted, telling the parents that he would not release anything to them without a court order. Again, they obtained one. But when the private investigator presented it to Malak in person, he refused to honor it, insisting he would not release the requested slides and samples.

Linda was furious. She wanted to pound her fists into something, do anything that would achieve some results. She called the state attorney general's office and explained the situation. Over the phone she read the court order to a deputy attorney general. To her amazement the state lawyer told Linda that he could not force Malak to comply, though he would strongly urge him to do so. By now Linda was used to encountering resistance where she would never have expected it. Later she would learn that she would have to take the matter back to court.

Larry was in no better shape. He felt as deflated, as confused, as she. Every instinct in him recoiled against notions of conspiracy. Yet none of this was working out the way he felt any ordinary person would expect. Larry went to work wishing that he knew what was going on. He came home braced for word of some new setback. As weeks turned into months, he yearned for just one thing: a good investigation, one they could believe in, one that would help them understand what had happened to their son and let them get on with their lives. With all his heart he wished that Malak had issued a less fantastic ruling and had had the decency to honor the court order. He wished that it had been easier to get the papers from the hospital. He wished that Sheriff Steed had shown an interest in the case and that someone could explain the tarp, instead of denying its existence. He hated fighting these battles. He hardly felt he had the strength, especially when, like Linda and Alicia and the Henrys, he had all he could do to battle the pain.

For Larry, the loss of Kevin was more than he could shoulder. Realizing that he needed professional help, he had started seeing a psychiatrist. Linda and Alicia were going to another therapist together. There were so many griefs to be sorted out—grinding, daily, relentless griefs. Many centered on the investigation. But others concerned the house. They arose from simple matters, like what to do about Kevin's room. Linda did not want to change a thing in it. Larry could hardly endure the reminder. The room became another sore spot in a family that was already badly hurting. Larry would walk down the hall and close the door to Kevin's room. Linda would walk down the hall, find the sight of the closed door unbearable, and open it as she passed. Later they would learn that theirs was a common dilemma, that the process of letting go unfolds at a different pace for every member of a family. But for now, all they knew was that each of them was trying to cope, and sometimes not very well.

The door to Kevin's room was not the only one that Linda kept trying to open. There were too many closed doors in this case. She and Larry, Curtis and Marvelle, might be up against the entire state, she decided, but they would force open what they could. The phone call to the attorney general's office had pushed her to a new resolve. She had started off angry at the media, a reaction born of hurt. But as the months had passed and officials had shoved the case aside, the media had stuck with the story. Where state and local officials seemed to see nothing irregular in the deaths or in the subsequent investigation, the media and ordinary people seemed to be fascinated by the story and to see quite a lot in it that was unresolved. Linda began to think that if the case of Kevin and Don was ever to be solved, it might come about only through public attention. Suddenly the media no longer looked like an enemy. One night, to her own surprise, she found herself telling Larry, Curtis, and Marvelle that the four of them needed to hold a press conference. On February 7, 1988, five months after the deaths, Linda opened the phone book and began calling newspapers and television stations.

The next day she and Larry, Curtis and Marvelle, stood together before a cluster of reporters at a local Holiday Inn. Linda thanked them for coming. She explained the families' frustrations with the investigation and their questions about Malak's ruling. She reported his blustery demand that they get a court order to release the remains, and then his refusal to honor it. Curtis Henry voiced the families' growing concerns about Malak's theory that the deaths had been caused by marijuana intoxication. Looking into the cameras, he said, "No one has assured us that marijuana will put you in a position to be unconscious. In fact, everything we have read or learned about it says no, it won't." The story ran statewide in newspapers and on television.

The move had its desired effect. The day after the press conference several reporters followed Larry and Curtis, along with their private investigator, into Malak's office at the state crime lab. This time Malak was the essence of cooperation. Of course he would release the samples. While the reporters listened and scribbled notes, Malak assured the fathers that a new investigation would not turn up any other cause of death. Still, he urged them, if it would satisfy their doubts, to have their sons' bodies exhumed and submitted for another autopsy.

"If it were my son, I would exhume the body and hire the best medical examiner in America," Malak told Larry and Curtis. "I am a father, too. My son is a teenager. I have two kids. . . . But this is the bottom line: those two children died because they were hit by a train."

The photographers packed up their cameras. The reporters left to write their stories. Malak then invited the fathers into his office. As they sat, an assistant brought in several jars. Malak unscrewed the lid of one. The room filled with the stench of formaldehyde. Malak took a pencil, moved it past the mouth of the jar, and touched an item inside. "That's a part of your son's heart," he told Curtis.

"And what is that?" Curtis asked, pointing to something else in another jar. Malak became angry and quickly resealed the jar he had opened.

Curtis recognized the move as another of Malak's threatening techniques, like trying to show the parents the autopsy photos, aimed at dissuading them from pursuing their inquiry. By holding his temper and asking about the contents of the second jar, Curtis hoped to send Malak the message that this tactic would not work. Curtis wanted to let Malak know that he had not hurt him, though, of course, he had.

Now that the reporters were gone, Malak shifted gears. He told the two men that it would be silly of them to send samples of their sons' bodies anywhere else to be tested. "You're just going to be spending a lot of money hiring quacks," he warned them.

"Don't worry," Curtis Henry replied, looking the doctor in the eye. "We've already heard the quack's opinion."

FOUR

HARMON AND GARRETT

FEBRUARY 1988

The two toxicologists reviewed Malak's autopsy conclusions. They did not mince words. As one put it, the Arkansas medical examiner's statements regarding the effects of marijuana were "bullshit."

ANOTHER LOOK AT THE CASE

Dr. Arthur J. McBay, chief toxicologist for the North Carolina medical examiner's office and a former medical examiner for the state of Massachusetts, told reporters for the *Benton Courier,* the *Arkansas Democrat*, and the *Arkansas Gazette* that he believed Malak must have been in error when he said the two Arkansas teenagers lost consciousness because they had smoked marijuana. McBay, who also taught pathology and pharmacology at the University of North Carolina at Chapel Hill, was considered one of the country's foremost experts in the study of marijuana. He characterized Malak's conclusion as "very bizarre," adding, "I don't know who would agree with it."

"I know of incidents where persons smoked twenty-one marijuana cigarettes, one right after the other," he said. "They become euphoric, but it doesn't make them unconscious." He added, "I don't know what kind of evidence you could possibly use to conclude this. I have never heard of anyone becoming unconscious from this under ordinary circumstances."

Moreover, he contested Malak's methodology in determining the concentrations of THC reported. McBay told the paper that no method of testing currently known could produce such accurate results. "I think the burden should be on the state or the individual who made that conclusion," he said.

"When I see this kind of result, it's usually someone who doesn't know a damn thing about marijuana or the testing."

The other toxicologist the parents had contacted also questioned Malak's results. James C. Garriott, Ph.D., of San Antonio, a specialist in drug detection, said that while many of Malak's methods were standard, he doubted the reliability of some of Malak's conclusions. "For confirmation of cannabinoids in blood, the only completely reliable technique available is mass spectrometry," Garriott said, adding, "I am sure that this was not done in this case. . . . "[1] Asked about the intoxicating effects of marijuana, Garriott told reporters, "Although it induces a 'dreamy' euphoric state, it does not directly induce sleep. . . . It is unlikely that an individual would be affected by marijuana, even in a high dose, to the extent that he would be totally unaware of his surroundings or be unable to respond to a threatening noise or other threatening circumstances."

Dr. Donald McMillan, chairman of the Department of Pharmacology at the University of Arkansas for Medical Sciences, cast further doubt on Malak's ruling. While McMillan had not reviewed Malak's reports, he was nonetheless willing to observe, "It is hard for me to imagine someone put into a sleep by marijuana from which they couldn't be aroused."

The Iveses and the Henrys took the statements as bitter validation. First they could not understand why the sheriff's office had been so ready to accept Malak's findings that, when reviewed by his peers, left him so open to ridicule. But what could they do? The boys were dead and buried, their deaths having been officially ruled accidents. The police were through with the case. It looked like there was no power in the county or state who could or would get to the bottom of it.

And then the improbable happened. The day after the press conference, the phone rang. When Linda answered it, the caller identified himself as Richard Garrett, a district deputy prosecuting attorney. Garrett told Linda that he had had no idea, until he saw the media coverage of the press conference, that the families of the dead boys had been dissatisfied with the sheriff's investigation. Garrett said he hoped to be able to help. He told Linda that he was considering holding a prosecutor's hearing to reexamine the case. He wanted to know if she would help.

She caught her breath. "A prosecutor's hearing?" she asked warily, reaching for a pen. She had not always been so cautious. There had been a time when she had not automatically made notes about calls. But Linda was different now from the trusting woman she had been just a few months earlier. Now caution was a reflex. Garrett explained that a prosecutor's hearing was a rather unusual event. In fact, it was highly unusual. It was intended for special inquiries, particularly when a cause of death was in dispute. He compared the process to a grand jury investigation in that both were fact-finding efforts. Unlike a grand jury hearing, however, which was held in secret, a prosecutor's hearing was open to the public. If new evidence were presented, the prosecutor could set aside a medical examiner's ruling and submit the case to a grand jury. There it could be examined anew. As Linda scribbled her notes, Garrett asked if she and Larry, along with the Henrys, would meet with him the next day to discuss the possibility of such a hearing and what questions would need to be asked.

When Larry came home, Linda reported the call with a mixture of hope and caution. Where once the two would have heard in the call a public servant doing his job, they now backed up to assess a bigger picture. Garrett's position of deputy prosecutor was an appointed one. He was now running for the top job, as a Democratic candidate for the elected post of prosecuting attorney. Linda and Larry realized that, with the campaign gearing up, Garrett's interest in their case might be entirely self-serving. But so what? Could a new look at the case—whatever motivated it—possibly hurt? And maybe it would help. They decided that if Garrett could revive the investigation and make some sense of the deaths, he deserved any credit—and any votes—he could get.

Linda looked out the sliding glass doors of her patio to where the first daffodils of spring were opening their blooms. What might a hearing accomplish? She longed to see Malak's ruling reexamined, to hear it challenged in open court in a way that she, Larry, and the Henrys had not been able to challenge it in Malak's office. But she also wanted to hear how Sheriff James Steed and all his deputies could defend the thinness of their investigation. She would like to hear Steed pressed to say more than that the deaths were just "a strange accident."

"There was nothing at the scene of the accident that was visible that would make anyone think it was a homicide," Steed repeatedly told the Benton paper. "That's the reason we do an autopsy. If there were injuries that were not consistent with being run over by a train, these would have been detected by Dr. Malak. Dr. Malak found no such injuries, and I have complete confidence in him." Questioned about Malak's credibility, Steed was unwavering. "If he says it, that usually makes it so."

He sounds so smug, Linda thought, watching as freezing rain pelted the stoic flowers. By then she had requested and received a copy of the deputies' investigative file. It was an inch thick, and that, Linda thought, was about how deep the investigators in this case had dug. Tallent's and Elmendorf's notes, dated almost entirely in the week or so immediately after the deaths, consisted mainly of interviews with high school students who had known Kevin and Don. They were asked primarily two questions: Had the boys been known to be suicidal? What do you know about their use of drugs?

Incensed by the shallowness of the work, Linda sat down at her kitchen table and wrote the sheriff a letter, a copy of which she sent to the *Benton*

Courier. "Sheriff Steed," it began, "You have stated that you are satisfied with the investigation your department has conducted into the death of my son, Kevin Ives, and his friend, Don Henry. You have also insinuated that our dissatisfaction with the investigation stems from the personal tragedy that we have suffered. I would like to point out to you, as well as the public, some of the reasons that we are dissatisfied:

"It is a fact that the area was never roped off and protected as a crime scene. The area could not possibly have been searched thoroughly for evidence of a crime. Whenever family and friends go down to the scene and recover a foot, the gun stock, and other parts of the gun Kevin and Don had, as well as other personal belongings, I consider this evidence of how 'well' the area was searched. . . . " The letter continued, citing the train crew's efforts to have the tarp retrieved and the fact that when Don's clothes had been returned to the Henrys, Marvelle Henry had found a second, small bag of marijuana in one of the pockets of Don's pants. The police had missed it entirely. "If something like this was overlooked," Linda's letter demanded, "what else?"

It was all she could think of to do. But Steed looked invulnerable. This year he was running for reelection to what would be his sixth term as sheriff. Until Garrett's call, it looked like everyone in authority was intent on ignoring the case. Now, when they least expected it, an official with authority to call a grand jury was proposing a serious inquiry. Larry and Linda let themselves indulge in some actual hope. That night, for the first time in weeks, they went to bed and dared to dream. Maybe, with Garrett's help, the truth about what had happened that night on the tracks would finally be brought to light.

MEETING GARRETT AND HARMON

Garrett was a large, disheveled man. In fact, he was a slob, Linda decided, as she, Larry, Curtis, and Marvelle took seats in his cluttered office. There was simply no other word for it. Half of his shirttail hung outside badly wrinkled pants, held up loosely with wide suspenders. Linda reminded herself of the man she had heard on the phone. Unseen, he had sounded competent. Another man, his appearance only slightly more professional, was also in the office. Garrett introduced him as Dan Harmon, his law partner and friend. Linda recognized Harmon's name, and although her mind raced, she could not quite remember from where. She would have to ask Larry. She did not want to miss a word as the lawyers got down to business.

Charitably, Linda decided to think of their look as "casual." She felt inclined to trust them. For one thing, they did not put on airs. They spoke like ordinary country folks. And while it might have been easy on first glance to write Garrett off as dumb, when the meeting got under way it became clear that he was not. He was sharp—and Harmon was sharper still. As Harmon spoke, Linda relaxed. He seemed confident, physically and mentally self-assured. There was a quickness about him and he spoke with a sense of commitment. After battling indifference for so long, Linda found Harmon's intensity reassuring. It represented all she had wanted for this case: a passion to get at the truth. Though Garrett, the deputy prosecutor, had called the meeting, Linda noticed that it was Harmon, who held no public office, who seemed to be taking charge. He spoke of the likelihood of a grand jury hearing as though he had been through it before.

That was it! Suddenly Linda remembered where she had heard of Harmon. It had been in the early 1980s, back when Kevin was in junior high. There had been a huge scandal involving Saline Memorial Hospital. The case had gone before a grand jury. Dan Harmon had been the special prosecutor. What had all that been about? She would have to think about that later. This meeting was too important.

For more than an hour the parents poured out their questions. They outlined the inconsistencies that had troubled them. "We aren't crazy," Linda told the two lawyers. "We just wish everybody would sit still a minute and look at what little we know. If they'd do that, we think that common sense will tell them that the investigation was superficial and that Malak's ruling must be wrong."

Garrett and Harmon seemed to agree. With the parents' help, they compiled a list of thirty-three witnesses, including Malak, who would be subpoenaed. Garrett promised to call a hearing before the week was out. At last it appeared that a real investigation was at hand. Larry and Linda left feeling encouraged, even ecstatic.

That night, as they discussed the day's events, Linda asked Larry what he remembered about the grand jury investigation Harmon had conducted about the hospital. That had been back in 1984. Four years had passed since then, and Larry's memory was sketchy, too. But between them, Larry and Linda pieced together a hazy recollection of the story. The hospital's chief administrator had been accused of embezzlement. There had been a state police investigation. The grand jury had met all summer, amid rumors of fraud, cocaine, sex parties, extortion, and—weren't there videotapes? Yes, they seemed to remember. Or at least that was what had been reported. And what had come of all that? Gradually, as they talked, details came drifting back. Harmon's grand jury had indicted six or seven people and the top administrator had gone to prison. And the rumored tapes? As best as Larry and Linda could recall, they had never been recovered.

Harmon had emerged a hero. The scandal had strained the small community, shaking its confidence in the county-owned hospital. With the indictments and the replacement of the hospital's upper echelon, residents of Saline County were able to put the affair behind them. In the secrecy of the grand jury, Harmon had conducted a sensitive investigation that touched some of the county's most prominent citizens. The more they reflected on it, the more Larry and Linda drew comfort from the episode. If Harmon could wade into that situation and get results, maybe he could do as well for Kevin.

THE SHERIFF'S DEAL

The prosecutor's hearing was scheduled to begin on February 18, 1988. The boys had been dead for six months. Late one afternoon, two days before the hearing was to begin, Harmon called to ask Linda if she and Larry could meet him at his office.

They arrived there before Harmon did. As they pulled into the parking lot, they could see Curtis and Marvelle Henry waiting in their car. In a car on the other side of the Henrys was a man they did not recognize. When Harmon pulled up, the man in the third car opened his door. Larry and Linda realized with a jolt that the man was Sheriff James Steed, the person whom they held most accountable for the investigation they were working so hard to reopen. Linda was incensed. "What the hell does he think he's doing?" she whispered to Larry as they followed Steed into Harmon's office. "I don't know," Larry whispered back.

Acknowledging the tension in the room, Harmon worked quickly to dispel it. "I invited you all here because I kind of thought I needed to get everybody together to work this out. The bottom line is, all of us want the same thing."

Linda gasped in disgust. Harmon turned to her. "Look, Linda," he asked, "what is it that you really want?"

"A good investigation," she snapped. "That's all we've ever wanted."

"Well," Harmon said, "that's what James here wants, too. He admits that some mistakes have been made. I've talked to him and he agrees that we need to step back and take another look at this case. But his feeling is that you've all been pretty hard on him, especially with that press conference. That doesn't make his job any easier."

Linda had no intention of making Steed's job easier. In fact, she hoped he would be trounced in the coming election—and that her letter to the editor would help that. But it was becoming clear, as the couples sat uncomfortably in the room, that Harmon had different hopes. Harmon wanted them to cooperate with Steed. In fact, Harmon announced that he had arranged a deal. The sheriff would assure the families of the investigation they wanted if they, in turn, would withdraw their criticisms of him and publicly state their support.

Linda's face clouded with doubt. "Look," Harmon urged her, "if someone else wins the election, you take whatever you get. They might take another look at the case or they might not. There won't be any assurance. This way you have a promise."

Linda stared at Steed. "Will you bring in the state police?" The sheriff promised he would.

Linda found the deal distasteful. Nothing Steed could say or do at this point could change the damage done early in the case. She felt reluctant to retract a word of the complaints she had outlined in her letter or voiced at the families' press conference. But Harmon was persuasive. All they needed to do, he said, was to soften their criticism of Steed. After all, Harmon cajoled, the sheriff was offering to correct the problem. That was more of a turnaround, Harmon reminded them, than they were getting from the medical examiner. They could still come down as hard as they wanted on Malak. That wasn't at issue here.

The couples talked it over. With or without their support, Steed might be reelected, as he had been repeatedly during the past decade. They had to consider that. If that happened, it would be better to be working with Steed than against him. Either way, it was a disagreeable situation, but the parents admitted that they saw Harmon's point, and by the end of the meeting they accepted his proposal. "I'd lie through my teeth to get an investigation," Linda told Larry as they drove home. "I'll do whatever we have to do." Larry heard an unfamiliar steeliness in her voice.

Harmon scheduled a press conference for the following morning. A half hour before the media were to arrive, the parents met Harmon at Steed's office. Harmon handed Linda a statement he had written. "Linda should be the one to read it," Harmon said, "because she was the one of the four of you who got most publicly crosswise with Steed."

Silently Linda looked at the paper and read: "The problems we have encountered in the investigation of our sons' deaths have not been with the Saline County Sheriff's Department. The sheriff's department has been cooperative and helpful and has devoted a great deal of man-hours to the investigation. It is unfortunate that the initial crime scene search did not uncover everything that it should have. However, the scene covered at least a half mile of railroad track and the surrounding woods and thickets. . . . "

Linda threw Harmon a look of disgust. "I'm not going to read this." She shoved the pages toward him. "Our agreement was that we would say our major dissatisfaction was with the crime lab. Steed would make a statement saying that the case wasn't closed. And Garrett would make a statement about the prosecutor's hearing—about how you were all going to work together and take another look at things. That's what we agreed."

Harmon begged her to change her mind, but Linda was adamant. "I'll stand here and keep my mouth shut while someone else reads it, but that's as far as I'll go. You'll never get me to say that anybody at that sheriff's office was helpful and cooperative." Finally, as the reporters began to arrive, Larry, in an effort at conciliation, said that he would read the statement. As the television lights switched on, Larry read the words that had incensed his wife. "We have encountered problems getting the state crime lab to cooperate and felt that a court order was necessary to obtain information. The sheriff's office has never refused to cooperate. We are pleased that progress is presently being made in the investigation and want every possible lead followed and pursued and have no other comment at this time."

Steed announced, for the first time, that he would request assistance in the case from the Arkansas State Police. And Garrett offered a few more details about his plans for the upcoming hearing. When a reporter asked what questions would be addressed in the hearing, Garrett mentioned almost offhandedly that he did not believe the boys' deaths had been accidental. Though he later complained that the reporter had published an off-the-record remark, Larry and Linda were gratified to hear it. Uncomfortable as they had been with Harmon's attempts to make peace between them and Steed, they had to admit that for the first time since Kevin and Don died, it looked like someone was taking their case seriously.

Billy Heath and Shirley Raper, the ambulance workers, were among those subpoenaed to testify at the prosecutor's hearing. Seeing their names on the list, an enterprising reporter cornered the two at the hospital. An article the next day quoted Raper as recalling that "for some reason," the color of the blood at the scene "stuck out like a sore thumb." Heath said that they had expected to find "fresher, more colorful" blood, because usually "when you go to a trauma scene you will see blood splattered everywhere." But it had not been that way at the tracks. Rather, Raper described the blood as looking "bland." She compared the pallor of the victims' mangled bodies to that of "a sawdust, colorless dummy. It was just strange," she told the paper. Heath acknowledged that he "didn't feel right about it" when a member of the train crew reported how still the boys had been. It was a sentiment Raper echoed, noting that she, too, had felt "funny vibes" about the scenes.[2]

The night before the hearing was to start, Richard Garrett, Curtis Henry, and Larry Ives went to the site on the tracks where the boys had died, arriving there about twenty minutes before a train was to pass. Garrett, wearing a pair of insulated overalls, lay down on the tracks, positioning himself as the crewmen had seen the boys. "It was very uncomfortable because of the rocks," he reported later. "The only way I could get halfway comfortable was to move, to rest my head on the rail." He noted that not only had the boys been in the more uncomfortable position, but they had been wearing T-shirts and jeans, not padded overalls. "I stayed on the track as long as I could," Garrett reported. "It was terrifying. I watched the train come. I heard it blow its whistles. I felt the rails shake. You could tell the train was coming from up to a mile away. I don't see how anyone could have slept through it. It scared the devil out of me."

THE PROSECUTOR'S HEARING

The century-old courtroom in Benton was packed throughout the three-day hearing. Linda, Larry, Curtis, and Marvelle sat in the front of the room at a table with Garrett. Seated before them on the bench was Circuit Judge John Cole, a sober, gaunt-looking man who lent the proceedings a no-nonsense air. Harmon, who had no official role in the hearing, bustled into and out of the room between whispered consultations with Garrett. Watching the two, Linda had the feeling that, as competent as Garrett appeared, it was Harmon who was calling the shots.

Whoever was behind it, the inquiry was producing surprising results. Police officers called to testify reported that on the night before the deaths they had received a "suspicious person" call complaining that a man near the Shobe Road crossing had jumped out of a car and pointed a pistol at another vehicle. He was never apprehended or identified. Friends of Kevin and Don called to the stand recounted the boys' whereabouts in the hours before they died. According to the accounts, the two had dropped by to see Don's sister, Gayla, who was staying at a friend's house. They had shot pool at a local video arcade and driven around with a third friend near an old swimming hole near Bryant.

When members of the train crew testified, Linda and others in the courtroom learned for the first time that soon after the police arrived, an approaching train that had been stopped nearby at the frantic crew's request had been given permission to continue on. It had passed alongside the halted train on a parallel set of tracks. When Garrett, astonished, asked who had allowed the second locomotive to pass through the scene of an investigation, the crew members testified that the decision had come from the Saline County deputies themselves.

Wayne Lainhart, the state trooper who had responded to the scene, testified that he had observed several pieces of particleboard near the point of impact. "I speculated that the children were lying on the particleboard because the other items, like the flashlight and scope, were found near the particleboard." The existence of a piece of particleboard had not appeared in any of the deputies' accounts. Linda found herself thinking of the piece of board Larry had brought to the state crime lab.

Billy Heath proved a reluctant witness. Only after persistent questioning by Garrett did he concede that the color of the blood and the relative lack of splattering would have been consistent with the possibility that the boys had died before being struck by the train. Raper, by contrast, set the courtroom abuzz when she related that, as she maneuvered her ambulance through the woods near the tracks in an effort to get closer to the boys, she had encountered three African-American men at a spot near the point of impact. The three men, whom Raper encountered on a rutted and rarely used road, told her that they were members of the Alexander Volunteer Fire Department. They had noticed the commotion, they said, and had come out to see if they could help. Raper's testimony—the first news of anyone being in the vicinity of the deaths—created a sensation. Garrett cast a puzzled looked at the Iveses and Henrys. Had they heard this before? The amazed couples shook their heads. Turning back to Raper, Garrett asked, "Why have you not reported this before?"

"Because no one ever asked," she answered.

George Moore, the hospital's ambulance supervisor, was called to explain why it had taken two court orders to force Saline Memorial Hospital to turn over its records from that night. Moore testified that at first he had been unclear about which records the families were seeking. "Once I realized whom they were speaking of," he said, "the record was produced."

The most sensational appearance, however, was that of Dr. Fahmy Malak. The state medical examiner climbed into the witness stand and bowed dramatically toward the parents. Before Garrett could address him, Malak said, "I want the families of these two boys to know that I forgive them for everything they have done." Linda turned to Larry. He looked stunned.

Malak carried with him a large valise, which he explained held enlarged photographs of the autopsies, photographs that would prove the correctness of his ruling. The parents immediately objected. Huddling with Garrett, Linda argued that there was no point to such a display. Malak's ruling had centered entirely upon toxicological evidence. The parents could see no reason for him to display their sons' cut-up bodies. "Kevin knew these people," Linda pleaded with Garrett, gesturing at the crowded courtroom. "He would not want them to see him like this." Garrett returned to Malak and told him that he would have to testify without showing his photographs. The medical examiner refused. He would not testify at all, he retorted, if he was barred from "revealing" his "evidence."

Judge Cole ordered a recess while Garrett placed a call to the state's attorney general. When Garrett returned, he reported that Malak had won. No state official was going to force Malak to testify on any terms other than his own. When Cole pounded his gavel calling the hearing back to order, Garrett made the announcement in open court. Malak, he said, would be showing some sensitive autopsy photographs. Anyone who did not wish to see them should feel free to step outside. Grim-faced, Larry and Linda, Curtis and Marvelle, left the room. Malak showed the photographs to those who remained, explaining the various injuries that the train had inflicted. When Garrett asked, however, what had caused the deaths, Malak reiterated his official position that the deaths had been an accident brought on by marijuana. And yes, he acknowledged under questioning, the critical evidence had been found in the blood. No, he further admitted, that evidence could not be seen in the photographs.

The families returned to the courtroom. Malak remained on the stand, where his testimony became the most sensational of the three-day hearing. One thing that had bothered the parents was that there had been no mention in the autopsy reports of the bodies having been examined for sexual assault. So Garrett asked Malak: "Did you examine either of these boys, Dr. Malak, to determine whether they had been sexually abused?"

Malak responded, "Absolutely. Yes."

"Why does that not appear in either of the autopsy reports?" Garrett asked.

Malak became agitated. "Well, Mr. Garrett," he said in fractured English, "you just was trying not to let me use the photographs, the first photographs of the autopsy, and citing about the sensitivity about the family, the parents. Rest assured, so many families object forcibly that we check their children for homosexuality. But I am here, under oath. I am telling you I examined these kids and they were negative. There was no homosexual act."

Listening, Linda felt a familiar mix of emotions. She was relieved to hear that Kevin had not endured a sexual attack. But she was appalled at Malak's rationale for not mentioning that information—information that might have been important to an investigation and could have eased the parents' minds. Looking at the medical examiner with contempt and pity, she thought, He doesn't even know the difference between sexual abuse and homosexuality. But Malak was unshakable. He insisted under Garrett's questioning that he would quit his job if it were ever proven that the boys had died before being hit by the train. "The definite proof they were alive at the time of the crash is the aspiration of blood in the lungs," he said. "The children bled from the crash. They died of the crash."

Garrett pressed further on the matter of the blood, asking Malak whether he had tested articles of the boys' clothing for the possible presence of anyone else's blood. Malak responded that his own visual inspection had been enough. "Mr. Garrett," he said, "I studied hematology for two years. Now, what I know about hematology, I don't believe a serologist knows what I know about it. If there was any evidence to tell me there's different distribution and different quality I am seeing, I will do something about it. You have to consider, too, the finding of their bodies. Like I read you are getting a witness to tell you the color of the blood on the scene."

"Uh-huh," Garrett responded, uncertain of what Malak was getting at. Was Malak referring to the EMTs' accounts of the unusual color of the blood?

"What do they know about blood?" Malak demanded. "What causes the color of the blood? What affects the color of the blood? This is inflammatory. It has no relation to the death. Don't make something more than what it is. These kids died because of the crash, the train passed on them, and the fact they were smoking marijuana. We are not tarnishing these kids. They are like my children. I am not putting this marijuana in them. It was found. It's a fact. We have to accept it. And this is life."

And then Malak added what many considered his most offensive statement. "Could it be a homicide?" he asked rhetorically. "There is one condition that fulfills the criteria of homicide. If the engineer is lying, he could stop and he wouldn't, if he was under influence of marijuana or alcohol."

The attack on the train crew's integrity leveled Larry. "I know these guys personally," he later told reporters. "Out of this whole investigation the one thing that I am completely satisfied with is what the train crew has done." Jerry Tomlin, the conductor, fumed: "All I've got to say about Dr. Malak's testimony is that I will go with him and be tested any day, any time he chooses. Then we'll go to the state mental hospital to have him tested for a brain."

Garrett concluded his questioning of Malak by asking if it was possible that the boys had received other wounds, wounds that had been masked by the violence of the train. "Not with me," Malak replied, relaxing in the chair. "Maybe other person would miss it, but not me."[3]

Malak and the deputies who testified seemed to be the only ones so self-assured. After the hearing had concluded, the mayor of Bryant reflected that it had been necessary because "I think there's doubts in everyone's minds." The principal of Bryant High School went further. "There's probably not a person in this community who feels it was a freak accident," he said. "How many times would two boys pass out at the same time, and in the same position?" When a reporter for the *Arkansas Gazette* interviewed students at the school, not one was quoted as believing the deaths had had anything to do with marijuana.

Richard Garrett reached the same conclusion. On February 26, 1988, five days after the prosecutor's hearing ended, Garrett issued a report that overturned Dr. Fahmy Malak's ruling. A half year after Kevin and Don died, Garrett ordered that the official ruling on the manner of death in their case be changed from "accidental" to "undetermined."

FIVE

EXHUMATIONS AND AUTOPSIES

FEBRUARY–APRIL 1988

In the difficult months between Malak's ruling and Garrett's hearing, as conjecture about what might have happened at the tracks swirled through Saline County, one of Linda's friends asked her if she had ever consulted a psychic. "No," Linda said. "I've never been to one in my life."

THE PSYCHIC

The idea had never entered her mind. But by now, much had entered Linda's life that had never been there before. She was reading autopsy reports and calling press conferences. She was talking with national experts about the effects of marijuana. She was paying a private detective, wrangling with a hospital, securing court orders, and arguing with a deputy attorney general. All of this, and still the anguish of Kevin's and Don's unresolved deaths hung around her like a shroud. By now she was willing to consider just about anything. If a psychic might help, she would see one. Even if the visit proved a waste of time, it could hardly be less productive than dealing with officials.

The friend recommended a Little Rock woman by the name of Carol Pate. She had a prominent clientele and had been consulted in other investigations, at times with some success. Linda called to make an appointment, saying only that she wanted to talk about her son.

"Well, she looks the part," Linda thought as the psychic met her at the door. Pate had long, dark hair and long, dark eyelashes. She had asked Linda to bring a photograph of her son and something that had belonged to him. Linda had selected a gold necklace that Kevin had always worn. It had been recovered with his body. Fingering the necklace, Pate said, "Your son died a violent death, didn't he?" Linda reflected that, given the media coverage, it would have been fairly surprising if Pate had been unaware of the violence of Kevin's death. But then, to Linda's surprise, Pate began to describe the deaths. She spoke as though she had somehow witnessed them, relating details Linda had never heard before, not even as speculative gossip.

Linda listened skeptically while Pate spoke with an air of certainty. She described seeing the boys in a field that was separated from the tracks by trees. She said Kevin and Don were sitting on a log and they were passing a cigarette back and forth between them, occasionally shining a light across the field. She described a car coming down a road in the middle of the field, the car stopping, and three men getting out. They had a young girl with them. "I want to say these men are policemen," Pate said, "but I don't know why, because they're not dressed like policemen. Whatever it is, they hold some position of authority." She said that the girl who was with them was in distress. She was screaming. The men were treating her roughly. The girl was very young, she said, and blond, with rather a long face. She described the clothes the girl was wearing.

Linda felt nervous. What Pate was saying sounded weird. But the woman continued with her story, speaking as if in a trance. The men, she said, had not noticed the boys where they were sitting in the dark. But the boys could see the men, and when they saw them mistreating the girl, Kevin shouted, "Hey, what's going on?" Startled, the men ran over to the boys. A brief skirmish ensued, during which Kevin was struck in the face with an object that Pate could not identify. Another man hit Don in the back. Don fell. The man jerked him up and stood holding him from behind. After the attack, an argument erupted among the men. Surprised to find the boys there, the men had reacted without thinking. Now they realized their brutality had created a problem. Both boys were severely injured. The men argued about what to do. Pate said that they decided to drag and carry the boys by way of a small dirt road through some trees to the nearby railroad tracks. There they covered the boys with something green. Pate's sense of the scene was that the men hoped that a train would pass over the boys without its crew ever realizing it had struck two human beings. But the fabric placed over the boys to cover them had partially blown off.

Now Linda was paying close attention. Pate's scenario had not struck her as plausible—until she mentioned the mysterious covering. It was a part of the story that had received almost no mention in the media. Larry and Linda had themselves only heard of it through their contact with the crew members. Certainly the deputies were not spreading the word. Linda wanted Pate to continue, but the psychic had little more to offer.[1]

That afternoon Linda could hardly wait for Larry to get home. She walked around the house wondering how she was going to tell him that she had been to see a psychic. But Pate's description had seemed so vivid that she had come home and made up her mind. Larry had been to the spot on the tracks where Kevin and Don had been found. So far, Linda had been loath to go. But now she decided she would visit the site, too. She would see for herself if anything about it resembled Pate's description.

"Linda, it's raining," Larry said, when she told him what she wanted to do.

"I don't care. I want to go down there."

As the two headed for their car, she asked, "Larry, is there a field anywhere down there?"

He thought, and answered, "Yeah, there is one. It belongs to a guy I know who works for the railroad."

They drove down a road to a field that looked to Linda like the one Pate had described. At a corner of the field near the woods was a small, rural baseball diamond. As they walked, Linda told Larry the scenario Pate had outlined.

"Linda, this field is a long way from the tracks," Larry complained, his skepticism clear.

The location of the boys' bodies on the tracks had always been rather puzzling. It was so far from any road that the police and ambulance had had trouble getting close. The deputies had parked on Shobe Road at the Alexander crossing, almost a mile away. If the boys had been injured or killed somewhere else and their bodies laid on the tracks in an attempt to destroy evidence, why would anyone have bothered to carry them so far? Or, if they had been attacked where they were found, what would their assailants have been doing in such a remote spot in the first place? Larry felt certain that whatever had happened to the boys had happened there on the spot. Walking through the field, he and Linda discussed various possibilities. "What if whatever happened, happened in this field?" Linda asked. Larry pointed to a dense stand of trees blocking access to the tracks.

"Look at how thick these woods are," he said. Linda realized he was right. Why would anyone struggle through woods like that all the way to the tracks? But as the two turned around, a train's horn pierced the air. As the thrum of the locomotive grew louder, nearing where they stood, Linda and Larry could see the engine through the trees. The tracks were much closer to the field than Larry had believed. As the cars flashed by, they estimated the distance from where they stood to be no more than about four hundred feet.

"Let's walk through the woods," Linda suggested, "and see where we come out on the tracks."

They found that getting to the tracks was also easier than they had expected. A little creek ran alongside the field. On this day in early winter, there was just a little water in the creek. They followed it through the woods for a short distance. When the woods opened up again, they found themselves looking at the trestle that marked the spot where the train had hit the boys. Larry was stunned. Linda told him that Pate had described the boys being carried on a dirt road through the woods. Larry reflected that in August, at night, with the creek dry, it might have looked like a road.

Abandoning any lingering skepticism, Linda came to hope that Carol Pate might truly hold some answers. It was a far-fetched hope, but by now Linda was committed to pursuing any lead that might supply answers where the police had not.

Curtis Henry disapproved of Linda's increasingly personal quest. He liked Harmon and Garrett. He believed they would solve the case. While Curtis had agreed with Linda that the media needed to be notified after Malak's ruling, now that Harmon and Garrett were involved, he wanted to leave the case with these officials, keeping the media out. He regarded Linda's contact with Garrett and Harmon, and her reports of information such as what the psychic had said, as needless interference. Over time, their different approaches would become a serious wedge between the two families.

Yet for now, the couples were still more together than apart. The Henrys and the Iveses were bound by the extraordinary deaths of their sons and by the extraordinary events that had followed. They alone had had the experience of burying their mutilated children and, afterward, of being told to accept the unacceptable. They alone could understand the depth of their respective traumas. And now, as spring was beginning to announce itself in the redbud and tulip trees at the cemeteries, they alone could appreciate the difficulty they were about to endure with the re-opening of the graves.

THE EXHUMATIONS

Immediately after the prosecutor's hearing, Richard Garrett and Dan Harmon asked the parents how they felt about submitting Don's and Kevin's remains to an out-of-state forensic pathologist. How did they feel about a second round of autopsies? The couples agreed that, in light of Malak's discredited ruling, new autopsies were a grim necessity. In March 1988, a month after Judge Cole overturned Malak's ruling and ruled the manner of the deaths "undetermined," the Henrys and the Iveses once again entered his courtroom, this time as Harmon presented their petition to allow the exhumations. The process was not the cut-and-dried affair Linda had expected. Cole asked several questions and at times seemed reluctant to grant the petition. Seated together at the table in the courtroom, Linda and Marvelle clutched each other's hands. Once again Linda found herself braced. If I can just get through this experience, she told herself, it will get easier after this. It was getting to be an old refrain. Now she wondered as she waited in court if it ever would get easier. Finally Cole pounded his gavel. "Petition granted," he said. Linda burst into tears. A throng of photographers and reporters surrounded the shaken parents as they stepped out of the courtroom. Linda headed for the car, while Larry remained behind to answer questions.

In the days ahead, as Kevin's classmates, the sons and daughters of friends, prepared for their prom and other graduation rites, Linda tried not to think of the cemetery or of the ground being opened and Kevin's coffin lifted out by a crane. Rather, she concentrated on the hope that the new autopsies would provide some better answers.

"A VERY CLOUDY ISSUE"

It was easy to hold the focus, particularly on Dr. Malak. Much of the state was also focused on the combative medical examiner as, almost daily, newspapers and television stations reported new revelations about his office, and pressure on him mounted. In 1988 the state was learning that even the legality of Malak's hiring nine years earlier was in doubt. Bill Clinton had approved Malak's hiring in May 1979, five months after Clinton had been sworn in to his first term as Arkansas's governor. A law passed shortly after Clinton's election had transferred the formerly independent office of the state medical examiner to the state crime lab, which was then part of the Department of Public Safety. As a result of that move, the director of the crime lab had hired Malak, and the director of public safety had approved the hiring, noting at the time that he did so "with the governor's approval."[2] Two years later, the Department of Public Safety was abolished, and the crime lab, with Malak ensconced as medical examiner, was again an independent agency.

But as criticism of Malak mounted, a check of the records revealed that, legally, Malak was supposed to have been hired by the state Medical Examiner's Commission, a body created in the late 1960s. That commission, however, had not met for years. When the commissioners were contacted, most reacted with amazement and declared that they had had no idea the commission even existed.

When this odd bit of history came to light, Arkansas Attorney General Steve Clark was asked to clear up the mess. He issued an opinion stating that, since the Medical Examiner's Commission had never been abolished, it was still a legal entity. Noting that the law authorizing the commission to hire the medical examiner had never been repealed, a spokesman for the attorney general commented: "If it's on the books, it should have the same force and validity that every other law should have." Despite the murky situation, no one made a move to oust Malak. As the spokesman put it, the attorney general's rationale was this: although Malak had not been hired as required by law, he had been "hired under the process which they thought was in effect at the time."[3] When the problem came to light in 1988 and reporters questioned the governor's office about the legitimacy of Malak's appointment, a Clinton spokesman reported, "From what we know about it, it's just a very cloudy issue."

By then other questions were dogging Malak as well. Reporters investigating the medical examiner's background learned that he had not become board certified in forensic pathology until 1985, despite the fact that he had been hired in 1979 and had testified in at least two trials that he had been certified since 1978. State law when Malak was hired required that the medical examiner be board certified or "eligible for board certification." Malak's status fulfilled neither requirement. The discrepancies were widely reported, but Malak weathered all storms. And there would be many more.

As confidence in Malak eroded, newspapers reported that a state legislator requested an attorney general's opinion after Malak issued a ruling of suicide in the case of a teenager from north Arkansas who had died from a rifle wound.[4] Witnesses said the boy, who had no history of depression, had been cleaning the gun when it discharged. Another disputed case centered upon a North Little Rock neurologist who had admitted himself to a psychiatric hospital suffering from severe depression. The doctor was later found hanged with his belt in a shower in his hospital room. His widow sued the hospital, alleging negligence. When the case went to trial, Malak testified on the hospital's behalf. He said that, while he originally had ruled the death a suicide, he had since concluded that it fit the description of autoerotic self-asphyxiation, a dangerous form of masturbation in which a person deprives himself of oxygen in order to heighten sexual pleasure. Malak, consequently, had changed his ruling on the manner of the doctor's death from "suicide" to "accident."

By March, as Linda and Larry began bracing for the exhumation of their son's remains, disputes over several of Malak's older rulings were also coming to light. One of the most controversial centered on a case five years earlier in which the victim had died of massive head injuries after a fight in a parking lot. While some witnesses had claimed that the young man had fallen off the back of a flatbed truck, others had said he was killed by a deliberate blow. The assistant medical examiner at the crime lab who performed the autopsy on the boy ruled the manner of death "undetermined." Nine months later Malak reversed the assistant's ruling and declared the death a homicide. Malak concluded that a bruise on the victim's broken collarbone matched perfectly with the butt of a .30–.30 caliber rifle owned by the alleged assailant. The man was charged with murder.

At trial, Dr. Malak illustrated for jurors what he described as a "one-to-one match" between the shape of the rifle butt and the injury to the collarbone. He did this by placing a transparency of the rifle butt over a life-sized autopsy photograph of the victim's upper body. Malak testified that the shape of the weapon and the shape of the wound corresponded "like a rubber stamp." When the defense attorney objected that he had not been previously made aware of the incriminating transparency, and questioned how long it had been available at the crime lab, Malak answered under oath, "For so long, several months." The transparency was admitted into evidence over defense objections, and largely on the strength of it, the defendant was convicted of first-degree murder. Five years after that trial, as press inquiries into Malak's background intensified, a check of records at the crime lab revealed that a work order for the transparency—the only one ever issued for the rifle—had been dated just six days before the trial. Days after that damaging story appeared, the two crime lab employees who had conducted the autopsy on the victim alleged publicly that, although Malak had testified that he had supervised the autopsy, he had not been present.

Linda read the news accounts with a mixture of outrage and hope. Every day the revelations grew more incredible. Not only did it appear that Malak had lied under oath about his presence at the autopsy, and lied again about when the transparency of the rifle was made, but now a third crime lab employee stepped forward to add another nasty twist. Mike Vowell, the photographer who had made the disputed transparency, charged publicly that Malak had deliberately misused the film by reversing it in its frame to make it conform to the injury to the collarbone. Vowell reported that six days before the trial, he had placed it in a cardboard frame and marked its correct viewing side. But he said Malak had removed the transparency in preparation for the trial. When Vowell saw the film out of its frame and reversed, he said he called the error to Malak's attention, but the medical examiner ignored him.

For weeks, as Linda watched, expecting the medical examiner to be fired, Malak dodged reporters' repeated attempts at interviews. When he finally acquiesced and was questioned about his perjurious testimony, Malak blamed his foreign roots. He insisted that he had not intended to be deceptive. "You have to remember the language barrier, things of that nature." He said the incident involving the transparency had simply been a mistake. "I reversed it," he told a reporter for the *Arkansas Gazette.* "I did it wrong and I have no sweat with that." Asked in 1988 about his sworn statement that he had "definitely, certainly, absolutely" been present at the 1983 autopsy, he responded, "I said that? No, if I said this, it is wrong. It would be a mistake."[5]

So serious were the revelations and so intense was the resulting criticism of Malak that state officials were forced to act. In March, at the height of Malak's negative publicity and a month after the Saline County prosecutor's hearing had overturned his ruling on the manner of death in the Henry-and-Ives case, Clinton's chief of staff, Betsey Wright, met with the crime lab commissioners to recommend the hiring of two out-of-state pathologists to review the way Malak ran his office.[6] Wright said Clinton would finance the review with up to twenty thousand dollars from the Governor's Emergency Fund. The board adopted the governor's proposal, and its chairman, Dr. J. Malcolm Moore, announced that when the out-of-state experts came, they would conduct a broad review of the Arkansas medical examiner's office, as well as look at specific controversial cases, "especially the case in Benton." The state legislature also appointed a committee to review Malak's office. Its chairman noted that the committee's purpose would be to "explore every area of interest and to be totally objective, not politicizing the investigation."[7]

Although Linda and Larry could not understand why Malak had been kept in office for so long, it looked to them as if some problems might finally be fixed. Surely, under a professional review, no medical examiner would be allowed to keep his post after his own staff had accused him of manufacturing evidence, backdating reports, and lying under oath.

NEW AUTOPSIES

At the end of March, Richard Garrett announced that Saline County had hired Dr. Joseph Burton of Marietta, Georgia, the chief medical examiner for north metropolitan Atlanta. Burton would conduct the new round of autopsies on the bodies of Don and Kevin. The pace of the investigation, which had languished for seven months, suddenly stepped up. Earth movers broke ground at one cemetery on April 4 and at the other on April 5. On April 6, Burton, who had flown to Arkansas with two assistants, scrubbed in a room near the morgue at the University of Arkansas medical school and began his own autopsies. The team worked on the bodies for six hours. After that, Burton examined X rays taken by the state crime laboratory. He asked to talk with Malak about some of his procedures, but Malak relayed word that he was unavailable. Burton made arrangements to have the boys' clothing sent from the state crime lab to his lab in Georgia. He then went to the site at the tracks where the train had struck the boys. Like Garrett, he lay down and took several photographs from that position. He also examined items found at the scene, including the gun, and collected tissue samples and samples of the marijuana that had been found with the boys' remains.

Before leaving Arkansas, Burton told Garrett that, according to his calculations, the boys probably had smoked only one or two joints of marijuana before their deaths. Garrett told reporters, "He said it certainly wasn't enough to make them pass out." Burton then met briefly with Linda and Larry and Curtis and Marvelle. "He told us he would do everything possible to find out what he could," Larry told reporters hopefully. "We may not get any better answers, but I believe we are seeing the end of this ordeal."

The following day, the boys' bodies were reburied. The day after that, Larry and Linda went out to dinner together as they always did on their wedding anniversary. This was their twenty-first and, despite the strain of the past seven months, they looked affectionately across the table at each other. They had suffered the unimaginable, but had managed to stay together.

Garrett asked Judge Cole to appoint his law partner, Harmon, to lead the grand jury investigation in the role of special prosecutor. Noting Harmon's experience conducting the Saline Memorial Hospital grand jury, Cole quickly granted the request.

For the Henrys and the Iveses, the appointment was another good sign. Both couples had developed a firm faith in Garrett and in Harmon. "I depend on Danny and Richard," Curtis told reporters. "If they say, 'Let's try it,' I say, 'Let's try it.' I'm behind them one hundred percent."

Linda and Larry felt the same. "We're hopeful that the truth of Kevin's and Don's deaths may finally be known," Linda said. "I believe the label of 'dopehead' that Dr. Malak has placed on their names and memories will be removed—and rightly so. They have been victimized enough."

On April 28, nine months after the deaths, the Saline County Grand Jury was sworn in. It would have been Kevin's eighteenth birthday. While news of the opening of the grand jury investigation, the biggest since the hospital scandal, dominated the front page of the *Benton Courier,* farther back in the paper, a poem Linda had written for her son appeared on the obituary page. It began:

Tangled in a web you did not weave,
Lies and questions—
Answers only a fool would believe . . .

SIX

A FINDING OF MURDER

APRIL–AUGUST 1988

"Is homicide a possibility? We think so," the *Benton Courier* announced in a May 1988 editorial, the day before the grand jury convened. "Two young lives were lost. We support the victims' families in wanting to know why."

Interest in the case was widening. Why the boys died was the primary question. But now there was another as well, and it was in some ways more disturbing: why had this case, which had begun so peculiarly, taken so many peculiar turns?

Speculation would have intensified considerably if the general public had been even slightly aware of a coinciding investigation. At the same time Dan Harmon was gearing up to lead the grand jury, he himself had become the subject of a federal drug investigation. But that information was highly secret, known only to a few people in the U.S. attorney's office, a few state police investigators, and some narcotics investigators working for the sheriff's office in adjoining Pulaski County. To most residents of the Seventh Judicial District, Harmon, who had volunteered to lead the grand jury without pay, was a hero.

THE SALINE COUNTY GRAND JURY

To Linda Ives, the *Courier's* editorial was a cup of cool water delivered in the heat of battle. For months, as she and Larry, along with the Henrys, had been fighting the sheriff, the hospital, and the medical examiner, they had often felt alone, cut off from their community. It was easy, when they went out, to feel that they were being looked at and talked about, for they where. Linda told herself to get over it. She would go out and life would go on, even if it had to include episodes such as a recent one at a local steak house. All through their meal, she, Larry, and Alicia had listened to the family seated nearest to them chatter about the case. It had been terrible.

Everyone had an opinion. Linda knew that in some circles Malak's ruling was roundly ridiculed. Marijuana—by the mid 1980s—was hardly an exotic drug. Linda suspected that in other circles, however, people accepted the medical examiner's ruling. Not so long ago, she herself might have accepted it. Now she was a different person. She knew quite a bit about marijuana. And she hated what Malak's ruling suggested about her son. To Linda, the ruling of death due to marijuana intoxication depicted him as a little dopehead, and it implied that he and Don had brought their deaths upon themselves. She could hardly bear to think that people were viewing Kevin that way. She wished that they could have seen him, as she could in her mind, skiing on Lake Ouachita, teasing her nieces, trotting so proudly onto the football field, buffing his car, or running in to grab a slice of pizza from the refrigerator. In so many of her memories of him, he was laughing. He was a good kid. But people who had not known Kevin would never realize that. He doesn't deserve this, she would think.

Of course, she wished that he had not been smoking marijuana or hunting illegally that night. These were things that she and Larry never condoned or allowed. But people wouldn't know that, either. Although their friends were always supportive, the Henrys and the Iveses went for months after the deaths feeling isolated, not only in their grief but in their sense of being judged by almost everyone they encountered.

Dan Harmon and Richard Garrett shattered that isolation. Garrett listened to their misgivings and responded. During the prosecutor's hearing, Linda began to realize that she, Larry, Curtis, and Marvelle had not been alone in their mistrust of Malak. When Garrett changed the manner of the boys' deaths to "undetermined," Linda felt the world become less hostile. Now, on the eve of the grand jury's investigation, she and Larry appreciated the newspaper's concern. Knowing that they were not so outcast—not so alone in their misgivings—made even the littlest things, like going to the grocery store, easier.

Judge Cole swore in six women and ten men for the grand jury. Under the guidance of Harmon, the special prosecutor, they were to investigate the circumstances surrounding the boys' strange deaths. They could subpoena, question, and request indictments. They could change Malak's ruling on the death. They could push the probe as far as they wanted. They began by calling Malak. When the medical examiner left the guarded chamber where the jury met in secret, he told reporters that he stood "absolutely" by his ruling that the deaths had been accidents caused by marijuana.

Later, Linda was to learn that Malak had told the jury much more. When portions of the transcript were illegally leaked to the press, she read that Malak had been asked about Kevin's foot, which Saline County deputies had overlooked at the tracks. Malak had not mentioned in his autopsy reports that either body was missing a foot. At the hearing, however, he testified that he had "noticed one foot was missing." He had, he said, "asked for that foot, and it was brought to the office some time later."[1] But Linda knew that that was not true. The foot had never been taken to the crime lab and had never, in fact, left Saline County. Perhaps the medical examiner had not paid close attention to the whereabouts of that foot, but Linda had.

She knew that the day after the boys died, a relative of the Henry family who was walking along the tracks had discovered the severed foot and notified the Saline County sheriff. The sheriff's office had dispatched a deputy to pick it up and to take it to the county coroner. The coroner, in turn, had called the state crime lab where the bodies had been sent. But officials at the crime lab had told him that the autopsies were already complete and the bodies had been sent to the funeral homes chosen by the boys' families. The coroner had called the mortuary where Kevin's body had been sent and the mortuary had sent a courier to retrieve it. Linda would have challenged Malak's assertion had she known about it in time. But she had not. The transcript of Malak's testimony did not appear until months after the grand jury ended.

And while the grand jury was in session, Judge Cole had imposed a gag order. No one involved was to talk about the case. Nonetheless, Harmon provided Linda with some information. And the witness list, reported almost daily in the papers, offered other clues. The witnesses fell into several categories. One of the biggest centered around Malak. The day after Malak appeared, Ralph Turbyfill, the acting director of the state crime lab, arrived in Benton and requested a hearing in Judge Cole's chambers. Cole granted the request, and there, in the presence of reporters, Turbyfill complained that Malak felt that, during his appearance, he had been "treated unfairly and rather rudely" by prosecutors Harmon and Garrett. Moreover, Turbyfill said, his boss considered the extensive press coverage he was receiving to be a form of "harassment," which was causing the medical examiner to feel "investigated" and "persecuted."

Reporters scribbled while Cole sat, as always, expressionless. Turbyfill continued. "Dr. Malak is, on a daily basis, being kept in the news. He is a very emotional person and it's difficult for him to do his job with the amount of press that he's getting at this time. He feels that this case is just adding to that pressure. It's not affecting his work as a pathologist, but it is affecting him emotionally and personally." Later, when reporters questioned Malak about Turbyfill's comments, the medical examiner replied that they had been, "if anything, an understatement."

The pressure Malak was feeling was real. A readers' poll conducted in the *Arkansas Democrat* in May 1988 gave a clear, if unscientific, sense of the public's opinion. Two weeks after the Saline County Grand Jury had convened, the paper asked: "From what you have read, do you believe the deaths of Larry Kevin Ives and Don George Henry were (A) accidental or (B) murder?" The readers' response, printed the following day, was: "Accidental—16.4 percent. Murder—83.6 percent."

The public was disenchanted with Malak, but law enforcement was not. Just as the grand jury was gearing up, the Arkansas Sheriffs Association called a press conference to announce its support for the embattled medical examiner and its agreement with Malak's assessment that he was being "persecuted." The organization had gone so far as to poll its members on Malak's behalf. The association's director reported that 64 percent of the sheriffs who responded to the poll thought Malak was doing an "excellent" job.[2]

Linda read the announcement with contempt. What could you expect? she thought. Saline County's own Sheriff James Steed was a former president of the association. She was by now convinced that some sheriffs and the medical examiner scratched each others' backs, their relationship being one of mutual support. But the sheriffs alone could not keep Malak in office. Linda wondered who was championing him.

By the time the grand jury had entered its second week, Linda suspected she knew. The legislative committee that had been established to examine Malak's office announced that it was holding its first meeting. Chairing the committee was Max Howell, the state's most powerful state senator. Howell opened the meeting by announcing his full support of Malak. While acknowledging that his committee's review of Malak's office was needed, Howell said that the complaints that had prompted the review were "political" and "not substantive." As Howell put it, "I have heard nothing but good things about Dr. Malak."

Linda heard a newscast reporting Howell's comments while on her way to work. When she got to her desk at the credit union, she called the senator's office, her temper rapidly rising. "The least you could have done was to try to present the appearance of being impartial," she told Howell, her voice shaking. "You could at least pretend that this legislative review means something!"

There was a pause. "Lady, do you know who you're talking to?" the senator bellowed.

"I know exactly who I'm talking to," Linda sputtered. The conversation, such as it was, degenerated quickly from there. If the senator sounded smug, Linda knew, she sounded like a banshee. She did not give a damn. Her screams were a wail of frustration in the face of implacable power. Ultimately, she realized, she was just another woman, feeling wronged and impotent, yelling at an arrogant official and getting nowhere. What did Howell care that nothing about the investigation made sense?—least of all Dr. Fahmy Malak's ruling? Her co-workers listened wide-eyed, transfixed. Sobbing, Linda slammed the phone down and retreated to the rest room.

Malak appeared invincible. Even the peer review ordered by Clinton was now being watered down. When the review was first announced, its mission, according to the chairman of the state Crime Laboratory Board, had been to check the medical examiner's procedures and methodology, as well as to examine Malak's rulings in several controversial cases, particularly the Henry-and-Ives case. But with the arrival of the two out-of-state pathologists who had been hired to conduct the review, Betsey Wright, Governor Bill Clinton's chief of staff, told reporters that the scope of the review had narrowed. Without elaboration she announced that the visiting pathologists would *not* be "evaluating cases."

While the two pathologists were in Arkansas conducting their now limited review, Harmon decided to question them before the grand jury. When deputies reported having trouble finding the doctors to serve them with subpoenas, Harmon requested a copy of the doctors' schedules from Clinton's office. When he did not get it, he subpoenaed Wright. A deputy attorney general appeared to argue against her appearance. In a brief but tense courtroom scene that seemed to pit Harmon against the governor, Cole advised the assistant attorney general that if the grand jury did not receive the information it wanted immediately, he would allow the jurors "to subpoena Governor Clinton, Betsey Wright, or whoever they want, in order to get that information." Within a matter of hours, Wright agreed to provide the schedules and she later appeared before the grand jury.

Though neither of the pathologists ultimately appeared before the grand jury, both expressed outrage at having been subpoenaed. One, contacted after he left Arkansas, said he had not appreciated having been invited into a controversy by the governor's office without being warned that he was stepping into a feud. "I may never come back," he huffed.

"Why such outrage?" the editorial page of the *Arkansas Democrat* asked the following day. The editors found it strange that "the very thought of having to testify panicked not only [one of the doctors], but also crime lab officials and members of the governor's staff who helped shield him from being served." When reporters asked Clinton about the new limitations that had been placed on the pathologists' review, the governor maintained that the consultants could examine Malak's office well enough without looking into "his opinion on each and every case."

That a tiff should develop between the grand jury and the governor's office during an investigation into her son's murder struck Linda as wrong.

She could not remember the governor's staff ever having wrangled with the prosecutor of a county grand jury. It struck her as more amazing still that this should happen in an investigation into the deaths, not of prominent citizens, but of two high school students.

It did her little good, however, to dwell on such complexities. Explanations were elusive and she had no time for speculation. What mattered far more to Linda and Larry was that Dr. Joseph Burton, the medical examiner from Atlanta, had sent the grand jury his preliminary report on the new autopsies. Harmon told Larry and Linda that, as a result of Burton's report, the grand jury was now extremely skeptical that Malak's ruling could be correct. Indeed, at the end of May 1988, just a month after it convened, the grand jury issued a preliminary report of its own, concluding that the deaths of Kevin and Don had not been accidents as Malak had ruled, but "probable homicides." As Garrett told reporters, the jurors were now convinced that Kevin and Don had died "as a result, or in connection with, some force other than the train."

Grim as it was, the news was also, in a way, good. The day after the "probable homicide" ruling, Harmon announced that the Arkansas State Police had joined in the investigation. The move struck many as overdue. Since the dawn when the boys' bodies were discovered, cooperation between local and state investigators had been rare and inexplicably strained, as in the confrontation with Wright. In an analysis of the latest development that ran in the *Arkansas Democrat,* reporter Doug Thompson observed that the grand jury's finding of "probable homicide" on the day after Wright's failure to honor her subpoena had "left the governor's office looking uncooperative in a murder investigation."

It was an impression the office moved quickly to correct. In the next few days, Wright did appear before the grand jury without having been subpoenaed again. At Harmon's request, a meeting was held between several investigative agencies to examine the year-old case. As Thompson reported on the meeting, "For the first time since the multiple investigations began, everyone actively involved—state police, sheriff's deputies, special prosecutors, grand jurors, and the medical examiner now being used [Burton]—were in the same room."

Now, when Larry and Linda talked over dinner about the day's events, they could not help but feel that, as Harmon had promised, they were about to get the investigation they had wanted from the start. Harmon and Garrett might be a scruffy-looking pair, but they were getting action. After the frustrations of the past year, particularly after having dealt with Steed and Malak, having Harmon and Garrett as advocates came as a tremendous relief.

Of the many factors that brought the investigators together, the most persuasive, observers assumed, was Burton's still secret testimony. The only information that had been released about his testimony was a statement Garrett had made to reporters that the pathologist had found wounds on the bodies "not consistent to being struck by a train."

Whether the sudden infusion of police into the case prompted what happened next, Linda could not guess, but the grand jury's investigation seemed to take a turn. Having started off to investigate two murders, its attention suddenly swung to drugs. In rapid order, several of the witnesses who earlier had been called to testify were now being charged with crimes. Harmon's grand jury rolled like a wave through the Saline County criminal community.

One of the first to be arrested was Tommy Lee Madison, one of the men EMT Shirley Raper had encountered in the woods near the tracks on the morning the boys' bodies were found. Madison, who had told Raper at the time that he was working for the volunteer fire department, was charged with eight counts of distributing cocaine. Days later, another witness was arrested. Ken Cook, a former employee of Callaway Motors, a used-car lot in Benton, was charged with three counts of having delivered cocaine to Madison. Next to fall was Richard G. Sampley, on a charge of aggravated robbery. Intriguingly, Harmon said that the arrests had nothing to do with the boys' deaths, but that during the course of the grand jury, information about other crimes had arisen when witnesses were questioned. "Naturally," Harmon said of the jurors, "any time they uncover any kind of criminal activity during testimony, they can't ignore it. It wouldn't be logical."

The most puzzling aspect of the proceedings—or of what could be gleaned of the proceedings from the published witness lists—was the number of police officers Harmon called, some repeatedly. It came as no surprise, for instance, that Harmon would call Rick Elmendorf. As a deputy for the Saline County Sheriff's Office, Elmendorf, along with Deputy Chuck Tallent, had been responsible for investigating the deaths. In the months since that investigation, Elmendorf had left the sheriff's office to take over as chief of police for the city of Benton, the Saline County seat. It was a big step up for Elmendorf. Benton was by far the biggest city in the county and one of the fastest-growing cities in the state. That Corporal Cathy Carty would be called to testify had come as no surprise, either. After her appearance, Carty told friends that she had repeated for the grand jury essentially what she had said at the prosecutor's hearing: "Then and now, my response was that the scene posed a very strange situation. . . . I do not believe that two young men would lay down, side by side, to have an accident."

What was new—and what struck Linda as vaguely frightening—was the number of other police officers Harmon had called; officers who, as far as Linda knew, had had nothing to do with the case. When she questioned him, Harmon told her that a witness had reported seeing two deputies from the

Pulaski County Sheriff's Office beating two boys near the tracks on the night that Don and Kevin had died. It was a shocking allegation. Though Harmon later told Linda and Larry that the witness's statement was not substantiated, the couple did not discount such rumors because of their by-now deep-seated mistrust of Steed.

During the months of June and July, the grand jury heard testimony from Sheriff Steed and one of his investigators. It also called Lieutenant Doug Williams of the Arkansas State Police Criminal Investigations Division, and his investigator Barney Phillips. It heard repeatedly from a handful of current and former officers with the Benton Police Department, in particular: Robert German, a former detective, and Sergeant James Smyth and Lieutenant Bob Holladay, who were both still with the department. And for reasons that many outside the courtroom found hard to fathom, it also heard from narcotics investigators from the sheriff's office from adjoining Pulaski County. One of those was Sergeant Jay Campbell.

Campbell believed he understood, if few others in the district did, why he and his fellow Pulaski County investigator, Kirk Lane, were being called. Beginning in the summer of 1987, shortly before Don Henry and Kevin Ives were killed, Pulaski County narcotics investigators had begun hearing from informants living near the Saline/Pulaski border that Harmon was buying and selling drugs and providing drug dealers with protection.[3] This information had been passed on to Assistant U.S. Attorney Robert Govar, who was coordinating a joint state and federal investigation of drug-dealing in the area. Campbell, Lane, and their boss, Major Larry Dill, suspected that Harmon had learned of their investigation. Recently, one of their informants, a man named David Zimmerman, had reported that Harmon and officers from the Benton Police Department had visited the house, first of Zimmerman's girlfriend, then of his brother, in the middle of the night, kicking in the door and imparting the message that they were looking for him. Zimmerman was in hiding. Campbell and Lane reported the incidents to the Benton police. The next thing they knew, Harmon was calling them to testify before his grand jury.

Later, Campbell would describe the subpoenas as a set up. He would observe, "My personal opinion was that Harmon used that grand jury to find out what he could about who had information on him—and to make it appear like we were suspects. We walked into the courthouse, and television cameras were flashing everywhere. Inside, he asked me exactly two questions: 'Do you know anything about these two boys that died on the railroad tracks?' We said, absolutely not. Then he asked, 'If you ever find out anything about them, will you be sure to tell us?' We told him, of course we would. That was it. I believe he called us blatantly, for the sole purpose of trying to discredit us, so that in case he got arrested and charged with drugs as a result of the federal investigation, he could say it was retaliation." Furious at Harmon's tactics, Major Dill had dismissed the proceedings, when questioned by a reporter upon leaving the jury room, as Harmon's "dog and pony show." When Linda read the remark in the paper, she found it astonishing that any law enforcement officer would demonstrate such contempt for a murder investigation. Harmon reinforced her low opinion of the Pulaski County deputies, hinting that he had indeed called them because of information he believed that they had relating to the boys' murders.

"THAT'S DANNY"

It was a confusing situation. Linda relied on Harmon. She consulted him often by phone and dropped in to see him frequently. She, Larry, Curtis, and Marvelle considered Harmon their personal knight. He had taken their cause as his own. Linda considered him a "bud." Their relationship had begun with her passing information to him from the calls that were still coming to her house. It had expanded with his willingness to report progress on the case, including hours and hours spent relating information from the grand jury. Though Linda, Larry, Curtis, and Marvelle were not as close as they had been at first, all were grateful to Harmon for his energy and commitment.

Over time they learned something about him, including how he had gotten to be such a fighter. Harmon's mother had died when he was an infant. His father had run off, leaving the boy in the care of his grandparents. When his grandfather died, twelve-year-old Danny went to work to help his grandmother pay the bills. He first came to public attention as a high school football player. Folks were proud of Benton's football team in the years when Harmon played tight end. Even twenty-five years later they still got excited remembering that glorious season in Danny's senior year when little Benton High, having gone undefeated, met Little Rock's Hall High, the second biggest school in the state, in a play-off. Hall beat Benton by two heartbreaking points.

Harmon played well. Fans appreciated his grit on the field, however rough around the edges the boy was otherwise. Around there, being poor was no disgrace. A former teammate remembered how, when Harmon needed money to attend the prom, he offered his teammates a deal. He passed around his helmet, asking how much everyone would bet that he couldn't run from the old high school to the new one and back, a distance of about ten miles. Having collected about a hundred dollars, "Danny set out running," the teammate recalled. "And we were following behind in cars, honking and urging him on. He ran like crazy and he made it. That's just how Danny was."

He never got any taller than five six, but he was always stocky. He won a football scholarship to Arkansas Tech as a 165-pound guard but left after a year to join the army. After that, he enrolled at the University of Arkansas, where he worked his way through law school.

By the late 1970s, when Harmon was in his midthirties, he had won election as prosecuting attorney for Arkansas's Seventh Judicial District, a district that served the three counties around where he had grown up: Saline, Hot Spring, and Grant. But in 1980, while running unopposed for a second term, Harmon had suddenly and without explanation dropped out of the race, leaving his office vacant, and the Democratic Party without a candidate for prosecutor just weeks before the primary election. Citing debts of almost $125,000 and assets of $33,000, Harmon filed for bankruptcy, then left the state. Four months later he returned, saying only that he had gone to California. He quietly reopened his law practice.

If Harmon had been aggressive on the football field, his reputation in the courtroom was that of a pit bull. Linda did not realize it at the time, but his best-known accomplishment to date—his service four years ago as special prosecutor for the hospital grand jury—was viewed quite differently by different segments of the community. The popular view, the one Linda shared, held Harmon in a favorable light. His detractors were more suspicious, though both sides generally agreed on what had happened.

In 1984, when the evidence surfaced that several top administrators were siphoning money from the county-owned hospital, Cole had tapped Harmon to be special prosecutor. A state police investigation brought evidence of the fraud, but the real buzz during the grand jury centered on stories of wild parties and secret videotapes made of unsuspecting guests using cocaine and engaging in sex.[4] Testimony established that the tapes had been made for purposes of blackmail. Although the names of a few prominent citizens and local elected officials did surface during the investigation, the complete list of guests who had attended the parties was never made public.

At the end of Harmon's grand jury, the chief administrator pleaded guilty to fraud and was sentenced to a short term in prison, and a few other participants in the scheme were ordered to make restitution. But no charges were filed relating to either cocaine or prostitution, and Harmon publicly complained that the videotapes were never found. That was the end of the affair. Skeptics in the district questioned the lack of drug arrests despite evidence and testimony of lavish cocaine use, and wondered privately if the videotapes might actually have been found and put to their intended use. But such dark suspicions were only whispered. Meanwhile, Judge Cole and the *Benton Courier,* representing the legal and civic establishment in the district, congratulated Harmon on his discretion and applauded his work with the grand jury.

Harmon's star rose quickly after that despite ongoing problems with money and unlawyerly flares of physical belligerence. The year before the boys were killed, while Harmon was arguing a juvenile case in a judge's chambers, he decked another lawyer who had had the nerve to call him a liar. Harmon was neither charged nor censured over the incident, either by the judge in whose chambers the incident occurred, or by the state's Committee on Professional Conduct, with whom the other lawyer filed a complaint. That was typical. People seemed willing, even anxious, to forgive Harmon almost anything: his generally disheveled appearance, his erratic departure for California, and his temper. They saw him as a scrapper, but a sincere one. That image overcame most objections. In a semirural community, where football heroes and county politicians were lifelong celebrities, Harmon was doubly qualified. He enjoyed widespread affection.

Linda could understand why. Harmon's passion for their case had turned it around. She and Larry felt that he had rescued them. At the same time, they worried that Harmon was struggling financially, partly because of all the time he was devoting to their case. Privately, Linda and Larry discussed how they might help him. At the time, Harmon was married to his third wife, Teresa, a woman in her early twenties who had been a friend of one of Harmon's two grown daughters. The two were not married long. Teresa had given birth to their son, Zack, at about the time Kevin and Don had been killed. More than once Harmon had referred to that fact in explaining his commitment to the case. "Fate gave me a new son," he said, "just as these people lost their sons." Linda felt that it was that personal, emotional charge that explained Harmon's dedication to solving the mystery of what had happened on the tracks.

Her relationship with Garrett was different. The deputy prosecutor told people he went to bed thinking about the case and got up thinking about it. But to Linda, Garrett always seemed distant. She liked him and she knew that he was smart. But Garrett was never as chatty or as informative as Harmon; he never seemed quite so involved. As she explained to one of her friends, while you had to ask questions of Garrett to get information, Harmon "would sit down and tell you everything he saw, everything he heard, and everything he thought." To Linda, after Steed's remoteness and Malak's coldness, Harmon's forthcoming style was a blessing.

As her fondness for him grew, so did her concern. Driving around in his ratty, old El Camino, he never seemed to have enough money and Teresa complained about the amount of time that Harmon devoted to the grand jury. While Larry and Linda appreciated his commitment, they felt almost guilty over the strain that it seemed to place on his new family. More than once, Teresa had called the Iveses' house looking for her husband. And there were times when she had called crying, claiming that he had hit her.

It was clear that Harmon's personal life was a shambles. Yet just as clearly, his family, especially his children, were always with him. The atmosphere in the law office that Garrett and Harmon shared was one of childish chaos. Toys were scattered on the floor. While secretaries came and went because the lawyers sometimes could not pay their salaries, children were a constant. Teresa would drop off two-year-old Zack and leave with Harmon's daughter, Tammy, who would have just deposited her baby with its grandfather. Harmon seemed to dote on them all. "It's not your typical legal environment," Linda sighed to Larry one night, "but they're trying so hard and they believe in the case so much." She and Larry offered to help offset Harmon's expenses for the extra work he did on the case. Over a period of several months, the Iveses paid him roughly three thousand dollars, the amount remaining, after funeral expenses, from a ten-thousand-dollar life insurance policy they had bought for Kevin a few months before his death. They would have helped the lawyer more if they could.

But for all the havoc Harmon's work with the grand jury seemed to be wreaking on his family, he would not let up. If Larry and Linda heard any information, he wanted to know about it. If they decided, as they once did, to travel to northwest Arkansas to talk to a person who said he had information, Harmon wanted to make the all-day trip with them—and did. But there were also areas where Linda and Larry were puzzled by Harmon's apparent ineffectiveness. One man, reputed to be a local drug dealer, had been identified by several callers to both police and the Iveses' as having seen the boys the night before they died. Harmon never called him before the grand jury. And when the grand jury sought to question Don Henry's sister Gayla about her contact with the boys before their deaths, Curtis Henry refused to disclose where Gayla was now living.[5] He said he had sent her away soon after the boys were killed for fear that she would be killed, too, and that he had no intention of disclosing even to the grand jury where his daughter could be reached. Linda found it strange that Harmon did not press the issue.

Linda knew that not everyone liked Harmon. He had some vocal detractors. But, she reminded herself, no prosecutor is universally liked. Once, she confronted him with the worst of the rumors she had heard. "People say you have used drugs," she told him. He responded by advising her to consider the source. "Find out who started that rumor," he said, "and you'll probably find out that I sent him to the pen." It made sense to Linda that a prosecutor would make enemies and that some of them might lie out of spite. But not all the rumors about Harmon could be as easily dismissed. Harmon admitted to another rumor whispered around the community that some people close to him had used cocaine. The problem was epidemic, he said. Linda sympathized. Here he was, she thought, working so hard on their case while also trying to fight the county's growing drug problem. Sometimes friends gently suggested to Linda that maybe it was a little strange for a prosecutor to be conducting a major drug investigation while associating with reputed users. But Linda could scarcely hear them. "All I know is that Dan helped us when nobody else would. If Dan was involved in drugs and all, he sure wouldn't be involved in this investigation. He wouldn't be opening this can of worms that might turn out hurting him."

An overwhelming majority of voters in the district shared that opinion. Harmon was rapidly becoming the county's most prominent antidrug crusader. His popularity, diminished by the defection to California in the midst of his 1982 reelection race, had rebounded. Harmon and Garrett had confronted Malak's ruling and attracted statewide attention. Now, it seemed, they were investigating wherever grand jury testimony led them. By all appearances, their probe was taking them deep into the local drug scene. As if to confirm that widening opinion, Harmon and Garrett sought and received permission from Cole to grant a rare press interview about the proceedings. Late one Friday afternoon in July 1988, after the close of a grand jury session, Harmon described for reporters how the investigation had widened.

"When we get to the bottom of these deaths," he said, "we believe they will be somehow drug related. That is the one consistent thing in all the testimony we have heard, even in the rumors. So we are investigating drug trafficking in that area. We feel that people connected in the drug business know something about these deaths. We are still investigating the deaths. If we find something else when we turn over a rock, we will deal with it."

Asked why he was calling so many police officers to testify who had not investigated the deaths, Harmon replied, "We know that, from the people we are talking to, it is not obvious to the media or the public where we are going. But I feel, without a doubt, we will eventually get to the true story. I know some folks would like this investigation to end right here. But we're going to stick with it. The cost to the county has been relatively small, and I think the grand jury will do a lot of good, exposing drug trafficking if not solving a murder."

The arrests continued. James Callaway, the used-car dealer whose employee was arrested earlier, was charged with aggravated robbery. Though the pattern of the subpoenas was not, as Harmon had noted, always "obvious to the media or the public," the inquiry's reach into the county lengthened. Then Harmon dragged in a witness named Teddye Carter.

Carter was a well-known drug dealer in Saline County—or he had been. On August 19, 1987, four days before Don and Kevin were killed, Carter had been arrested by two officers of the Benton Police Department—Detective German and Sergeant Smyth, both of whom later testified before Harmon's grand jury. Carter was charged with dealing drugs. He posted a twenty-thousand-dollar bond and the charges against him were dropped. Now, almost a year to the day later, Carter was being questioned along with the arresting officers. When Carter left the courtroom, he told reporters that since his arrest he had been working as an informant for both the Benton police and the FBI. When reporters pressed for details, Carter refused to elaborate. He referred all questions to Benton police Lieutenant Holladay, whom Harmon had also called before the grand jury, and who, Carter said cryptically, "knows more about what I do than anybody." But Holladay, citing the gag order, declined to comment.

Carter's statement left reporters turning to Harmon with the summer's burning question: why was he subpoenaing so many police officers? For Linda, the possible answer to that question was horrifying, but the idea was never stated. Harmon only said, "We think they have information we can use."

If wrongdoing had been found on the police force, no charges were ever brought. In early August, Elmendorf, in his new role as Benton's chief of police, suspended Lieutenant Holladay with pay.[6] Sergeant Smyth was reassigned. And by then, Detective German had left the force.

During Arkansas's sultry August, with the grand jury's investigation droning on and the first anniversary of the boys' deaths approaching, a crew for the television show *Unsolved Mysteries* came to Saline County to film an episode about the case. Chip Clements, the field producer for the show, had found the case "intriguing; a story with a real question as to what happened to these two." Clements observed, "There's a lot of different theories, but I don't think the evidence shows that these boys laid themselves down in identical positions and lay motionless until a train ran over them. I think that sounds pretty absurd." Larry agreed to participate in the production in the hope that the show might, as he put it, "stir things up."

Dottie Polsgrove was one of the people the crew interviewed about the boys. A physical science teacher at Bryant High School, Polsgrove described Don Henry as "very considerate, but more of a cutup and a tease." She remembered Kevin Ives as calm, classy, neat, and clean-cut, "a lot quieter than Don." She told the film crew that she did not believe Sheriff Steed's and Dr. Malak's assessment of their deaths. "I think someone did something to them," Polsgrove said on-camera. "Always have, always will."

"DEFINITELY HOMICIDES"

By then it was becoming clear that Dr. Burton had reached the same conclusion. In a surprising move, considering the secrecy imposed on the grand jury,

Harmon suddenly arranged to make public the most crucial testimony the jury had heard: Burton's autopsy findings. Harmon made the decision, it appeared, because Judge Cole was growing impatient. In early September 1988, after the grand jury had been meeting for four months, Cole complained to the foreman that it was taking too much time and costing the county too much money and that it seemed to have strayed from its original charge. Its investigation into drugs and other crimes had been broad, but so far, its action on the train-deaths case had been limited to a finding of probable homicide. Cole demanded a sealed, written report on the status of the investigation and on the grand jury's expectations. He threatened to disband it if progress was not made.

Within a week the jurors presented Cole with a videotape of Burton's testimony. They told the judge that they had decided to make the testimony public because it formed the basis of their written report, which they submitted to Cole with the tape. The jury's report was to the point:

"Our conclusion is that the deaths are definitely homicides," the foreman wrote, "and we should continue our investigation."

Asked why, after guarding the evidence so closely, Harmon was now allowing its release, he replied, "I just felt like there were so many rumors that the benefits outweighed the losses." The following morning, Curtis, Larry, and a handful of reporters got to view the tape after clerks set up a television screen in the front of Judge Cole's courtroom. After Malak's obscure ramblings, Burton's testimony sounded startlingly clear. "I'm sorry I could not be present with you today in Arkansas to discuss the case....

"To begin with, one of the things I feel is most disconcerting and very important to this case is the shirt that was worn by Don Henry, or allegedly worn by Don Henry. This is the shirt that was not on the boy's body when he was found, that was some distance away from the track, where the torso and body of Don Henry were recovered.

"This shirt, as you know, has a lot of tears and defects in it. A question was raised as to whether these tears or defects were made by the body being pulled down the track by the motion of the train over the body of the victim. What I did was, I took the shirt to a private laboratory that I work with here in Atlanta, and we took one of these tears on the lower back area of the shirt that kind of was in the area where this injury was on the back of Don Henry, and we took a scalpel and cut this defect out, which measured a little bit over an inch in length. We then took this defect and it was analyzed under a scanning electron microscope, which is a very powerful microscope, and with this microscope you can tell whether fabric has been torn or cut with something like scissors or a knife.

"The shirt in this area does indeed exhibit all the characteristics of a defect caused by something with a sharp blade, such as a knife. As I said, it's a little over an inch in length; the markings of it are similar to the markings made by the cut of the scalpel in the fabric. There is no question that this particular defect was not a tear, and it was made by something cutting through the fabric. Also, around the marking of this defect are a number of red blood cells or objects consistent with red blood cells under the scanning electron microscope. So not only do we have a defect in the shirt, but there is also blood around this defect. I think this is important because, first of all, the shirt was not on the body when it was found, and secondly, the defect was not a tear that you might expect from the shirt snagging on a crosstie or on a railroad spike or on something underneath the train itself, but is consistent with something actually cutting the fabric. It is also important because the defect is in the area on the back where this injury, which I have described to you previously, is located. I think this is very important as far as the investigation into the deaths of these two boys is concerned."

Burton said he was also concerned about an injury found on the left cheek of Kevin Ives, an injury he said he did not find "consistent" with any pattern that might have been made from being struck by the cowcatcher in front of the engine. He explained that he had sent photographs of both boys' injuries to computer-enhancement specialists with the Dade County Medical Examiner's Office in Miami, where he had trained, but that the results were not yet back.

"Also, since we last met," Burton continued, "Dr. William Anderson, the pathologist here in Atlanta that I've talked to you about, has looked further into this case. He has gone over the slides of the tissue sections again and is very much concerned about the degree of reaction and the congestion and fluid in the lungs of both boys. He feels that it is inconsistent with the type of injuries that one might expect from someone being run over by a train, when you have sudden death occurring. He feels like the possibility exists that this information alone would strongly suggest that the boys were injured, rendered unconscious, or even killed prior to the bodies being run over by the train. He also shared my same concerns that the evidence supplied by the engineers and conductors of the train is consistent with the forensic evidence, and at this time we have nothing to account for the fact that these boys apparently did not try to move away from the oncoming train."

Burton made no pronouncement on the videotape about the specific cause or causes of the boys' deaths. That, he suggested, would have to await the results of the photographic enhancements from the specialists in Dade County. But the refutation of Malak's findings was clear enough.

After the viewing, Curtis Henry was asked if he had any qualms about releasing information about the boys' autopsies. "The public deserves to know," he answered. "This never would have gotten off the ground without the public and the news media standing with us."

Reaction was also sought from Sheriff Steed. "I'm not completely convinced that it's a homicide," he said. "But by the same token, I'm not completely convinced it's not."

The dramatic refutation of Dr. Fahmy Malak's ruling set off a lively round of reactions. Within the next seven days:

- Dr. Fahmy Malak, who had promised to resign his job if proven wrong in his ruling, declined to comment on the grand jury's ruling, citing Judge Cole's gag order.
- Sheriff Steed refused a request from the grand jury that he pay the panel's expenses out of his office's special drug enforcement fund. "They are not getting it," Steed said. "I am not financing the grand jury with my drug money. And I don't know a nice way of saying that."
- Richard Garrett said of Steed's refusal to pay, "We can't make him. But it really gripes me to hear people talking about the cost of this when the governor can spend whatever he wants to hire two out-of-state [pathologists]."
- Steve Cox, the chief criminologist at the Arkansas Crime Laboratory and head of the laboratory's trace evidence section, publicly stated that he had found an apparent cut in Don Henry's shirt and had reported it to his superiors, but that that information had been dismissed. "I checked all of the clothing and do recall noting all the damages, including the defects that Dr. Burton noted," Cox said. "I know for certain that I did report punctures in the clothing. They just were not coupled with the body." Cox said that by the time he examined the clothing, the autopsies had been completed and the rulings as to cause of death had been made. He said he suggested to his superiors that "the damages should have been looked at with the body to see if they were relevant" and that the clothing should have been further examined to look for bloodstains, but his suggestions had been rejected. Cox said his administrators had insisted that the agency "didn't have the time" to investigate the clothing further because, they said, "We need to get the case out." The criminologist said he considered his bosses' rationale in the case "illegitimate." As he put it, "I'm all for

speedy results, but sometimes you have to sacrifice that. We're all there trying to find the truth."[7]

- A coroner's jury in Pulaski County ruled that a nursing home resident—whose death Malak had ruled was due to natural causes—actually was a homicide that had resulted from a beating.
- The *Arkansas Democrat* mused in an editorial on Friday, September 16, 1988, that "wherever the grand jury search leads, the Saline County case raises real questions about the medical examiner's office, questions not easily resolvable." The same day, the crime lab's new director announced that he was raising Malak's salary by fourteen thousand dollars.
- Burton reported to Garrett that the computer enhancement performed by Dade County on photographs of the boys' bodies identified a stab wound in the back of Don Henry and a blow from a blunt instrument to Kevin's cheek.
- Governor Bill Clinton said that he would leave the decision of whether to retain Malak to the crime lab's new director, a retired Arkansas sheriff whom Clinton had recently appointed. Asked about the numerous complaints about Malak's performance, Clinton responded, "I want to wait and see what the new director has to say about that." Asked about the raise that the new director had just announced, Clinton defended Malak by noting that he had "a lot of supporters" and that he had done a "good job" as medical examiner despite understaffing at the lab. The governor said he would recommend a substantial increase in the lab's budget in the 1989 session of the Arkansas General Assembly. He said he wanted to make sure that "nobody is worked to the point of exhaustion" and that "that should solve most of the problems."
- The editors of the *Arkansas Democrat* decided to find out whether the paper's readers agreed with the governor. On September 22, 1988, the day after Clinton declined to take action regarding Malak, the statewide newspaper asked its readers, "Should Dr. Fahmy Malak be fired?" The unscientific but overwhelming response was: Yes—81.2 percent. No—18.8 percent.

SOME ILLUSIONS SHATTERED

Linda Ives surveyed the battlefield. August 23, the first anniversary of the boys' deaths, arrived with a flood of memories, giving rise to a flood of tears. But amid the grief there was some consolation. The landscape had changed. At last, some things were making sense. Malak's ruling that the boys had, essentially, smoked themselves to death on the tracks had been thrown out, as it deserved to be. Burton's evidence was chilling and clear. Kevin and Don had been murdered; Don with a knife in his back, and Kevin with a blow to his face, a blow that might have come from a rifle butt. It was a year late in coming. But Harmon and the grand jury, as well as investigators from several police agencies, were finally looking for the murderers. Moreover, a motive for the murders had emerged. The jurors' search was leading them into the county's underworld of drugs. It looked like cocaine—not marijuana—might be the drug behind the deaths.

Now that it was clear that they had been murdered, the tarp seen by the train crew made sense, as did the boys' unnerving stillness. Linda could imagine the killers laying the boys' bodies on the tracks and covering them, hoping that the crew of an oncoming train would not notice them and that the violence of the train's passing over them would obliterate the very evidence that Burton had found. Now the ambulance crew's testimony about the condition of the blood also fit into the puzzle. The blood did not look fresh and oxygenated because it was not. It also made sense that something more valuable than marijuana may have led to the murders: It was not something the boys had smoked, but something they had witnessed. Some of the "illusions," optical and otherwise, that had been dismissed despite the complaints of so many witnesses, had not been illusions at all.

When the *Benton Courier* interviewed Linda on the anniversary of the deaths, she explained, "I think many people thought it was a case of parents not being able to accept what had happened, which occurs in a lot of cases. People don't want to believe their kids are involved in drugs. But in this case, other people didn't have all the facts that we did. If they had, they would have understood our position." For their help in bringing some of the facts to light, Linda expressed her family's heartfelt gratitude toward Garrett and Harmon. "I feel that we're closer to the truth now than we've ever been."

Even so, as September 30, Don's birthday, neared, Linda reflected on the questions that remained unanswered, questions that went beyond who had murdered the boys. As murders go, these deaths—or at least the subsequent mutilations under the wheels of a freight train—were as strange as they were awful. The investigation had also been strange. And the medical examiner's ruling, in the view of professionals and laypeople alike, had been absurd. Even now, with a revised ruling of homicide, the persistent strangeness that had permeated the case seemed to hover over the grand jury's investigation. Harmon was investigating police officers and drug dealers but producing no one, it seemed so far, who knew anything about the deaths. Legislators and sheriffs were rallying to Malak's defense. And despite pronounced public disapproval of the medical examiner, the governor seemed to be bending over backward to keep him in office. Linda did not know what any of it meant.

Whatever the reason, she consoled herself, their maneuvers did not matter anymore. The battle with Steed and Malak had been won. The Arkansas State Police were now involved in the case. Kevin and Don would get the investigation they deserved. It would not be long, Linda and Larry told each other, before they would be able to look their son's murderer—or murderers—in the eyes.

SEVEN

KEITH McKASKLE'S MURDER

SEPTEMBER–DECEMBER 1988

Early in the fall of 1988, as the grand jury investigation continued, Linda Ives came home to find the door leading from her garage to her house open. It was only slightly ajar, but she always locked her doors when she left the house. Larry was running his train route to Missouri. Alicia was in Little Rock, attending the University of Arkansas. Linda was alone, and while ordinarily that did not bother her, finding the door open was unsettling. She told herself she must be slipping; she must have left it unlocked. She would overlook it. But a few weeks later, a similar incident occurred. This time the door she found open was the one leading to the patio. Unnerved, she got her neighbor L.A., to whom she had turned when the boys were found dead, to come over and check the house with her. They could find nothing that looked disturbed. When the incident was repeated a third time, Linda called L.A. again, and again they searched the house. They found nothing amiss. On each occasion Larry had been away from home. Linda felt she was being toyed with. She felt as though someone was telling her, "See how easy this is."

MURDERS AND MESSAGES

After voting on election morning, she came home—again alone—to find a pickup truck parked near her house. House lots in the Iveses' subdivision were large, averaging two-and-a-half acres, so it was strange to see men who had no business at her house parked so close to it, doing nothing. The men drove off when Linda drove up. She followed them, hoping to see the license plate or get a clue as to who they were, until they pulled off onto a shaded lane that led to a house that was under construction. It was an isolated area and Linda did not feel safe following them off the road. The license plate was bent and unreadable. She never found out who they were.

By now Linda was used to living with questions. So much that had happened was murky—dark, like the lane she had not wanted to turn down. She had the feeling that she and Larry, the Henrys, and prosecutors Harmon and Garrett had challenged some unseen foe. She knew they were in battle. But who was the enemy? Just as she did not know the identities of the men who had parked near her house, or who seemed to be so easily opening her doors, she had no idea who wanted the mystery of the boys' deaths to remain unsolved.

As Arkansas's colorful autumn faded and the grand jury neared its mandated dissolution at the year's end, reporters began to ask Harmon if the killers would be found. "I think every day we've got to be getting closer," he said. "We've done too much work. It's a process of elimination. Eventually we'll get the right suspect." Even if the grand jury failed to name a suspect, he added, he felt certain that the Arkansas State Police, who had recently joined the probe, would solve the mystery. The days grew shorter and darker.

THE SHERIFF'S RACE

The "deal" Harmon had worked out among Steed, the Iveses, and the Henrys had not improved their relations. Linda's contempt for Steed remained a major difference between her and Harmon, an irritating thorn in the side of their otherwise close relationship. Despite the grand jury's announced suspicion that the boys' deaths were drug related, Steed had resisted freeing his office's drug funds to aid the investigation, insisting that he would not be a "sugar daddy" for the grand jury. Linda had considered his decision outrageous. But that had not been the worst of it. The last straw had come when Linda learned that, after agreeing to send the boys' clothes to the FBI for analysis, Steed had secretly reneged on his promise and ordered them sent instead to the Arkansas Crime Laboratory. Linda flew into a rage. She did not trust Steed, Malak, or the crime lab. Her efforts to get the evidence out of their hands and into the hands of a neutral agency had been overtly and covertly blocked. She wanted to scream.

She drove to the courthouse and burst into Steed's office. The sheriff was on the telephone. He kept raising his hand, motioning her to be patient. She waited for about five minutes. Then she lost what little patience she had left. She walked to Steed's desk and put her finger on the phone's button, disconnecting the sheriff in midsentence. At about the same time, Linda Hollenbeck, a reporter for the *Benton Courier,* walked in, hoping to see the sheriff. "I want you to hear this," Linda Ives told the reporter. Turning to Steed, furious and on the edge of losing control, she asked, "Why did you send those clothes to the crime lab? You were supposed to send them to the FBI. We never wanted them in the Little Rock crime lab. You knew that. I knew that. Everyone in this fucking county knew that." She was almost nose to nose with Steed. "James Steed," she said, pointing a finger at him, "you are in deep shit."

He looked at her with disdain. "Lady, I don't care."

Hollenbeck reported the incident, quoting Steed's final remark. It did not play well in the county. A member of the county Quorum Court commented later that he and other members had been "offended" by Steed's attitude toward the murders, as illustrated "when he told Mrs. Ives that he didn't care."

Letters to the editor of the Benton paper reflected a change in the political air. A man who had been a pallbearer at one of the boys' funerals wrote of the pain the victims' families and friends had endured. But the most painful aspect of the deaths, he wrote, had been "watching our authorities and our medical examiner try to ignore the fact that a tragic murder was committed." Another correspondent noted, "We have homicides either directly or indirectly related to the drug trade in Saline County. We have a Drug Enforcement Fund. And we have a sheriff who believes he has a better place to spend the money currently in the fund. Where can this place be? If someone in the drug trade is willing to murder two teenagers, then this person must be awfully deep in the drug trade. Does Sheriff Steed prefer to chase the minnows of the drug trade rather than hook the big shark that murdered two teenagers?"

Harmon, however, had continued to defend Steed to Linda. He had argued that Steed was valuable both to the case and to the community. He contended, "Steed might be kind of lazy, but he knows the county, and he's probably unbeatable anyway. What kind of investigation do you think you'll get from Steed once he's reelected if you and Larry work for his opponent?" But by now, Linda did not care. Anything would be better than what they had gotten from Steed. The only change Linda could see in Steed since the deal was that Steed was distancing himself somewhat from Malak. When he realized that, for the first time in his career, public sentiment might be turning against him, Steed shifted gears. He announced that he now found it "very difficult to understand" why Malak had exhibited "so little regard for a thorough investigation of the forensic evidence presented to him by the Saline County Sheriff's Department."

What a laugh, Linda thought On October 11, 1988, a month before the sheriff's election, Linda held another press conference, this one by herself. She chose as the site the tiny post office at the community of Alexander, about a mile from where Kevin and Don were killed. Her voice as she stepped forward was firm. "While I feel that politics should not play a role in any murder investigation," she told the assembled reporters, "I feel it has been a major stumbling block in the investigation of my son's murder. This matter is not a political issue to me at all, but a very personal one. The murder of my son, Kevin, is a very real fact that we must deal with at my house every minute of every day. I am here because I am tired of the political games and deals that are played and made in the Saline County Sheriff's Office. My family and I have been made victims of those games." She announced that she was endorsing Steed's opponent, Larry Davis.

That night, KARK-TV, Little Rock's NBC affiliate, broadcast the *Unsolved Mysteries* program with the segment about the boys on the tracks. It included a reenactment of the scene at the tracks, with a videotape shot from the cab of a locomotive as the train's headlight illuminated two partially covered figures. The show's host, Robert Stack, asked Garrett about his personal view on the deaths. "I think that the boys saw something they shouldn't have seen and it had to do with drugs," Garrett answered, "either with a crank lab, which manufactures methamphetamine, or certain individuals involved in those matters, and those people felt like the information the boys then had was such that they could not allow them to live." He added, "I think there is a distinct possibility that there are other parties involved. The thing is, the case is so complex that the solution could lie in something as simple as a vagrant or a migrant on the railroad track doing it and going away and us never hearing anything from him again, or it could be as complicated as police involvement."

For many Saline County viewers, the most intriguing part of the interview came when Garrett told Stack that "Saline County and the central Arkansas area are overrun at this time with drug trafficking—and it's drug trafficking at a high level that extends to other states and other counties." Linda herself was surprised by the remark. Other counties and other states? All this time she had thought that the investigation, such as it was, was entirely local in focus. What did Garrett's comment mean? She wondered alone because Larry was away at squirrel camp, a long tradition this time of year. He had missed squirrel camp last year. The season had come just two months after the boys' deaths. Until then, Kevin had accompanied Larry and the men since he had been old enough to hunt. Linda could see that it was hard for Larry to pack for the trip this year without Kevin. But he had gone and she was glad. They were learning to go on.

But the past was always hovering. The day after the TV show ran, reporters called Linda for her reaction. "It was hard to sit and watch it," she acknowledged. But she added that she hoped the program would elicit new leads now that there was a fifteen-thousand-dollar reward fund. She and Larry had put up most of the money themselves.

Two days before the sheriff's election, Linda sent out a prepared statement in which she acknowledged that she and Larry had made an agreement with Steed back in February, in which they'd agreed to soft-pedal their problems with the sheriff if he would give the investigation proper attention. Steed had not upheld his end of the deal, Linda wrote. The story ran on the *Courier's* front page on election eve.

Turnout was so heavy that poll watchers had to send out for extra ballots. By the time they were counted, Steed had won only 42 percent of the vote, to Davis's 58. The five-term incumbent Democrat had been defeated in a Democratic stronghold by a thirty-one-year-old former deputy who was not only a political newcomer but a Republican. The upset made statewide news.

By then the grand jury had issued its sixth indictment, the third on drug-related charges. But Harmon had no progress to report on the investigation into the murders on the tracks.

THE KEITH McKASKLE STORY

On November 10, 1988, two days after the sheriff's election, as Linda and her co-workers at the credit union thought about lunch, Dan Harmon rushed into her office and shut the door. Something was wrong. He looked ashen, visibly shaken. His voice was trembling: "Keith McKaskle has been murdered."

Seeing Harmon so rattled and hearing the news about McKaskle scared Linda to her core. She was already on edge over the open-door incidents and the men watching her house. Now she became truly frightened. She called Alicia. She called Larry. She wanted her family around her. She wanted everyone to come home.

Linda had never met McKaskle, but she knew about him. Harmon had told her that, as McKaskle was a skilled photographer, he had been asked to take aerial photographs of the area where the boys had died. But there was more to McKaskle's reputation than just his ability with a camera. He managed the Wagon Wheel Lounge, a private club on "the county line," a stretch of liquor stores and bars along Interstate 30 where the highway crossed the north edge of "dry" Saline County into the southern edge of "wet" Pulaski County. When Saline County residents wanted a drink, they headed for the county line. Linda knew that the Wagon Wheel was a popular spot with a lot of people in the area, including Richard Garrett, Sheriff Steed, Deputy Elmendorf, and other police officers from both Saline and Pulaski counties. McKaskle's club was as decent as the rest, but fights broke out in them all. When that happened at the Wagon Wheel, the altercations were brief. McKaskle stood six two, weighed 205 pounds, and was a veteran of barroom brawls. Patrons recounted stories of McKaskle wading into drunken knife fights without a weapon and quickly breaking them up. In the demimonde of county-line bars, McKaskle was something of a legend.

Curtis Henry counted him as a friend. "He knew everything," Curtis said, "and when he found out something, he'd tell me." But McKaskle was not just talking to Curtis. Harmon had told Linda that McKaskle was acting as an informant in the case. He had agreed to pass along any information he heard in the bar or from his many contacts in the Saline County underworld. That was one of the remarkable things about McKaskle: he was rumored to be a drug user and probably a drug seller and he had friends in a lot of low places, but he counted cops among his closest friends. Cathy Carty, the deputy who had objected so strenuously at the tracks to treating the deaths as an accident, considered McKaskle a buddy. Before getting into law enforcement, she had worked at a liquor store on the county line. "Keith was my protector," she said. Carty was one of many women who were fond of Keith McKaskle and considered him a friend. Carty's friendship with McKaskle continued after she joined the sheriff's office. She knew that McKaskle used drugs, principally methamphetamine, and that he sold some on the side. But after she became a deputy, he never used drugs in her presence. "Maybe it's not exactly the way things ought to be done," she reflected later, "but Keith gave me a lot of good information on things I was investigating, and in exchange for that, I turned a blind eye to some things I might not have approved of."

One crucial piece of information Carty said McKaskle passed on to her would not become public for many years. It concerned Harmon's grand jury and Harmon himself. Harmon's name had come up when Carty and McKaskle were talking about drugs. "Keith told me I might want to watch Dan Harmon," Carty recalled, "that he was one of Saline County's largest suppliers." Carty had stored the information away, lacking any evidence to support it. But after McKaskle's death she bitterly recalled how she had learned of her old friend's murder. She was at work when Sheriff James Steed came into the office shouting, "You ain't gonna believe who just got his damn throat cut."[1]

Linda did not know of Carty's relationship with McKaskle or of the information McKaskle had given Carty. All she knew was that her trusted friend Harmon was shaking in her office. Harmon said he had just come from the death scene—the driveway of McKaskle's home. He told Linda that McKaskle's body had been wrapped in a tarp, a circumstance that he considered "a message to us all, so we'll connect it and back off."

Later, a neighbor who lived across the street from McKaskle reported that he had been awakened by a dog barking at about 1:30 A.M. "I heard some groaning," the man told police, "but just about as quick as it started, it quit. It almost sounded like someone had drank too much and was vomiting." The man said that he had looked out his window, seen nothing unusual, and gone back to bed. The next morning a female friend discovered McKaskle's body, wrapped in a flower-patterned plastic shower curtain, lying in the carport of his Benton home near a door leading to his kitchen. The woman, who had stopped by with another woman for a visit, was almost hysterical by the time police arrived.

When Investigator Don Birdsong of the Arkansas State Police arrived, Benton's chief of police, Rick Elmendorf, was already at the scene along with a lieutenant and three detectives. Birdsong took detailed notes. " . . . The left hand is in a clutched or fist-like position with what appears to be hair in the grasp of the hand. . . . There is what appears to be blood on the victim's face and a deep wound under the left ear. There are wounds located on both arms with what appears to be a severe wound on the left arm near the elbow. The blue shirt has numerous slits located on the back area. There is a large pool of a red substance believed to be blood located on the right side of the body appearing to have come from under the body. . . .

"There is what appears to be blood in nearly all portions of the walkway. There is an area where there appears to have been a scuffle where there is what appears to be a large pool of blood, with smears and footprints. . . . " Birdsong entered the house, describing the scene as he went: a blood splatter on the doorframe and a smear below the knob, a brown briefcase open on a kitchen counter with "assorted documents" in it, blood flakes around the edge of the briefcase, blood spots on the floor, bloodstains on the walls.

The following day, on November 11, 1988, a headline in the *Arkansas Democrat* read: INFORMANT IN 2 TEENS' DEATHS SLAIN. The paper reported that Malak would be performing the autopsy. Noting that McKaskle was "a big man in his forties—strong—who has personally prevented many incidents in establishments he has managed," Elmendorf told the paper that his department had "no leads whatsoever" as to who might have killed McKaskle. But, he added, "Nothing at this point in the investigation has led us to believe that this is connected to the Henry and Ives case."

But McKaskle had indeed been involved with the case. Harmon and Garrett acknowledged publicly that McKaskle had assisted in their investigation, Garrett describing the bar manager's role as one of "keeping his ears open." McKaskle was, Garrett said, "an extremely intelligent man, able to communicate with all levels of society. He was a man of many talents. He undertook roles ranging from a bouncer at bars he managed to a nationally recognized expert on and author of magazine articles about the Civil War."

Garrett's boss, prosecuting attorney Joe Kelly Hardin, noted that Garrett had recently interviewed McKaskle, but Hardin would not say what the interview concerned. Nor would Garrett himself comment on the information McKaskle had provided, other than to say that it was "not earth-shattering."

Asked whether he saw a connection between his interview of McKaskle and McKaskle's murder, Garrett said that he did not. He considered the timing of the events "a coincidence."

Within hours of McKaskle's murder, a story began circulating in Saline County. Within days it was so well known that it became impossible to ascertain whether it was true. Many found it plausible, others were skeptical. The story was that on the night of the sheriff's election, two days before McKaskle's murder, he had thrown two pennies onto the bar at his Wagon Wheel Lounge. "If Jim Steed loses," he announced, "my life isn't worth two cents." Many felt that whether or not McKaskle's death was connected to information he had about the murders of the boys, the timing of his murder was almost certainly connected to the defeat of Sheriff James Steed. The widely accepted interpretation of the story was that McKaskle had passed information to Garrett and Harmon that implicated Steed in the boys' murders and that this information had gotten back to Steed. When McKaskle tossed the pennies onto the bar, he was announcing that if Steed became vulnerable by losing the election, people like him—people who knew too much—would have to be eliminated.

Linda tried not to get tangled up in such wild speculation. Besides, to accept that version of events, she would have to believe that someone close to the prosecutors had betrayed McKaskle after he had given them evidence implicating Steed in the murders. It was too frightening to consider. Linda had heard so many unsubstantiated rumors in the months since Kevin had died. This was just another.

Moreover, after his first, nearly hysterical reaction, Harmon now appeared convinced that what Elmendorf was saying was true: McKaskle's murder had had nothing to do with the murders of Kevin and Don. If it had been related to the defeat of Sheriff Steed, then that reinforced Linda's perception that Steed had been controlling some nasty business in the county—business that was going to unravel now that he was out of office. Horrified as she was at the brutality of McKaskle's murder, she was glad to have Steed out of office. She and Larry had worked hard against him, and his defeat was worth the effort.

"QUESTIONABLE CIRCUMSTANCES"

The Arkansas Sheriffs Association continued to support Malak by questioning the credentials of Dr. Burton. In a letter to the grand jury, Burton wrote, "I must admit that I am somewhat hurt by the allegations that I have spent all of this time and given my opinions for reasons that are not completely professional. I think that my conclusions are based on solid forensic facts and evidence . . . and unless someone can explain adequately the questionable circumstances and the forensic facts which I have brought to light, by some other logical and reasonable hypotheses, then to criticize my opinions and conclusions in such a way is totally unfair and unjust."

In his final report, Burton added little to what he had already told the grand jury, except for one thing. He told the panel by videotape that, prior to being run over by the train, Kevin Ives had been struck in the face by an object, perhaps the butt of a gun. "The butt of the rifle that was found near the bodies of Don Henry and Kevin Ives is shaped almost exactly like his injury on the face."

Since Burton's earlier report, Linda had accepted that Kevin had taken a possibly lethal blow to the head. But she was not prepared for the shock she received when she eventually read a complete copy of Burton's report. In the middle of a section labeled "head," she learned that during its brief stay at the Arkansas medical examiner's office, Kevin's skull had been sawed into pieces. "It is difficult to ascertain exactly what fracture lines were present at death," Burton had written, "due to the fact that the skull has been sawed at various angles to remove the maxilla, mandible, and dome of the calvarium at the first autopsy." Linda was aghast. She called Burton and asked him about the notation. He told her that he had performed thousands of autopsies. He had never seen this done before. He could provide no explanation as to why Malak might have sawed the head as radically as he did. "You'll have to ask Dr. Malak," Burton said.

No matter who had been involved in the murders, Linda had expected that information about the crimes would have been discovered during the autopsies in the state medical examiner's office. Instead, Malak had backed up the sheriff in his pronouncement that no crime had been committed. If people were being protected at the county level, who was protecting them? And what about Garrett's reference on *Unsolved Mysteries* to "drug trafficking at a high level that extends to other states"? It was too much to process. Linda tried to keep her head clear. I'm just too close to this, she told herself. I need to stand back and look at it rationally.

But it was not easy to look at things rationally in the days after Keith McKaskle's murder. Reminding herself that both the Benton police and the state police investigators had immediately dismissed McKaskle's murder as having nothing to do with Kevin's and Don's, she drew back and followed the investigation the way most other people in Saline County did—safely from a distance, in the newspaper, as though it had nothing to do with her.

SHANE SMITH, DEFENDANT

Benton police investigators focused their suspicions in the McKaskle murder immediately on one of his neighbors, a nineteen-year-old teenager who lived with his parents across the street. When the murder was discovered, Ronald Shane Smith told his father that he had witnessed something during the night, and Smith's father had walked across the street to the police to report that his son might have some information. But soon after interviewing the boy, the officers arrested him. Within forty-eight hours Shane Smith stood charged with the murder of Keith McKaskle.

What was known—or what had been reported by Dr. Malak—was that during the fatal struggle McKaskle had suffered "in excess of 115 stab wounds," all of them above the waist. Many of the cuts were "defense" wounds, signs that McKaskle had tried to resist with his arms and had attempted to grab the knife during the assault. The most serious wound, and the probable cause of death, was one that had entered the heart. In addition, Malak noted, there were approximately thirty wounds in the left lower back which had been inflicted after death. Malak said wounds to the back of McKaskle's head and to his left shoulder had also been administered after his death.

Smith, a slight, quiet young man with no criminal record, initially told police that he and McKaskle had been friends. He said that he had seen "three people in clown masks" waiting for McKaskle late in the evening, before the bar manager came home from work. But detectives found bloody clothes in an outbuilding behind the Smiths' house. After he was arrested, Smith changed his story.

In later interviews he said he had been at McKaskle's house waiting for him to come home when five men arrived. They were not wearing clown masks, but black masks, as well as black shirts and black pants. Smith said he lied about the clown masks at first because the men threatened to kill him and his family if he told police what had actually happened. Without releasing details of Smith's statements, Elmendorf noted that the young man had "changed his story several times" and that the evidence against him was persuasive.

Smith's fourth statement, made two days after McKaskle's murder, was his most extensive account of what he said he had witnessed.[2] He stuck to it from that day forward. Smith said he had gone to McKaskle's house because he had arranged to buy a silver tray for his mother from McKaskle, along with some pornographic videotapes for himself, and he was there to pay part of what he owed. McKaskle arrived, and as the two went into the kitchen, five men burst in behind them.

"Two came in immediately," Smith said. "One came to me and held a gun to me and pushed me down in a chair and told me to stay still. Four of them was around Keith, held guns to him, and one told Keith to get out. Keith kept on saying, 'Who are you? What do you want?' and they said, 'Out,' pointing guns for him to go to the carport. And they went out there and shut the door behind them and I heard wrestling going on and Keith yelled out, 'Help me,' about two or three times; after that, about forty-five minutes later, they came in and told the one [holding me] to bring me out there. I went out there and I tripped. I fell on Keith and got blood all over me, and they started laughing and I got up and he handed me a knife and he told me to stick it over Keith and act like I was going to stab him so he could take a picture of it. And he did. After that, he took the knife back and cut my hand two places at the same time, and they told me to leave. I left."

Smith said he recognized one of the men by his voice. He told police that once, during the summer, when he had stopped by McKaskle's house, another man had been there, who had been introduced only as "James." Smith said he had used the bathroom while the two men stepped outside to talk. "When I opened the bathroom door there was about seven marijuana plants in there, and briefcases and pills and all sorts of things lying around," he said. "James came in there and talked to me. He asked me if I was going to tell the police and I said no. I kept telling him no and he just reached in his pocket and pulled out five-hundred-dollar bills and handed them to me. . . . Keith came in and James told Keith that I had found the stuff. . . . [Then] they asked me to help them put the stuff in the van, and I said I would do it. I helped him put the stuff into the van, and after I did that I come into the house and James had a picture of me putting one of those plants into the van, and he said he was going to use that snapshot to get to me, to make sure I didn't tell you all anything. Keith looked at him and he told him that wasn't necessary."

Later that day, Smith said, when he left work, he went to his motorcycle and found two photographs on the seat. One was a picture of his sister riding in a car. The other was a picture of himself walking into the Kentucky Fried Chicken store. Smith said he became extremely nervous. Over the course of the next few weeks, he said, he received photographs in the mail of his father getting out of his car at work, his mother getting out of her car, and of his sister with her friends. All of them, he said, had come with the same message. He interpreted the message for the police as: "If I talk, I'll die. Me and my family will die." Smith said he had destroyed the photos for fear that his mother would find them while cleaning his room.

The knife that had been used to kill McKaskle—a big one, according to Malak, with a blade at least five inches long—was not found, and police still had established no motive for Smith to have killed McKaskle. Nonetheless, Elmendorf said he was confident the killer had been found.

Linda wanted to believe the affair was that simple. But like others in Saline County who'd known McKaskle or known of him, she found it almost impossible to believe that a nineteen-year-old boy, five feet eleven inches tall and weighing 180 pounds, who had been considered slow in school, who had never been hunting and who had never been known to fight in his life, could have overcome the six-foot-four, 205-pound Keith McKaskle, and in a fight with a single knife, no less.

As it turned out, as early as the first week of their investigation, the police had gathered plenty of reason to question Smith's guilt, as well. Although Linda did not know it at the time, and Elmendorf was not saying it, investigators for the Benton Police Department and the Arkansas State Police had uncovered other disturbing allegations in interviews about McKaskle.

- One friend told state police investigators that McKaskle had said repeatedly in the weeks before he died that "somebody was going to kill him." "He was always pointing out small cars, saying they were following him," the friend said. "[He] kept saying the law was following him."
- Another friend admitted that McKaskle had supplied her and her husband with drugs. "She said Keith was worried recently about the police looking at him because he had been called to testify before the grand jury," Investigator Birdsong noted. The woman said McKaskle had been involved with some methamphetamine labs, and she named five local men, including two who happened to be named James, who she said had been involved with him in the business. The woman said McKaskle had talked to her about the labs and about how money was being laundered at the county-line clubs. "The last time she talked to Keith was about two days before he was killed," the investigator wrote. "Keith sounded very depressed. He said his heart was bothering him and he was scared. . . . "
- Another of McKaskle's friends told Birdsong that "McKaskle told her that there was some people following him."

It is not uncommon for drug users to experience paranoia. But other reports in the possession of police had reinforced the image of McKaskle as an exceptionally worried man:

- After interviewing one witness, an investigator wrote, "About two or three weeks ago, Keith started to tell him about the murder of Ives and Henry. He said Keith did not give any names or much information, except that he did say that [authorities] were involved. He said that before and after that conversation, Keith told him that he was being followed by [police]."
- Another report on an interview with a woman noted, "Keith tape-recorded information he knew about the Henry and Ives deaths and about his being followed. She said Keith never told her exactly who was

following him, except that he thought it was [county police]. She said Keith told her that he told Richard Garrett information in reference to being followed."

- Another man told police that "McKaskle came by his residence about three weeks ago and said that people were following him and that he was scared. [He] stated that two weeks ago McKaskle told him he had some very important papers and pictures that he wanted to bring to him because he was afraid that he was going to get killed over them."
- A lieutenant from a Little Rock suburban police department contacted the state police to report that "McKaskle had told him that there were several young guys following him around in rental cars, and that they were making it very obvious that they were following him."
- Finally McKaskle's brother, a businessman in Conway, a city thirty miles northwest of Little Rock, told police investigators that a week before he died, Keith had told him that he was living in fear for his life. He said that McKaskle had visited his aging mother and that, although she did not realize it, he had told her good-bye.

Police, but not the public, knew all this by the time the prosecution began preparing its case against Shane Smith. While people meeting for coffee in the cafés around Benton tried to figure out how any single person, let alone a teenager like Smith, could have gotten the jump on McKaskle, Linda was pondering another question. That day when Harmon had burst into her office, ashen and clearly frightened, to tell her the news of McKaskle's murder, he had added that he had been among the first to get to the scene. He had arrived just minutes after Elmendorf. Later, Linda asked Harmon how he had heard about the killing so quickly. He said that they had been sitting in Garrett's office with a police scanner on when the call came across.

Linda did not dwell on the incident. She had enough murder to think about. At least in the case of Keith McKaskle, the police had nabbed a suspect, however unlikely he seemed. That was more than Steed had done in the case of Kevin and Don. Don Birdsong, the state police detective, had told her personally that, although the fact was not being reported, police had concluded that McKaskle's murder had been "a crime of passion." As evidence, they pointed to the excessive number of wounds. Linda trusted Birdsong. She wanted to believe that there was an explanation for McKaskle's murder—one that had nothing to do with Kevin and Don or with messages being sent.

Besides, Christmas was coming. Linda wanted life to be a little more normal. Despite her mistrust of Elmendorf, she wanted to believe him. The implications she would have to consider if she doubted him were too nightmarish to contemplate. And she desperately wanted to believe Harmon and Garrett. She was tired of mulling over questions about the informant's murder. What mattered was what Harmon and Garrett had done. They had challenged Malak's ruling, called a prosecutor's hearing and a grand jury, and though they had not yet solved the case, they had gotten the ruling in the boys' deaths changed from "accident" to "homicide." When she and Larry and the Henrys had felt that everyone else was against them and there was nothing they could do, Harmon and Garrett had taken their side. And they had done a lot. Against the backdrop of all that, Linda's doubts seemed petty and niggling. She put them out of her head.

That would have been harder for Linda to do had she known about Deputy Cathy Carty's close relationship with McKaskle. Linda had always appreciated the way Carty had objected that night on the tracks to the deputies' decision to treat the deaths as an accident. It was one of the few moments of clear common sense on the part of a local or state official that Linda had heard of since the case began. In light of her respect for Carty, Linda would have been disturbed to know that Carty suspected McKaskle's death was indeed related to the murders of Kevin and Don. Carty was convinced that McKaskle had passed information on to certain authorities. "We'd talk about it," she said later. "He'd say, 'Don't worry about it, baby. It's all going to come out before long.' "

But McKaskle was wrong. Whatever he knew about the deaths—if anything—never did come out. His murder ensured his silence. Just as Carty could not accept that Don Henry and Kevin Ives had lain side by side on a railroad tracks, as she put it, "to have an accident," she found it hard to swallow that Shane Smith had overpowered Keith McKaskle. While Linda Ives was hanging on to her belief in Harmon and the investigators, Carty was telling her closest friends that the police were wrecking the case again. "I will never believe that Shane Smith attacked Keith McKaskle and that Keith could not have fought him off. I've seen Keith in too many fights, and none of them lasted long. I think Keith was killed to send a message to everyone who knew anything about anything in Saline County, and that message was to keep your mouth shut."[3]

EIGHT

DEATH TOLL MOUNTS

JANUARY 1989–MARCH 1990

Linda continued to receive dozens of phone calls a week, from people both known to her and not. Some of the callers purported to have information, tips which she jotted down and passed along to Harmon and Birdsong. She read the papers, kept up with the television news, and listened, as people do in any small town, to the word of mouth passed by neighbors. Even so, her view was limited. She had learned a lot since Kevin had died, but she realized now that there were secrets in Saline County, dark and tightly knotted secrets that she could not—and perhaps would never—unravel. She focused on trying to loosen the knot she could see.

ALIGNING AGAINST MALAK

Beyond keeping in touch with Harmon and, to a lesser extent, with Birdsong, there was nothing Linda could do to further the investigation. But she decided that there was something she could do about Malak. She could still feel the grief he had caused her and Larry, and she knew how the Henrys despised him. In the wake of the grand jury's decision overturning Malak's ruling, she was beginning to learn just how many other Arkansans shared her estimation.

The calls would come in the evenings. "Mrs. Ives," one caller began, "we were hoping you might help us." The man lived in northwest Arkansas. His daughter Janie, like Kevin and Don, had also been in high school when she died. The last time he saw her alive was when she left to attend a party given by a classmate near their rural home. By all accounts, the circumstances surrounding Janie's death were suspicious. The man related how her body had been sent to Little Rock, where Dr. Malak had performed the autopsy. As in Kevin's and Don's case, he had ruled her death accidental, concluding that Janie had broken her neck after falling backward off a porch. The problem was that the porch was too low and close to the ground. Later, Janie's father learned that her body had been bathed and her clothes changed before it was taken to the crime lab. When he asked for the paramedics' reports from the night of the alleged accident, he was told that some were "missing." Janie's father believed that his daughter had been beaten at the party and that her killer was being protected.

Linda empathized with her caller's anguish. She could understand his frustration at not knowing where to turn. "You got a grand jury investigation," he said. "You got Malak's ruling overturned. Can you offer us any advice?"

Another caller reported that after a family member had been found with his head cut off, Malak had ruled that the death was from natural causes. According to the medical examiner's report, the man had died from a perforated ulcer and the family dog, having come across the body, had eaten the dead man's head. Malak explained that he had reached this conclusion because the dog had regurgitated, and police had brought him samples of the vomit, in which he had detected pieces of human tissue. The family found the explanation preposterous. They pointed out that the head had been cleanly cut off, not gnawed. There had been no sign of bites or chew marks. When they consulted veterinarians, they were told that a well-fed dog will not normally eat a human, particularly its owner, and that if a dog was going to chew on a body, it would eat like animals in the wild, devouring the soft tissues first. But questionable as Malak's ruling might be, it held the force of law.

Other callers told of relatives who were in prison due to Malak's rulings of homicide and his testimony in their cases. Linda became well acquainted with the relatives of the man who went to prison after Malak's presentation in court using the allegedly doctored transparency. Still other callers related how Malak had ruled a loved one's death a suicide, when they felt sure the victim had been murdered.

After months of such reports in which Dr. Malak's questionable rulings and challenged testimony, families who were struggling with unresolved deaths lacked any confidence in his credibility. Linda knew from her own experience how dealing with such uncertainty compounded a family's grief. Her heart went out to the people who called her. She knew that rulings of suicide in particular, even if correct, were often hard for survivors to accept. The pain was harder when families were not sure the medical examiner could be trusted. Even if Malak had been correct in the rulings that affected some of her callers, Linda felt that they should not have to endure such uncertainty.

But she did not know what to tell them. And she already felt that she was coping with more than she could handle. Though life with Larry had settled down to something resembling the calm of the past, the emotional strain remained. They no longer discussed Kevin's death very much, nor even the case itself. Larry, a private person anyway, was even more private in his grief. They had come to understand the difference in their responses to Kevin's death and to respect each other's approach. But the result was sometimes strange. It felt like they were tiptoeing around each other in the house, always trying to protect each other, being careful not to disturb their hard-won emotional balance. So long as the grand jury had been in session, their equilibrium had been tentative; revelations could emerge at any time. There had been little events, such as the open doors in the house, and big events, such as Keith McKaskle's murder, to be reckoned with. They traveled to Little Rock a couple of times a month to sit in on meetings of the legislative committee and the Medical Examiner's Commission, both of which were "investigating" Malak. There was nothing normal about their lives, no matter how much they tried to pretend. No, Linda thought, after hearing from yet another caller who felt trampled by Malak. She had enough going on in her own life. She could not let herself be drawn into anyone else's problems.

But the calls continued to come from communities across Arkansas. "You're the first person who's even listened to us," many of the relatives would say. Linda understood. She remembered trying to talk to a sheriff who would not listen and feeling hopeless in the face of Malak's official ruling. She knew how hard it was for ordinary people, such as Larry and herself, the Henrys, and most of her callers, to mount a private investigation. And she ached to recall the difficulty of confronting all of these obstacles while overcome with grief. Just getting out of bed and combing one's hair required a superhuman effort. So Linda listened patiently to each caller because she knew that, after the loss of their loved one, the feeling of abandonment was the worst of what they had to bear.

Linda assured them that she and Larry were attending the hearings about Malak in Little Rock, as representatives for all those he had hurt. She also notified others of the meetings, so that they, too, could attend. Buster Schmidt, the uncle of the young man who had been imprisoned after Malak's testimony using the allegedly reversed transparency, became one of the regulars. Like Linda, he hoped to see Malak removed from office.[1] Linda got to know him well. The two talked about how many other people who were not at the hearings had had similar problems with Malak.

"At least we should all keep in touch," she told him after one of the sessions. It looked like no one had any intention of removing Dr. Malak and that, after all the reports about him, the meetings were an attempt at damage control. Linda had begun to feel they were mostly for show. Still, she and Schmidt kept attending, if only to keep up some pressure.

Schmidt said he had been thinking the same thing, and as the two descended the steps of the capitol, he added, "I've been thinking we should start an organization. Maybe we could call it VOMIT."

"VOMIT?" Linda looked at him aghast.

"Yes," Schmidt said. "It would stand for Victims of Malak's Incredible Testimony."

Linda laughed at the joke. "Oh, yeah," she said. "I'm sure I would want to be part of something called VOMIT."

"But think of it, Linda. We *are* all victims of Malak's testimony. And that *is* what you feel like doing."

Linda was still chuckling as she drove home to Bryant. But as the miles passed, she realized Schmidt was right. An organization was needed to give voice to Malak's opponents. And if the situation was sickening, state officials had made it so. Over the course of the next few months, she spent a couple of hundred dollars having bright yellow T-shirts printed with the word VOMIT in big, black letters on the front, with the acronym spelled out underneath. Larry fumed about the cost, but Linda sent the shirts to the people who had called her, and the idea, which had started out as a touch of humor, a gesture of solidarity among some disaffected citizens, took hold. While the hearings continued, Linda sent out newsletters with updates about what was happening—and more often, what was not. When Linda and Schmidt held an organizational meeting at a bank in Benton, several members drove from across the state to attend. A newspaper ran a photograph of the two wearing their VOMIT T-shirts, and thereafter Linda became an unofficial spokesperson for the growing anti-Malak movement in Arkansas.

It was a strange thing, she realized. Rarely do medical examiners attract much attention, much less organized, grassroots opposition. But what had not been strange, she reminded herself, since that morning of Kevin's death?

For many who have suffered a loss, helping others becomes part of the healing. But Linda had not become involved in the effort to oust Dr. Malak as a step toward her own recovery—at least, not consciously. And that was a good thing, as it turned out. No matter what she and the other families did, and no matter how many of Malak's outrages came to light, it was becoming distressingly clear to Linda that he would not be removed. In fact, it looked like no one in a position of power was willing to so much as shake a finger at him.

MANIPULATING JUSTICE

On top of their disappointment that Malak was still in office, the hope that Linda and Larry had placed in the grand jury had come to naught. And now federal officials were criticizing Harmon.

In December 1988, the last month before the grand jury disbanded, Assistant U.S. Attorney Bob Govar in Little Rock became furious with Harmon about an informant who was about to testify in a federal case. The informant, David Zimmerman, had been an associate of Teddye Carter, the drug dealer who said he had been an informant for the Benton Police Department. Federal agents had been investigating that department, and if Zimmerman was expected to testify, and to offer what prosecutors described as "very damaging information" about officers stealing drugs out of the department's evidence locker for sale on the street. When Harmon unexpectedly charged Zimmerman with manslaughter and possession of methamphetamine in connection with a year-old traffic fatality, Assistant U.S. Attorney Govar was irate. In a rare display of anger directed by one prosecutor toward another, Govar complained that Harmon's charge against David Zimmerman was little more than an attempt to discredit the witness by saddling him with a criminal record. Govar told reporters that it looked like the criminal justice system in Saline County was being manipulated to impede a federal investigation into drug trafficking. "In the case of David Zimmerman," he added, "the manipulation was apparently successful."[2]

Linda knew nothing about the scale of Govar's investigation, but she was surprised to hear a U.S. attorney lash out against the workings of a local grand jury. By now she understood that drugs were a huge problem in Saline County and thought that Kevin and Don had probably died because of them. But, as Harmon frequently reminded her, it would be a mistake to assume that all evidence of drug activity was related to their case. She tried to keep that in mind. Despite Govar's complaints, as far as Linda and most others in Saline County could see, it had been Harmon who had brought drug problems in the Benton Police Department to light through his work in the grand jury.

Harmon usually had a quote or two ready for reporters, but he was uncharacteristically short when asked about Govar's accusations. "I don't understand anything the feds have done in this case, or the police department case, or anything else," he snapped. "So don't ask me."

By the year's end, the questions were piling up. Harmon promised that the grand jury's final report would "tell it like it is." But to Linda's disappointment, whatever was in the report was doomed to remain secret. The jury prepared a five-page report that included a two-hundred-page attachment containing the testimony of Dr. Fahmy Malak. But Judge Cole ordered that neither the report nor the attachment be released. Instead, he allowed the jury to release a one-and-a-half-page edited version. Stating only that the boys' deaths were probably drug-related murders, it contained no indictments, no recommendations for additional charges, and none of Malak's testimony. Cole said that state law barred the release of grand jury testimony without the witness's permission, and Malak had not given his permission. That decision did not sit well with the sixteen jurors. "It's a disappointment in the final analysis, the way it all turned out," said foreman Carl Allen.

Judge Cole put the best spin he could on the endeavor's fruitlessness. "I think if we've accomplished nothing else," he said, "we've at least caused the citizens of this county to know that there is a body, there is a way, there are people with dedication, there are people with perseverance who will do everything humanly possible and within the law to see that the administration of justice in this county is served." Larry and Linda agreed with Cole that Garrett, Harmon, and the members of the grand jury were indeed people of dedication. Yet it was hard for them to find comfort in Cole's words when, after nine months and one hundred and twenty-five witnesses, the grand jury had produced not a single clue that related to the murders of Kevin and Don.

SILENCED WITNESSES

Comfort, in those weeks after the close of the grand jury and Keith McKaskle's murder, was in short supply. Just three weeks into 1989, on January 22, another young man from northern Saline County was murdered. Greg Collins, twenty-six, died from three shotgun blasts fired at close range. His body was discovered in a pine forest in a county south of Saline. Though Collins had been called, to testify before the grand jury, he had never appeared. Newspapers reported that Harmon and Garrett had questioned him privately about the train-deaths case. After Collins's body was found, Garrett commented on a rumor that Collins and others had been with Kevin Ives and Don Henry on the night the two had died. Garrett said the rumor never had "panned out."

It was the kind of news that made Linda feel sick. It reawakened grief and gave her a heightened sense of the evil around her because what was known as a fact in Saline County was that Collins had been a friend of another young man named Keith Coney—and Coney too had recently died. Linda had noticed the small news item reporting Coney's death just a few weeks after the start of the grand jury, in May 1988, but she had attached no significance to it. At the time, the parade of witnesses appearing before the grand jury dominated Saline County's news. But after McKaskle's murder, Coney's death six months earlier began to attract belated attention.

The official report had been that Coney had run his motorcycle into the back of a semitrailer truck while traveling on the highway at a high rate of speed. But there may have been more to the death than that. Friends reminded Linda that some people had told investigators that Keith Coney's cousin,

Michael Coney, had been one of the last people to see Kevin and Don alive on the night they died. Keith Coney, like Collins, had been one of the witnesses whom Garrett and Harmon had called to testify before the grand jury. The whisper now circulating was that Keith Coney's death had not been a highway fatality. The rumor, which authorities did not dispute, was that Coney had jumped on his bike to escape an attack on his life and that he was being chased when he swerved into the back of a truck. Witnesses who saw Coney's body reportedly stated that his throat had been slashed, a wound they did not believe had been caused by the accident.

Linda tried to keep the story in perspective. She would go crazy if she let herself think that every unexplained death in Saline County was linked to Kevin's and Don's. She tried to remain calm, even after Garrett commented in the paper that "in light of what's happened since, the possibility that Keith Coney was being chased is looking more suspicious."

Not everyone felt saddened by Coney's death. Deputy Cathy Carty told friends that she considered the young man's death an improvement to the county. Having encountered him in the line of duty, she explained, "He was what we in law enforcement used to call a dirtball." Once, she said, after she had arrested Coney on an outstanding warrant, he sent her a message that, as she recalled it, "One of these days he was going to slit my throat and piss on my face as I died." She added, "So no, I can't say as I was upset to hear what happened to him."[3]

It was unusual for a rural area like northern Saline County to experience so many violent and unexplained deaths in such a short period of time. First there had been Kevin and Don on the railroad tracks. Nine months later came Keith Coney's questionable death on his motorcycle. Then the brutal stabbing of Keith McKaskle six months after that. And now the murder of Gregory Collins, just a couple of months after McKaskle's. Each of the last three victims had had some connection to the now defunct grand jury. It could not be a coincidence, Linda thought. Her home felt like the eye of a hurricane, with Saline County, a maelstrom of intrigue, drugs, and murder, swirling outside. Unable to do anything else, she placed her trust in the ongoing investigation by the Arkansas State Police.

MALAK CONTRADICTS HIMSELF

Judge Cole had sealed the grand jury's report, but in the weeks after the grand jury disbanded, Harmon leaked critical parts of Malak's testimony—segments in which the medical examiner had contradicted himself—to reporter Doug Thompson of the *Arkansas Democrat*. In the days that followed, newspapers around the state reported verbatim key excerpts from Malak's grand jury testimony. The discrepancies in Malak's testimony centered on an important question concerning the weight of Kevin's and Don's lungs.

In his first appearance before the grand jury, Malak reported that Kevin's lungs weighed 1,250 grams, and Don's 880. Noting that a weight of about 700 grams would have been normal for the boys, he explained the extra weight by saying that the boys had inhaled blood.

"Okay," Harmon said. "And how does the inhaling of blood, what does that have to do with the traumatic death?"

Malak: "The inhaling of blood, what this means, this means that these people were alive when they were hit. If I am dying or if I am dead and I receive injury, I am not breathing. No blood will go to the windpipe."

Harmon: "All right. Let's back up a minute. Say you're run over by a train. Would you expect death to be how quick, within a matter of seconds?"

Malak: "Yeah. It is, it is immediate death."

Harmon: "All right. If you had suffered a blow to the head or some other sort of injury and then you were laid down on the track and ran over by a train—if you died a slower death—would your lungs weigh more? Or would they weigh more as a result of the train running over you?"

Malak had seemed stymied. "I don't know the answer for that," he replied, "because this is a hypothetical question."

Harmon: "Well, you're an expert."

Malak: "I don't know the answer to that."

When Burton, the Atlanta pathologist, testified, he had not been so equivocal. Burton stated clearly that the extra weight of the lungs indicated that the boys had been alive for some time after being injured, time during which the blood had entered their lungs. That blood would not have had time to accumulate, he testified, had they died suddenly, as would have been the case if they had died from being struck by the train.

When Malak returned to testify before the grand jury in November, he revised his theory about the weight of the lungs when a juror asked him about the discrepancy between his findings and Burton's. "But you keep bringing up the weight of the lungs," the juror said. "And it turns out that when Dr. Burton did his check, that's one of the determining factors in why he thought it was that they were already killed. Do you think that?"

"No," Malak had answered. "I tell you, ma'am, exactly what this is. If we weigh the lungs separate, they have a certain weight. But if you weigh the lungs with the throat, with the tongue, voice box, and the windpipe, they weigh a lot."

Harmon: "Is that what you're telling us now you did?"

Malak: "Look in the photograph and you'll find the whole thing."

Harmon: "And that's what you weighed?"

Malak: "This is the technician—what they weighed, sir."

Reports of the testimony created another media stir. Harmon justified his decision to release it. "Dr. Malak is a disgrace to the judicial system and to the people of the state of Arkansas. He is the sole reason we couldn't get a meaningful and thorough investigation into the boys' deaths, and we won't get one until he's gone because everyone is so concerned about protecting him."

There appeared to be little doubt that officials in Arkansas, from the governor to the state legislature to the Arkansas Sheriffs Association, were keen on defending Malak. Almost immediately after Harmon released the testimony, the sheriffs association reiterated its support for the embattled medical examiner. "We're not saying Malak was accurate in the Saline County case or in any case," the association's director said, "but he's human and can make mistakes." The sheriffs' spokesman attributed part of Malak's problem to the fact that "he's Egyptian, has dark skin, wears thick glasses, and has a language problem."

Harmon, who was seeing his popularity in Saline County and statewide grow with every assault he made on Malak, lashed back. A person's skin color has "nothing to do with honesty and integrity and the administration of justice," he proclaimed. And he added, "I guess anyone who doesn't agree with Dr. Malak now is prejudiced." Again the *Arkansas Democrat* polled its readers, and again the results overwhelmingly favored Malak's ouster. But by now Linda knew better than to hope that any show of public dissatisfaction would dislodge the man from office. For reasons she could not understand, he seemed entrenched.

Further Malak support came in early 1989, soon after Greg Collins's murder, when the Crime Laboratory Commission released the review of Malak's office by the out-of-state pathologists. It was glowing. The reviewers found Malak to be a "diligent, dedicated, and capable forensic pathologist" whose credibility as state medical examiner had been tarnished by an "unenlightened press." The report cited no examples of incorrect or "unenlightened" reporting, but it noted that, as a result of the stories about the medical examiner, "We perceived that Dr. Malak has lost the professional confidence of some of the public and private sectors." The reviewers offered a suggestion for improvement of his office's operations: increase Malak's salary by about 25 percent. Dr. Joycelyn Elders, the director of the Arkansas Health Department and chair of the commission, said that, due to the favorable evaluation, the commission was grateful to have Dr. Malak on board.

The discrepancy between official support for Malak and the public's mistrust of him had become more than Linda could bear. Governor Clinton especially seemed to want to distance himself from any issue concerning Malak and the state crime lab. Faced with wave after wave of criticism of Malak, Clinton had nothing to say. Instead, he passed the question of what to do about Malak on to the legislative committee, to the revived Medical Examiner's Commission, to the team of out-of-state pathologists his office had hired, and finally to Bill Cauthron, a former sheriff whom Clinton had recently appointed as the new director of the state crime lab. By now it was clear that none of those committees or commissioners was going to find the least fault with Malak.

In the summer of 1989 Linda tried another approach to getting him removed. In a short, passionate letter, she appealed to the Arkansas Medical Society to curtail what she regarded as the abuse of the medical examiner's authority. Recalling the nightmares he had caused her family—the ordeal of overturning Malak's now discredited ruling that Kevin and Don had died from too much marijuana, his opening of the specimen jar containing Don Henry's remains in front of the dead boy's father, and his needless introduction of the enlarged autopsy photos at the prosecutor's hearing—Linda accused the state's medical examiner of conducting himself in a "grossly unethical manner." She also made it clear that she was not writing for herself alone. "I have spoken to families all over the state and our experiences are not unique. This man's decisions have had a devastating and lasting impact on many lives, and he must be held accountable for his actions. You have no idea how hard it is to deal with the loss of a child or loved one with the added complication of 'having to fight the system,' as well—only to find that justice is out of your reach because of the incompetence of our medical examiner." She asked that Dr. Malak be disciplined. The society took no action. Linda received no response to her letter.

Before Kevin's murder, Linda had never been involved in causes. She had never been vocal, never feeling she had anything to be vocal about. When she stood up with Larry and the Henrys at their first press conference, she felt that what she was doing was out of character for her. But under the circumstances, she was learning that speaking out was both in her character and essential to survival. Many times she would think, I've done all I can do. I'm just going to have to step back and go on with something else. And then there would come some new affront and she would be riled all over again. There were nights when she could not sleep because she felt so frazzled. But gradually she was finding out that she was tougher than she had thought. She was committed. For the sake of Kevin's memory, she would not be brushed aside.

Linda began a petition drive with other members of VOMIT. In a matter of weeks, standing at shopping malls, she and her supporters collected more than two thousand signatures on a petition asking Governor Clinton to step in and fire Malak. When reporters stopped by to ask about this latest effort, she explained simply, "We are tired of nothing being done." She told them that ordinary citizens recognized that Malak was not fit to hold his job. They could not understand why the governor did not recognize that fact, as well.

As Linda was making those statements, they were underlined by a small drama in a courtroom just west of Saline County. Four of thirty-eight prospective jurors called to sit for a capital murder trial had to be dismissed because they said they were not sure they could believe Malak's testimony. One of the dismissed jurors said she was concerned about Malak's ruling in the train-deaths case "and what he put those boys' families through." Another potential juror was excused for stating his opinion that Dr. Malak was "a fake." Malak's credibility problem was having an effect on the state's justice system.

MORE MURDERS

As the public controversy surrounding Malak unfolded in the state's newspapers, Saline County's murder rate accelerated. In March 1989, about six weeks after Greg Collins was found shot, police began searching a remote site for the body of yet another man whom Garrett and Harmon said they had attempted, without success, to subpoena to testify before the grand jury. Daniel "Boonie" Bearden of Alexander, Arkansas, had been reported missing for the past eight months. Now, in the aftermath of the other murders, authorities said that they had received information that Bearden's body might be found buried near the little town of Redfield, east of Saline County, on a site near the Arkansas River. They searched the remote area, but the body was not found.

The fruitless search heightened a growing sense of unease in the county. As Garrett publicly noted, Boonie Bearden, who had vanished, Greg Collins, who had been shot, and Keith Coney, who had inexplicably run his motorcycle into the back of a truck, had all been close friends. The two deaths and the third suspected one, all from within a circle of friends, all from the same part of the county, and all with ties to the grand jury, struck many as underlining in blood the message implicit in the murder of Keith McKaskle: in Saline County, to know too much about certain matters was a dangerous thing. It looked like Larry Davis, the newly elected sheriff, had taken over the job of policing a county where death and intimidation were used to ensure silence. Davis tried to reassure the public. "Right now," he told residents, "the only thing connecting these deaths is that it is strange that four people who knew each other died or disappeared in so short a time."

The strange events grew stranger. In April, just a month after the new sheriff made his remark, he faced the unpleasant task of reporting that yet another young man—Jeffrey Edward Rhodes—who had connections to the county's drug underworld, had also turned up missing. A week later, the charred and cut-up body of twenty-one-year-old Rhodes was found in a local landfill. He had been shot twice in the head.

By now Saline County's murder rate was attracting statewide attention. Linda followed the stories in the newspapers with more than average interest. Rhodes's story, like those of the other murders, had many chilling aspects. Soon after police discovered his body, reporter Doug Thompson of the *Arkansas Democrat* contacted the young man's father in Houston, Texas. Eddie Rhodes told Thompson that his son Jeffrey had called him two months before he died, saying that he was desperate to get out of Benton.

"He wanted to know if I could get him a job here in Houston," Eddie Rhodes reported. "I asked him why. He said he had to get out of Benton, that he knew something about the Keith McKaskle murder."

Eddie Rhodes said that he had reported the conversation to Benton police officials at the time Jeff disappeared, and that "they listened and took me seriously. But the sheriff's office dismissed the whole idea. The sheriff's investigators said that everybody wanted to connect everything that happened in Saline County to either that case or the case of the two boys who were left on the railroad tracks. They never did a thing about it."

By now the county had set a murder record.[4] Sheriff Davis insisted that the death of Rhodes was unconnected to the other killings. Linda would have liked to believe him. But when a twenty-six-year-old Pulaski County man, Frank Pilcher, was arrested and charged with Rhodes's murder, testimony at his trial reawakened her suspicions.[5] Marissa Bragg, Pilcher's girlfriend, having turned state's evidence testified that she had witnessed the killing and helped to dispose of Rhodes's body. Bragg testified that Rhodes had been working for Ron Ketelsen, a Benton hairdresser, whom Bragg identified as "a big cocaine dealer." Bragg also mentioned during the trial that she had met Ketelsen once, when she had gone to his shop with a friend of hers by the name of Dee Anne Parker. Parker, Linda noted, was the woman who, a few months earlier, had discovered the body of Keith McKaskle. Sheriff Davis could insist as much as he wanted that these deaths were not connected, but by now, Linda figured that anyone who believed him was more naive than even she had once been.

THE TRIAL OF SHANE SMITH

In August 1989, as the second anniversary of Kevin's and Don's deaths approached and the county gossiped about its rash of unsolved murders, Linda attended the trial of Shane Smith, McKaskle's young accused killer. She was not prepared for what unfolded in the courtroom. For starters, a prospective juror was excused because, when told that Dr. Fahmy Malak would testify, he said he could not accept that Malak was an expert. The satisfaction Linda drew from that was all she would find in the trial.

Smith, described by a defense psychologist as being of below-average intelligence, socially withdrawn, and emotionally immature, was charged with capital murder. Saline County prosecutor Gary Arnold built his case against Smith upon discrepancies in various accounts Smith had offered of what he had seen and heard on the night that McKaskle died. Smith had given four interviews to police. In the first three, he reported that McKaskle was killed by three men who burst into the house wearing clown masks. In the fourth interview he changed his story, claiming that five men had actually come to the house wearing black masks and black clothing. In all four accounts, Smith said that he had been held in the kitchen at gunpoint while the slaying took place in the carport, and that after McKaskle was dead, the assailants had taken Smith out to the carport, where they'd photographed him holding a knife over McKaskle's body. After making the final statement, he did not depart from it.

The state's two key witnesses against Smith were Arkansas State Police investigator Don Birdsong, who discussed the changes in Smith's accounts, and Dr. Fahmy Malak. Malak testified that McKaskle had received more than one hundred knife wounds, all of them above the waist, and that at least thirty of them had been struck at McKaskle's head. When Malak brought out autopsy photos of McKaskle's body, Smith's attorney, Curtis Rickard, objected, arguing that the photos were "highly prejudicial" and served "no appropriate purpose." But the objection was overruled and Judge Cole allowed the photographs to be introduced.

In Rickard's cross-examination of Malak, he attempted to question the medical examiner about the allegations made by crime lab employees that Malak had altered evidence. Prosecutor Arnold objected, and Cole sustained the objection. Rickard was able only to establish that the medical examiner could not ascertain from his autopsy whether more than one knife had been used, or if there had been more than one attacker. The prosecution never produced a murder weapon. It claimed robbery was the motive.

In Smith's defense, Rickard tried to establish that discrepancies in the boy's statements to investigators were the result of threats made against him and his family while he was held by McKaskle's assailants. Rickard attempted to introduce evidence contrasting McKaskle's size with the defendant's and the vast difference in their experience at fighting, but Judge Cole allowed no testimony in either of those directions. After Prosecutor Arnold objected that "anyone who strikes the right blow with a knife . . . can stab to death anyone else," the judge prohibited any references during the trial to the victim's physical strength, his legendary fighting ability, or to his reputation as a bouncer.

With two of his defenses thwarted, Rickard tried to zero in on McKaskle's widely reported fears that his life was in danger. But when Rickard produced a witness who said he had been offered four thousand dollars by an Alexander man to kill Keith McKaskle[6], Cole ruled the testimony inadmissible. Rickard next tried to present several witnesses who were ready to testify that McKaskle had feared for his life. Cole ruled their testimony inadmissible, as well. In chambers, away from the jury, Cole listened as David Hart, a former police officer from a small municipality in Pulaski County, testified that McKaskle told him that three men—one black and two white—had been following him in a compact car. Hart said that McKaskle had told him he was afraid because he "knew something about the railroad-track thing." Stating that fears for one's life were relevant only for a defendant claiming he killed in self-defense, Cole ruled that the jury would hear no testimony in this case about the victim's fears for his life.

Though he had been stymied at almost every turn, Rickard did manage to mount a minor defense. He was able to establish that hair found clutched in McKaskle's hand after his death did not match Smith's, nor did a bloody handprint that was found on a wall inside the house.[7] It was evidence the prosecutor dismissed.

"Shane Smith's description of the events on the night of Keith McKaskle's murder is so implausible," he told the jury in closing, "it amounts to a confession." Rickard countered that the investigation into McKaskle's death by the Benton Police Department and the Arkansas State Police was "sloppy" and "pitiful." "There is a reason Keith McKaskle is dead," Rickard told the jury, "and whoever had that reason still walks the streets."

The jury considered the case for two and a half hours, then found Shane Smith guilty of second-degree murder and sentenced him to ten years in prison. Linda was flabbergasted. "The only thing I was convinced of on the defense side is that they were not allowed to present a defense," she told the *Benton Courier* after the trial. She said she found it odd that the jury would sentence "someone who supposedly committed such an incredibly vicious crime" to only ten years in prison.

Smith's father, Ronnie, was heartbroken. He recalled how he had encouraged his son to cooperate with Garrett and the police, and that in doing as he had advised, Shane had provided the prosecution with "everything they had." Ronnie Smith said he felt betrayed. "They took my honesty and they used it against me," he said, his voice faltering. "Keith McKaskle's killers are walking the streets, laughing at Saline County." As he walked down the courthouse steps, the elder Smith added, "Now I know what Linda Ives feels like. We're victims of Saline County, too."

For many, Smith's words struck a nerve. Just before the Shane Smith trial began, a member of the 1988 Saline County grand jury made a public statement requesting a new grand jury investigation into the train-deaths case. He said he had come to question "the lack of concern by law enforcement as a whole for doing anything to investigate even the leads we as a grand jury came up with." The former juror said that when his grand jury was in session, investigators "went through the motions" of checking out leads in the case, and presented jurors with a "stack of affidavits" to prove that they had talked with potential witnesses. But now the disillusioned former juror said, "They may have talked about fishing, for all we know." Asked which law enforcement agencies were dragging their feet, he answered, "I think they all are."

Sheriff Larry Davis disputed the juror's remarks. "I can assure you," he told reporters, "that we're working very hard and heavy" on the case. He added there would be no new grand jury.

ACCUSING A CORONER OF MURDER

During that same hot August of 1989, Little Rock's KARK-TV reported that Malak was accusing Mark Malcolm, Pulaski County's chief deputy coroner, of murder. According to Malak, Malcolm had murdered a fifty-year-old man who had been brought to a hospital with a .22-caliber bullet wound to his head, the result of an apparent suicide attempt, by ordering the hospital to disconnect the man from life-support systems.[8] What happened, in fact, was that after arriving at the hospital, the man was declared brain-dead, the attending physician, in consultation with the man's family, removed the life-support systems, the man died, and Malcolm was notified. When Malak reviewed the hospital's records of the incident, however, he interpreted a medical symbol to mean that Malcolm had ordered the life support removed. He then contacted the Little Rock police, alleging, as the police sergeant who took the report noted, "that the patient did not die as a result of the gunshot and that Mark Malcolm killed him."

After Malak leveled his accusation of murder, Malcolm's boss, Pulaski County coroner Steve Nawojczyk, and Malcolm's lawyer, John Wesley Hall, Jr., went to the office of Betsey Wright, Clinton's chief of staff, to formally complain about Malak. They were told that Wright was too busy to see them. Meanwhile, the Little Rock police, who investigated the incident, were able to sort out the confusion of Malak's mistaken interpretation of the medical symbol. The police reported that Malcolm had merely been notified of the hospital's decision.[9]

The incident finally received Betsey Wright's attention when the Little Rock police sent her their report outlining Malak's latest error. She recommended that the newly reconstituted Medical Examiner's Commission convene immediately to review the case. Once again Dr. Joycelyn Elders, head of the Arkansas Health Department and chair of the commission, was presented with the problem of what to do about Dr. Malak. Going into the meeting with the commissioners, Elders said, "People have been accused and we need to know what we are talking about." But she added, "My opinion is that there was perhaps a misinterpretation of the medical symbol used, and that is not unusual."

Linda was freshly indignant but not surprised by Elder's easy defense. At a meeting earlier in the year, she and Larry, along with Buster and Kathy Schmidt, had met with Elders to talk about the expanding controversy surrounding Malak. Elders had advised them to submit a formal written complaint that outlined their specific grievances and to attach supporting documentation. The families felt it was a lot to ask of private citizens, particularly after so many of Malak's problems had been documented in the press. But, gratified by Elders's interest, Linda had complied. She compressed her family's experience with Malak into seventeen specific complaints. She then gathered records of the testimony from the prosecutor's hearing and the grand jury hearing—fifty-two pages in all—to support each of her complaints.

The project took time and effort. When it was completed, Linda's allegations against Malak focused on his questionable actions regarding the deaths of Kevin and Don, including his now debunked finding about the influence of marijuana; his omission of the critical wounds identified by Dr. Burton; his failure to note in his autopsy report that Kevin's foot was missing; his contradictory testimony regarding the weight of the lungs; his refusal to order testing of the clothes; and his offensive suggestion that members of the train crew might have been using drugs. She also highlighted statements Malak had offered in his testimony at the prosecutor's hearing that medical examiners have a "social message" to decry the use of marijuana.

"Ladies and gentlemen," he had said, "the job of the state medical examiner is more than to find the cause of death. We have a social message. What is a social message? . . . [We must use] all our efforts in the community to go to schools to tell the kids, our children, 'Stop marijuana. Say no to marijuana. Say no to drugs.' " Admitting that his own son had used marijuana, he told the jurors, "I am here, ladies and gentlemen, to tell you that I am a father, and I have this problem with my kids. And one of them dropped, dropped in grades.

My wife is a chemist. We took his urine, found he is using marijuana, and I stopped him."

Linda had found the speech shocking. It reflected the blurring in Malak's mind between the role of a minister or an educator and the role of a forensic scientist. Proselytizing against drugs was one thing, but it had no place, Linda wrote in her complaint, in either a medical examiner's ruling or in his testimony about a death.

Linda completed the document at the end of July, just as the Malcolm affair was about to break. When a special meeting of the commission was called to consider the Malcolm debacle, Linda asked if she could present her report to Elders and the other members at that time. In a cover letter attached to the document, Linda wrote, "Dr. Elders requested that our complaint be documented with court transcripts where perjury has been alleged, etc. I have done this in our case where it was possible. However, there are many instances of purported wrongdoing where we, as private citizens, do not have access to legal records. I believe that the burden of documenting alleged wrongdoing by Dr. Malak lies with the Medical Examiner's Commission, rather than with private citizens, who have neither the time nor resources to do so."

The letter continued, "My family, like many others throughout the state, has spent thousands of dollars, as well as precious time, overturning Dr. Malak's asinine rulings—at a time when it is a struggle just to cope with ordinary, everyday problems. The nine months that we spent proving that a murder had been committed could have been spent searching for the murderer. After researching various rulings and speaking with other families throughout the state, I believe that erroneous rulings by Dr. Malak are far from the exception—they occur with frightening regularity. . . . Putting all particulars aside, the total lack of credibility and integrity in the medical examiner's office has had a devastating impact on the entire justice system in Arkansas. I believe that you have a responsibility to the people of Arkansas to terminate Dr. Malak without delay."

At the meeting, which was attended by Malak's attorney and several members of the Little Rock media, Linda outlined Malak's string of errors, the allegations against him of evidence tampering made by members of the crime lab staff, and the erosion of Malak's credibility with the general public and before juries. "What will it take for him to be fired?" Linda asked Elders directly.

"The facts," Elders replied.

Linda explained that Malak's "facts" regarding the death of her son, Kevin, and his friend, Don Henry, had been refuted by Dr. Joe Burton of Atlanta—refuted so decisively that a grand jury had overturned Malak's ruling. Elders listened quietly. When the meeting was over, reporters asked her what she thought about Linda's arguments, particularly as they concerned Burton's scathing refutation of Malak's findings in the train-deaths case. Elders suggested that discrepancies in the testimony of the two pathologists may have resulted from "a lack of communication."

After that experience with Elders, it came as no surprise to Linda when she opened the *Arkansas Democrat* on Aug. 10, 1989, to read: "The state commission with the authority to fire state Medical Examiner Fahmy Malak isn't capable of rating how well Malak does his job, the commission chairman said Wednesday. 'As far as his abilities, I do not feel this commission feels we have the technical skills to judge Dr. Malak,' said Dr. Joycelyn Elders, chair of the state Medical Examiner's Commission. 'For that reason, we hired outside consultants.' "

Elders pointed out that the consultants brought in earlier at the expense of the governor's emergency fund had lauded operations at the medical examiner's office. As to Malak's recent accusation of murder against the Pulaski County deputy coroner, Elders said: "We found no reason to make any personnel recommendations. We are going to recommend there be better communication between the medical examiner's office, the coroner's office, and the crime commission board." When reporters pressed as to why Malak was being retained despite his dismal record, Elders replied, "Everybody in the world makes mistakes. There are no hard facts that Dr. Malak made a technical mistake on specific cases."

Reporters next turned to Bill Cauthron, Clinton's newly appointed director of the state crime laboratory, for comment on Malak's mistaken accusation of murder against Pulaski County's deputy coroner. But Cauthron said that he, too, lacked the expertise to supervise Dr. Malak, even though he granted that Malak was his employee. Noting that only the Medical Examiner's Commission had the authority to hire or fire Malak, Cauthron said that Malak, in effect, operated independently. "My relationship with Dr. Malak," Cauthron said, "is similar to that of a hospital administrator. An administrator doesn't go in there and tell a doctor what to do."

The pronouncements left many admirers of both Governor Clinton and Dr. Elders bewildered. Clinton had deferred to either Cauthron or the Medical Examiner's Commission every time he was asked about Malak. But now Cauthron was saying that he did not have the expertise to evaluate Malak, and Elders and the other commissioners were saying that their commission—the only one that, by law, had authority over Malak—did not have the expertise to evaluate his performance, either. By deferring to the team of out-of-state pathologists who had evaluated Malak, the board appeared to be suggesting that no one in the state of Arkansas with authority to censure Malak was qualified to judge his performance.

The commission's stance prompted a sharp reaction from Malcolm's attorney. "What purpose are they there for?" he asked. "If they don't think they have the needed abilities, what are they going to do the next time they have to hire or fire a medical examiner?"

If Governor Clinton shared any of the concerns that were being voiced, he showed no sign of it. To the contrary, Clinton agreed that, despite the latest embarrassment, he saw no reason to fire Malak. "I think the big problem is that he's been out there a long time working more or less by himself, and he's obviously stressed out, and he did something he shouldn't have," the governor said. Referring to Malak's charge that Malcolm had committed murder, Clinton conceded, "He did make a mistake and I think he ought to apologize to the guy for it." If Malak apologized and if he were to "get up to speed on the symbols issue," Clinton added, "I wouldn't think that this issue alone would be sufficient to let him go."

The next day the headline on the *Arkansas Democrat*'s editorial page read: MALAK AN UNTOUCHABLE? The editorial began, "Fahmy Malak is off the hook again." It went on to ask, "Why is it that politicians and bureaucrats always seem to do the sidestep shuffle when questions are raised concerning Malak's performance? What is it about Malak that makes them want to shield him from objective scrutiny? He's so autonomous that he didn't even bother to appear before the commission. . . . Apparently, no one has the ability to tell whether Malak's a good medical examiner or a bad one." It concluded, "The public doesn't need for its appointed medical examiner to be truly answerable to no one or for the commission that oversees him to be powerless."

John Brummett, a political columnist at the rival *Arkansas Gazette,* was no less offended. "Dr. Fahmy Malak is the Teflon medical examiner," he wrote. "The man can survive anything, and has." Brummett noted that "For $81,429, we get a man who performs nearly two autopsies a day and gives testimony at trials that supports the positions of local law-enforcement officers who like him for that. Meanwhile, he averages only two or three high-profile outrages a year." When editors of the *Gazette* met with Clinton, specifically to talk about Malak, the governor again insisted that Malak's mistakes were attributable to mental exhaustion due to an excessive workload. But when a *Gazette* reporter polled medical examiners in Texas and Tennessee, both reported that their workloads were comparable.

Newspapers around the state echoed amazement at the commission's stance, and the *Benton Courier* was no exception. "Seemingly every few weeks," that paper's editors wrote, "there's a new charge that state Medical Examiner Dr. Fahmy Malak has botched an autopsy and come up with the wrong cause of death . . . "

On August 21, 1989, Linda wrote a letter to Governor Clinton, enclosing a copy of the complaint she had submitted to Dr. Elders. Referring to Clinton's defense of Malak, Linda wrote: "While I would certainly concede that Dr.

Malak has a communication problem and that he is perhaps stressed out, these are all situations he has brought upon himself. I would also agree with Dr. Elders's statement that everyone makes errors. However, it is crucial that a professional person in Dr. Malak's position be willing to admit their errors and do everything within their power to rectify them. Dr. Malak has historically lied to cover his errors."

Noting that Malak's credibility had become an issue in qualifying juries, she stated, "I believe that the lack of credibility in the medical examiner's office has absolutely crippled the justice system of Arkansas." And she added, "I feel that your statements and the most recent findings by the Medical Examiner's Commission are an absolute insult to the intelligence of the people of Arkansas and certainly raise questions about your own credibility and that of the Medical Examiner's Commission."

Linda would have liked to speak with the governor personally, to explain the treatment that she, Larry, and the Henrys had received from the overburdened Dr. Malak. Twice before she had requested a meeting with the governor, but her requests had been denied. In September, three weeks after she sent Clinton a copy of her complaint against Malak, she came home to find a letter from the governor's office. "Dear Mrs. Ives," it began. "Thank you for your very thoughtful and pointed letter of August 21. Please be assured that I am taking your request and your advice very seriously. Sincerely, Bill Clinton." That was all Linda would ever hear from her governor.

A few weeks after the Malcolm outrage, Linda began to wonder about the wording on Kevin's death certificate now that the grand jury had overturned Malak. She ordered a copy of the document from the state's Bureau of Vital Statistics. When it arrived, Linda was infuriated once again to see that nothing had been changed. Kevin's death was still listed as an "accident." She and Larry had the feeling that they were constantly fighting to regain ground already won—to take care of business that should have been handled by authorities. Linda and Larry made a formal request to the medical examiner's office and filed a formal petition in Circuit Court in Saline County to have Kevin's death certificate changed. The Henrys joined in the petition. Linda felt that she was fighting for Kevin's life. If she could stand up to the monster who had murdered him, then some basic decency and fair treatment for Kevin would result. Yet again and again she reminded herself that, while these miserable battles mattered, no victory, no matter how big, would ever bring Kevin back. She would fight, but she had to be clear about the goal. It was a measure of justice she was seeking, a truthfulness of record, a dispelling of illusions and of the slander that had been perpetrated against the boys. She would never have Kevin alive again, but she could at least demand the truth about his death.

In March 1990, two and a half years after the boys were killed and a year and a half after the grand jury ruled the deaths homicides, Judge Cole granted the families' requests that the death certificates be changed. By that time, Cauthron had died and Clinton had named Jim Clark, a former Arkansas state policeman, to replace him. Like Cauthron, Elders, and Clinton, Clark continued the defense of Malak. When reporters reminded Clark of the promise Malak had made at the Saline County prosecutor's hearing two years earlier—"If it turns out to be that these kids were beaten, I say in front of you all, I quit this job"—Clark insisted that that would not be necessary. And he added, "I don't think it's proven at this point that he made a mistake on this case."

NINE

THE GOVERNOR'S MOTHER

JANUARY–MARCH 1990

In early 1990, near the time that the boys' death certificates were changed, the families, along with the rest of the state, learned about a heretofore unknown juncture in the careers of the Arkansas medical examiner and Virginia Dwire Kelley, the mother of Governor Clinton. Linda was watching the local television news when reporter Mel Hanks broke the story on KARK-TV. It was an odd piece of reporting. The events were already years old, some dating as far back as 1977. They would not have ranked as news at all had it not been for Dr. Malak's and Clinton's prominence.

THE LAURA SLAYTON STORY

The story began in the late 1970s, a little more than nine years before Don and Kevin were murdered. The boys were in elementary school at the time.

Virginia Kelley, then Virginia Dwire, was a nurse anesthetist working in the resort city of Hot Springs, a half hour's drive south of Benton. In many ways, Hot Springs suited her. Nestled in the Ouachita Mountains and warmed by a series of hot natural springs, the city had started as a spa. For decades it had been famous as a gambling town, all of the gaming illegal except for the thoroughbred horse racing that took place every spring at the city's Oaklawn Park. Kelley was an avid fan of the races. After the 1970s, when the illegal gaming was shut down, the city rested its fortunes on the money brought in by tourists. They came for the horse races—which continued to be legal—for the national park that adjoined Hot Springs, and for the fishing and skiing on the mountain lakes to the west and south of the city. It was a lively, often rambunctious town where Kelley's son Bill had attended high school and which he would always consider home. She had campaigned hard for him in and around Hot Springs, first in his unsuccessful bid for the U.S. Congress in 1974, and again in 1976 when he ran successfully for the state's attorney general. But her own profession was nursing, and it was in this role, in the late 1970s, that her life intersected with the life of a young mother named Laura Lee Slayton.

Slayton had given birth to her first child—a girl—in August 1977, at Ouachita Memorial Hospital, the county-owned facility where Kelley worked. The child was delivered by cesarean section, but while Slayton was still in the hospital recovering, a staph infection attacked the incision and threatened her life. Dr. John H. Brunner performed several surgeries, and when Slayton began to recover, her family attributed her survival to Brunner's care.

Six months later, in April 1978, Brunner felt that Slayton was strong enough to return to the hospital so that he could remove a piece of mesh that had been left in her abdomen to help her heal from the earlier surgeries. The operation was considered minor. Kelley administered the anesthetic. But the surgery proved to be more complicated than expected due to scarring from the infection and the prior operations. The work was tedious and the operation took longer than anticipated. Suddenly, however, Slayton went into cardiac arrest. Brunner got her heart beating again, then completed the operation. He told her family about the cardiac crisis but reported that she was now out of danger and in the recovery room.

Less than fifteen minutes later the family was notified that Slayton had again gone into cardiac arrest. A tracheotomy was performed, but within minutes the young woman was dead. Privately, shocked staff members at the hospital pointed an accusing finger at Kelley.[1]

Three years later, just before the statute of limitations would have expired, W. O. Slayton, Laura's widower, sued Brunner and Kelley for negligence. Other members of the family said that, though the doctor was named in the filing, they never thought he was to blame. By then it was April 1981. Bill Clinton had already served one two-year term as governor and been defeated for reelection. He was temporarily out of office, organizing his comeback campaign.

By then, Kelley had formed her own anesthesiology group that held the contract at Ouachita Memorial. But as she later recalled in her autobiography, "Medicine was changing, and with the change came bitter new truths."[2] Increasingly, around the country, hospitals that had once used nurse anesthetists were replacing them with physicians trained in anesthesiology. Partly due to changes in Medicare and Medicaid, those hospitals that still used nurse anesthetists no longer allowed them to practice without the supervision of an

M.D. anesthesiologist. The requirement for physician supervision had rubbed against Kelley's independent grain, but she had submitted and found a doctor willing to sign on with her group.

It had not been easy. Privately, physicians in Hot Springs were complaining about Kelley's work. They said she wore inappropriate costume jewelry into the operating room, was not always attentive to patients, and filed her nails, wiped her shoes, and left patients unattended during surgery. There was concern in the medical community that Kelley, who had received her training twenty-five years earlier, had not kept up with developments in her profession. In the months when the horses were running at Oaklawn, she had a reputation for reading the daily racing form during surgery. A consensus was growing among the city's physicians that the longer and more complicated a surgery, the more risky it was to use Virginia.

By the late 1970s, physicians had begun refusing to work with her. They effectively restricted her practice to the publicly owned Ouachita Memorial Hospital and to fairly simple procedures. They performed most of their surgeries, and certainly the more complicated ones, at the privately owned St. Joseph's Hospital, Ouachita's business rival.

Following Laura Slayton's death, the pressure on Kelley intensified. "It could have been any anesthetist there the day she didn't come out of it," Kelley said in her autobiography, "but it happened to be me. . . . I was shocked. I hated it for her family, of course. Life isn't fair. But I believed I had done all I, or anybody, could have done for her. . . . Nevertheless, you could almost hear the drumbeats starting. All over town, my enemies had caught the scent of blood." In fact, Slayton's death might have quietly been forgotten if not for two significant events: W. O. Slayton, Laura's widowed husband, filed his lawsuit; and a second death occurred.

THE SUSAN DEER STORY

The lawsuit in the Slayton case had been on file for barely two months when, on the morning of June 27, 1981, another young mother named Susan Deer came into Ouachita Memorial for surgery. Kelley was called to administer the anesthetic. Deer died on the operating table.

The tragedy had begun a day earlier. Deer, seventeen and the mother of an eight-month-old baby, had gone to Hot Springs with a relative for a Friday night on the town. At about 4:15 A.M., after a night of drinking and dancing, the group was driving along one of the city's main thoroughfares when, according to notes later taken by the police, they got into a shouting match with an African-American couple walking along the street. The women hurled racial insults, followed by a can of beer. In return, the man on the street picked up a rock-sized piece of concrete and threw it at the moving car. It sailed through an open window and struck Deer, who was riding in the backseat, on the right side of her face.

Her friends took her directly to Ouachita Memorial. She was bleeding, but doctors did not believe she needed immediate surgery. Nonetheless, they were reluctant to transfer her. A few hours later, a team of doctors was assembled to repair the damage done by the rock to her nasal cavity, mouth, and jaw. They assured Deer's relatives that she would be fine. Despite her facial injuries, Deer was sitting up in bed before being taken in to surgery, talking and asking questions.

While the doctors worked on Deer's mouth, Kelley administered the anesthetic to the teenager through a tube inserted through her nose. During this portion of the surgery, Deer was "stable, vital signs were excellent, blood pressure stable, and there [were] no abnormalities of cardiac rhythm," according to notes made by Dr. William Schulte, the chief physician in the operating room, as reported later in the *Los Angeles Times.* Nurses reported to the waiting relatives that "Susie was doing fine."[3] When work on the girl's mouth was complete, the surgeons asked Kelley to move the endotracheal tube, placing it into her mouth so that reconstruction could begin on her nose. That was when the trouble began.

Kelley later conceded that she had had trouble with the second intubation. Vomit came up through the breathing tube, which indicated to the doctors that the tube had been improperly inserted and was delivering air to Deer's stomach, not to her lungs. Schulte later recalled that Kelley tried "at least two times, maybe more," to insert the tube correctly into Deer's lungs.[4] When those attempts failed, Kelley asked Dr. James Griffin, an ear, nose, and throat specialist, to take over. But by then it was too late. "Immediately following the reintubation of the patient orally, she developed badycardia [a slowed heartbeat]," Schulte wrote in his notes, "and within a matter of seconds [she] went into complete cardiac arrest." Schulte and Griffin tried for an hour to revive the girl before pronouncing her dead. Schulte reportedly said later that, as they left the operating room, all three of the doctors present believed that Kelley had caused Deer's death.[5]

Deer's death marked a turning point. The Hot Springs medical community was through with Kelley.

"I didn't realize I had been blamed for Susie Deer's death until later," Kelley wrote in her autobiography. "Not by the girl's family, but by members of the Hot Springs medical community who pointed the finger at me—saying that I'd had trouble moving the air tube. . . . The rumors were nasty. One I particularly abhorred was that I had been shining my shoes during surgery. Can you believe that? Before the crisis occurred, I'd noticed that a little blood had splattered onto my shoe, and I had leaned over for a second to wipe it off. The patient was breathing fine at that point, everything was under control. But the rumor made it sound like I'd been blithely shining my shoes while Susie Deer lay dying."

Though the tragedy was widely discussed in the Hot Springs medical community, it was little known beyond that circle. But for Kelley, Deer's death could not have come at a worse time. Depositions about her role in the death of Laura Slayton were scheduled to be taken that month. Because of the rock-throwing incident that had brought Deer to the hospital and the uncertainty surrounding her death, Deer's body was sent to the Arkansas Crime Laboratory at Little Rock.

The following Monday Dr. Fahmy Malak performed the autopsy. He concluded that the victim had died of "blunt trauma" to the head and from injuries to her brain that were suffered when the rock hit her face. He ruled the death a homicide. His autopsy report contained no mention of the difficulties the doctors had reported over the insertion of the breathing tube. He did not question any of the medical care she had received. He did not address the question of why Deer had suffered cardiac arrest. Dr. Griffin later complained publicly that Malak at least should have considered the possibility that Deer had died because of inadequate care provided during noncritical surgery performed hours after the original injury.[6]

A week later the Hot Springs police arrested twenty-two-year-old Billy Ray Washington, the young man who had thrown the rock, and charged him with negligent homicide. The public knew only that a teenager had died as the result of a rock-throwing incident and that Washington had been arrested. Kelley went to her depositions in the Laura Slayton lawsuit cleared of responsibility for Deer.

But Malak's ruling was not enough to help Kelley. After Deer's death no physician in the city was willing to perform surgery with her at Ouachita Memorial. By September 1981, two months after Deer's death, the hospital's board of directors, facing a financial crisis, voted to award its anesthesia contract to a local physician, replacing Kelley's group. The board had its back against the wall, and its decision caused Kelley to fight for her professional life. "The truth, I believe, is that they weren't trying to get rid of me because of those two deaths," Kelley wrote later. "They wanted me out because I was a nurse anesthetist and anesthesiologists were determined to take over anesthesia in Hot Springs the way they had in a jillion other cities. But since I wouldn't go quietly, they were seizing on these two cases to discredit me." Kelley might have found some support for her contention if the physician who had subsequently contracted to serve as her supervisor had stuck with her. But after Deer's death, he, too, severed their relationship. The total abandonment effectively ended her career.

In October 1981 Billy Ray Washington was preparing to go to court on his negligent homicide charge when his lawyer, Sky Tapp of Hot Springs, heard that there might have been more to Deer's death than even Washington had known. "Billy Washington was facing ten years," Tapp later recalled. "We were working, preparing his case, when I was tipped off that I should look at the medical records." Tapp requested the records from the prosecutor's office. "They never surrendered them to me," he said. "Instead they offered a deal—six months instead of ten years. I got my client a six-month sentence on a negligent homicide charge merely by subpoenaing the records." On Tapp's advice, Washington accepted the prosecutor's deal.

The suppression of Deer's medical records in Washington's criminal case was not the only legal decision that year that benefited Virginia Kelley. Circuit Judge Henry M. Britt of Hot Springs dismissed the damage suit that had been filed by the estate of Laura Slayton. The Slayton family lawyer had sought to introduce the expert testimony of Dr. Robert King, an Oklahoma anesthesiologist who was prepared to say that, based on standard professional practices, Kelley had been negligent. Judge Britt rejected King's testimony on the grounds that, being from out of state, he was not competent to testify about the standard of care available in Arkansas. Judge Britt then granted a summary judgment to Kelley and Dr. Brunner.

No longer allowed to practice nursing in her hometown, Kelley applied for work at nine other hospitals, but none offered her a job. She then filed an antitrust lawsuit that named as defendants the anesthesiologist who had replaced her at Ouachita Memorial, the hospital's entire medical and dental staffs, and all the members of the hospital's board. But none of her efforts succeeded. The doors to the operating rooms of Arkansas had been permanently closed to her. "With nowhere left to go," she wrote, "I had no choice but to retire from anesthesia."

Bill Clinton won the election in 1982, but his mother suffered another setback. The Arkansas Supreme Court ruled that Judge Britt had erred in refusing to allow the testimony of the Oklahoma anesthesiologist. The case was remanded and trial scheduled for July 1983. But only days before trial, the case was settled out of court. Brunner had been dropped as a defendant. Kelley alone was ordered to pay the settlement of ninety thousand dollars, an amount roughly equivalent to her annual income when she had been allowed to work. The following year, Kelley's federal antitrust lawsuit was dismissed. She let her nursing license lapse.

By the spring of 1990, when news reports began to surface about how

Malak's career had touched upon the career of Governor Clinton's mother, Linda Ives could only add the information to her file of unanswered questions. By now she had dozens of them. She reminded herself that Malak's ruling in the Susie Deer case may have been perfectly appropriate. Maybe the rock had caused the girl's death. On the other hand, she could not dismiss the question that had been raised by many in the state, including editors and columnists at its two leading papers: Why, despite all the controversy around him, was Malak being kept in office? Could this be an explanation?

There was so much she did not—could not—know. But in the end, all the unanswered questions led to only one: What had happened that night on the tracks to her Kevin and his friend Don? While other questions lapped at the edges of her life, that was the one—the only one—anchored in her heart.

TEN

INVESTIGATING OFFICIAL CORRUPTION

APRIL–JUNE 1990

Linda sat in a small, unoccupied office at the Arkansas State Police headquarters in Little Rock. She was on her own. The sheriff's investigation had been botched, Malak's ruling had impeded it, and Harmon's grand jury had produced not so much as a single suspect. All the standard approaches to law enforcement had been stymied—or foiled. It was in the hands of the state police now, but Linda knew better than to expect the diligence she had, in the beginning, taken for granted. She would check up on the state police.

She had no idea what she was confronting. For some reason, the investigation of this case had been thwarted. At first she had assumed that she was up against a dishonest sheriff. Now she suspected that certain state officials were also blocking the investigation. Since Kevin's death, she had awakened to the often cozy relationship that can exist between law enforcement and politicians. And she had learned that the relationship between criminals and law enforcers can sometimes be cozy, as well. She had come to see how law enforcement can serve as a link between politics and crime. The realization frightened her.

She would have been terrified if she had been able to see the true scope of the problem she faced: how the strand she had picked up in Saline County and followed to Little Rock would lead to the nation's capitol; how it was not just low-level politics that had its connections to crime. But she had a lot more to learn before that awakening would come. As Linda saw it on that April day in 1990, her battle was against local thugs and local officials.

Spread out on the table before her were mounds of files from the agency's criminal investigation division. By now the state police had been investigating the deaths for almost two years. They had amassed a file of more than one thousand pages. Yet detectives told Linda that so far they had been unable to find a suspect, a clue, or a thread of reason. With the investigators' notes before her, Linda hoped that she might succeed where they had failed. She opened the first file and began to read, making notes for herself as she went. Then she opened the next.

But even as she sat there, in the little office the state police had provided for her, she could not help but wonder. Officially the case was still open. According to state police policy, no one but police were supposed to be allowed to view the investigative file of an "open" case. Linda could not imagine why she had been granted this unusual access, unless it was that the state police regarded the case as essentially closed, but she was not about to question the decision. She accepted it and plowed in.

THE STATE POLICE FILE

The reports ran in a hundred directions. There seemed to be no central focus, no logical narrowing of scope. There was no indication of a systematic investigation. The files reminded her of Harmon's grand jury: long and fruitless. She searched for anything of importance there that might have been overlooked. But it was hard for her to know what was and was not of significance. She decided to organize her notes based on her own common sense. It could not be less productive, she told herself, than the professionals' approach had been.

A report that immediately caught her eye had been dictated by state police sergeant Barney Phillips in March 1988—barely seven months after the deaths. It was one of the earliest reports ever generated. It even predated the county grand jury.

- The report was of a meeting Sergeant Phillips had had with a confidential informant. Phillips wrote, "The CI states that she has been told that the area where the two boys died is a drop zone for dope coming out of Texas. The CI states that there is a good possibility that the two boys were not ripping off a marijuana patch, but trying to rip off a drug drop that had either been dropped from an airplane or from a passing train."

Linda was intrigued on several counts. She found it significant that the report had come so early in the case. And it startled her that, at a time when speculation had been focused almost exclusively on the notion of drugs being shoved off of trains, this report from a confidential informant—one of the earliest to appear in the Arkansas State Police file—had pointed to the possibility of drugs being dropped from planes.

The reference to the site where the boys had died as possibly being a "drop zone" was a surprise. The idea that drugs might have been coming in by airplane was a new one.

Linda and Larry were well aware of the speculation that the boys had stumbled onto a marijuana field somewhere near the tracks, or that they had interrupted the retrieval of drugs that had been shoved off a passing train. A search of the area by a friend of Curtis Henry's soon after the boys were killed had turned up nothing that looked like it was or ever had been a marijuana patch. Larry knew enough about the complexity of routing freight trains that he had profound doubts that drugs were being shipped that way. Reading this report, Linda wondered if the air-drop scenario had not been mentioned because it was so far-fetched—or because someone in authority knew it led in the right direction.

- Another file that caught her interest was dated June 1988—still early—just weeks after the grand jury started. It detailed a call made to the state police by an unidentified man. The caller said he was contacting the state police because he did not trust Sheriff Steed due to what he said were Steed's apparent "connections" to the local drug dealer whose name had repeatedly surfaced, but whom Harmon had never called before the grand jury. The report concluded that the caller wanted the state police to know that Don Henry and Kevin Ives had been at the home of another alleged drug dealer on the morning before they died.

- A month later, the files showed, Investigator Birdsong had arranged through Curtis Henry to interview Don's sister Gayla by phone. According to Birdsong's report on that call, Gayla confirmed that Don had been at the alleged drug dealer's house on the Thursday or Friday before he died. She said, according to Birdsong's report, that "while he was there he had tried to buy a quarter ounce of marijuana," but none was available. Birdsong wrote that Gayla Henry told him that she had never heard Don "say anything about ripping anyone off for drugs . . . but she does remember him saying something about the ultimate dealer, who is supposed to be a subject out of Little Rock. This was approximately three weeks before the boys were killed." Gayla Henry also confirmed in that interview that she had seen Don on the night before he died, but that Kevin was not with him.[1]

- Another report noted that Investigator Dave Dillinger of the state police had interviewed Chris Ballard, a young man to whom Gayla Henry had once been married. The two had separated a few months before the boys' deaths. According to Dillinger's notes, "Ballard stated that he saw Don Henry on the Thursday night before his death. Henry was going to steal some cocaine. Henry allegedly showed him three one-quarter-gram packages. Ballard said that he got the impression that someone had fronted Henry the cocaine . . . The last time Ballard saw Henry, Henry said that he had found this 'ultimate guy' in Little Rock, and he was fronting Henry all of his drugs. All Ballard ever saw Kevin Ives with was some marijuana. . . ."

- State police sergeant Barney Phillips, in the summer of 1989, had interviewed a friend of Don's and Kevin's who said that on the night the boys were killed, they had dropped in on a party he was attending at a mobile home. "Before they left," the boys' friend told Sergeant Phillips, "someone came out and told one of them that they had a phone call. When they were leaving, they said that they were going to get some cocaine to sell and make some money." According to Phillips, the source told him: "The next morning, I think it was around 8:00 A.M., we were asleep in the trailer when Chris Ballard came by and told us that Don and someone else had been run over by a train and killed. I asked Chris how did he know and he said he had talked to Gayla, Don's sister, who was also Chris's ex-wife, and that she told him."
- Investigator Don Birdsong also entered notes in the summer of 1989 about a conversation with another confidential informant. According to Birdsong, the informant said that two men—one of whose names Linda recognized as the one she had heard mentioned often—were heavy coke dealers in the Saline County area. "Information was," the report read, "that Don Henry and Kevin Ives overheard a phone conversation between [the dealer] and an unidentified individual about a large drug drop near the area of the tracks. Information was that Don Henry and Kevin Ives decided to rip off the drugs but that [the two men] caught them and were going to rough them up, and things got out of hand, and one of the boys was hit with the butt of a weapon and killed so they had to kill the other boy because he was a witness." Birdsong's report also quoted the informant as saying that the drug dealer and his associate had hired two other men to kill Keith McKaskle. "Information was that Shane Smith, the kid who was arrested for the killing of Keith McKaskle, was across the street and did see [the murder]," the investigator's notes continued. "The informant advised that on one occasion [one of the men] beat up a kid to remind him to keep his mouth shut about [the dealers]."

The reference to Keith McKaskle reminded Linda of the numerous other deaths that had followed McKaskle's throughout 1989—perhaps more "roughing up," Linda thought, that had gotten "out of hand." Then, toward the back of the file, she found a report on an interview Birdsong had conducted with another young man who identified himself as having been a friend of Don's. The subject said that on the Wednesday before Don and Kevin were killed an acquaintance had contacted him, wanting to buy an ounce of cocaine. He mentioned the name of Jeff Rhodes. The young man said that he had been unable to obtain the cocaine, so he had called Don, and that Don and Kevin had come over and met with the would-be buyer. It was the caller's impression that they had made a deal to obtain the requested cocaine. The report was dated August 1989. By that time, Linda reminded herself, Rhodes's burned body had already been found in a landfill with two bullets in its head. According to the report, Don Henry thought he could provide the cocaine for Rhodes through his contacts with—once again—the reputed drug dealer who was never questioned. Linda read on.

- Investigator Birdsong's notes from an interview with Linda Hollenbeck, a reporter at the *Benton Courier,* revealed that Hollenbeck said a woman who worked for the Bryant Police Department had told her "that a call had come in to the department reporting gunshots in the area of the tracks on the night of the train incident. Ms. Hollenbeck stated the woman advised that Trooper Lainhart [of the Arkansas State Police] somehow heard on the police radio about the gunshots and was headed to the call, but before he got there, information came out about the boys being hit on the train tracks and he went to the train incident instead." (Linda remembered that Trooper Lainhart had been one of the first persons on the scene. She had heard that he had been somewhat critical of the Saline County deputies' investigation. Rifling to the front of the state police file, she looked for his report—it should have been the first. No report from Lainhart was there.[2])
- An interview, also by Birdsong, with Steve Cox, the former state crime lab employee who had examined Kevin's and Don's clothes, revealed: "Cox stated that when he examined the T-shirts of the subjects, the most interesting one was the black T-shirt with the tears on the sides and the linear cuts in the back. Cox stated he thought this was most peculiar. Cox stated he brought this to the attention of the administration of the crime lab and advised them that there was a possibility of reconstruction. Cox stated that he said he was wanting to do more concerning the testing of these shirts and had set up with another employee to help do a reconstruction on a mannequin to show the wound pattern and to see if it was consistent with any wounds that were found on the bodies of the boys. Mr. Cox stated that he had a meeting with his superiors at the lab, and that he was advised that he should not go any further with the

testing of these items and that they wanted him to get the report on the case out that day."

Linda read all of the reports, trying to keep her mind open and alert to patterns. The reports suggested a possible motive for the murders, if, as some had suggested, the boys were planning to "rip off" some "ultimate" drug dealer. Linda did not like to think that her Kevin might have gotten involved in such a scheme, but even if he had, at seventeen, he did not deserve to be murdered for it and then to have his murder covered up. If that was what had happened, Linda wanted to know it. If he and Don had gotten mixed up in cocaine, she wanted to know that, too. And she wanted to know who was supplying them with the drug. Who was this "ultimate dealer?" But as she searched the file for other pieces of the puzzle, she found herself looking for an element that she knew by now was not there. It was the same as in the sheriff's investigation and even in Harmon's grand jury: nowhere in this file was there a sign that anyone with the Arkansas State Police had ever interviewed the local drug dealers whose names kept popping up. Disheartened, she turned back to the file.

- A diagram made in 1988 by a man named Ronnie Godwin was accompanied by a statement. Reading Godwin's statement, Linda was surprised by the clarity of its details. On the night the boys were killed, Godwin had told the state police, he spent three or four hours at Gigi's, a private club near the county line.

  "I had seven or eight beers and left after midnight," he said. "When I left, I went down Highway 5, turned down County Line Road through Alexander, then turned right on 111. When I approached Shobe Road I saw an unmarked police car. It was tan or gray and had three antennas, police hubcaps, and spot lights. Instead of turning right onto Shobe Road toward my house, I went straight to avoid being noticed. I had been drinking and was concerned about getting another DWI. I shut off my lights and turned in between two of the trailers that were lined up in two or three rows in the lot across from the store.

  "When I drove by the store, I saw two cops with two boys. My first thought was the police had caught the boys breaking into the store. One of the boys was taller and heavier set with light-colored hair. This boy was shoved up against the phone booth by the larger cop, who had on a white pull-over shirt and jeans. The other boy was on the ground outside the passenger side of the unmarked car on his knees with his head down. He was not moving. The smaller cop with a khaki-colored shirt picked that boy up and threw him in the backseat of the car.

> "The larger cop hit the boy at the phone booth in the head with the phone receiver. The boy was not resisting. The boy went down when he was hit, and the cop picked him up and threw him in the backseat of the car, also. The smaller cop was then looking around. The cop by the phone booth picked up a little .22 rifle and threw it in the car with the boys."
>
> "The larger cop got into the passenger side and the smaller cop drove. They drove up the hill to where it dead-ends and it looked like they went to the left. They stayed up there ten to fifteen minutes, then came down and turned right on 111. I could see something that looked like a garbage bag slapping against the window, from the wind because the front window was down. They turned north on 111 and came back in about ten or fifteen minutes and turned right on Shobe Road. I sat there another ten minutes or so. They never returned and I left. I was waiting to make sure they left the area so I wouldn't run into them. When I left, I noticed a medium-size car sitting back off the road across Hwy. 111 from where I was parked.
>
> "I did not tell this story to anybody. This is just not something I would have gone around talking about. When I heard about the murders, I didn't connect it at first, but as I heard more and more, I made the connections, and I was convinced after a time that it was Kevin Ives and Don Henry."

Linda looked up from the paper she was holding. Could this have happened? Could Kevin and Don have tried to run to the phone booth there on Shobe Road, only to be caught by two cops who were involved with drugs? Had Kevin and Don run to the phone booth to call for help? Was it possible that the crushing blow to Kevin's face—the one Dr. Burton believed might have been caused by a rifle butt—had been inflicted with a phone receiver? Linda knew the grocery store on Shobe Road to which the report referred. If there had been a phone booth there at the time, it had since been removed.

Linda rose to put on her coat. She felt a familiar mood wrap around her. It was anger, an emotion she had felt at almost every stage of this so-called investigation. It was clear how much could have been done that was not. No wonder the state police, like everyone else, had turned up nothing.

That night she and Larry talked about what was in the file—and what was not. By the time they turned off the lights to go to bed, they had decided to request a meeting with Col. Tommy Goodwin, the director of the state police.

When the day of the meeting arrived, Larry and Linda were shown into Colonel Goodwin's office. Linda listed for him all the points that she considered to be obvious flaws in the investigation, starting with the failure to interview the oft-mentioned alleged local dealer. The more she talked, the more her frustration grew. She heard herself ranting and raving. Goodwin listened courteously and tried to calm her down. As he spoke, she began to believe that he recognized that she and Larry had come to him with a legitimate complaint. "If this were your child," she had asked him, "would you be satisfied that everything that could be done by the state police had been done?"

"No, I would not."

Goodwin turned and instructed Lt. Doug Williams, the head of the agency's Criminal Investigation Division, to make a list of every remaining lead in the case that needed to be pursued. He ordered Williams to personally make sure that an investigator followed through on every one of those leads. The group stood up and politely shook hands. As Linda walked out of the building she promised herself that she would be right behind Williams, checking on his progress.

DISASTER AT HOME

A few weeks after the meeting with Goodwin in March 1990, a reporter for the *Kansas City Star* called the Iveses' house to inform them that he had heard of their case and become intrigued by its peculiarities. When he asked how the investigation was going, Larry offered a simple summation. "You go through life believing that when something like this happens, the authorities step in and take care of it," he said. "But we realized that if you don't push for something, it doesn't happen."

When the article was published and Linda and Larry received a copy, they saw that the reporter had also contacted Jim Clark, Dr. Fahmy Malak's new boss at the Arkansas Crime Laboratory. When Clark was asked about Judge Cole's order to change the boys' deaths to homicides, his response was what Linda and Larry had come to expect. "It is still our contention," the former state police officer said, "that these deaths were accidental."[3]

A few weeks after that interview, Governor Clinton made a campaign appearance at the Saline County Courthouse accompanied by his daughter, Chelsea. Linda waited in the crowd. As the governor approached, shaking hands, it became clear that he would pass directly in front of her. She knew exactly what she wanted to say. Greeting people as he went, Clinton finally arrived at the spot where Linda stood. "Let me shake your hand," he said, as he had been greeting all the well-wishers. Linda extended her hand. "Yeah," she said, looking him in the eye. "I'd like to shake the hand of the man who's refused to see me for years." Clinton stopped. He looked concerned. Linda introduced herself. She explained that she had been trying to call his attention to problems in the medical examiner's office ever since Malak's ruling in the deaths of Kevin and Don. Clinton asked, "What if we brought in a panel of out-of-state pathologists to review what he does on a case-by-case basis?" Linda fired back, "Why don't we just fire Malak and get a medical examiner who can do the job right? I think it would save the state money." Clinton nodded and said, "Well . . . " But by that time he was moving on, and the conversation was over.

After the governor had passed, a reporter who had noticed the exchange approached Linda and asked her what had transpired. She told him, and the reporter later caught up with Clinton and asked him for a response. "He seemed surprised that it was still an issue with you," the reporter later told Linda. "He said, 'I thought she left satisfied.' "

Linda had to laugh. She was far from satisfied. But she would pursue the case single-handedly if need be.

Then catastrophe intervened. On a May day in 1990, late in the afternoon. Larry, who had been doing spring chores around the house, fell off the roof while trying to remove a metal cap from the broad stone chimney. He struck the concrete driveway, breaking both of his arms. His left elbow was entirely shattered. Both arms required surgery.

A week later, when Larry returned home from the hospital, his right arm was in a cast that ran from his shoulder to his hand; it was held to his body by a sling. His left arm was a reconstruction in metal, held together by three screws inserted at the elbow. It had to be held out in front of him. Bent at a right angle, it rested on a brace attached to Larry's waist that held the arm perpendicular to his body. For the next several months, he would be utterly helpless. Until the injuries healed, Linda had to bathe him, shave him, dress him, and feed him.

As she and Larry had learned to accept each other's differences in coping with their grief, they now learned to accommodate each other through the ordeal of Larry's recovery. The cool days of spring passed into the heat of summer. With her attention so occupied at home, Linda had little energy left for Fahmy Malak or the Arkansas State Police. She barely had time to read the newspaper reports about Dan Harmon and the trouble he was in.

BENEFIT OF THE DOUBT

Dan Harmon had decided to run for prosecuting attorney again. By early 1990, twelve years had passed since his first election to that post at the age of thirty-five. He had served one two-year term and had run for reelection in 1980, as expected. But that was the year he suddenly withdrew from the race, declared bankruptcy, and left for California. Since his return and his work as special prosecutor for the district's two most sensational grand juries, the Democratic party had forgiven him, and so, apparently, had the voters.

Harmon charmed people, not with sweetness but with swagger. Clients were beguiled by him the way Linda and Larry were. They liked his shirt-sleeved, aggressive manner, and his smart but down-home style. Because of his appeal, people tended to take up for Harmon where they might have pilloried someone from outside the county. Did Harmon have a reputation as a bully? Were his marriages and finances a mess? No matter what rumors flew around him, the response of many citizens was the same as Linda and Larry's had been: Harmon was a hardworking, crusading lawyer. Anyone could have problems in his personal life. People gave him the benefit of the doubt.

And he had used that benefit to good advantage, polishing his confrontational style and capitalizing on run-ins with the powerful. People liked it when Harmon was quoted in the papers attacking Dr. Fahmy Malak or mocking assistant U.S. attorney Govar as a meddling bureaucrat. "That's Danny," folks would say, mixing admiration with affection.

But Harmon's appeal was not universal. A segment of the district's population, a wary minority, saw him as a dangerous enigma. They wondered why Harmon seemed perpetually broke. He drove raggedy old cars and cared little about his clothes. His family life looked equally unkempt. At forty-five, Harmon had two grown daughters, a four-year-old grandson, and a three-year-old son. He now also had three ex-wives, since he and Teresa, who was the age of one of his daughters, had recently divorced. If no one could fathom what Harmon did with his money, what he did with his women was more easily grasped. Stories floated about Harmon with women and drugs, and that Harmon had a complicated, nasty streak. The speculation was that Harmon could erupt into violence and disgust because, while one part of him liked women and using drugs, another part of him, the antidrug crusader, truly hated mind-altering drugs and people who were drawn to them.

Such talk was necessarily muffled. In the spring of 1990, about the time that Larry fell off the roof, as Harmon was seeking his second stint as prosecutor, the rumors burbled like an underground spring, well out of the hearing of most people in the three-county district. On the surface, Harmon was a respected public servant, albeit a character. People appreciated how, as a divorced father, he had coached his daughters' softball teams. They liked the vigorous campaigning he had done for several local charities. And they liked how, when appointed by Judge Cole, this spunky country lawyer had handled the hospital and train-deaths grand juries. Even though the results in both had been minimal, Harmon trumpeted them as successes. And his self-serving assessment stuck. Now, as he renewed his bid for prosecutor, he frequently referred to the Henry-and-Ives case, telling audiences, "I honestly feel I have unfinished business with the prosecutor's office resulting from the grand jury investigation. I feel like we got a good start on gaining information about the drug problem, and this needs to be followed up on."

At a meeting of the Saline County Democratic Women, he noted that "since 1987, there have been nine execution-style killings in Saline County alone." All of those killings, he said, had been related to drugs. He never mentioned, however, that by the summer of 1990, only one of those murders had been solved.

"GET IN THERE AND TAKE A LOOK"

As Harmon campaigned around the district, few in his audiences knew that he was being investigated by the FBI. Certainly Linda Ives did not. But in fact, federal agents had been watching him for almost a year, since late 1988, around the time of Keith McKaskle's murder and soon after the election of Larry Davis as sheriff. Linda had no idea that Harmon, her hero, was himself the target of a federal probe.

Davis had campaigned on a promise that the deaths of the boys on the tracks would receive a proper investigation. But he realized soon after assuming office that the promise might have been more than he could deliver. Such a sensitive investigation within his own county was no job for a sheriff, especially a new one like Davis, who had no prior police experience. If Davis was tempted to forget his promise, he quickly realized that Linda Ives, his most visible supporter, would not let him. Davis took the only route he saw. He pitched the problem of possible official corruption in Saline County into the hands of Charles E. "Chuck" Banks, the Republican-appointed U.S. attorney serving the eastern district of Arkansas.

Banks agreed to look into the case. While murder typically is not a federal crime, official corruption can be, if it occurs under the color of law or leads to the denial of civil rights. Violations of national drug laws are also a federal crime. In either event, federal agents would have jurisdiction. That settled, Banks handed the assignment to his top narcotics investigator, assistant U.S. attorney Govar. Two years earlier, in 1988, during Harmon's grand jury investigation into the train deaths, Govar had headed a team of state and federal agents who were investigating allegations of drug dealing by Harmon, members of the Benton Police Department, and others along the Saline-Pulaski county line.[4] Toward the end of that investigation, Govar had made the surprising announcement that his team had found evidence of "a rather large conspiracy" involving drug dealers and members of the county's judicial system.[5] When Harmon's grand jury had indicted David Zimmerman, the midlevel Saline County drug dealer who was one of Govar's informants, Govar had erupted and complained publicly that "the criminal justice system in Saline County is apparently being manipulated . . . to impede a federal investigation into drug trafficking."[6] Since then, Harmon had been just as clear in expressing his contempt for Govar.

As Govar would later recall, when Banks called him into his office to discuss a new investigation, he asked his boss "what the parameters of the investigation would be." Banks told him, "Just get in there and take a look at it, and see what happens."[7]

Govar was pleased with the assignment. He knew about the deaths of Don Henry and Kevin Ives and that the crime remained unsolved. He was aware of the grand jury's finding that the deaths had probably been drug related. He understood that the mystery of the boys on the tracks would not be central to his new assignment, but he assumed that, if there was drug-related public corruption in the county, the deaths and the fact that they had remained unsolved might be connected to it. And if they were, he decided, that was something he wanted to look into.

At the same time, Govar knew that the assignment could be a minefield. He had already voiced his concerns about the county, particularly that certain events might be being "manipulated." If, as it appeared, politics were at play, the situation could get sticky. Experience warned Govar to be cautious. He did not want to launch the investigation only to find himself abandoned once the political gunfire got heavy. He did not want, as he explained to Banks, to be "left twisting in the wind."

"I'll go into Saline County, and we'll look at this," he told his boss. "But I have one thing I want to ask you, and I want to be clear on this: If you want to start this war, I'll start it, but I want to make damn sure I can finish it." According to Govar, Banks assured him that he would have his full support.[8]

The effort was uphill from the start. Govar planned to organize a team of federal investigators but had a hard time getting help from other agencies, with the exception of the IRS. "The FBI didn't seem too interested," he said. "They didn't want to dedicate any investigative resources to it. At that time they were convinced that there wasn't anything to the investigation." The DEA was not much help, either. "At the time, in 1989, they didn't even have the manpower in Arkansas to address that type of investigation. At the point when we started this, they only had six agents working in the state."

Months later, when Govar related his frustrations, Banks promised to make some phone calls. Within a few weeks, the FBI had committed two agents to the probe, and the Arkansas State Police had contributed two undercover agents.[9] By the spring of 1990, about the time that Larry fell off the roof, it looked to Govar like his investigation into Saline County's official corruption had finally acquired some teeth.

Absorbed as she was with Larry, Linda had little time for much outside of her home and her job; she could not have learned about an operation as secret as Govar's. But even if she had known what the federal agents were up to, she would not have been impressed. From early on, soon after Kevin's and Don's deaths, she had pleaded with federal officials—especially with the FBI—to get involved in the case. They had repeatedly refused, explaining to her that not every local murder is necessarily a federal case.[10]

Now, three years later, she would have placed little trust in Govar or the FBI agents who were helping him. The agency had ignored her pleas for help when its involvement might have done some good. On the other hand, she knew that Harmon, who in her eyes had worked hardest to solve the case, held Govar in contempt. Between the two of them, Linda trusted Harmon.

Harmon was unabashed, both with Linda and in public, about labeling Govar as a meddling "outside" investigator. It was an old, populist ploy, and it played well in the county, where disdain for federal agents could be traced back for generations—to the enforcement of integration, to bootleggers' bouts with "revenuers," to the heavy hand of Reconstruction, and beyond. Harmon realized that with many of the county's voters, an attack on any federal intrusion into Saline County was a sure win for himself. He played the card for all it was worth.

Govar's investigation was to be a general investigation of drug-related corruption in the county. Harmon was not initially a target, though he quickly became one. By May, Harmon knew, though the audiences at his campaign stops did not, that Govar's team of DEA and FBI investigators was breathing down his neck. He also understood that Govar's team was not his only problem. There was a new team of undercover agents working in his own judicial district that focused specifically on illegal drugs. It operated outside his control and its existence infuriated him.

Federally funded drug task forces were born in the late 1980s when the federal government released millions of dollars to states to augment their police and sheriff's departments. Arkansas responded by forming special task forces with undercover officers whose only assignment was the elimination of drugs. These drug task forces were organized and administered by judicial districts. In the Seventh Judicial District, which included Saline County, prosecuting attorney Gary Arnold, who was not seeking reelection, appointed one of his deputies, a woman named Jean Duffey, to be the new drug task force's director. Duffey hired a team of undercover agents and introduced a new and unpredictable element into the law enforcement mix in the district. Harmon wasted no time in denouncing Duffey and her task force as incompetent. Campaigning, he swore that the first thing he would do when elected prosecutor would be to fire her.

"THAT CRAZY JEAN DUFFEY"

Linda had little contact with Harmon these days—certainly nothing approaching the daily phone calls during the grand jury session. But when they did speak, and when Harmon mentioned Duffey, his assessment of her was scathing. "That bitch is crazy," he told Linda. Whenever he mentioned the task force director, it was always as "that crazy Jean Duffey." It was a harsh assessment, but from what little Linda had heard about Duffey, she thought that Harmon might be right. Though Duffey had grown up in the district, in adjoining Hot Spring County, which made her a local girl, she had gained a reputation for bucking the legal establishment. According to what Linda had heard, within a year after Duffey was hired as a deputy prosecutor in the district, she had already had run-ins with several of its attorneys and with at least one of its judges.

Duffey hardly looked like an opponent worthy of Harmon. Tall and slender, she had a reedy quality. Though the two were close in age—both in their early forties—physically, Duffey was at the other end of the spectrum from Harmon's stocky, pugilistic build. Their personalities were no less at odds. Duffey and her husband, James, whom she called Duff, had both been schoolteachers until he had taken over Jean's parents' moving business and she had gone to law school. They led a quiet home life with their three children. But Duffey was an activist at heart, and while attending law school in Little Rock, she had co-founded an animal-rights organization, Arkansans for Animals.

When Gary Arnold became prosecutor in the same election that saw Steed defeated, he had hired Duffey as one of his deputy prosecutors and placed her in charge of the district's drunk-driving cases. By the end of her first year, Saline County's DWI conviction rate had jumped from 68 to 96 percent. But not everyone appreciated the improvement. While the added revenue pleased Prosecutor Arnold, and while police and sheriff's deputies were heartened, some defense lawyers began to grumble. After losing a case, one red-faced defense attorney hissed at Duffey under his breath that she would be gone within six months.

But Duffey was enjoying herself. Though her job also included cases in juvenile court, she liked it, despite its heavy workload and, more ambiguously, the problem she had come to regard as "good-ol'-boyism" in the district. In one memorable theft case involving a thirteen-year-old boy considered by police to be "a one-man crime wave," his defense attorney, Harmon, said Duffey had not provided him with a critical file. Duffey told the judge that she had given the file to the court's probation officer. The probation officer testified that she had personally placed it into Harmon's hands. "Your honor," Harmon persisted, "I never saw that file." And that, apparently, was good enough.

Ignoring the two women's testimony, Judge Pete Lancaster sided with Harmon. He dismissed the case. The police officers who had come to testify stared at Duffey in amazement. Then, as she described the scene to Duff later that night, "I lit into the judge verbally. I was raising some hell. I said, 'This is absurd. You'll listen to Dan Harmon, but not to the sworn testimony of your own court's officer.' Lancaster stood up to leave. I walked up toward the bench. He said, 'Madam Prosecutor, if you don't shut up . . . '

"I said, 'You'll what?'

"He said, 'I'll hold you in contempt of court.'

" 'Then do it,' I said. I had some files in my hand and I threw them at him."

Pandemonium was breaking out in the courtroom. As Duffey stood yelling at the judge, Harmon approached her with his fist drawn back. It was not an idle gesture. As many in the courtroom knew, Harmon had decked a lawyer before. Now it looked like he was about to deck Duffey, when a third lawyer ran up to restrain him. Duffey turned to the interloper and yelled, "Let him go. Make my day." Judge Lancaster just walked into his chambers.

Shortly afterward, when Duffey returned to her office, her boss, Prosecutor Arnold, was on the phone with Lancaster. "Gary," Duffey told Arnold when he hung up, "whatever Lancaster told you I did, trust me, it was worse."

Arnold reported that Lancaster wanted him to remove her from juvenile court. If he refused, Arnold said, the judge threatened to hold her in contempt of court and file assault charges against her as well as an ethics complaint. Duffey told Arnold to tell Lancaster, "Go for it." She told him she would like to see the episode investigated because she wanted to hear how Lancaster would explain his decision to dismiss the case.

In the end, Arnold did not remove Duffey from juvenile court and Lancaster did not follow up on his threats. To Duffey, the result was a vindication. But the episode ended tragically. Months after the boy's theft case had been dismissed and while his crime wave continued, two deputies from a nearby county were killed when a helicopter in which they were riding crashed as they searched for the fleeing teenager.

When federal funds became available, Arnold formed a board of directors, including the sheriffs and the chiefs of police in the district's three counties, to oversee the new drug task force and to hire a director. Duffey was an obvious choice because of her record prosecuting drunk drivers and her rapport with local police. When she was offered the job, however, Duffey declined. She explained that she liked what she was doing. When the board pressed her to accept, she agreed, but on the condition that the post would be temporary, until the end of 1990, by which time she expected the board to have found a permanent director. Duffey began hiring undercover officers in April 1990, and by May, a few weeks before Larry Ives took his tumble off the roof, the seven-member task force was up and running.

It went to work with little fanfare. Duffey was proud of her crew, particularly of two young men, Scott Lewellen and Carl Carlson. Others she hired, like Jim Lovett, she was not so sure about. But Lovett was older, he had more experience, and he had worked for Govar, which was itself a recommendation. Plus, when she asked Benton police chief Rick Elmendorf his opinion of Lovett, Elmendorf had advised her, "He's the cop type that you need."

Duffey figured she would need all the experience she could get. Directing a team of undercover narcotics officers would be tough enough in itself. But Prosecutor Arnold made it clear immediately that it would be even harder in this district. According to Duffey, on her first day on the job as director, the prosecutor walked into her office and told her, "Jean, you are not to use the drug task force to investigate any public official." (Arnold's recollection of the exchange was that he "reminded Ms. Duffey that the U.S. attorney was already investigating allegations of misconduct by public officials in the Seventh Judicial District.")

Under ordinary circumstances, Duffey would have found the order strange and very troubling. But by then Jean was aware that the circumstances in Saline County were anything but ordinary. As part of the district's judicial staff, she had been apprised of Govar's investigation into suspected public corruption. She understood that that investigation was believed to involve illegal drugs, and thus that it might overlap some of the work of her own drug task force. Fair enough, she figured. She would be glad to pass any parts of her investigation that related to public officials on to Govar. Her team would be stretched thin enough as it was. She saw no need to duplicate a federal investigation. Without going into detail, she told her undercover officers that if they came across information relating to public officials, they were to include it in their reports and copy the reports to Govar.

THE CONFIDENTIAL MEMOS

Ordinary citizens like Linda did not know how serious Govar's probe had become—or how intensely it now focused on Harmon. In April 1990, soon after Duffey was made director of the task force, Prosecutor Arnold showed her a copy of a memo that Govar had written three months earlier, in February. In it Govar had outlined much of the information, all of it highly confidential, that his team had thus far assembled. Not long after that, Lovett showed her a second memo—this one written by Govar in March—that also detailed allegations about officials in Saline County.[11] It was clear to Duffey that if Govar could substantiate even a fraction of what was alleged in the two memos, important heads would roll. One of those heads would be Harmon's.

It was unusual for U.S. attorneys' memos to be circulated. Duffey assumed that only a few people in Arnold's office and perhaps in law enforcement had seen the memos. She wondered if Harmon had seen them.

Linda Ives did not know the memos existed. But if she had, something in her would have been shattered. For months now, Linda had believed Harmon's claim that Govar wanted to overturn the county grand jury's murder ruling. She had even had a meeting with Govar about it—a meeting during which she recalled she had not been "too nice." Still, Linda's faith in Harmon had also come under assault. She did not want to admit it to herself, but the grand jury's lack of results, combined with the rumors linking Harmon to cocaine, were assailing her image of Harmon, however much she wanted to believe in him.

"At this point in the investigation," Govar had written in his memo to Banks, "Dan Harmon, an attorney from Benton, Arkansas, has been identified as a target in this investigation. . . . As of this date, we have developed a pretty substantial amount of information concerning his drug use and dealing activities. It appears from the information that we have so far, that Dan Harmon was not only involved in the use of cocaine, but that he distributed it. . . . With regard to his law partner, Richard Garrett, I am most distressed about some cases that do not appear to make any sense. . . ."

"KILLED OVER COCAINE"

At the end of May 1990, voters overwhelmingly elected Harmon as the Democratic candidate for prosecuting attorney. That same week a young woman named Katherine Brightop stepped into the witness box in federal court in Little Rock. In testimony that would send ripples throughout Saline County, she talked not only about the drug case that was on trial, but about possible connections between it and the deaths of Kevin and Don. For Linda and Larry, Brightop's testimony added one more incredible scenario to the dozens they had already heard. There had been the sheriff's and Malak's notion that the boys had died accidentally, asleep or in a marijuana stupor; there had been the psychic's vision of the men and the girl in the field; there had been the speculation Linda had seen in the state police files, including the graphic description of the boys being beaten near Shobe Road—and now there was this.

Brightop had been called as a witness against twenty-five-year-old Paul William Criswell, a Saline County man who now stood charged with distributing cocaine. Brightop, who had dated Criswell for about a month, testified that during that time Criswell told her that Don Henry and Kevin Ives were killed after attempting to steal cocaine from James Callaway, the used car dealer. According to Brightop's testimony Paul Criswell told her that

Callaway and three other men had chased the boys down and killed them.[12]

Linda read the account in the paper and recognized Callaway's name. He had been among the first people indicted by Harmon's 1988 grand jury. He had only been charged with aggravated robbery. "Was he ever tried on that charge?" Linda asked Larry. Neither of them could remember the case ever having gone to court. But they remembered that Callaway's name had surfaced again within the past four months. This time a federal grand jury had charged him with providing an illegal sawed-off shotgun that had been used in the attempted robbery of a crap game in Lonoke County, northeast of Little Rock. One of the robbers, a Saline County man named Richard Winters, had been killed in the exchange of gunfire. Now here was Brightop alleging that Callaway was responsible for the murders of Kevin and Don.

According to Brightop, Criswell had told her that the boys had gone to Callaway's house "to steal a bunch of cocaine." She said that Criswell and another man had discovered them and given chase. One boy had been stabbed and the other beaten. The boys were unconscious when the four men carried them to the tracks. Brightop told the court, "He said they had been killed over cocaine."

Moreover, Brightop testified, when Criswell found out that she was talking to federal officials, he attacked her while she was sitting in her car. She said Criswell grabbed her by the hair, yelling, "I know what you've done," while beating her head against the steering wheel. The judge ordered Criswell held without bond, while Govar, who was prosecuting the case, had Brightop housed at a secret location.

The testimony pushed Kevin and Don once again to the top of the news. DRUG SUSPECT LINKED TO RAILROAD DEATHS, one newspaper reported the next day. A headline in another paper read: TESTIMONY COULD HELP SOLVE CASE. Dan Harmon told the *Benton Courier* that he was "very pleased" with Brightop's testimony. "Obviously they believe this young lady or they wouldn't be holding Paul Criswell without bond." The paper quoted Richard Garrett as saying that he was "tickled to death" by the development.

In the days that followed, Harmon's excitement over Callaway's new status as a murder suspect grew. He told the *Benton Courier,* "This could be the break we're looking for. I don't know how to evaluate the woman's testimony, because I haven't ever seen it, but these people were suspects almost from the beginning of the grand jury. We tried to locate Paul Criswell, but he was in Texas and we could never find him." Asked why he and Garrett had not been able to find Criswell, Harmon blamed the failure on police indifference. "When we first started, we were strictly on our own," he said. "We did subpoena Finis Criswell, the father of Paul Criswell, and he did testify before the grand jury. Callaway testified and was charged with aggravated robbery."[13]

For those who had grown suspicious of Harmon and Garrett, the explanation rang hollow. If the two had focused as closely as they were saying they had on Callaway and the Criswells during the grand jury, if solving the deaths of Kevin and Don had been the main purpose of that grand jury, and if Brightop's testimony was as believable as Harmon now seemed to think it was, how was it that Harmon and Garrett had never gotten close to linking the men with the murders? As Linda read the news, she wondered about an even more basic question: If, as Brightop testified, Callaway and Criswell had been involved in the distribution of cocaine in Saline County, and if both men had come to the attention of the 1988 county grand jury, why was it that neither had ever been indicted on drug charges? After all, though the jury had done nothing about Kevin and Don, other than to declare their deaths murders, it had supposedly spent a lot of energy delving into the local drug scene.

But Linda could not bring herself to distrust Harmon. When doubts came knocking, she tried not to let them in. She had lost Kevin. She had almost lost Larry. After Larry, Harmon had become the most solid presence in her life. No, she reassured herself. Danny would not have betrayed his role in that crucial county grand jury. He and Garrett would not have sabotaged the very process they had begun. It was unthinkable.

ELEVEN

THE SALINE COUNTY UNDERWORLD

JUNE–DECEMBER 1990

A full-page photograph of Linda ran in the June 1990 issue of the *Arkansas Times,* a slick, monthly magazine aimed at educated, affluent subscribers. She looked angry in the picture. Wearing a dress suit and patent leather heels, she stood in the gravel between the tracks where Kevin's and Don's bodies had been found, one foot resting defiantly on a rail. In front of her she held a T-shirt. Her expression left no doubt that she considered herself, as the T-shirt explained, one of the "Victims of Malak's Incredible Testimony."

The accompanying article by reporter Rod Lorenzen was titled "Why Fahmy Malak Should Be Fired . . . And Who's Protecting Him." Harmon, never one to mince words, was quoted in the article as saying, "I think the man's dangerous. I think he's mentally unbalanced. He has no honesty, no integrity—and you can quote me on that."

POLITICS AND MALAK

The article outlined what little was known at the time about Malak's autopsy of Susan Deer. It quoted crime lab employees who complained that the review of Malak's office ordered by the Medical Examiner's Commission had been cursory at best. It related how the commission's chair, Dr. Joycelyn Elders, had told reporters that her board did not "have the skills" to judge Malak, while at the same time Malak's boss, the crime lab's director, admitted that he, too, lacked "the expertise" to assess Malak's performance.

The article concluded that the chief defender was Max Howell, a powerful veteran state senator who had headed the legislative committee formed to review Dr. Malak's work. Howell had announced at the start of that review that he "had an admiration" for the way Malak had handled his job. He had gone so far as to express his concern that Malak "not be indicted" for the deaths of Don Henry and Kevin Ives. Reading the article, Linda was reminded how that remark had jolted her at the time. No one was talking about indicting Dr. Malak. She wondered why Howell would have said such a thing. But when she told Howell how inappropriate she considered his remarks, she remembered angrily how he had bellowed back at her: "Lady, do you know who you're talking to?"

Now, as she read further, Linda saw that her experience with Howell did not seem unique. According to Lorenzen, several of Howell's critics, including Harmon, charged that Malak and Howell had a deal through which Howell and members of his law firm used Malak when they needed testimony to support their clients' claims. They suspected that, in turn, Howell used his considerable influence to keep Malak in office.[1] The senator vehemently denied the charge. A former crime lab employee, Lee Beamer, told Lorenzen that not long after he had gone to work for Malak, Howell had called the medical examiner's office, asking for the results of a certain autopsy. "Malak was out of the office," Lorenzen wrote, "and Beamer initially refused to give out the information. 'Boy,' exclaimed the caller, 'don't you know who I am?' Beamer released the information."

The article noted that, along with Howell and Elders, Governor Clinton and Jim Clark, the new crime lab director, continued to express support for Malak even in the face of what the magazine alleged was Malak's "lying on the stand, tampering with evidence, and manufacturing of convictions." The article concluded, "As long as state officials continue to allow Malak to play the role of supreme investigator for the state of Arkansas, he remains secure in his domain, accountable to no one. But outside, the cries of indignation grow louder and more insistent."

Linda closed the magazine with a sense of grim satisfaction. Malak was being protected, but at least his outrages were recognized. Sighing, she carried the magazine into the room where she kept her files. Three years ago she could not have imagined herself in a magazine, standing in such an unlikely place, scowling, and holding a T-shirt proclaiming such an ugly word as VOMIT. She had preferred her quiet life. But events had obliterated that life. Lorenzen's article was good. She slipped the magazine into a folder. It had been worth the trip to the tracks.

"QUITE SUSPICIOUS"

At the federal building in Little Rock, Bob Govar went over his notes. By now, in June 1990, he had become familiar with a large cast of suspects in Saline County, a group that ran the gamut from known criminals to prominent lawyers. Govar was certain he did not have the whole picture, but he felt he knew some of the players. A couple of them, Govar reflected, had won the confidence of Linda Ives, the mother of one of the boys on the tracks.

Of particular interest to Govar was James Callaway, the used-car dealer whose lot stood on the western edge of Benton. Govar's information was that as far back as 1987, the year the boys were killed, Callaway had headed "a significant cocaine distribution operation." In one of the two memos that were later shown to Jean Duffey, Govar had written to Banks:

"There is a possibility that Callaway may have been involved, indirectly, in the murders of Kevin Ives and Don Henry on the railroad tracks in Saline County. There is also the possibility that he was involved in the murder of an unidentified Mexican drug dealer who is currently in cold storage at the Arkansas Crime Laboratory. And lastly, he is probably involved in the killing of Richard Winters, who was shot to death during an attempted robbery of a crap game in Lonoke County, Arkansas, in July of 1989."

Govar sat back in his chair. There was not much to look at in his office: a few family pictures, a few framed law school honors, a few awards from the Department of Justice. If there was a motif to the neatly kept office, aside from its federal furnishings, it showed up in a few understated representations of his passion for duck hunting. He settled back in his chair, contemplating the attempted robbery at the gambling house where Winters had been killed. Winters's death during that aborted robbery had occurred during July 1989—that same murderous year when so many young men with connections to drug dealing in Saline County had died or turned up missing. It was an ugly situation, Govar mused. The question was, how much of the mess in the district could he bring to light and prove?

The Saline County case was a tricky one. Unlike state prosecuting attorneys, a U.S. attorney cannot directly charge a person with a crime. Under the federal system, a federal grand jury must issue a "true bill," after hearing evidence against a person, in order for that person to be charged. Govar had first to gather his information. Then he had to present it to the federal grand jury that was seated at the time. And then, if the jurors were persuaded, they and they alone could begin the process of indictment. Before he took his information to the grand jury, Govar wanted to make sure that he had all his ducks, so to speak, in a row.

The problem Govar faced was typical for this kind of case. His sources were not the most upstanding of citizens. It was a reality of drug investigations: the people who knew who was using and selling drugs were often using and selling drugs themselves, which tended to taint them in the eyes of a jury.

Woodrow May was a good example. May testified before the grand jury that he had worked as a middleman in the Saline County drug trade for years, buying cocaine from a dealer in Hot Springs and distributing it in Saline County through a network of friends and acquaintances.[2] May testified that during the years he was active, three other people had had similar arrangements with his dealer, two of whom were personally known to Harmon. In another disturbing revelation, May reported that Daniel "Boonie" Bearden, the young Saline County man who had disappeared in the summer of 1988, while Garrett and Harmon were reportedly seeking him to testify before the county grand jury, had worked as one of May's distributors.

If May had been the only person making such allegations, Govar would have put less stock in them. But the underworld of Saline County, Govar was learning, was full of people with similar stories about Dan Harmon and some of the people around him. One witness said that in 1987—the year the boys were killed—he had bought drugs regularly from a woman known to be close to Harmon and that Harmon had been present for two of those purchases.[3] The witness testified that, as the prosecutor's hearing was getting ready to start, his supplier had warned him "that Dan Harmon was getting nervous about her dealing . . . because of his position in the community." Thereafter, the man said, he dealt with his supplier more covertly.

Another admitted drug dealer, Myron J. Harrison, told investigators that the same woman had started to buy cocaine from him at the end of 1987. He said she was both using and selling, and that she had introduced him to Harmon in 1988, shortly after the start of the county grand jury.[4] According to Harrison, Harmon paid for one of the woman's drug purchases with a check for approximately eighteen hundred dollars drawn on Harmon's law firm. That particular check cleared the bank, but Harrison said that on three subsequent occasions, Harmon had come to him to borrow money to cover hot checks he had written. Harrison told investigators that he had loaned Harmon a total of twenty-seven hundred dollars in cash, money that was never repaid, and that by the time he quit doing business with Harmon, he and the woman owed him an additional twenty-three hundred dollars.

But the favors had not been one-sided. In return for the loans, Harrison said, Harmon kept him apprised throughout 1988 of what was happening in the grand jury. Moreover, as Govar explained to Banks, "on several occasions Harrison asked Dan Harmon to check people out before he sold drugs to them, which Harmon did." This witness, Govar reflected, had more to offer than most. Federal agents had fixed him up with a body mike. As a result, Govar had in his possession tape-recorded conversations between Harrison and Harmon, tapes he was anxious for a federal grand jury to hear.

Govar also called Harmon's ex-wife Teresa to appear before the federal grand jury. Twice, Govar later told Duffey, Teresa Harmon testified that she had seen Dan Harmon use cocaine in their home. She also told him in an interview that she had seen him use the drug on at least five occasions. In addition, a legal secretary who had worked for Harmon in 1987 reported that twice during that year she had seen her employer at his desk sniffing lines of cocaine with a straw. She said she had quit the job because of that and because her paychecks from Harmon were beginning to bounce.[5]

Again Govar sat back in his chair. Drug deals, he reflected, were numbingly similar. But there was something odd about the reports from Saline County. It was the testimony about Garrett and Harmon that troubled him most. Govar let his mind go over what the informants had said about Garrett's activities, some of which, Govar reflected, struck him as "awful fishy."

On May 6, 1988, for example, the very month the train-deaths grand jury was impaneled, Saline County investigators had arrested a man whom they had found in possession of some 240 marijuana plants, as well as some equipment for growing marijuana. The arresting officer had had a valid search warrant, and after his arrest, the man gave the officers a tape-recorded confession in which he admitted growing the marijuana for sale. But seven months later, in December 1988, at the end of the grand jury and in the last month Garrett served as deputy prosecutor, the case had been dropped. To Govar and others familiar with the case, the decision looked "extraordinary."

In another instance, the son of a man who was believed to be a close friend of James Callaway struck and killed a person in Saline County, reportedly while driving under the influence of drugs and alcohol. The driver "never was arrested or charged in connection with the vehicular homicide," Govar had written to Banks. This situation, too, he said, he considered "quite suspicious."

And what about Sheriff Steed? As with Dr. Fahmy Malak, some of the most damaging reports about Steed were coming to investigators, not from drug dealers and convicts, but from men who had worked for the sheriff. One of Steed's former deputies told agents working on Govar's team that once, when a state police officer had turned in approximately nineteen thousand dollars in cash to Steed in the aftermath of a Saline County drug arrest, the sheriff had asked the officer to sign a receipt made out for three thousand dollars less. The startled investigator had declined.

Another time, the former deputy reported, he had received a report about gambling at a home outside of Benton. When the deputy checked the house, the lights were on and it was surrounded by cars. He returned to the sheriff's office and was preparing to raid the place when another deputy suggested that they should notify the sheriff first. Steed, who lived a few blocks from the sheriff's office, ordered his men to do nothing until he arrived. According to the former deputy, when Steed arrived at the office forty minutes later, he sent one deputy home for the night and told the other that he would ride with him "to look at this so-called gambling operation." When the two men arrived at the house, the place was dark and the cars were gone.[6]

Govar tried to piece together his case. It was interesting, he mused, how Callaway and his used-car lot turned up in so many of the informants' accounts. Had Callaway, Harmon, and Steed, and possibly some other figures in the county, formed some kind of racket? Were they engaging in some crimes, covering up others, and possibly protecting some behind-the-scenes backers? Govar believed he had evidence that all of that was possible. Part of it had come from Jerry Arnold Easom, a former detective sergeant in charge of Steed's Criminal Investigation Division. During 1985, Easom told Govar's team that he had gotten to know Callaway fairly well, having responded to several domestic-disturbance calls at Callaway's house. After one such call, Easom said, Callaway had taken him aside and confided that he had been robbed by three men at a gambling house in nearby Lonoke County.

According to Easom, Callaway had asked Easom how much he would charge to harm the men who had robbed him. Easom said he'd been surprised, but he'd played along. Easom had reported the incident to Steed and asked for permission to go back to Callaway wearing a tape recorder. But Steed had refused permission. As Govar later told Banks, "Sheriff Steed told Investigator Easom to stay away from Callaway and not to do anything else on the matter unless the sheriff told him to do so. According to Investigator Easom, he never heard from the sheriff on the subject again." Nor, apparently, did anyone else. As Govar noted, "Investigator Easom told me that he tried to bring this matter up while testifying before the Saline County Special Grand Jury that was investigating the deaths of Kevin Ives and Don Henry, but special prosecuting attorney Dan Harmon cut him off and told him that the grand jury was investigating other matters and that his statements concerning that matter were not relevant to the grand jury investigation."[7]

Govar sighed. Just over the horizon, to the south of Little Rock, he could imagine the landscape of Saline County. So far in his investigation, all roads into that place seemed to lead to Harmon. Yet Harmon had just won the district's Democratic primary. If something did not happen soon, Govar thought as he gathered up his notes, next January Harmon would be sworn in as the district's new prosecuting attorney. He would take control of the district's drug task force and he would fire its director, Jean Duffey, whose undercover officers, even now, were supplying Govar's team with new information.

His mind wandered to Linda Ives, the mother who was trying so hard to make sense of her son's murder. God knows, Govar thought, what Harmon is telling her.

QUESTIONING CALLAWAY

By now it appeared that a sinister thread was unwinding, one that might end up connecting Callaway, not only to the deaths of Kevin and Don, but also to the rash of unexplained murders. Harmon himself was intimating as much.[8] Soon after Katherine Brightop delivered her surprising testimony, Harmon revealed an element of the case that federal prosecutors had not yet disclosed. He reported that the fourth man in the group who allegedly had carried the boys' bodies to the tracks was probably Richard Winters, who was later shot in the gambling-house robbery. At first Callaway had just been charged with providing one of the would-be robbers with an illegal shotgun. But now Callaway stood accused of having planned the ill-fated robbery.

Govar's team had learned a lot about Callaway. Agents knew that he was a friend of the man who ran the weekly crap game that Winters had been sent to rob. Govar had to consider the possibility: an attempted robbery, followed by a shooting in self-defense, all staged to cover the elimination of a potential witness. Of the four men whom Brightop testified Criswell had said were involved in Kevin's and Don's murders, two—James Callaway and Paul Criswell—were now under federal indictment, and the other two—Winters and Criswell's father, Finis—were dead. The elder Criswell had died at his home in Alexander at fifty, reportedly of natural causes.

"I would not rule out the possibility of another grand jury," Harmon announced to reporters. But Sheriff Davis struck a more cautious tone about the train deaths. "We will take our investigative file to Little Rock and compare information," he said. "Our case file is five to six inches thick, and this is the first time Criswell's name has come up. It makes me a little wary of Brightop's statements."

Callaway, meanwhile, was insisting that the deaths of Kevin and Don could not have occurred as Brightop alleged. "She said the two boys were caught stealing cocaine from my house," Callaway told Doug Thompson of the *Arkansas Democrat.*[9] "In the first place, I've never sold drugs or had them in my home. In the second place, I'd lost my home in the divorce settlement before those boys were killed." Linda noted with interest that Callaway did acknowledge, however, that Kevin and Don had visited his house. "My oldest daughter and Don Henry were good friends who had known each other all through school," he said. "We lived five houses down from him on the same side of the road." He said that when Kevin and Don came over, "they'd play basketball and they'd use the trampoline in the backyard." But Callaway insisted that by the night the boys were killed, he was no longer living in that house.

For Linda, the world in June of 1990 centered around Larry and the news that was breaking about Callaway. Larry's arms were healing, but now the reports linking Kevin to Callaway had caught Linda off-balance. For more than two years she had been praying for some kind of development in the case—but not this. Could it be that Kevin and Don had died while attempting to rob a local cocaine dealer? When the *Benton Courier* called her for comment, Linda responded with caution. "This has gone further than anything they have done before," she told the paper, "but right now, it's one of a lot of stories we've heard. Hopefully, they'll be able to prove something at some point."

She tried to maintain her equilibrium. But the stories that were surfacing about Callaway seemed to take one strange twist after another. For example, Linda came across this odd bit of information tucked into the middle of a piece in the *Benton Courier* about how Callaway, who had been released on bond pending his federal trial for supplying the shotgun for the gambling-house robbery, had been rearrested the following day, after selling cocaine and marijuana to one of Duffey's undercover officers. The paragraph that startled Linda read:

"A report from the Saline County Sheriff's Office shows that James Callaway was involved in a vehicle accident at the Shobe Road crossing on Jan. 7, 1979. At that time, Callaway reportedly told deputies that the engine of his pickup truck had died after he drove onto the track. He said he saw the lights of an approaching Missouri Pacific train and could not get the vehicle started, but that he managed to get himself out of the vehicle before the train hit the truck. After impact, the vehicle traveled approximately 375 feet south of the intersection. This incident occurred about a quarter of a mile from the spot where the bodies of Ives and Henry were recovered."

Linda shuddered. It was too strange. Kevin and Don are murdered. Callaway is implicated as a suspect in their deaths because of Brighton's testimony. Richard Winters and Finis Criswell, who were also named as suspects, die. And now this: a report that Callaway had personally witnessed the destruction that a locomotive can cause—not to human bodies, but to his own pickup truck. And it had happened at almost exactly the location where Kevin and Don were later run over.

While Dan Harmon was hinting at the possibility that a new county grand jury might be called to further investigate Callaway, most of his energies were focused on winning the election as prosecutor. "If there's a problem of someone being ripped off, or injured, or someone selling drugs to children," he promised shortly after the May primary, "we'll try to put a stop to it." Reiterating his intention to fire Jean Duffey as deputy prosecutor and head of the new drug task force, he announced that he would replace Duffey with his old friend

Richard Garrett. If the board of the drug task force refused to back his firing of Duffey and kept her on as task force director, he vowed not to prosecute a single drug case on information provided by the task force until she was replaced.

It was a strong stand, but Harmon had powerful reasons for wanting Duffey gone. Between her group and Govar's, a net was being drawn around him. It is likely that he knew, for example, that in mid-June, a few weeks after his victory in the primary election, Jim Lovett, one of Duffey's agents, had teamed up with Sheriff Larry Davis to interview Callaway, who was being held in the Saline County jail. In the middle of the night, hours before Callaway was to be picked up by federal marshals, Lovett and Davis asked Callaway if they could interview him, and he agreed. At 2:56 A.M. the officers clicked on a tape recorder, and Callaway began to talk.

The first question the two men asked was whether Callaway knew Richard Garrett. Yes, he said, the two had been card-playing buddies, and in 1987, when Callaway was seeking a divorce, he had hired Garrett to represent him. After the divorce, Callaway said he had occasionally staked Garrett money when they played poker together. Callaway said the money was never repaid, and that he had personally written it off as payment for the legal work Garrett had done on his divorce.

In the months after Don Henry and Kevin Ives were killed, Callaway told his interrogators, Garrett came by his car lot on a few occasions to ask if he knew anything about the case. Callaway said he told Garrett "what little things" he had heard. One evening Garrett brought Harmon to the car lot with him. After questioning Callaway again about the deaths, Garrett and Harmon had left at about 8:00 P.M. Callaway said: "At about two o'clock in the morning, the phone rang and it was Dan Harmon and Richard Garrett again. I said, 'Damn, don't y'all ever sleep?' And they said, 'We need to talk to you tonight . . . right now.' "

According to Callaway, he met Harmon and Garrett at their office, and there the two lawyers spelled out for him a theory they had that involved him in the deaths of the boys. The two said that they believed that he and another man had learned that some black men were dealing cocaine at a site near the railroad tracks. They speculated that Callaway, who knew the boys because he was friends with Don Henry's father, Curtis, had sent the boys to the site to steal the black men's drugs.

Callaway told Davis and Lovett that he had felt he was being set up and that he had let Harmon and Garrett know it. "When Harmon finished laying out his theory," Callaway said, "I told him, I said, 'Well, I'll tell you one thing right now: You may get me for two murders, but it won't be for the two boys. It'll be for you two son of a bitches if y'all ever try something like that on me.' " Callaway insisted that he had had nothing to do with the boys' deaths, and that the suggestion by Garrett and Harmon that he had had surprised him.

Sheriff Davis: "Why are they trying to dump on you, James?"

Callaway: "I think I know who possibly killed the boys, and with the information that I have given them, they're scared to death that I may know something about them or some other official. Now, that's my opinion."

Davis: "Do you want to tell us about it? Do you know something about some officials?"

But Callaway stiffened and balked. "I don't know anything about any officials," he said.

The night and the interrogation wore on. "Whoever's trying to cover all this—and it's going to be some people here in Saline County," Callaway continued, "—it's going to be some officials who are making money off selling dope. Harmon comes in to lead this grand jury, and they use me as a smoke screen to make it look like they was really doing something, and they wasn't doing shit the whole damn time. I'm not stupid, Larry," Callaway said to Davis. "I've figured this shit out."

Then, rather abruptly, he added, "All right, let me say this much. Another reason Dan Harmon don't like me—I made a statement on the stand to the grand jury that one of his best friends sold those boys the marijuana the night that they got killed."

"And who was that?" Lovett asked.

Callaway named one of the men whom informants had identified to state police as having supplied Don Henry with marijuana.

"How do you know that?" Lovett asked.

"[He] told me, hisself, personally."

As Callaway warmed to the subject of the boys' deaths, he began talking about the relationship that had existed between himself and the two allegedly prominent drug dealers whose questioning had been so overlooked by both the county and state investigators.

Callaway said that when Harmon and Garrett started "stirring their little shit" with the grand jury, one of the reputed dealers had started "coming around" his used car lot. "Man," Callaway quoted the dealer as saying, "I need to get hold of some cocaine. I've got some heavy-duty lawyers and doctors and stuff and they need some and that means I've got to get some." When Callaway told the man he couldn't be of help, he said the dealer replied, " 'Well, see what you can do for me' . . . and that's when he told me that he sold them—the kids—and that he was good personal friends of Dan Harmon. I testified to that in the grand jury. If you'll look in the record, you'll see. I told Dan."

Callaway told Lovett and Davis that after he had offered that testimony, Harmon had asked, "Do you know anything else about this case that you need to tell us?"

"And I said, 'Yeah,' " Callaway continued. "And he said, 'What's that?' And I said, 'It's my understanding that one of your best friends sold them the marijuana the night they got killed.' 'One of my best friends?' And he turned as white as a piece of paper. I said, 'That's what they say.' He said, 'Who might that be?' "

Callaway said he then named the reputed dealer. "And Dan Harmon didn't say another word," Callaway told his questioners. "They let me leave."

Lovett asked Callaway if he thought there had been a cover-up of the crime. "I've always said that," Callaway answered. Lovett asked him why. "Just the way they handled it, the way they handled the case—and the main thing, which was that they didn't question anybody I told them about. They never went to interview the people I told them about."

The sky was beginning to lighten when Davis and Lovett turned off the tape recorder. They walked out of the building sure of only one thing: Even if Callaway had been lying on some points, some of what he had told them was true.

"SMOKE SCREEN"

Linda had no more idea that her son's death was being discussed that night in the bowels of the Saline County jail than she did that Dan Harmon was suspected of dealing drugs. It would be several years before she would see a transcript of Callaway's statements, and even then, she would not know how much of it to believe. But if she had known what Callaway was saying on that summer night in 1990 to Sheriff Davis and Agent Lovett, Linda would have been deeply disturbed. After seeing the references in the state police files to the reputed dealers whom no one had questioned, she would have been keenly interested to hear that Callaway not only echoed the file information, but that he also linked one of the reputed dealers to Dan Harmon. She would have pondered Callaway's allusions to "officials that are making money off of selling dope," his description of the grand jury as "a smoke screen," and the implication that Sheriff Steed had been protecting the other dealer. But the line that would have troubled Linda most would have been Callaway's assessment that there was a cover-up of the murders.

Linda had quit her job at the credit union to stay home with Larry. But she was tired. For years now, she had been carrying, in addition to her anger, a heavy weight of grief. She understood that the death of a loved one was not supposed to hang over a person forever. But what could she do? Soon it would be three years since Kevin's death, and there was not a shred, not a trace, of closure. This isn't right, she told herself. She decided she would seek help another way. And so when she heard of a support group for parents who had lost children, Linda and her daughter, Alicia, decided to attend a meeting. Alicia's reaction surprised her. Linda had seen Alicia cry only a few times since Kevin's death, all in the days just before and after the funeral. But when they sat down at the meeting of Compassionate Friends, Alicia had barely begun to introduce herself when she broke down in tears.

Alicia never returned to the meetings, but Linda continued to attend. She found a perspective there that she needed. One night, after a meeting, she drove home thinking about a couple she had just met whose three children had all died together, burned to death in their home. The couple's grief was overwhelming. With one of the family's cars out of commission, the mother had left the children asleep in bed while she drove her husband the short distance to work. When she returned less than twenty minutes later, the house was ablaze. Linda began to realize that it helped to tell one's own tragic story to other parents who had lost their children. Beyond sympathy, survivors could offer hope.

It wasn't that others had suffered that made her feel better. But there was consolation in the communion of loss. Often, people whose children have died complain that friends drift away from them. But it's not that, Linda thought, pulling into the driveway of her home. It's that we push them away. We change. We have different cares and priorities. We don't think anyone who hasn't been through what we've been through could possibly understand.

Yet as time went on, Linda realized that, even at the meetings of Compassionate Friends, she felt a strain of alienation. Here were people whose children had died, yes; but it was different when your child was murdered. And different still when the murder was unsolved. Even so, the comfort of the group was better than the isolation she had been feeling. She continued to attend the meetings and to draw strength from the friendships she found there. Eventually she became the chapter's chairwoman. But no matter how energetically she threw herself into the organization, there remained a part of her grief that hung beyond the reach of even these compassionate friends.

HARMON ATTACKS

Jean Duffey was one of the few people in the Saline County area who suspected the depths of the intrigue that had enveloped Linda Ives. Knowing what she did about Harmon, Duffey imagined she understood the treachery of the situation better than Ives herself. She also understood that her own situation had taken a turn for the worse. As Duffey's investigations of Harmon intensified, his attacks on her kept pace. He accused Duffey of spending thousands of task force dollars to equip her agents with automatic weapons and high-tech surveillance gear. The task force's board denied the charge. Despite the denial, Harmon repeated the charge relentlessly, convincing many voters in the district that "that crazy Jean Duffey" had spent a fortune equipping her agents with snooping equipment. Duffey went about the task force's business, reminding herself that she would be resigning at the end of the year.

James Callaway went on trial at Little Rock amid allegations of intimidation and double-crossing. He was charged with supplying the twelve-gauge shotgun used in the gambling-house robbery. According to various witnesses, a dice game was held at a mobile home owned by Sylvania Peeks every Thursday night after a local used-car auction. But this was no gentlemen's operation. According to the testimony, Callaway and Peeks had once together pulled off a robbery of Peeks's game, netting themselves fifty-thousand dollars to split. Later, according to witnesses, the two had had a falling out and Callaway had mentioned that "he'd like to see Peeks's game hit." It was after that that Callaway recruited Winters and another man to attempt the robbery. When Callaway took the stand, he denied having had anything to do with the robbery, but the jury took thirty minutes to find him guilty.

So far as Linda could tell, Callaway's trial had cleared up nothing. On the contrary, many things now looked murkier. The day after the trial, for instance, a reporter asked Prosecutor Arnold about the status of the charge of aggravated robbery that had been brought against James Callaway by Harmon's 1988 grand jury. Admitting that the charge had been dropped, Arnold explained that it had been nol-prossed "to facilitate a continuing investigation." He added, "That's really all I can say." Skeptics in the county, including Duffey, read the statement with contempt. Harmon had bent over backward to remind voters that his grand jury had indicted Callaway on that charge of aggravated robbery. No one—certainly not Prosecutor Arnold or candidate-for-prosecutor Harmon—had bothered to mention that the charge against Callaway had been dropped.

Duffey typed up her agents' reports and mailed them to Govar. But she was careful, even within her own office. Whenever she wrote to Govar, she copied her letters onto disks, erased her computer files, then brought the discs home and hid them. If the information she was sending to Govar fell into the wrong hands, the lives of her informants could be in jeopardy. She had only to remember the number of people with connections to Harmon's grand jury who had died or turned up missing. Only weeks earlier, Jordan Ketelsen, a convicted drug dealer who some thought might be linked to the murder of Keith McKaskle, had been found shot to death in his truck. Jordan was the son of Ron Ketelsen, a Benton hairdresser and a reputed drug dealer himself. If Govar's team could develop the information, get it before the federal grand jury, and get some of the chief suspects indicted, Duffey consoled herself, she could resign at the end of the year as planned, and the strain of the past few months would have been worth it.

But pressure on her task force was building, and Duffey realized that Harmon's attacks were having an effect. In a few months Harmon almost certainly would become prosecutor and take control of the task force. Perhaps in preparation for that and to avoid a confrontation with him, the board was willing to look for ways to quietly force Duffey out.

At the same time, reports surfaced about another incident involving Dan's ex-wife, Teresa. By now the couple had been divorced for several months, and according to Teresa, they had been arguing for most of that time about Harmon's delinquent child-support payments. On the night of July 10, 1990, Teresa Harmon reported, Harmon kicked open her front door, barged in, and began to hit her. She brought her complaint to Duffey, who seemed to be the only person in the district willing to stand up to Harmon. Others involved in the incident gave their accounts to police and to at least one newspaper reporter.

According to Duffey's notes of her meeting with Teresa, "Harmon stopped [hitting her] when Teresa's boyfriend, clad only in a towel, walked into the room that they were in. Harmon shouted that he would kill them both and threw the boyfriend against a wall. The boyfriend ran through the house, grabbed his pants, and ran out the front door with Harmon chasing him. The three stood in the front yard shouting. The boyfriend was shouting for someone to call the police, Teresa was shouting at Harmon, and Harmon was shouting at both of them.

"A neighbor came over and after a brief but angry exchange between the neighbor and Harmon, the neighbor turned around and walked back to his yard. Just as he reached his driveway, Harmon jumped on the neighbor's back and started hitting him in the head. The force of the attack threw the neighbor into the side of his pickup. With Harmon still on his back and still hitting him, he reached into the back of his pickup, grabbed an iron pipe, and knocked Harmon to the ground with one swing. Harmon got up, ran to his truck, and sped off, almost hitting a parked car. Harmon was arrested later that day on a charge of driving with a suspended license. Within 45 minutes, he was released on a bond of $250."

Ultimately Teresa Harmon decided not to press charges in the incident. The neighbor who had filed a complaint against Harmon also changed his mind about filing charges. A newspaper report three weeks after the event noted that the boyfriend who had been visiting Teresa when Dan burst into the house had left the state.

No one in an official capacity had seemed offended by the candidate's behavior. The assaults brought neither comment nor reprimand. The Saline County establishment was similarly mum when, as a result of that incident, reporters checking state traffic records learned that Harmon's driver's license had been suspended twice in the past eight months—and had never been reinstated. Harmon brushed off the problem, suggesting that it was insignificant in light of all the good he was trying to do. Voters seemed willing to agree. Many said that they rather liked Harmon's too-busy-for-details style. "That's Danny," they laughed.

All Duffey hoped for was to hang on. Govar seemed to be moving the case forward, and there was a chance that Harmon would be indicted before the end of the year. His assaults had not seemed to bother anyone. Nor had his apparent disdain for traffic court. But maybe if he were under a federal indictment, Duffey thought, someone might object to having him sworn in as the district's prosecuting attorney.

"NOT JUST A FEW ROGUE INDIVIDUALS"

But hanging on was more difficult than she'd imagined. In the summer of 1990, Linda and Larry quietly observed the third anniversary of Kevin's and Don's deaths. James Callaway pleaded guilty in federal court to an additional charge of selling drugs, after he was nabbed by Duffey's task force. And Jean Duffey began the fight of her life.

From the moment Harmon was elected Democratic candidate for prosecuting attorney, Duffey and her task force endured a barrage of accusations, some legitimate and most not. During that summer, Duffey discovered a discrepancy of nearly four thousand dollars in the task force's account, and that the task force's fiscal officer had been signing Duffey's name to checks. Duffey reported her findings immediately to Prosecutor Arnold and to the state police. A state audit cleared Duffey of responsibility for the missing funds. The financial officer said she signed the checks because Duffey had authorized her to use her signature. But the investigation took its toll because, regardless of the police findings, many believed Harmon's accusations that Duffey was responsible for the missing money.

The second blow occurred when it was revealed that Duffey and her husband had housed Richard Sampley, a convicted felon released from the Saline County jail, at their home. Because of Sampley's connections to the Saline County underworld, Sheriff Larry Davis had released Sampley from jail prematurely on the condition that Sampley cooperate as an informant for the drug task force. Duffey had arranged for Sampley to work at her husband's moving company and to sleep in the basement of their house—conditions that she felt offered reasonable supervision. But when newspapers learned of the arrangement, which lacked the requisite court authorization, Duffey—though not the sheriff—faced the most serious and valid criticism of her term.

There had been a third, more personal and underhanded attack. One day in the middle of the week, Duffey's children were taken from their classes and interviewed by state child welfare officials because of an anonymous call charging Duffey with child abuse. The inquiry lasted only a couple of days, and in the end the social worker apologized to Duffey for what she concluded had clearly been harassment.[10]

But the storm of controversy continued to batter the task force, and by November, Duffey was fired. Several of her agents resigned in protest. The task force was shut down. Despite its dissolution, however, Duffey and some of her agents continued to cooperate with Govar. The fruits of months of investigation—all they had worked for and endured for the past nine months—hung on whether the federal grand jury would hand down indictments.

In December 1990, Duffey and Agent Scott Lewellen met with U.S. Attorney Chuck Banks to explain the scope of the problem they had confronted in the Seventh Judicial District. "What you have in Saline County is lawyers, judges, police officers, and businessmen involved," Lewellen told the federal prosecutor. "It doesn't seem to end. Information about one elected official leads to information about other elected officials, or to attorneys or businessmen. This is not just a few rogue individuals. What we're seeing in Saline County seems to be interconnected."

A few days later, Duffey and Lewellen met again at the federal building in Little Rock. Govar was bringing witnesses, many of whom had been developed by Duffey's drug task force, before the federal grand jury. One of the witnesses Govar had scheduled was Harmon's daughter, Tammy. Duffey and Lewellen waited on the ground floor of the marbled federal building while Tammy Harmon was questioned in a courtroom above. The area where they waited was packed with reporters who had been alerted that Harmon had accompanied his daughter to the courthouse. Suddenly, as the doors of an elevator opened, the bright lights of the television cameras flashed on and photographers scrambled for position. As Duffey and Lewellen watched, Dan Harmon stepped out of the elevator, cocky and confident, escorting his daughter, Tammy. With them was Linda Ives.

Duffey had never seen the mother of Kevin Ives before, though she had seen her face often on television and in the papers. Duffey was startled to see her with Harmon. Didn't she know that Harmon was himself involved with drugs? Did she really still trust him?

Poor woman, Duffey thought. She's been completely fooled. Turning to Lewellen, she said, "Scott, that's Linda Ives with Harmon."

Lewellen's face registered surprise. "When is she going to figure it out?" Duffey whispered. "When is she going to wake up?"

TWELVE

NO CORRUPTION FOUND

NOVEMBER 1990–DECEMBER 1991

As the photographers struggled to get a shot of Harmon and his daughter, they had no idea of what had just transpired in the rooms above. After bringing Tammy to the room where she would wait before testifying, Harmon asked to have a word with Banks. It is not common for a subject of a federal grand jury investigation to seek a meeting with the U.S. attorney. It is even more unusual for such a request to be granted. But Harmon was not a typical suspect. He was a fellow lawyer, and more than that, having won the general election, he would soon be sworn in as an Arkansas prosecuting attorney. Banks invited Harmon to have a seat in one of the office's stuffed leather chairs. He then invited Govar to join. But the courtesy Banks extended to Harmon quickly blew up in his face.

THE "CONFIDENTIAL" MEMOS

Harmon was a powder keg whose fuse had been burning for months. He exploded at the sight of Govar. Office workers in adjoining rooms stopped what they were doing and ran into the hall at the sound of pounding from Banks's office. Stopped speechless outside the door, they could hear Harmon cursing Govar: "You lying, no-good son of a bitch . . . " The situation had clearly gotten physical, though none of the worried listeners felt it appropriate to intervene. The listeners were expecting something to crash when a U.S. marshal appeared and dashed into Banks's office. It was unclear who had summoned the marshal, but he emerged a few minutes later, escorting Harmon from the room. Witnesses said Harmon looked calm and in control. Some thought he looked amused.

But there was no doubt that Harmon had been feeling some pressure. This was not the first but the second time that his daughter, Tammy, had been called to appear. Harmon almost certainly knew that his former wife Teresa and at least one of his former friends, Sharline Wilson, had also been sworn in and questioned about him by the grand jury. Wilson had testified that, among other things, she had dated Harmon while he was married and that the two of them had snorted cocaine.[1] It is unlikely, though possible, that Harmon knew the entire list of witnesses Govar was calling. Harmon's outburst in Govar's office led Duffey and others to suspect that, by early December 1990, he had seen both of the memos Govar had written to Banks earlier in the year. That—if nothing else—would have explained his fury.

In the two memos Govar quoted witnesses as describing numerous occasions on which they had seen Dan Harmon consume drugs. Different witnesses reported seeing him buy drugs on at least six occasions, talk about wanting to grow and manufacture drugs at least twice, and watch on six occasions while a woman he knew purchased drugs. Prosecutor Arnold, Duffey, Lovett, and others in the district had been privy to the memos for months. Harmon would almost certainly have been given a copy of the damning documents when he was elected prosecuting attorney—if not before.

Linda Ives was waiting for Harmon when he emerged from Banks's office. Larry had gone back to work a few months earlier, and life was beginning to return to normal when, to their surprise, Harmon had called to ask Linda if she would accompany him and Tammy for Tammy's appearance in federal court. He told her he needed her moral support.

While Duffey and other officials had seen the allegations in Govar's memos, Larry and Linda, like most ordinary citizens, had not. They knew that Govar was investigating Saline County, but not that Harmon was a target. There were rumors, to be sure. And Harmon made no secret of the fact that he believed Govar was out to get him. When Linda asked him why, he vaguely referred to the case of Kevin and Don and to the 1988 grand jury. He hinted that he had turned up some information during that grand jury that was embarrassing to Govar. Harmon told Linda that Officer Robert German had been working with Govar's antidrug task force, and that while serving in that capacity, he had worked with Teddye Carter, a drug dealer whom Govar had enlisted as an informant. The findings of the grand jury, as they related to the testimony of Carter and German, had been kept secret. But in a subsequent court appearance, Carter confirmed that, even while he was working as an informant for Govar, he had continued to deal cocaine. Harmon suggested that by opening the train-deaths case, he had embarrassed Govar's federal drug task force and that revenge for his having exposed that episode was prompting Govar's vendetta.

In his battle with the federal officials, as in all his battles, Harmon positioned himself as an underdog. He was a scrapper for what was right, taking on bigger but unjust powers. It was the same stance he had taken against Malak. It was a stance to which Linda could relate. She and Larry had felt like underdogs, trying to wrest some justice from forces bigger than they. Harmon had been a friend to them in their most desperate hour. If he needed Linda's help now, she was not about to refuse.

But as Linda waited at the courthouse while Tammy testified and while Harmon blew up in Banks's office, she had to admit to herself that there was something wrong with the scene. In all the time she had known Dan, she could not remember one instance when he had needed moral support. Why had he really asked her? Linda could not let go of the question. After Tammy's testimony, Linda accompanied Harmon and her into the courthouse elevator. When it stopped at the ground floor and the doors slid open, the three of them stepped out of the elevator into a blaze of media light. In a flash, Linda understood. Harmon was playing defense. She was being used as a prop, a sympathetic figure whom Harmon had assisted. On her behalf, he had battled Malak and won. By appearing at his side, Linda was not offering moral support. She was a public relations asset.

A change came over her. A crack spidered across her confidence in Harmon. As Duffey and Lewellen watched in pity, Linda walked past them feeling used.

The next day, to Govar's horror, the confidential memos that he had written to Banks were leaked to the media. Mel Hanks of KARK-TV was the first to report on them, offering viewers detailed information about the allegations relating to Harmon. The next day, December 12, the rest of the state's media followed.

Linda and Larry opened the *Arkansas Gazette* to a front-page photograph of Dan Harmon with the headline PROBE TARGETS PROSECUTOR. Linda looked at it, still reluctant to believe, but remembering how many people had related stories linking Harmon to drugs. She remembered how he had always dismissed them. "You prosecute people, and there are always people who will hate you," he had told her. "They spread those kinds of stories. It's something I have to live with." The response had made sense.

But now that explanation had worn bare. She picked up the paper and read. "Seventh Judicial District Prosecutor-elect Dan Harmon is a primary target of a federal grand jury investigation into public corruption and drug-trafficking in Saline County, according to U.S. Attorney's Office memorandums. The memos—one dated Feb. 13, 1990, and the other March 29, 1990—indicate the federal investigation also focuses on Harmon's law partner, Richard Garrett, whom Harmon has picked as his chief prosecutor. Federal indictments could be returned soon, officials said Tuesday . . . "

The crack in Linda's beleaguered confidence in Harmon widened.

In an article in the *Arkansas Democrat* two days after that, she and Larry read: "Former Saline County Sheriff James Steed was also the subject of an Internal Revenue Service tax investigation, the memos revealed. Steed, Harmon, and Garrett all are accused of helping protect James Callaway, who the memos claim had 'a significant cocaine distribution operation in Saline County during 1987 and 1988.' " Linda and Larry went numb as they read the dates. Kevin and Don had been killed in 1987, in the very period when this report was suggesting that Harmon, Garrett, and Steed were protecting Callaway. The couple had long had their doubts about Steed. But it was almost too much to imagine that he, Callaway, Harmon, and Garrett had all been in league together. Relentlessly the report continued, "There is a possibility that Callaway may have been involved, indirectly, in the murders of Kevin Ives and Don Henry on the railroad tracks in Saline County. . . . "

It was too much. Linda could not hold her shattering confidence together anymore. It was nearly impossible for her to think that Dan Harmon, in whom she had placed all her hopes, might actually have been involved in protecting a murderer. Yet, now it was also becoming impossible for her not to think that that might have happened.

After the leak of the memos, John Deering, an editorial cartoonist for the *Arkansas Democrat,* captured the growing public perception of the situation in the central Arkansas county in one of his year-end cartoons. It showed two lanes of Interstate 30 approaching an overpass sign that read ENTERING SALINE COUNTY. Beneath that were two other highway signs: SLOWER TRAFFIC KEEP RIGHT over one lane, and DRUG TRAFFIC over the other.

Linda sought reassurance, but none was to be found. Harmon was about to be sworn in as prosecutor. He had already announced his intention to make Roger Walls, a former drug counselor, the new director of the drug task force. At the same time, it looked like Govar was closing in. In the days following the leak of the memos, Govar's federal task force arrested several drug suspects, including a man named Marvin Stegall of Hot Springs. Stegall had been named in Govar's memos as an alleged major supplier of drugs to counties in the Seventh Judicial District, including to some of the witnesses who were now testifying against Harmon.

Slowly, painfully, Linda and Larry felt their world reshaping itself around them. The shock was too much to be absorbed at once, but it was becoming clear to both of them that, just as they had had to accept the reality of Kevin's death, they were also going to have to accept the sting of Harmon's apparent betrayal.

CONVICTION OVERTURNED

Events kept nudging them to finally believe the unbelievable. Then, just before that Christmas of 1990, the Arkansas Supreme Court handed down an opinion that added another twist to Saline County's knot of drug-related murders. The court ruled that Shane Smith, the teenager convicted of murdering Keith McKaskle, had not received a fair trial. McKaskle's murder had bothered Linda from the start—ever since Garrett and Harmon disclosed that McKaskle had been "keeping his ears open" for information relating to the murders of Kevin and Don. Now the state's high court was ruling that much about his trial had been improper.

In considering Smith's appeal, the state Supreme Court found that Judge Cole had erred when he refused to allow testimony that McKaskle had told several people that he was living in fear for his life. While holding that certain evidence of McKaskle's fighting ability had been properly excluded (since the jury had been allowed to hear testimony that McKaskle had been a bouncer and "a multiple badass"), the justices held that Judge Cole should not have barred testimony from a prison inmate who'd said that he had been offered four thousand dollars to kill McKaskle. Nor, the appellate court said, should Cole have excluded the testimony of a police officer who was prepared to say that McKaskle had come to him ten days before his murder to report that two black men and a white man had been following him. The state Supreme Court also held that the trial court should have admitted statements from other witnesses who "were going to testify that McKaskle had been in fear for his life because of something he knew."[2] Smith's conviction was reversed and his case remanded to Judge Cole's jurisdiction. When asked what would happen to Smith, Cole answered, "If the prosecutor wants a new trial date, then we'll set it."

Linda knew that Smith had been the only person the Benton police had ever suspected in McKaskle's murder. During his trial, she had been appalled at how much of the defense's case Judge Cole had barred. Now that the state Supreme Court was sending the case back to the county, with the order that much of that evidence be admitted, Linda could not imagine how a jury would reconvict Shane Smith. And if Smith were not tried again, who—if anyone—would be? Who had really killed Keith McKaskle? Why had this investigation, too, apparently broken down? Was the drug culture in Saline County so invulnerable that murder upon murder could be committed without any final dispensation of justice? And if all of that were true, what did it say about Harmon, who seemed to have one foot in the courthouse and—Linda was now allowing herself to admit—another in the county's underworld of drugs?

LEWELLEN'S NOTES

Scott Lewellen was off the drug task force. But he was not ready to leave Saline County. Convinced that the place was rife with corruption and that the murders of Don Henry and Kevin Ives were related to it, Lewellen dedicated himself for several weeks, before moving to his next job, to finding out what McKaskle had known. Lewellen had never spoken with Linda, but by now he shared her passion to see some justice restored to Saline County.

By early January 1991, Lewellen had composed thirty-five pages of notes detailing interviews with more than a dozen sources. He slipped them into an envelope, sealed it, and passed it on to Govar. Lewellen felt satisfied that, in a county overrun with speculation, he had worked hard to distinguish what was myth from what was fact. In his notes, Lewellen reported to Govar that Betty Alexander, the mother of Keith Coney, the young man who was killed in the suspicious motorcycle accident in May 1988, said that her son had told her that he knew some important information about the deaths of the Henry and Ives boys, but that he did not want to worry her with it. According to Lewellen's notes, Betty Alexander "stated that Keith was becoming very nervous during the three months prior to his death, but again, he would not tell her why."

Another of Betty Alexander's sons, Eugene Coney, was now in prison. Mrs. Alexander told Lewellen that on one of her visits to Eugene, she had met another inmate by the name of Mike Crook, a former manager of Gigi's, a club on the county line. As Lewellen reported Mrs. Alexander's account, she and Crook were talking when Crook told her about a customer who had frequented the club, and an incident the customer said he had observed at the little grocery store near Shobe Road—the one with the telephone outside. He referred to the store, which is the only commercial establishment in the area, as a dairy bar. According to Crook, the customer said "that on the night of the boys' deaths, he was parked at a dairy bar in Alexander close to the railroad tracks waiting for his wife, when he observed three teenage boys, two of which came in a car and the third on a motorcycle, by the dairy bar, and that the three were smoking some marijuana. A police car pulled up and the boy on the motorcycle sped off. Then two officers got out of the car and 'beat the shit' out of the boys. Afterwards, the boys were thrown into the back of the patrol car. The man heard the next day that Henry and Ives had been found dead on the tracks and he thought what he had seen the night before could have had some connection.

"When the man told Crook about this, Crook convinced him that it may have been tied in to the deaths and that the man should go report what he had seen to the Saline County Sheriff's Office. The man did so and was immediately thrown into jail by Sheriff Steed for not paying back child support. The man spent approximately 90 days in the county jail before being released. He then went to the lounge and told Crook what had happened and that he was leaving Saline County and was not going to return."

Betty Alexander also told Lewellen about a local tough who was suspected of running a large-scale theft ring that specialized in robbing Wal-Mart stores in Tennessee, Texas, and Louisiana, who was also considered a suspect in the motorcycle death of Betty Alexander's son, Keith Coney, the shotgun death of Greg Collins, and the disappearance of Daniel "Boonie" Bearden. Betty Alexander was familiar with the man. She told Lewellen that on the night the television show *Unsolved Mysteries* aired the segment about the Ives-and-Henry deaths, the man was at the Coney house. "When the part about a man wearing military fatigues came on," Betty Alexander said, "He tugged at his shirt, which was camouflage, and said, 'Who do we all know that wears camouflage all the time?' This statement shook up the Coney family because they knew he liked to brag about his accomplishments by making comments like that one. No one in the Coney household felt that he was joking when he made that statement but rather that he was boasting. . . . "

Elsewhere in his papers Lewellen noted that:

- A young man who claimed to have been "best friends" with Keith Coney said that Keith had been running drugs for James Callaway.
- "According to Govar, Garrett called Govar toward the end of 1988 and said that he wanted to meet and talk with him. They met in a bar after work, but all Garrett would do was cry in his beer and tell Govar that he wished he could tell him some things, but he couldn't. This coincides with the time period that Garrett's windshield was shot out, according to sources, as a warning to keep his mouth shut."[3]
- Sharline Wilson told Lewellen that she dated Dan Harmon five or six times in 1987, the year the boys were killed. Usually they went to a private club in Little Rock. "Sharline says that Harmon always had cocaine powder in the glove compartment of his car and they would 'do a line' on the way to the club."

- One informant reported that Roger Walls, the man Harmon selected as director of the revived drug task force, had once had several teenagers in his hometown of Sheridan working for him, selling marijuana. The informant said that when he was thirteen years old, he himself had sold drugs for Walls. At the time, Walls was a drug counselor for teenagers in Grant County, the third and—with a population of fewer than fourteen thousand—least populous county in the district.

In Lewellen's mind, the most interesting interview he conducted had been with Curtis Henry, who had moved with Marvelle to Magnolia, in southern Arkansas. Noting that on the morning the boys' bodies were discovered, Don's shirt had been found inside out, about a hundred yards from the point of impact, Curtis mentioned that when he and Don would wrestle, Don would frequently "corkscrew" completely out of his shirt to get out of his father's grasp.

Regarding James Callaway, Henry said that he knew the used-car dealer quite well and he suspected that Callaway probably knew something about who was involved in the boys' murders. But, Henry told Lewellen, "Callaway is the type that will never be able to be 'squeezed' hard enough to talk about what he knows because he would rather do ten years in prison and take that chance of staying safe than talking and possibly being killed."

Regarding Keith McKaskle, Henry noted that he and McKaskle had been good friends. "He said that he would meet Keith at the Wagon Wheel Lounge quite frequently and they would go into the office where Keith would tell him what he had just found. He said that he was sure that Keith had been killed because of what he had learned."

Regarding Linda Ives, Henry offered his opinion to Lewellen that she was "an emotional freight train." He said he felt she jeopardized the investigation by discussing it publicly, and that "the last straw" in his relationship with her had been "when she told him that a psychic said that his own daughter" knew something about her brother's death.

Lewellen talked with Henry about numerous people involved in the investigation, and Henry offered information and opinions about many of them. One person he did not want to discuss, however, was his daughter, Gayla. Lewellen felt that Henry seemed to be a sincere parent who wanted nothing more than answers as to why he had lost his son, but not at the expense of dragging his daughter into the morass. As the investigator would later recall, "Gayla was an issue we skirted around, because he made his feelings quite clear about that."

CURTIS HENRY'S THEORY

Of particular interest to Lewellen was Curtis Henry's theory about what had happened on the night that his son, Don, and Kevin Ives were killed. In his notes Lewellen summarized that theory, as outlined by Henry:

"Don and Kevin walked down to the area of the woods off of the tracks where the field is only about 400 feet away. They may have walked up upon some cocaine that had been thrown off of the train that passed southbound at approximately 1:30 A.M. or people picking up the cocaine. At the time of their deaths, it was possible to walk up on something near the tracks without being seen because there were heavy thickets growing on both sides of the tracks. He does not know for sure if there was another boy with them or not.

"Or, more possibly, the boys were in the field when a cocaine drop was made from an airplane." Curtis told Lewellen that after the boys' deaths, he had spent "night after night" at the tracks trying to figure out what had happened, when he noticed that a small airplane was making regular landings, once a week, between 2:00 and 3:00 A.M., on a grass airstrip located on property near the tracks. The area is very dark at night but near the field is a large institution known locally as the children's colony, and that place is brightly lighted. Curtis said he made some inquiries and believes that the plane was making regular cocaine pick-ups in Louisiana or possibly Texas, dropping them off in the field and using the lights of the children's colony as a beacon. Henry told Lewellen that he had given his information about the airstrip to Investigator Birdsong of the Arkansas State Police, along with aerial photos of the area, "but he learned that they had never conducted any type of investigation on the information he had given them."

Henry said he believed the boys may have approached the drop, when they were confronted by their assailants. "If they were confronted," Lewellen wrote, based on his interview with Henry, "Curtis knows that there would have had to be someone present that Don felt comfortable around or he would have run off into the woods. Curtis is positive that no one would have been able to 'get the drop' on Don out there because Don had hunted in that area for all his life and he was too good an outdoorsman to be caught if he didn't want to be. There is also the possibility that the boys had been put up to meeting the shipment and stealing some of it by someone who knew about the cocaine operation and was offering them money to do so and therefore the boys may have been a little too brazen in their attempt to get some of the shipment.

"Either way, once the boys were apprehended, they were walked to the part of the tracks where they were laid, since it was close by. Curtis feels at this point the men who had the boys began to beat them and interrogate them as to either who had sent them out there, who knew they were out there, or who the third boy was, if there indeed was a third person who managed to get away. Then Kevin was smashed in the head with Don's rifle and he fell to the ground, possibly dead at that point. Don took off running and was chased for about a hundred yards before being caught again. He was then stabbed from behind while maybe being held, when he did his 'corkscrew' maneuver and came out of his shirt, turning it inside out. The stabbing either was that severe or he was knocked to the ground where his head was smashed open by one or several blows from his rifle."

U.S. ATTORNEY CHUCK BANKS

Linda Ives did not know of Curtis Henry's theory, as related to Scott Lewellen, that cocaine was being dropped from airplanes at sites along the railroad tracks. She did know that, while many investigators suspected that Don and Kevin had stumbled upon a drug drop, the prevailing conjecture was that the drugs were being pushed off trains. But to Linda, the wife of an engineer, that theory did not make sense. Many nights she and Larry talked about what could have happened the night that Kevin was killed. They had discussed the widely held theory that the boys' bodies were found where they were because of drugs that were being brought into the county by train. Larry told her he knew too much of how trains were routed to believe that that was possible. Trains are continually being broken up and reassembled, depending on the routing of individual cars. Larry discussed with his co-workers the possibility of smugglers using the trains to move drugs. But the trainmen could not see how that could be done—at least not for long or with any consistency.

Jean Duffey had always found it difficult to understand the drugs-by-train theory, too. She would have considered the idea that drugs were being dropped by airplanes if anyone in the Benton Police Department had ever mentioned that for years they had been investigating complaints about low-flying planes in the area around the tracks. But that information had never come up. Only after Scott Lewellen questioned residents along the tracks was he able to confirm that the night flights had occurred and that, for some residents, they had become a nuisance. Duffey did not know how Curtis Henry had come to suspect that drugs were being dropped by air, but once other residents in the area supported that theory under questioning by Lewellen, Duffey brought the information to Govar.

She and Lewellen made a special trip to Little Rock to discuss the idea with Govar. But when they arrived, Govar's boss, Chuck Banks, intercepted them. Saying he wanted to talk to them, he took them one by one into his office and questioned each of them individually about the source of the leaked memos. Duffey was irritated. She had what could be important information relating to two unsolved murders in the county—to say nothing of possible drug running. But Banks seemed more concerned about the leaks from his office. She told Banks that she had no idea who had provided them to the media. Lewellen also disavowed any knowledge of the leaks.

Then Banks turned his attention to the murders. Lewellen related what Curtis Henry had said and what residents near the tracks had reported about the low-flying planes. Then he and Duffey rolled out aerial maps on the table in Banks's office. Lewellen pointed out the tracks, the Shobe Road crossing, the children's colony at Alexander, and the location of homes belonging to residents who had told of hearing low-flying planes at night. "These murders can be solved," Duffey interjected, "but Scott and I can't do it. You have the investigative authority. You have the power to subpoena. If you would do it, you could solve these murders." Banks assured the two that he would let them bring their information before the federal grand jury. If the murders could be solved, he promised, they would be.

In the next few weeks, Duffey was called to appear before the grand jury, as promised, but to her amazement and disappointment, Banks, who handled the questioning, did not ask her about airplanes, or cocaine in Saline County, or the Henry-and-Ives murders. Instead, he focused on the leak of the memos. Banks asked Duffey if she herself had not leaked the memos because she had a "vendetta against Dan Harmon." Duffey answered calmly that she had no vendetta against Harmon. Then she waited. Banks did not turn his questioning to the issues of drugs and corruption in Saline County—the matters at hand before the grand jury. He ended his questioning of her without raising the topics. As he was about to excuse Duffey from the stand, one of the jurors raised her hand. The juror asked a question about goings-on in Saline County. Duffey answered it. Then another juror asked a question, then another. Duffey appreciated their intelligence and initiative. But Banks ended the day's testimony then, promising that Duffey would be called to reappear, but the call never came.

While Duffey wondered what Banks was up to, Govar had reasons of his own to worry. His investigation was coming apart at the seams. He did not know who had released his memos, but their appearance in the media had dealt him and his investigation a blow. Banks was furious and Govar was deeply concerned.

"One of the most devastating things that could happen to a criminal investigation is to have a wholesale disclosure of witnesses and what they have said," he would later reflect. "The thing that most concerned me was the fact that the leak had placed these people in danger. If you were a witness and the prosecutor told you he would do everything to protect your identity, and then a week later you read what you've related in confidence in the paper, it's frightening. Some of the people we had talked to felt they were in serious jeopardy. They feared that Mr. Harmon might retaliate."

Another effect of the release was to stifle other potential witnesses. Even before the leaks, in light of what had happened to McKaskle and the others, many considered the risk of talking about activities in Saline County to be unacceptably high. After the leaks—when it became known who was talking, what they were saying, and about whom they were saying it—the sense of risk that already permeated the county turned to outright fear. The leaks had been more than embarrassing. They threatened to sabotage Govar's investigation.

But that was not the only thing going wrong. After the arrest of Marvin Stegall, reputed to be one of the biggest cocaine suppliers for Saline County, Govar had hoped that Stegall would roll over to avoid prosecution and that once he started talking, he would provide valuable information. But Stegall had disappointed him. As Govar would later put it, "Mr. Stegall was not inclined to cooperate with the United States government. He did his time. He never made a statement."

Another problem facing Govar was that federal grand juries typically are released at the end of a year. This one was no exception. At the end of 1990, the jurors who had heard all the testimony offered so far about the Seventh Judicial District were told that their work was done. Banks could have held them over, but he did not, so Govar entered 1991 facing a new panel of grand jurors.

Serious as those setbacks were, they paled next to Govar's biggest frustration. Banks wanted Govar to have every witness he called in the Saline County investigation submit to a polygraph test. It was an unusual demand. And it was the last thing Govar wanted. Many witnesses had already testified, but Banks wanted them to be polygraphed, as well.

The meeting to discuss the issue was a tense one. Banks and some of the other deputies in the office were of the opinion that, because of the nature of the investigation and the prominence of some of its subjects, it was imperative that the witnesses called upon to testify should have passed a polygraph examination. Banks also was understandably concerned about the appearance of allowing people with criminal pasts to testify against elected public officials. At least six Saline County residents had been granted immunity from federal prosecution in the course of the investigation. Banks claimed that the unsavoriness of their backgrounds worried him. Among those granted immunity were Richard Sampley, the inmate who was released from jail early on a robbery conviction to work with Duffey's task force; William Carl Samples, the other gunman in the fatal attempted robbery of the Lonoke County gambling house; Marissa Lynn Bragg, the woman who testified that she had been present during the 1989 murder of Jeff Rhodes, whose burned and dismembered body was found in a Saline County dump; Woodrow "Woody" May, the methamphetamine dealer who had testified that Harmon alerted him whenever police were getting "too close" to discovering his operation; and two other men whom Harmon had charged with selling cocaine as a result of the 1988 grand jury. It was a motley crew of witnesses.

But Govar reminded his co-workers of what they already knew: that the upstanding members of a community are never going to be the ones who are intimate with public corruption. In other words, often it takes crooks to know crooks—and to know what crooks have been up to. And people with these sorts of backgrounds are likely to have problems passing a polygraph examination. But to eliminate such witnesses entirely, Govar argued, would be to undermine all the investigative work that had been done on the case. In an impassioned plea to Banks and his associates, Govar outlined his resistance.

"First, polygraphs are a useful investigative tool, but their findings are not conclusive. If they were as scientific as some people like to think they are, they would be admissible in court, and they're not. We all know that these examinations are subjective. The responses can be interpreted differently, depending on the opinions of the examiners. My second reason for not wanting these witnesses polygraphed is that, as most of you also know, all witnesses lie—especially people who have been involved in drug trafficking. If there's anything at all they don't want to reveal, it can show up as a lie on the test. I say, don't do the polygraphs. When we put these people under oath, we're placing them under penalty of perjury. If they lie as to a material fact under oath, they've committed a felony for which they can be prosecuted. That's what we normally do, and what we should do in this case. On the other hand, what will happen if we polygraph these witnesses before we put them on the stand? Assuming that they don't all pass with perfect scores, all we've done is create a lot of Giglio material."

Govar's audience understood. As federal lawyers, they were familiar with the U.S. Supreme Court decision known as *Giglio* v. *United States.* It was basic to their careers. In it the court ruled that if a prosecutor has information that can be used to impeach the credibility of a witness, the prosecutor has an obligation to reveal that information to the defense. Ever since the ruling, information prosecutors develop that could be harmful to the credibility of one of their witnesses has been called "Giglio material." From a tactical point of view, prosecutors try to avoid developing such material.

But that was what polygraphs might do and what Govar was arguing against. "If we polygraph all these witnesses," Govar told the other U.S. attorneys, "I bet my meager federal investigator's salary, all of them will fail. They'll fail even if they're telling the God's truth about the investigation here at hand. And if they fail, we have torpedoed our own investigation, because we'll have created a ton of material that we'll have to turn over to the defense attorneys. So we ourselves have made them useless as witnesses."[4]

The issue was put to a vote and Govar lost. In the weeks that followed, he watched as most of the witnesses who had testified about Harmon, or who were going to, were subjected to polygraph examinations. In all the years he had been a federal prosecutor, he had never seen a situation in which every witness who had information relating to a specific subject was required to pass a polygraph. But that was happening now. And, as Govar had predicted, none of the witnesses polygraphed passed with perfect scores. "I saw my witnesses dropping one by one," he later lamented, "and I knew that it was just a matter of time before the investigation was completely gutted."[5]

HARMON SUBPOENAS DUFFEY

Almost immediately upon taking office as prosecuting attorney, Harmon, the subject of a federal grand jury investigation into public corruption, announced that he would impanel his own county grand jury to investigate public corruption. It was a ludicrous situation, one in which Harmon was trying to seize the initiative. Linda, like most others in the county, could only watch the maneuvering, uncertain what any of it meant.

In February 1991 one of Harmon's first official acts, in conjunction with his new grand jury, was to subpoena Jean Duffey. But Duffey had no intention of being questioned under oath by Harmon about an investigation in which he figured. Govar was still holding out hope that he would be able to indict Harmon. Duffey wanted to protect the witnesses who had provided her and her agents with critical information. Duffey talked the situation over with Govar. He advised her to ask Banks to petition Judge Cole's court, explaining that Harmon's subpoena of Duffey could frustrate a federal investigation. But when Duffey took that request to Banks, the U.S. attorney refused.

So Duffey did not pick up her subpoena. She could not carry on with her normal life and avoid being served. During a tense week in early February, Duffey and her husband got up early every morning and, before their children awoke for school, discussed the situation over coffee. Both saw the writing on the wall. As Duffey finally expressed it, "It's a simple matter of either giving up to Harmon and Cole all the witnesses Scott, Carl, and I developed, or refusing to say anything and being held in contempt of court. If they hold me in contempt of court, I will be jailed. And if that happens, I seriously feel my life will be in jeopardy."

Scott Lewellen was facing a similar situation, though he had not yet been subpoenaed. He offered the Duffeys a suggestion. Lewellen's parents owned a rustic, three-bedroom house that they sometimes used for vacations in the mountains of southwestern Arkansas. Surrounded by nothing but pastures and woodlands, it would make a comfortable, temporary hideout. He was going to go there, and there would be plenty of room for Duffey and her family if they wanted to join him.

The Duffeys explained the situation to their children. Jean would be staying at the cabin, and Duff and the kids would visit her on the weekends. On Friday, February 8, 1991, Jean Duffey got up, cleaned the house, washed some clothes, and packed for her flight from Saline County.

ACCEPTANCE

Linda knew nothing of Govar's disappointments, or of the fears that had led Duffey to such a critical turning point, persuading her to leave her home and family. But even without that information, Linda had also reached a turning point. In the quiet of her soul, the weight of what she had learned about Harmon had finally tipped the scales. The defensiveness, the doubt, the wavering was over. An implacable certainty settled over her, accompanied by a bitter calm. She had been fooled, but she forgave herself. When you want to believe something badly enough, she thought, you can make yourself believe—and she and Larry had wanted desperately to trust Dan Harmon. It had been horrible to the point of impossibility to imagine that, not only the police, but also Harmon, their supposed defender, had been involved in crimes that were, perhaps, linked to Kevin's death.

But now the last of that hard-held faith slipped from Linda's grasp. She and Larry had been betrayed—she saw that clearly. They had suffered the agony of Kevin's death and they had also suffered the insult of Harmon and Garrett. The tragedy of Kevin's and Don's deaths went beyond the manipulative investigation headed by Sheriff Steed. It went beyond Malak's incompetence and bullying. It went beyond all of the frustrations she and Larry had experienced with the Arkansas State Police and with the FBI. The malevolence, Linda realized, had been pervasive—and insidious. It had come into her home in the guise of a dedicated prosecuting attorney. It had sought and gained her trust. And it had turned the investigation to its own perverted purposes.

Linda let out a sigh she had been choking back for months. Devastating as the realization was, she now found that facing it was easier than holding onto a rotted faith. She let go of that faith forever, allowing the loss and the grief to wash over her. Once again she found herself finally accepting what she thought she could not bear. And, as had happened the first time she did that, in the aftermath of Kevin's death, she found that with acceptance came a strengthening, an intensification of her will. She had experienced murder and betrayal, and, to her own amazement, it had not destroyed her spirit. It had not made her afraid. "Don't worry, Kevin," she whispered. "They won't get away with it."

During the next few days, Linda remembered with some embarrassment how she had paid a call on Bob Govar after the memos about Harmon had been leaked. Govar had listened courteously as she had defended Harmon. He had been more polite, she recalled, than she had been. Linda also thought about "that crazy Jean Duffey." Duffey had not been so crazy after all. Linda picked up the phone and called Govar. She apologized and made an appointment to see him in Little Rock. Reaching Duffey was harder. The television and newspapers were reporting that she was hiding to avoid being served with Harmon's subpoenas. Duffey's brother, David Keesee, was speaking on her behalf. Linda contacted him and asked him to have Duffey call her. She wanted to tell Duffey that now she understood. She knew the truth about Harmon. But it seemed that Duffey had disappeared.

RETALIATION

The next few months, March, April, and May 1991, saw a flurry of activity. Judge Cole issued a warrant for the arrest of Jean Duffey, charging her with failure to appear. Cole announced that if she was apprehended, Duffey would be held without bond in jail. James Duffey told reporters that his wife believed that coming out of hiding would endanger not only her own life, but the lives of many other individuals who had testified before Govar's grand jury. On a popular Arkansas radio talk show, he said that his wife would come forward only if Harmon was removed as prosecutor of the county grand jury. Cole blasted back that he would not consider removing Harmon in order to appease a fugitive.

In early April, Harmon startled members at a meeting of the Benton Kiwanis Club by launching into a tirade during a lunchtime talk. Harmon attacked the former prosecutor, Gary Arnold, for not having done his job properly and for leaving Harmon with a huge backlog. He complained that the Saline County Sheriff's Office was made up of bunglers and incompetents who were not capable of properly investigating a case and bringing it to his office for prosecution. And he accused the local news media of contributing to the stress that had caused his deputy prosecutor, Richard Garrett, to suffer a recent stroke. One amazed Kiwanian remarked, "He just fired off at everyone."

In early May, Harmon switched tactics. He offered to step down as prosecutor for the grand jury, and asked Judge Cole to appoint someone else. "Hopefully," he wrote to Cole, "this step will encourage some of the witnesses we have been having difficulty getting to testify before the grand jury to cooperate." Harmon mentioned Duffey and Lewellen as two who were critical to the investigation but unwilling to testify as long as he was involved. After receiving Harmon's letter, Cole requested assistance from Arkansas Attorney General Winston Bryant, who had grown up in nearby Malvern, another city in the district. Bryant suggested that the county grand jury be dismissed since its focus on public corruption duplicated efforts of the federal grand jury under way in Little Rock. Cole rejected that advice and the county grand jury continued throughout the summer. When it finally disbanded, having accomplished nothing, its members released a report saying that they had found no evidence of public corruption in the district. Cole lauded Harmon for his diligence, applauding the "exemplary job" he had done.

Having failed in his efforts to force Duffey and Lewellen to testify, Harmon did what he could. He announced that he and members of his staff, including Richard Garrett, had voluntarily submitted to a drug test and that all had checked out negative. Then he turned to prosecuting the people who had been identified in Govar's memos as having testified against him. In the weeks that followed, Harmon racked up an impressive series of convictions in Judge Cole's court. Woodrow May, who had testified before the federal grand jury about Harmon's alleged involvement in drugs, was arrested by the district's revived drug task force and charged, as a habitual criminal, with dealing drugs. May stood trial and, under Harmon's prosecution, drew a sentence of eighty years. Sharline Wilson, who told federal investigators that she and Harmon had used cocaine together, was arrested by the task force and sentenced to thirty-one years in prison. On one day in May, the task force, led by Roger Walls, made a sweep of the county and rounded up twenty-three individuals whom Harmon charged with drug-related crimes. In announcing the arrests, Harmon made a point of noting that several of them had been witnesses for Govar's federal grand jury.

While Harmon boasted of his conviction rate on drug arrests, he failed in one significant case. James Callaway, who had already been convicted in federal court of supplying the shotgun that was used in the attempted robbery at the gambling house, was acquitted in Judge Cole's court of having planned the robbery.[6]

There was one more peculiar bit of business that troubled some of Saline County's more astute observers during that tumultuous spring of 1991. Since the Arkansas Supreme Court had reversed the conviction of Shane Smith in the murder of Keith McKaskle, courthouse watchers were wondering when Smith would be retried. The decision was up to Harmon. But he did not mention the case, and Smith stayed out of prison. It looked to many like the message in McKaskle's murder had a dangerous postscript: people with information could die—and their killers would never be found.

It was a message that, despite herself, Linda Ives was beginning to believe.

"HOTHEAD AND WOMAN-CHASER"

Before Duffey and Lewellen had gone into hiding, they had visited the offices of the monthly *Arkansas Times* magazine to meet with John Brummett, the state's most popular political reporter. Duffey had brought several files with her. She was running out of places to try to tell her story. Saline County would not listen. Running unopposed for prosecutor, Dan Harmon had won the election in November with 60 percent of the vote, despite the well-publicized physical attacks on his ex-wife, Teresa, and others. Duffey's main hope had been Govar. He kept promising that the new grand jury would hand down indictment, but that prospect was growing dimmer. Before she was fired from the task force, Duffey had even raised the problem of corruption in Saline County with Governor Bill Clinton. The exchange, in the hallway outside a meeting of the state's drug task force officials, had been brief. Blurting out her concern that under Harmon, the Seventh Judicial District's prosecutor's office would be used for racketeering, she'd pleaded, "Governor, you've got to help us." He had been gracious, saying he would look into it. But Duffey had walked back into the session knowing that, for all the governor's charm, she had been brushed off. The approach to Brummett was her swan song.

As Jean spread her files on the table, Lewellen outlined the scale of corruption that they had been confronting in the district. The reporter was clearly skittish. For months Harmon had gone well beyond the limits of professional disagreement in his attempts to humiliate Duffey. Lewellen could see in Brummett's reaction that Harmon's tactics had worked. Her credibility had been destroyed. At the end of the interview, much of it about the allegations contained in the leaked federal memos, Brummett asked Duffey and Lewellen what they expected Banks would do. "He has ambitions," Lewellen replied. "He's got his eye on a federal judgeship. I don't think he'll do anything. Why stir up a lot of turmoil with a bunch of public officials? It's a two-edged sword. If you open that box, you never can tell which way the insects will swarm." As Duffey packed up her files and replaced them in her briefcase, Lewellen added an afterthought. "I think Bob Govar wants to do the right thing. I think Chuck Banks wants to do the right thing, too—if it will benefit him or his office."

Brummett wrote a cover story for the *Arkansas Times* and titled it "Out of Control in Saline County." The piece began: "Dan Harmon was reared in Benton by his grandfather, a union man, who taught him that there are two ways to survive in this world. One is education. The other is with your fists. Outsmart a man if you can, but fight him if you must." Echoing that refrain, that Harmon was at once clever and uncouth, Brummett noted that, even as the prosecutor was being investigated by federal officials on suspicions that he might be protecting some local drug dealers while prosecuting others, his personal finances were a shambles. In the early summer of 1991, Harmon was renting an apartment and driving a 1988 Chevrolet pickup that he had had to finance fully because he lacked money for a down payment. Brummett wrote, "He smiles agreeably when a visitor tells him that a friend had called him an incurable hothead and woman-chaser who would resolve many of his problems if he would overcome those weaknesses. 'Yeah, that's probably about right,' Harmon says."

With the threat of federal prosecution hanging over his head, Harmon put his thoughts about Govar into a letter from which Brummett quoted: "The American justice system is able to withstand the abuses of a punk assistant U.S. attorney and his bloated ego," Harmon wrote. "If Mr. Govar wants to charge me with any offense, I will kick his butt all over the courtroom. If he wants to bring his yuppie ass to Benton, I will kick it all over the streets of Benton for the shameful way he subjected my family and friends to such unwarranted and unnecessary grief."

As for the biggest case in Harmon's career, the unsolved murders of the boys on the tracks, Brummett noted that Harmon's 1988 county grand jury had "determined only the obvious, which was that Malak's finding—that the boys died because they were comatose on the railroad tracks from smoking too much dope—was absurd. . . . Harmon himself theorizes that the boys happened upon some crooked cops from Benton or maybe adjoining Pulaski County, who beat them so badly that the boys had to be killed." Then, after a lengthy recounting of Harmon's various wrangles, Brummett noted that, nonetheless, "Most of the leading townspeople in Benton like Harmon and say Duffey is unstable. Both are probably slightly paranoid, but Harmon is the hometown scrapper, and they can't help but root for him."

Duffey came off looking slightly mad. As described in the *Arkansas Times,* during her six turbulent months as head of the drug task force, she was "spending more time attacking Harmon and infighting with other officials than pursuing drug dealers, and concocting a wild tale of a drug ring that supposedly includes Harmon and just about every other public official in Saline County. . . . She also spread charges, to Govar and this magazine, that Harmon is part of a corrupt court system in Saline County and is behind an extensive drug trafficking operation that might have had something to do with the deaths of the teenagers." But, Brummett added, "Duffey and her astonishing allegations have been widely discredited."[7]

"RUMORS AND INNUENDO"

On June 27, 1991, Linda Ives at home in Bryant, Jean Duffey at the Lewellens' cabin in the Ouachita Mountains, and Bob Govar at home in Little Rock unfolded their morning papers to jarring news. U.S. Attorney Chuck Banks announced that he would not be seeking indictments on drug charges against Dan Harmon. The papers reported that in an unusual move, Banks had called a press conference to underline his decision not to act. But he had not stopped there. Going an extra mile, Banks specifically cleared Harmon and his family from the taint of allegations raised in the embarrassing leaked memos. He told reporters that the allegations of Harmon's drug use and involvement in drug trafficking were "based on rumors and innuendo and didn't have merit." Asked about allegations of misconduct, corruption, or drug use by Harmon or other Saline County public officials, Banks said, "Quite frankly, there is none. We found no evidence of any drug-related misconduct by public officials in Saline County."

Harmon thanked Banks for his statement. "It took courage for him to come out and say that." Describing the federal investigation as "three years of pure hell," he told reporters, "I regret that it took so long to do that and that federal investigators listened to a crazy person like Jean Duffey." Public support for Harmon swelled, especially in Saline County. As many saw it, Harmon had been smeared by lowlife drug dealers and an arrogant U.S. attorney who had been willing to take the word of informants—informants greased with promises of immunity—to get back at a smart county prosecutor who had embarrassed him. At coffee shops around Benton, men mocked Govar's contention that information about persons involved in drugs usually came from informants who were also involved in crime. That might be true for "trash," as folks referred to the lower classes, but where did the federal lawyer get off thinking that he could apply the same rules to a man like Harmon—a lawyer and a prosecuting attorney, for God's sake? Of course drug dealers were out to get him. Harmon's stance on drugs was well known. He was the drug dealers' biggest enemy.

Brummett, the reporter and columnist, quickly put into print the questions that went buzzing around the state after Banks made his announcement: "Was Harmon persecuted by federal authorities, as he claims? Did the drug investigation of Harmon and his family constitute harassment? Do the federal authorities feel like the jerks that they appear to be?"

Meanwhile, Duffey had even more reason for concern as a result of Banks's decision. Her brother, David Keesee, appeared on a Little Rock radio show and reported that his sister, Jean, remained in as much danger as ever, since, as he put it, it was now apparent that "she and her informants are the only ones that haven't been silenced by Saline County officials."

Govar was crushed. "I can tell you," he told a reporter, "that there were several members of the federal grand jury who were willing to indict Mr. Harmon, but Mr. Banks made the decision that there was not enough evidence. The grand jury was never given the opportunity to indict Dan Harmon because Mr. Banks made the decision that there would be no federal felony indictment presented."[8] In the wake of that decision, Govar stepped down from his position as head of the federal Organized Crime Drug Enforcement Task Force in Arkansas. "I voluntarily resigned in protest of this action," he said. "I told Mr. Banks, 'You need to put somebody in this position that you have confidence in. I do not feel that you have confidence in me. Pick somebody you can trust.' " Exactly what Govar had feared at the investigation's outset had come to pass. He had pursued the investigation, and when it had gotten hot, he had been abandoned, "left twisting in the wind." "If I start it, let me finish it," he had asked when Banks had given him the assignment. Instead, Banks had finished it. His announcement clearing Harmon, followed by Govar's resignation from OCDETF, left federal agents who had been involved in the Saline County investigation demoralized. "They thought the whole thing was just a big cluster fuck," Govar said. "They got out there. They tried to do their best. They tried to do their jobs. I'm sure they were disappointed that, after all that, nothing came to fruition."

Govar found his situation bitterly ironic. He understood the climate in Saline County, and that it could be traced back at least to 1984 and the scandal surrounding Saline Memorial Hospital. At that time there had been testimony of cocaine and extortion, though no charges were brought. But Govar believed the combination of cocaine and extortion had become a way of life for some in the district.

Reflecting on the hospital grand jury, Govar noted, "It looked like extortion—blackmail is the short way to put it. And when that situation occurred, what did Circuit Judge John Cole do? He called a special grand jury and he put Dan Harmon in charge of it. No one was charged for drugs. No one was charged with prostitution. They said they never found the tapes. That thing ran for almost a year, and not squat came out of it.

"The next big scandal to hit the county was the deaths of Don Henry and Kevin Ives, in 1987. What happened? The same thing. They call a special grand jury. Harmon gets put in charge. It runs for almost a year. There's a lot of publicity and a tremendous expenditure of money. And what comes of it? Not squat. They concluded that the deaths were probably homicides. Well, the fact that someone has been murdered is usually the beginning point of an investigation, not the final point—not the place to stop. The important questions were: Who did it and why? And those questions were never answered."

What distressed Govar now was that, as a result of Banks's decision, his own federal grand jury probe had been as effectively neutered as Harmon's. A lot of work had gone into it, by Duffey's team and his own. It had taken a lot of time and a lot of money. And what had come of it? Not squat.

When Linda and Larry read the news that Harmon would not be indicted, they felt another shift in the earth. They had been struggling to stand for the past four years. After Kevin's death, they had tried to keep their balance through the shabbiness of the county investigation. They had held each other up through the jolts dealt them by state officials—particularly Fahmy Malak and the Arkansas State Police—as the investigation had been further confounded. Recently they had accepted the stabbing duplicity of Dan Harmon and the charade of his investigation. Finally, they had placed their hopes in Govar and the U.S. attorney's office. And now there, too, the bottom had fallen out.

Where do you go, they asked each other helplessly, if crimes as horrendous as murder are committed, but no one—not a county, state, or even federal official—is willing to confront them? Larry and Linda choked with outrage.

CLINTON RUNS FOR PRESIDENT

Almost all news in Arkansas during that summer of 1991 was eclipsed by the fevered anticipation of Governor Bill Clinton's announcement for president. He was expected to make it official by Labor Day. But as reporters from around the world began filing into Little Rock to do "backgrounders" on the unannounced candidate, a story that few of them could fully appreciate was unfolding in the local papers. Linda read the accounts with grim satisfaction.

For the first time since Dr. Malak had taken office, his defenders were backing away. In March Malak had embarrassed the medical examiner's office again in another murder case. This time a twenty-one-year-old man stood charged with murdering another man at a Hot Springs apartment building. The prosecutor had witnesses who were prepared to testify that the accused had shot the victim from a distance. Nothing in the autopsy report disputed that scenario, and the prosecutor built his case around it. But when Malak testified, he surprised everyone when he announced that the victim had been shot "point-blank." In a few words from Dr. Malak, the state's case had been destroyed. The case was dismissed. The defendant left the court a free man. The prosecutor, the police, and the victim's family all were fit to be tied.[9]

As usual, when the first sign of furor erupted over the episode, Jim Clark, director of the state's crime lab, stood up for the embattled examiner. But then Clark's position suddenly and unexpectedly changed. Shortly after he had publicly defended Malak's testimony in the Hot Springs case, Clark told Malak that he needed to find a new job. When reporters questioned Clark's sudden change in position, he insisted, "It was mainly a personal suggestion. I was under no pressure from the governor to get rid of him." But many reporters and government workers found that hard to believe. "The state has gone to the wall for Malak," a former state legislator said. "This looks like a complete about-face." As the months passed, the withdrawal of support for Malak became increasingly conspicuous. But Malak seemed oblivious. In late April, Malak told reporters that he had no intention of seeking new employment. So Clark made his new position clearer. "Somewhere down the line, enough is going to be enough."

"What in hell does he consider enough?" Linda asked a reporter seeking a comment on Clark's observation. "How many people will have to go through what we did? Does the victim have to be someone influential before it finally matters? We think it was 'enough' a long time ago."

Media reaction to the administration's about-face on Malak was unqualified in its approval. "Years late comes the welcome news that Dr. Fahmy Malak's twelve-year stint as state medical examiner may be drawing to an end," Max Brantley wrote in the *Arkansas Gazette.* "Clark's willingness to relate his conversation with Malak is significant. Clark is an appointee of Gov. Bill Clinton. Clinton has been a staunch supporter of Malak through the years. He has often brought the might of his office to the task of defending Malak. Powerful state Sen. Max Howell of Jacksonville has also been a Malak ally. Now, it would seem, they are willing to let him go."

Columnist Meredith Oakley, writing in the *Arkansas Democrat,* chimed in: "It seems too good to be true, and it is certainly years overdue." Citing Malak's "ignominious record," she bemoaned the fact that his tenure had lasted so long. "Having been in office for 10 of the past 12 years," Oakley wrote, "Clinton has had ample opportunity to sack Malak, and he has always had the ability to do so."

But even as applause for Malak's exit swelled, Clinton insisted that the decision to remove him rested, not with him, but with the newly revamped Crime Laboratory Board. In May, after Linda and members of VOMIT brought petition sheets with thousands of signatures to the governor's office, Clinton told a Memphis reporter, "Should I call the medical board or the Crime Lab Board and say, 'Get rid of this man; I've got four thousand signatures and a newspaper article, and never mind the merits'?" He added, "I am very sympathetic to Mrs. Ives, and my heart goes out to her. But I am still going to defer to the Crime Lab Board."

"If he's so sympathetic," Linda told Larry, "you'd think that just once when we begged for an appointment, he would have met with us."

As the furor around Dr. Malak intensified, the reclusive medical examiner submitted to a rare interview. He told a reporter, "If I had known the social structure of the state—they don't like to say somebody was using marijuana and hit by a train—I would not care," he said. "I would not do it. I would not keep it. I would not say a word. I would not lose anything if I said the cause was undetermined."

The article also noted that Clinton had gotten some bad press in his 1990 campaign for governor when his Republican opponent had promised that, if elected, he would fire Malak. Now, with a presidential campaign in the works, Clinton acknowledged for the first time that it was getting tougher for Malak to weather criticism. "We don't fire people for bad press," Clinton said. "But what I've told Clark is, if the credibility issue keeps coming up, maybe it's time we call it quits."[10]

Again reporters contacted Linda for her reaction. Noting that this was the first time in more than three years that Malak had spoken about his ruling in Kevin's and Don's deaths, Linda asked, "And what's the first thing he does? He admits he tells people what he thinks they want to hear."

Even Malak's supporters in the sheriffs association started to sniff the wind. In June the association's president conceded that Malak should resign. "I think with the publicity he has received in the last year or so," Sheriff Dick Wakefield said, "his credibility has been damaged. I'm not sure it might not be a good time for him to help himself and perhaps save Arkansas by possibly looking for some other employment."

By July, Malak was still medical examiner, but the Crime Laboratory Board announced that it would review his five most disputed cases. Topping the list was his ruling in the 1987 deaths of Don Henry and Kevin Ives. To Linda the news was too little, and its arrival far too late.

HARMON BEHIND BARS

By now, almost four years had passed since the boys' bodies were found, but despite the lapse of time, in the summer of 1991 the case was still in the news. It was still a political football. In a speech in July, Harmon reminded the Senior Democrats of Saline County of his first meeting with Larry Ives and Curtis Henry. "We were all forty-three years old and God had just blessed me then with what had been taken away from them—my only son." The prosecutor vowed to rededicate himself to finding the boys' killers and bringing them to justice. "I will not rest until this case is solved."

But if the four-year-old murder was to be solved, it would not be through any cooperation between Harmon and Sheriff Davis. After all, it was Davis's visit to Banks that had prompted the federal investigation. Minutes after Judge

Cole sentenced Govar's informant Woodrow May to prison, Harmon picked up a phone inside the sheriff's office and had Davis paged. The call, like all calls on the system, was recorded. When Davis answered, Harmon gloated, "Your buddy just got eighty years."

Davis: "Eighty years."

Harmon: "And I tell you what. He said he was going to escape, and if he escapes . . . "

Davis: "Uh-huh?"

Harmon: " . . . I'm going to come looking for you and I'm going to stomp your ass so hard you may never walk again."

Davis: "For what!"

Harmon: "If he escapes. You got that?"

Davis: "He's not going to escape."

Harmon: "All right."

Davis: "All right."

When Davis made the tapes public, Harmon was asked why he'd threatened the sheriff. "I didn't threaten him," he bragged. "I made him a promise."

Harmon had always gotten away with bullying. Few complained about it. Many seemed to like it. He wore his toughness like a medal. "When I was playing football in high school, I was 5 foot 6 and weighed 145 pounds," he told reporter Doug Thompson of the *Arkansas Democrat*, "and coach Tom Hardin had me convinced there wasn't anybody I couldn't take down." He recalled the legendary game against Hall High. "Our team was undefeated until the last 30 seconds," he reflected. "Our whole line didn't average 160 pounds. Shoot, the backfield outweighed the line. We shouldn't even have been in the same stadium as Hall High, as far as everybody else was concerned. But Tom Hardin convinced us we could do anything as long as we tried and worked hard." It had been a defining experience for Benton and for Harmon. After his grandmother, Harmon's coach had been the biggest influence on his life.

But a tougher scrimmage lay ahead. In mid-August 1991, a month after Banks cleared Harmon of accusations of felony public corruption, he held another press conference to announce that he was charging Harmon with four misdemeanors. According to Banks, Harmon had failed to file his income tax returns for four years—1985 through 1988. In two of those years, 1985 and 1988, Harmon had served without pay as a special prosecuting attorney for the grand juries investigating the hospital scandal and then the deaths on the tracks.

"It's a straight failure-to-file case," Banks announced. "There won't be any charges of income tax evasion based on the information we have now." Then he added, "I want to emphasize that these are misdemeanor tax counts. While, in my view, they are important and cannot be ignored, they are not related in law or fact to that previous investigation. They are related only by time and as an offshoot of that investigation." The charges would have no effect on Harmon's role as prosecutor. "Only a felony charge would prohibit him from serving," Banks explained. "This is like any other misdemeanor from the standpoint of impairing his ability to serve."

Reading the news, Linda thought about Jean Duffey, now frightened enough of Harmon to have gone into hiding somewhere away from her home and family. She thought of Teresa Harmon and of the reports the previous summer of Dan's attack on her, her boyfriend, and her neighbor. At the time it had come out that Harmon was driving with an expired driver's license and had failed to appear in court on two traffic violations within the past year. Now it turned out he had not filed his taxes—not in the year of the hospital grand jury, or the following year, or the year when Kevin and Don were killed, or the year of his so-called grand jury investigation into how they had died. Most of us ordinary citizens, Linda thought, do better than that. Yet despite his disregard for the law, Harmon would remain in his job as the district's prosecutor—a job that included the police powers inherent in his role as administrator of the district's undercover drug task force.

For his part, Harmon was combative. He announced that he would seek a jury trial on his misdemeanor tax charges. "If the federal fools would leave me alone, I'd send more people to jail accidentally than they could on purpose."

The boast backfired within a week. When Harmon pleaded innocent at his arraignment in federal court, U.S. Magistrate H. David Young told him that, to be released on his own recognizance, Harmon would have to submit to a drug screening, drug counseling, and any treatment "deemed necessary by the probation office." Harmon consulted briefly with his attorney, Robert A. Newcomb of Little Rock, who asked the judge that the drug screening be waived because Harmon stood charged with misdemeanors, not felonies, and there were no allegations of drug use in the charges. Young refused and insisted that the drug-screening requirement was his standard practice for everyone wishing to be released before trial. Harmon addressed the magistrate himself. "I am innocent," he said. "I will not submit to probation before I'm found guilty. I will not sign that." Young explained that the conditions were considered "pretrial supervision," not probation, but Harmon balked again. "I will not submit to any infringement of my constitutional rights before I'm found guilty."

Unable to persuade the judge, Newcomb asked him to impose the least restrictive conditions possible. Harmon was "a person who is in the public eye every day," and stringent supervision would not be necessary to ensure his appearance for trial. "I disagree with you," Young replied, "and those are the conditions I'm going to impose." If Harmon did not want to accept those conditions, he could await his trial in jail.

"Lock me up," Harmon told the judge. "I am not guilty. I will not submit to probation before I'm found guilty. I will cloak myself in the Constitution of the United States and I will not submit to any infringement of my liberty." Young ordered his bailiff to take Harmon into custody. Thus, on August 27, 1991, almost exactly four years after the boys' murders, U.S. marshals escorted Dan Harmon, in handcuffs and leg chains, out of the federal courthouse in Little Rock. "This is ridiculous," Harmon told reporters. Newcomb said that Harmon was not afraid to take the drug test. "It's the principle of the thing. He's been a law-abiding person all his life, and we're talking about the same conditions imposed on bank robbers."

Within an hour, Newcomb appealed to U.S. District Judge Henry Woods for Harmon's release. Harmon was willing to post a cash bond, the lawyer said, but he objected to having to submit to a drug screening on a misdemeanor tax charge. Woods refused. "I am not going to make an exception in this case," he said. "I would be accused of taking care of a public official when an ordinary guy named Joe would have to comply with these conditions." Noting that all Harmon had to do to get out of jail was to submit to the drug test, Woods added, "The man has the key to the lockup in his pocket."

The defiant prosecutor was taken to the jail in North Little Rock, the capital's sister city across the Arkansas River, to be held until his trial, which had been set for late October.[11] Harmon's decision to choose jail over a drug test set tongues wagging in his judicial district, which was now without its chief prosecutor. To the surprise of many, Sheriff Davis came to Harmon's support. He said he hoped to persuade the U.S. Marshals Service to let him hold Harmon in the Saline County jail because the district needed its prosecutor. "I'm going to do my best to get him down here in my jail," Davis announced, "so he can do his work." Garrett said that cases would still go to court. "We will continue to kick ass and take names. We will carry on with business just like we always do."

An odd alliance of defenders spoke out on Harmon's behalf. With near unanimity, columnists and civil rights advocates questioned the legality of the pretrial drug test that was being required of Harmon. The practice, which was not standard in most of the country's ninety-three federal judicial districts, had been adopted in Arkansas's eastern district in 1989, after the district participated in a federal pilot program that allowed pretrial drug testing of everyone charged with a federal crime.[12] An estimated five hundred to six hundred people had undergone pretrial drug testing in federal courts in the state's eastern district, but the issue had not become a cause célèbre until Harmon challenged it.

The local and national offices of the American Civil Liberties Union decried the drug-test requirement, explaining that the organization opposed any drug tests not based on probable cause and a warrant. Little Rock attorney John Wesley Hall, who had complained about Harmon's behavior in the past, now rose to his defense. "There has to be some individualized suspicion that the defendant might use drugs," Hall argued. "You can't do it to everybody to try to catch one or two."

Newspaper columnists were unanimous in their support of Harmon's stance. "I am not going to argue that Dan Harmon is the kind of person you would like to see your daughter bring home for dinner," wrote John R. Starr, the generally conservative managing editor of the *Arkansas Democrat.* "He is, if published accounts are to be believed, immature, irascible, and prone to violence. Too often, he seems to act more like a spoiled brat than a responsible public official. He is not, however, an animal. That is what federal authorities treated him like Tuesday when they threw him into irons and marched him off to jail. . . . " Starr argued that when Harmon declined to meet the magistrate's conditions to be released on his own recognizance, the judge should have permitted him to post a cash bond, as Harmon had offered to do. "Some might say Harmon should be willing to give up his rights to get out of jail," Starr wrote. "I do not agree. Principle looks good, even when it is being demonstrated by the likes of Dan Harmon."

In a rare instance of agreement, columnist John Brummett, the paper's more liberal voice, weighed in on the same side. "The conditions are common in federal cases, we were told, but I can't say that I blame Harmon, considering the string of indignities that the federal government has inflicted on him in recent months. . . . It makes you wonder what happens to a man's constitutional rights when the feds get the idea that he is a crook."

Under a headline that read HARMON SETS AN EXAMPLE, the rival *Arkansas Gazette* editorialized: "Whatever the outcome of Dan Harmon's income tax trial, he's earned respect for resisting judicial tyranny. . . . A defendant charged with misdemeanors that have nothing to do with drugs or violence shouldn't be denied release because he objects to drug screening. It's not fair to Dan Harmon and it's not fair to John Doe. These people have not been convicted of anything, and they are presumed innocent of the charges against them."

Columnist Max Brantley, also of the *Gazette,* chimed in. "It offends fair play to submit a man to drug testing while he stands innocent of any crime." But, he added, "Make no folk hero of Harmon, who brags about the butts he has kicked in a life of brawling. Remember instead that Harmon, the chief law officer of Saline County, failed to file income tax returns for four successive years. What kind of justice would you expect from a prosecutor who doesn't think the income tax law applies to him?"

While Harmon's attorney appealed to the Eighth Circuit Court of Appeals in St. Louis for his release, the prosecutor held a jailhouse press conference. He claimed that he was being held as a political prisoner. He compared himself to Soviet freedom fighters. He said he was being harassed because he had disturbed the "bloated egos" of federal bureaucrats. Wearing an orange jail jumpsuit, Harmon insisted that he would not resign.

"Just because everybody else wants to give up their constitutional rights damn well doesn't mean I have to," he said. "Three years ago I showed that members of assistant U.S. attorney Bob Govar's drug task force were trafficking drugs, and the members of his task force have given me hell ever since." In his unique position as both prosecutor and prisoner, he posed a hypothetical situation: What would federal authorities do if, as prosecutor, he had done to someone else what was now being done to him? "Say [federal Judge] Henry Woods was traveling through Benton and was charged with four traffic violations," Harmon said. "I tell him to come back down and enter a plea, then, after he was down there, tell him we won't let him go until he pees in a bottle. He'd be just as outraged as I am. What would they be writing about Saline County in the papers? Do you think I'd get away with it?"

While Harmon waited for the decision of the Eighth Circuit, he offered to submit to a urinalysis, but not one conducted by federal authorities, whom he said he did not trust. But the court stood firm. "I'm starting to smell bad," Harmon told a newspaper in a phone call from jail. "I'm ready to smell a little fresh air, and I'd love a package of Red Man chewing tobacco." In the meantime, he said, "The Gideons brought Bibles, which I've read twice, so my time hasn't been wasted."

At the end of August, Harmon received a two-hundred-dollar contribution toward his defense from Tommy Robinson, a former congressman from Arkansas and former sheriff from Pulaski County. Earlier in his career, Robinson had been the state employee who had hired Malak as medical examiner. "You are correct to take the stand that you have," Robinson wrote in a note accompanying the check. Verbal support came from Judge Cole's sister, state senator Charlie Cole Chaffin of Benton. Speaking at the dedication of a new public building in Saline County, Chaffin drew a rousing round of applause from what a reporter estimated was "the vast majority of the hundreds of people gathered" when she said, "I'm so sorry Dan Harmon cannot be with us tonight because he is defending his constitutional rights." The ACLU and the National Association of Criminal Defense Lawyers jointly filed a friend-of-the-court brief in Harmon's behalf with the federal court of appeals. "The war on drugs," the brief concluded, "should not be permitted to degenerate into a war on the Constitution."

On his twelfth day in jail, Harmon repeated the theme. "When you ask a policeman or a prosecutor why he can't get anything done about drugs," he told *Democrat* reporter Doug Thompson, "he'll probably tell you that the constitutional rights of defendants won't let him, rather than admit his own laziness or incompetence. He'll say there's nothing he can do until we surrender our rights, so he might as well stay in that coffee shop and munch his damn doughnut. There's a wave of hysteria over drugs in this country, and we're all going to police and asking them what to do. They're telling us the answer is to become a police state, and if we listen to them, we'll lose our liberty and the drug war both. Well, let me tell you something about the so-called war on drugs. Drugs can be fought and fought effectively without giving away our constitutional rights. The reason I ran for prosecutor is to prove that you can do the job within constitutional limits. The reason I'm in this jail is because I do not recognize that surrender of constitutional rights is necessary to fight drugs."

After Harmon had been in jail for eighteen days, the Eighth U.S. Circuit Court of Appeals agreed with him. A three-judge panel in St. Louis struck down the requirement that Harmon submit to a drug test in order to qualify for release. With his shirttail hanging out and sporting several days' growth of beard, Harmon was taken back to federal court, where he reluctantly accepted other terms of release and was freed. "I've spent eighteen days in jail on something anyone with a sixth-grade education could have figured out was illegal," he said as he left he courthouse. "The average citizens are lucky they don't have to deal with the federal government, because they don't know some of the things that are going on in this country."

Linda Ives watched Harmon's drama unfold with a new and grim awareness. Of course he had not wanted to submit to a drug test, she thought. That business about cloaking himself in the Constitution had been nothing more than a bid for time. Harmon was playing his supporters like he had played Larry and her. And he will betray them, as well, she thought. Watching the outpouring of support for Harmon, and his own brilliant challenge to the court, Linda consoled herself that she had not been entirely stupid for having believed in him for so long. Here were legal scholars, newspaper editors, and ordinary citizens in the district rallying to his defense. They were doing what she had done: accepting the picture of Harmon that he wanted to project and ignoring the parts of the picture that did not fit. He's got his bluff in on just about everyone, Linda thought. They applaud him for standing on principle when that is the one thing he has most brutally betrayed.

Linda did not feel the urge to confront Harmon. That day would come. Nothing would be served by forcing it. For now, she would be discreet. She could be calculating, too. And there might still be something to be learned in an occasional conversation with Harmon. She would smile, she told herself, if she ran into him on the street. Let him think that she was still as naive as she had been for the past three years—as naive as everyone else still seemed to be.

MALAK'S TIME TO GO

During the same week in August that Harmon was taken to jail in chains, Jim Clark, the director of the state crime laboratory, let it be known that Governor Clinton was trying to imagine the crime lab without Malak. It was hardly a decisive pronouncement, but political observers had no trouble recognizing its significance. As the *Arkansas Gazette* noted in a front-page article on September 1, Clinton's opponents in a presidential campaign would focus on "weak spots" in his Arkansas administration, and Fahmy Malak was definitely a blot. "The state medical examiner has been under fire for years for a number of controversial, sometimes curious rulings on causes of death," the paper observed. "An aggressive opponent might hit Clinton with questions about Malak's competence, but there are signs now that the governor is reviewing Malak's role."

Two days after that story appeared, Clinton publicly discussed for the first time the possibility that Malak was not right for the job. One night, as Clinton fielded questions about his anticipated presidential candidacy during a statewide television broadcast, a viewer called in to ask about Malak's future. "It would be better if he recognizes that he's worked hard and long for many years and that he probably should not keep trying to do this anymore," Clinton said. He added that not all of the criticism of Malak was valid but that "his credibility has been so strained and his effectiveness so exhausted that I question whether he can go on without causing more difficulties for the crime lab and therefore more anguish and doubt for the families of people who die." The next day Clinton told reporters, "It's just become clearer and clearer. It seems to me that whether he's right or wrong, instead of having a presumption of accuracy, there's almost a presumption of inaccuracy in the press, and when the presumption runs against you, your credibility becomes an issue in every criminal trial." Asked whether he thought Malak was doing a poor job, Clinton refused to answer.

Malak, who had been entrenched for the past twelve years, dug in deeper. The day after Clinton's televised suggestion that he should resign, Malak announced through his lawyer that he would not. But it was a position he could not hold. As Linda Ives and many others in the state had thought for years, once the governor wanted Malak gone, he would be gone. And he was. On September 10, 1991, with Clinton's national announcement of his candidacy looming, the *Arkansas Gazette* reported on page one: MALAK RELINQUISHES POST. Alongside a large, color photo of Malak, he was quoted: "I was never pressured by anyone. I did this of my own volition, my own choice." Beneath that was a quote from Linda Ives, Malak's best-known opponent: "I certainly think it's a political fix. That's all they did is make a deal with him."

Few in the state thought otherwise. The same article that announced Malak's resignation reported that he would immediately move into a new job, under the direction of Dr. Joycelyn Elders at the Arkansas Health Department. The job was created especially for him, in the department's communicable diseases division. His salary was to be seventy thousand dollars, forty-six thousand dollars less than he had earned as medical examiner. But even Malak's move was controversial. Peeved employees of the health department pointed out that the agency had been under a hiring freeze for months and that during that time, several important existing positions had been left unfilled.

The move seemed to satisfy no one. When Linda was asked what she thought about it, she replied, "We used to pay him to do autopsies. Now we're paying him not to do them." Harmon, who was still in jail when the news broke, said he was glad that Malak had been removed as medical examiner. But, he added, "The way they did it is disappointing and smells of chicken manure. What this does is save Fahmy Malak's state retirement." Richard Garrett commented, "It's strange that the state spent thirty thousand dollars on outside experts to try and prove Malak was right. Then, when it was no longer politically expedient to keep him, and the governor decides he needs to go, he's gone."

But Clinton denied it. Asked if Malak's sudden resignation was related to his national political ambitions, the governor testily replied, "Absolutely not." But accounts of Malak's last days in office were emerging, and it became evident that the governor's office had, in fact, been involved in removing him. Malak's lawyer, Larry Carpenter of Little Rock, told a Little Rock TV station that the governor's office had played a key role in negotiating Malak's resignation. "Some of those details had to be worked out . . . with the health department and the crime lab, and the governor's office helped in that. When the governor says it's time to move on," Carpenter observed, "it certainly creates a lot of pressure."

As details of the governor's role solidified, Clinton continued to downplay it. "We didn't make any deal," Clinton said. He added that it was "almost coincidental" that the health department job opened up just as Malak became available. Later that day, however, a Clinton spokesman confirmed that a member of the governor's legal staff had helped to bring Malak's lawyer and health department officials together.[13]

Dr. Joycelyn Elders announced that, far from having offered Malak a golden parachute, she was delighted to have won his talents for her agency. Proclaiming him "a true asset," she said, "I have a great need for several physicians. Dr. Malak is trained in clinical and anatomical pathology, as well as forensic pathology, and he has been a public health officer, so he has a lot of good things that we need in a person." Elders said that she had been looking for a physician to work in the department's expanding sexual diseases division, and Malak was willing to take the job for a salary that most doctors would have rejected. Describing Malak as a "very bright man," as well as a dedicated and competent physician, Elders added, "It's almost like the heavens opened up and dropped him on me."

For the second time in a month, the usually discordant voices in the state press were in harmony. Max Brantley, of the *Arkansas Gazette*, noted that Malak's resignation made sense because "Clinton didn't want the Malak controversy dogging his presidential campaign." Brantley wrote, Malak "wanted us to believe that two Saline County teenagers would choose a railroad track as a bed after smoking themselves into a pot-induced stupor. A stupor so deep, Malak said, that a blaring locomotive couldn't waken them. Other experts found other causes of death, questioned some of his tests, and doubted that marijuana could cause such a sleep. Experts aside, Malak's notion just didn't make sense. His resignation does." The *Gazette* editorial when Malak resigned announced: "For once, everybody agrees with Malak."

The *Arkansas Democrat,* whose opposition to Clinton's presidential bid was well known, took a harder look at the governor's role in Malak's sudden departure. "In a decade of bureaucratic embarrassments," *Democrat* columnist Meredith Oakley wrote, "Fahmy Malak was perhaps this administration's keenest embarrassment. He didn't know a marijuana high from a stab wound. Before his scalpel, suicides looked like accidents and murders looked like natural causes. He couldn't keep his testimony straight from one minute to the next. He treated evidence like a 4-year-old treats a jigsaw puzzle: When the pieces didn't fit, he tried to pound, push, and mold them into place. Malak's tenure in the state Crime Laboratory was one fiasco after another, undermining public confidence not only in the system but in the administration. Yet, by his refusal to confront the obvious, Clinton remained Malak's staunchest defender. For reasons known only to him, the governor chose to ignore the criticism of Malak's abilities as a forensic pathologist, criticism leveled by colleagues in the field as well as by citizens."

For the Ives family, the departure brought scant satisfaction. Malak had caused incalculable suffering. But Malak had not been fired. He had not even been censured. Even at the end, he had been able to negotiate with the governor's office for a soft landing in another state agency, a landing that would allow him to keep his state benefits. To Linda, the manner of Malak's departure added insult to injury.

On the heels of his resignation, the newly reconstituted Crime Laboratory

Board announced that, since Malak was now gone, it would not be reviewing his decisions in five controversial cases as it had announced. Since one of those was the case of the "train deaths," Linda began hearing again from reporters. There was a hard-edged weariness in her voice by now. "Two times I've been told to gather up all the information on my son's death and present it to a state board," she said. "Nothing happened the first time. Now nothing's going to happen the second time." Linda had given up hope that Kevin's and Don's deaths would be investigated fairly at the county level. And since U.S. Attorney Chuck Banks's decision not to bring indictments in the federal investigation of Saline County, she had lost hope for justice there. In light of state officials' long support of Malak and their reluctance to examine even his most controversial rulings, she told the reporters that no one at the state level wanted the deaths to get a fair investigation, either.

Dan Harmon was released from jail on Friday, September 13, 1991. The following Monday, Dr. Malak started his new state job at the Arkansas Health Department. At seven-thirty that morning, Linda Ives and eleven members of VOMIT gathered outside the health department building to protest. One woman carried a sign that read, CLINTON FOR PRESIDENT, MALAK FOR SURGEON GENERAL? The protesters explained to television reporters that they felt Governor Clinton had shielded Malak by slipping him into a new state job. "Our message to Bill Clinton is we're tired of having Fahmy Malak crammed down our throats," Linda told the reporters. "We want him to take Malak out of state government. We're just very angry that he has been allowed to sweep everything under the rug, to close that chapter in his life, when it's not a closed chapter to us at all."

When a reporter asked Elders about the protest, she supported Malak and criticized Linda Ives. "The people demonstrating, they know Dr. Malak did not kill their son," Elders said. "Secondly, there has been no data to suggest the results of his autopsy were wrong. I feel if these people would pursue as hard the possibilities of who gave their son marijuana or how they got the marijuana as diligently and as hard as they pursue Dr. Malak, I feel something constructive could come out of their efforts." When asked about the allegation that Malak had mixed up blood and tissue samples in a recent Hot Springs murder case, Elders, as head of the health department, answered, "That does not concern me at all."[14]

Three weeks after Malak's resignation, on October 3, 1991, Bill Clinton appeared before reporters from around the world and a throng of excited admirers to announce his candidacy for president. He made the announcement on a glorious fall day from a balcony at Arkansas's elegant Old State House, the original capitol. The lawn was filled with men, women, and children who had gathered for the historic announcement. Linda Ives was among them. Standing near the wrought-iron gate at the entrance to the grounds, she carried a sign that read NOW MALAK'S A NATIONAL SCANDAL. She knew her appearance would be fruitless. She did not expect to accomplish a thing.

"It was just a statement," she would later reflect, "just a stand. I think that with Malak out of the way, they thought it was all over with, it was smooth sailing, that everything had been handled. And to all intents and purposes, it had been. I just wanted Bill Clinton to know that, for some of us, nothing had been handled. Nothing was over with. I hoped that he would see me. I wanted him to know that I wasn't going away."

THIRTEEN

WIDENING THE CONTEXT

JANUARY 1992–MARCH 1994

Linda could not share the state's excitement over Clinton's race to the White House. But in July 1992, as Clinton campaigned in Ohio, an event there reopened the old wound of Kevin's death. The incident occurred at an outdoor rally in Utica. A woman standing near the front row held up a homemade sign that read GOV. CLINTON, I MUST TALK TO YOU. Newspapers identified the woman as Karen Conwell, the mother of a young woman who had been murdered in Arkansas while she, her fiancé, and a friend were sailing down the Mississippi River en route to the Virgin Islands. The couple's boat had broken down near Helena, Arkansas, and while twenty-six-year-old Susan Conwell's fiancé went for help, she and the couple's friend were assaulted and stabbed to death.

Police charged two Helena men with the slayings, but one trial had already ended in a hung jury. Karen Conwell wanted assurance from the Arkansas governor that the next trial would be fair. Linda was sympathetic. Every parent of a murdered child wants justice. What infuriated her was the way Clinton responded when Conwell held up her sign. As the Ohio woman gratefully told reporters, "He came over and kissed my hand. He said he'd do something about it."

THE FIVE-YEAR MARK

Linda did not begrudge the woman the Arkansas governor's attention. All she wished was that she and her family had been accorded the same consideration. Almost five years had passed since Kevin and Don had been murdered. During those five years, Linda and Larry's requests to meet with the governor had been denied. She had sought a hearing about Dr. Malak, and that request, too, had been ignored. She had appealed for help to every agency she could think of, and none had been willing to help. But now, all a woman in Ohio had to do was hold up a sign saying that she needed to talk to the governor and Clinton was there for her, kissing her hand and promising action.

The day after the Ohio event, Linda and other parents of murdered children called a press conference on the grounds of the crime lab. "I guess it was our bad luck that my child was killed in what was not a presidential campaign year," Linda said. "In the year after our son was killed, my husband and I tried to get an appointment with Governor Clinton, and after many, many, many attempts, we were allowed to meet with an aide. He told us, 'We can't get involved in one specific case because if we got involved in one, everybody would want intervention.' " Now that Clinton had promised intervention to the Ohio woman, Linda said, "I hope he does help her. I just was insulted that so many people here have been denied that kind of help from him."

The following month, Linda and Larry paid for a memorial ad in the *Benton Courier,* commemorating the fifth anniversary of Kevin's death. Linda marked the passage of time in a poem she wrote for the ad: "The room that you grew up in doesn't look the same; the friends who used to call you rarely mention your name . . . "

Time was passing. The newspaper war that for years had pitted the *Arkansas Gazette* against the *Arkansas Democrat* ended when the *Democrat* bought the *Gazette*. But still the train deaths haunted the news. At the close of 1991, the renamed *Arkansas Democrat-Gazette* ranked Clinton's presidential campaign as the state's top news story, and Malak's resignation among its top ten. Year-in-review stories credited the train-deaths case as having turned popular opinion against Dr. Malak.[1] They described Linda Ives, the once quiet housewife, as having led the opposition. Some intimated that it was she who had forced the governor's hand. But Linda harbored no illusions about the impetus for Malak's departure. When a reporter asked why she had never relented in her battle to remove him, Linda answered, "We only did this because we had no other choice, except believing the unbelievable. We were forced into it. And yet, the only reason Malak had to leave was because Clinton wanted this problem swept under the rug before he ran for president. That's what put him out, not us."

She told an interviewer as the year came to a close: "What I want is justice, and that's simple. Justice is when mistakes are admitted. Justice is when a murder, or even the possibility of a murder, is given more priority than protecting a fellow state employee's ego. Justice is when investigators look at new evidence in a death from whoever presents it, instead of grumbling because they feel they're being second-guessed." She continued, in what had become to reporters her familiar, unvarnished style, "There are some good people in law enforcement, but as a whole it attracts a type of person who likes to wear a gun and doesn't question authority, and who doesn't like it when his authority is questioned. That was our 'crime.' We questioned them, and that's a no-no, even when what they're saying obviously and provably clashes with common sense."

Linda renewed her visits to the Arkansas State Police. But she found no satisfaction there. When she checked on the status of the follow-up interviews that Colonel Goodwin had ordered, she found that several noted there was no need to requestion individuals who had previously been questioned by Harmon. She left state police headquarters in disgust. Only Jean Duffey might be as hurt and disillusioned as she. But Linda had been unable to locate Duffey. All that Linda knew was that the former deputy prosecutor was unreachable, hiding for her life from Harmon and the legal establishment of the county she once had served.

In fact, Duffey had not merely left the county but the state. After two months in the Lewellens' cabin, the loneliness and separation from her family had become too much. The cabin was comfortable enough, and Duff and the kids had visited on weekends. But the isolation and idleness were draining. In March 1991, at about the time Callaway was acquitted in Judge Cole's court, Jean and Duff agreed that she needed to be with her family, somewhere where she would be safe. But that could not be in Arkansas. Duff placed a phone call, and the next day Jean drove to Houston, to the home of her brother-in-law, where she would live for the next few weeks more restfully than she had in months.

Returning to Saline County had never been an option so long as Harmon remained prosecuting attorney, the warrant Cole issued remained in effect, and the forces that controlled the county's drug business remained more powerful than the forces of law. Within six months after Jean left Arkansas, Duff and the children joined her in Texas. Duff sold his business and their house. They settled near Houston, in the town of Pasadena, where Jean took a job teaching high school algebra and Duff taught eighth-grade science. Occasionally one of Jean's brothers in Arkansas would report that one law enforcement agency or another was trying to get in touch with her. But Duffey would not respond. She asked her brothers to relay word that Govar had all the information she had gathered and that the callers should contact him. Once, her brother reported that Linda Ives had called. But so far as Jean knew, Linda was still in Harmon's thrall. He might have put her up to making the call. In the case of Linda Ives especially, Duffey saw no point in responding.

Though her family had uprooted itself from family, friends, schools, and business and started over in Texas, Duffey was sick about what had happened in Arkansas. But if she had to do it again, she would. And she had no intention of turning the information about her sources over to Harmon.

In January 1992 the *Arkansas Times* published an article on the unsolved murders in Saline County. It was the first article to link the deaths of Kevin and Don to the deaths of McKaskle and six other Saline County men.[2] Larry Ives was quoted in the piece: "I think the main reason we didn't get a thorough investigation to start with is that there's a big drug ring operating in Saline County and a lot of people in the know are involved and they didn't want an investigation because they thought it would mess up their little party."

To Linda's surprise, as she read the article, Curtis Henry was quoted as saying that James Callaway had come by the Henrys' house frequently in the days after the murders to ask how the investigation was going. Marvelle Henry recalled that on one occasion "he came down to the house and he said, 'Curtis, I wonder if you didn't just beat up Don and put those boys on the tracks yourself.'

"Of course," Marvelle said, "we were still in shock at the time, and I couldn't believe he was saying that. But then James has always been kind of uncouth. When Curtis asked him why he would say a thing like that, James sort of brushed it off. He said something like, 'Oh, I've just been trying to figure out things that could have happened.' Of course, that was long before we even knew that they'd been beaten."

But the story that would dominate 1992 was Clinton's bid for the presidency. In May 1992, at the height of that effort, the *Los Angeles Times* ran an article about Clinton's relationship with Dr. Malak.[3] Titled "Clinton's Ties to Controversial Medical Examiner Questioned," the piece reported how, for several years, Clinton had refused to dismiss the doctor "whose controversial decrees [had] included a ruling that helped Clinton's mother, a nurse-anesthetist, avoid scrutiny in the death of a patient . . . " Quoting an Arkansas Democratic state legislator who said that Malak had been "sort of protected by the governor and the [state crime laboratory] board," the writers noted that Clinton had issued a written statement to the paper in response.

"There has never been any connection between my mother's professional experiences and actions I have taken or not taken as governor of Arkansas, and I resent any implications otherwise. In fact, it was several years after the incident that I became aware, through the media, that the ruling made by Dr. Malak in the case was controversial." Clinton then repeated what he had said many times in Arkansas: "I do not have the professional knowledge necessary to judge the competency of a forensic pathologist. For several years prior to Dr. Malak's resignation as medical examiner, I requested that reviews of his performance be conducted and that appropriate action be taken by the crime lab board and/or the Medical Examiner's Commission. It was their decision to retain him."

While Clinton forged ahead in the polls during that summer of '92 as "the comeback kid," the surreal quality that, to Linda, infected much of the news took an almost psychedelic turn. Dan Harmon and Sheriff Larry Davis, who had been at odds for months, were now reported to have taken a trip together from Saline County to Evansville, Indiana. Even stranger was that, according to newspaper reports, they had gone there to testify *in behalf* of an accused drug dealer. Kevin DePriest of Arkansas and five other men had been indicted six months earlier in a crackdown on what authorities described as a multi-million-dollar drug operation, with a network that allegedly stretched from California to Arkansas to the Midwest. According to federal prosecutors, the operation had imported more than seventy pounds of methamphetamine to the Evansville area between 1985 and 1990. DePriest's lawyer was David E. Smith of Benton, Arkansas, the same lawyer who had represented Harmon in part of his tax case. Smith subpoenaed Harmon and Davis to testify in DePriest's defense, even while he insisted that neither Harmon nor Davis had ever met his client.

The pair's testimony was noteworthy. Both Harmon and Davis stated under oath that, although they did not know DePriest, they did not believe he was a drug dealer. They said that DePriest's lifestyle and his work as a self-employed plumber were inconsistent with a person dealing drugs. When an Arkansas reporter asked John Thar, an assistant U.S. attorney who was prosecuting the case, whether Harmon and Davis were reluctant witnesses, Thar replied, "Not the way they testified."[4] Thar said it struck him as odd to see a county prosecutor and a sheriff travel hundreds of miles to testify in the defense of an accused drug dealer, a man they said they did not know. "I have not ever seen it, and I've been involved in drug prosecutions since 1982," Thar said. "I have seen law enforcement officers called by the defense to testify as to what they did in an investigation, but I've never seen either a sheriff or a prosecutor come in and testify that, not only have they never heard a particular person's name, but because they never heard it, they knew he was not a drug dealer. That was what was so surprising."

Thar said that Davis, who testified in uniform, was adamant when he said that he would know if DePriest were selling methamphetamine. Under cross-examination, Thar asked, "Are you saying that Kevin DePriest doesn't fit the mold of being a drug dealer, or are you saying he absolutely is not?" Davis replied, "I'm saying he is not a drug dealer. If he was, I would know."

Harmon testified that he found the charge against DePriest surprising. He had never heard DePriest's name mentioned as a drug dealer when he was a special prosecutor for the 1988 Saline County grand jury. He told the Indiana jury that about 450 drug users and dealers were interviewed during the course of that investigation. Later Harmon told Arkansas reporters, "I had him checked out and we didn't have any kind of information on him of any sort. I didn't hesitate to go testify."

Davis also stood by his story. "I don't feel like Mr. DePriest is involved at all," he told the *Arkansas Democrat-Gazette*. "Because if he's dealing that much methamphetamine, as many drug arrests and as many informants as I have, I would have heard his name."

Despite Harmon's and Davis's testimony, DePriest was convicted, largely on the strength of testimony from two men who admitted to being his accomplices. All three men were sentenced to prison. The following month, in Little Rock, Harmon was sentenced in federal court in Little Rock to one year of probation and thirty days' home detention on his misdemeanor tax conviction.

Linda kept up with the news, but these were hard times for her. Harmon's behavior suggested that he thought himself invincible, and indeed, he seemed to be. The case of Kevin and Don had come to a standstill and there was nothing she could do to push it forward. Blocked in her legal efforts, she turned her energies to Parents of Murdered Children. The Compassionate Friends had lived up to their name, but Linda was relieved to learn of the existence of a more specialized group, one that addressed the grief that she and Larry felt. After meeting with four other women who had had children murdered, Linda became one of the founding members of POMC's Central Arkansas chapter. She and Larry both became active, working, as the group's charter states, "to put pain into action to help others similarly bereaved."

For Linda, involvement in the organization meant extensive travel around the state, to cities where she would speak on behalf of victims' rights and sometimes organize a chapter of POMC. Winston Bryant, the Arkansas attorney general, also advocated victims' rights, and the two of them appeared at many of the same events. Occasionally they arranged to travel together to cities where they were scheduled on the same program. Linda got to know Bryant and liked him. Sometimes, riding in the car with Bryant and his aides, Linda would stare for a time out the window, lost in thoughts of Kevin and how her life had changed since he'd died. How odd, she thought. As a result of Kevin's murder, she had gotten almost chummy with the state's attorney general—and ended up a critic of the nation's new president.

A NEW SHERIFF, ANOTHER TRY

Bill Clinton was elected to the country's highest office in November 1992, and Harmon, despite his tax conviction, was reelected as prosecutor. To Linda,

Clinton's ability to brush off the Malak affair, combined with Harmon's gift for staying in office underscored her new belief that power worked for the powerful—and against people like herself. Harmon's hold on power in his judicial district was unquestioned.

But there had been a few complaints. The Arkansas Supreme Court's Committee on Professional Conduct had notified Harmon that he was being suspended from practicing law for a three-month period as a result of his misdemeanor conviction. Responding with typical belligerence, Harmon insisted he would continue as prosecutor while he appealed the committee's decision. He requested a public hearing, which automatically delayed the suspension.

Thus, on a Saturday morning in March 1993, while Clinton and his staff were settling into the White House, Harmon appeared before the Arkansas Supreme Court's Committee on Professional Conduct to argue that he did not deserve the suspension. He brought with him a lot of support. In addition to numerous affidavits, several prominent lawyers appeared in person to testify in Harmon's behalf. Chief among them was Arkansas Attorney General Winston Bryant, the state's attorney general. Judge Cole also spoke in Harmon's behalf, as did two other judges and several lawyers, as well as many public officials from the Seventh Judicial District.[5] Afterward, Harmon's lawyer for the proceeding told reporters that the affidavits and testimony had stressed much the same thing: that in spite of Harmon's recent conviction, he remained "trustworthy and honest, and his fitness as a lawyer was clearly proven." After listening to the parade of witnesses, the committee voted to rescind the suspension and, instead, to issue Harmon a reprimand.

The district's broad show of official support for Harmon galled Linda. But she had been amazed at Bryant's support, and she called him to tell him so. Privately she told Larry how she hated the way Harmon was still exploiting his role in their family's tragedy. As the *Benton Courier* reported, Harmon's lawyer at the suspension hearing had referred to "the community service Harmon gave when he served, free of charge, as a special deputy prosecutor for an eight-month county grand jury that investigated the deaths of two Bryant teenagers."

But the election in November 1992 had brought a glimmer of hope. Larry Davis had decided not to run again for sheriff. A good thing, as far as Linda was concerned. He had never reinvestigated the train-deaths case, and when Linda had gone to his office and demanded to see the case file, she had found it was a mess. They were glad to see Davis go.

Judy Pridgen, the new sheriff, had been an officer in the Benton Police Department. She was the first female sheriff to serve in Saline County, and even in 1992, she was one of the few female sheriffs in the nation. As soon as

Pridgen was sworn in, Linda and Larry went to see her. Again they pleaded for a sound investigation. Pridgen agreed and promised to assign one of her new deputies, John Brown, to the case. Linda was not pleased. Brown had experience in investigations, but he came from south Arkansas. He was new to Saline County. "How many times do we have to go through this?" she fumed at Pridgen. "Breaking in a new investigator, getting him familiar with the case? How many times do we have to start back at square one?"

Just give him a chance, Pridgen urged. And indeed, when Linda and Larry met Brown, they began to think that he might be just what their case needed.

Brown paid his first call on them at their home in February 1993. He told the couple that he had heard of their case even where he had lived before, in a small town near the Louisiana border. When Sheriff Pridgen gave him the assignment, he was anxious to tackle it and asked to see the case file. But it had been just a cardboard box that contained what he called "a jumble of nothing." Brown talked to Linda and Larry for a long time that night. As he was leaving, he told them that he would keep them apprised of what he was doing and of anything he learned. Closing the door as he left, Larry and Linda reminded each other that this was the first investigator for any agency who had ever told them that.

For the next several months, Brown proved as good as his word. By the summer of 1993, he had brought them two remarkable pieces of information. The first was that he had learned what the Benton police had known about low-flying aircraft that had been troubling neighbors near the tracks in the mid-1980s, around the time the boys were killed. Moreover, he reported that by the early 1990s, many police agencies, particularly in the South, had learned quite a bit about drug rings that relied, for the first stage of their distribution, on drops from low-flying airplanes.[6] The north edge of Saline County—rural but just minutes from Arkansas's biggest city—would have made an ideal site, particularly if some local law enforcement officers were included in the operation.

Brown's theory was the first that made sense to them. "I never did think it was possible they were bringing in drugs by train," Larry said. They did not know that Scott Lewellen had come to the same conclusion. Or of Lewellen's interviews with Curtis Henry when Curtis reported that he had watched aircraft make landings at night on property near the tracks. Or that Curtis had told Lewellen that he had taken that information to the state police. Or that Lewellen and Duffey had already presented the theory to U.S. Attorney Banks, while they spread aerial maps across his desk and implored him to explore the deaths of Kevin and Don as related to the interstate transportation of drugs. All Larry and Linda knew was that moving drugs by plane sounded more feasible than moving them by train ever had.

SHARLINE WILSON

The other startling news Brown delivered was that he had interviewed a woman by the name of Sharline Wilson. Linda and Larry did not know who she was. Wilson, a vivacious woman in her mid-thirties, had been one of Duffey's confidential informants. Wilson had told Duffey—and later, Govar's federal grand jury—that she had "dated" Harmon throughout most of the 1980s and that he was "a big cocaine user." Harmon had been married at the time, Wilson said, but she added, "He was good to me. He bought me clothes. He called me his little country bumpkin, but evidently I had an air of something he liked. . . . He took care of me."

Now charged by Harmon with possession of drugs with intent to deliver, Wilson awaited trial in the Hot Spring County Jail in Malvern, where the district confined its female prisoners. In May 1993 Detective Brown sought her out for an interview. What she told him was shocking.

Brown announced to Linda, "Well, I've cracked the case." He said he had a signed confession, a written statement from Wilson, in which she admitted that she had been at the tracks the night of the murders. Linda was floored.

The statement was written in Wilson's own hand. She wrote that she had accompanied Dan Harmon and Keith McKaskle to the tracks on the night the boys were killed. She said that two other men had been there, as well, and that all of the men were agitated because "there had been a small band of kids that had tried to already rip off the drop. There was supposed to be a drop of three to four pounds of coke and five pounds of weed. Several of the boys had got away, but they had caught two—Kevin Ives and Don Henry—one being deceased at that point." She claimed that McKaskle had killed the other.

Brown was exultant. But Larry and Linda were skeptical. Talking it over, they both agreed that even with Wilson's signature, the story of her involvement, as Larry put it, "was just another theory, another possibility." To him, there had been so many of them, "so many angles," as he told Linda, "that it's hard to get excited unless there's just some ironclad proof." Linda agreed.

As it turned out, the couple's wariness was wise. They had no way of knowing it at the time, but Wilson had already given police a number of statements about that night on the tracks, with important variations in each. But the statements also held some disturbing consistencies. Of particular interest to Linda, when she discovered them on a later visit to the Arkansas State Police, were statements that Wilson had made to state police investigators a full two years earlier, in May 1991—about the time that Harmon was beginning to prosecute the witnesses who had testified before Govar's grand jury. Wilson's two statements to the state police had been given less than two weeks before U.S. Attorney Banks had cleared Harmon of all wrongdoing in connection with Saline County public corruption. There was another reason why Wilson's statements stood out. They were unique among the hundreds of pages in the state police file because of the format used. Other interviews were recorded in the form of investigators' notes—brief, dictated paragraphs highlighting the interview's main points. The Wilson interviews, by contrast, were in the form of very specific, typewritten questions, prepared by the state police, which Wilson had answered in her own hand.

Q. Tell us about your drug dealings with Dan Harmon.

A. He kept me high a lot. On occasion I would make specific drops to different areas for him. I got high with him a lot.

Q. If you were going to conduct an investigation on Dan Harmon, how would you do it?

A. I would go to his ex-wife Rebecca. Then I would check his money background with a fine-tooth comb. Then I would go through drug task force records to see who all they let go on pay-offs, drugs, etc.

Q. List the five most important causes that would have led to Dan Harmon selling drugs and using drugs.

A. (1) His family history. (2) Letting people go that had enough money to buy him off. (3) Drugs confiscated but not actually being reported. (4) Letting big-time dealers off free. (5) Common knowledge of his use for years.

Q. Write in detail one drug deal you conducted with Dan Harmon.

A. Le Bistro Club, with Dan Harmon, Roger Clinton, and myself, known as the "Lady with the Snow," in 1978–79. One Saturday night we met in the parking lot and made an eight-ball exchange.

Q. Do you know who else deals drugs with Dan Harmon?

A. [Wilson listed four men.]

Q. While filling out this form, what were your emotions?

A. Scared but ready to come clean.

The second state police questionnaire, which Wilson filled out on the same day, dealt with the deaths of Don Henry and Kevin Ives.

Q. Tell us what you know about the circumstances that might have led to the deaths of Don Henry and Kevin Ives.

A. I feel that Dan Harmon has more knowledge of the two boys' deaths than he has ever told. In late summer, in August, I drove Harmon to Alexander to meet with, I assume, Keith McKaskle to make a pick-up. A couple of days later they have on TV the two boys' deaths, supposedly ran over by a train.

Q. Write in detail what happened on August 22, 1987, from when you got up till you went to bed that evening.

A. I got up, did some coke and crystal mixed—called high-balling—cleaned up the house, left, and went to find some more. Later on that afternoon Dan wanted to show me a house and we went in his car and looked at a house at Alexander. We came back to my house and I ate a sandwich and put on more makeup. Dan asked me to take a ride back out to Alexander with him and asked me to pull down, I think, the old quarry road and wait. I got high while waiting on him to come back and when he came back he said, "Let's go!" We left and went back to my house. He told me to take a shower. I asked him if anything was wrong and he said NO. I took my shower, went and laid down, and we made love, and he showered and left. I went to sleep.

Q. What would you say if it was later determined that you lied on this form?

A. No way.

Q. While filling out this form, what were your emotions?

A. Pissed off.

Q. Were you afraid while completing this form?

A. Yes, because Harmon doesn't like me.

THE CLINTON CHRONICLES

After Clinton's election as president, and Malak's removal from office, reporters' interest in the aging mystery of the murdered boys all but disappeared. For years, Linda had tried to focus media attention on the twisted circumstances of the case. She had hoped that public awareness would force answers. But now that hope was beginning to fade. On August 23, 1993, Linda and Larry went to the cemetery to quietly mark the sixth anniversary of Kevin's death. They could not have imagined that his almost forgotten murder case was about to attract renewed attention on a scale neither of them could have anticipated.

The transition began with a phone call. John Hillyer identified himself as a freelance video photographer, formerly with NBC, who was in town for a few days from Atlanta. He told Linda that he and an associate, a man named Pat Matrisciana of California, were working together on a project, talking to people in Arkansas who "had a problem with Bill Clinton." Hillyer had heard of the situation involving Dr. Malak, and of the battle Linda Ives had waged to see him removed. He asked if he and Matrisciana could come to the house and meet her and Larry.

Such a call was not surprising. Ever since Clinton announced his run for president, reporters from around the world had been in and out of Arkansas, and now that he was in office, the spotlight on Clinton—and his past—remained intense. Linda had spoken with any reporter who expressed an interest in the case.

It was a decision she had made long ago. At first she had hated the media, particularly when they intruded on the funerals. But when it became clear that no genuine investigation would be forthcoming, she, Larry, and the Henrys had had nowhere to turn for help. Since their first press conference, Linda had had a policy of speaking with any reporter who called. She had one overriding purpose: to find out what had happened to her son. For that to happen, she had to do whatever she could to see that his murder was not forgotten. The story had to be told—and retold, as often as necessary, until those behind the murders were exposed. In the past six years, Linda had told her story more times than she could count. The telling never varied, except where elements were added as they occurred or became known. Now here was this Hillyer fellow. It was clear he was no admirer of Clinton, but by then, neither was she. She told him how to get to her house.

The men who appeared at her door the next night looked like Mutt and Jeff. Hillyer was short and stocky, with close-cropped hair; Matrisciana, tall and thin, with well-cut silver hair. Both men were polite, warm, and personable, especially Matrisciana. Hillyer, however, seemed driven. As Linda later remarked to Larry, "His passion was so intense you could feel it." To Linda, Hillyer was almost obsessive, fueled by righteous fury over what he saw as Clinton's failings. Matrisciana did not seem to burn so hot, but his company, Jeremiah Films, reflected an equally conservative mission: producing videotapes on religious themes and warnings against such perceived dangers as New Age humanism and cults. During Clinton's campaign for president, Jeremiah Films had branched into a more political arena when it produced a video opposing equal rights for homosexuals. After the election, Hillyer had contacted Matrisciana, and the two had formed an informal partnership. Their intention was to inform as wide an audience as possible about all that, as Matrisciana put it, "wasn't right" about Clinton.[7] Meeting with Linda and

Larry, the two explained that they were talking to as many people as they could and gathering information, without a clear idea of what they were going to do with it.

Larry and Linda understood that what they were gathering would not be flattering to Clinton. But Linda told her story. The men stayed for two or three hours, discussing mainly the ordeal with Malak. Linda noticed that the men were particularly interested in the reports of airplanes in the vicinity of the tracks. They asked if Linda would be willing to repeat some of what they had discussed on tape, and she said she would. But after they left, she told Larry that she doubted anything would come of it.

A couple of days later, Hillyer called because he had left his schedule book at the Iveses' house. When he arrived to retrieve it, he was carrying his equipment. "John," Linda said, "what are you doing?"

"Well, I was going to get you on tape while I was here."

Linda was startled, but she acquiesced. While Hillyer carried in his lights, she went to her bedroom, combed her hair, and applied a little lipstick. She did not change out of her sweat pants but put on a respectable sweater. She instructed Hillyer, "Don't show anything below the waist."

He sat her in a rocking chair in front of the stone fireplace in the family room. Then he turned on his camera. Almost conversationally he asked questions about the topics they had discussed. Linda answered them, unrehearsed. She answered as she had for years. The session lasted about ninety minutes. As Hillyer packed up his gear to leave, Linda assumed that the session had been a test run, a warm-up for something more formal that might or might not come later.

A BOY WITH A STORY

As 1993 wore to a close, Linda did not know whether Detective Brown was close to solving the case, or whether a solution was more remote than ever because so much time had passed. But in December, just before the holidays, a young man named Mike called the house. He said that he and Kevin had been friends in high school. Mike explained that he now worked at a car dealership, and that the other day a young man had come in and talked as though he knew something about Kevin's and Don's deaths. Mike told Linda that the boy, who was about eighteen, appeared to be frightened yet compelled to talk. After listening to the boy, Mike said, "Look, if this is true, you need to be talking to Kevin's mother." Mike told Linda he was not sure the boy would talk to her, but he gave her a phone number where he thought the young man could be reached.

The boy seemed truly frightened when Linda called. He begged her not to tell anyone who he was or what he had to say. Doubting that he had much to offer—after all, he would have been twelve when the boys were killed—she nonetheless promised to protect his identity. He relaxed a little and told her that he knew of a box that contained evidence relating to the deaths of Kevin and Don because he had watched his aunt and a friend of hers bury it beside a barn. Linda listened impatiently. But then the boy startled her. He said that he and some other boys had been in the woods near the tracks that night—they said they had been hunting for a rumored marijuana patch—when they saw a group of men. The boy said he had seen "two kids walking up the tracks with a light" and that one of the men in the group, a man whom he claimed was Harmon, motioned to the boys with the light. According to the boy's account, the boys on the tracks approached the men and were casually talking to them when suddenly a shot rang out. The boy on the phone said that the two friends who were with him had taken off running at the sound of the gunshot. He collected his wits and took off after them.

Be careful, Linda thought. She asked the boy how, if he had been only twelve at the time, he thought he could even recognize Dan Harmon. "Because he used to be my mother's boyfriend," the teenager stated. "They dated off and on for years." He then named one of the two drug dealers with alleged ties to the case who had come through the investigation unquestioned, adding, "We lived in the same apartment complex as him."

Linda pleaded with the boy to talk to John Brown. Finally he agreed, but after Brown interviewed the boy, he told Linda that he found his story "pretty far-fetched." He said he would check out what parts of it he could. A few days later Brown called Linda again, a note of amazement in his voice. He said that while talking with an FBI agent about another matter, he had offhandedly mentioned the eighteen-year-old boy and related his peculiar story. To Brown's surprise, the agent had said, "Bring him in. Let's polygraph him."

Brown took the boy to Little Rock, where agents interviewed him and immediately placed him in protective custody. For the teenager, the situation was like being under arrest. He was constantly under guard. At that moment, Brown said, the FBI agents told him that they were entering the train-deaths case directly, something the agency had refused to do for all of the past six years. Brown was incredulous. He told Linda that when he asked the agents why they had taken such a sudden, dramatic turn, they replied that the teenager's story had "corroborated part of what we already knew."

Days later, agents polygraphed the boy. Brown told Linda that the teenager had passed the lie-detector test on all points except one. He'd said he did not know the name of the man who had helped his aunt bury the box. When asked again about that episode, the boy identified the man as Keith McKaskle, and that statement registered as truthful. But the boy did not want to remain in protective custody. According to Brown, he refused to cooperate further, and so did his mother. But the event changed the dynamics of the case. As a result, FBI agents in Little Rock told Brown that they were taking control of the investigation. They asked Brown to turn over all his records to them.

Linda never did find out any more about the reported box, whether it existed or not. She knew, however, that Brown was relieved that the FBI had entered the case. She was not. She was furious. So far as she could tell, every time the FBI had come near the case, the case got squelched. What else had those silly sound tests been about? And why, with all of the evidence on Saline County corruption that the FBI had developed, had the 1990 federal grand jury sputtered to its conclusion without issuing indictments? Linda thought Brown had produced the first real investigative work that had ever been done on the case. As she saw it, the only reason the FBI wanted to take over now was so they could shut down the case again.

DUFFEY VIEWS THE VIDEO

John Hillyer, the video photographer, had succeeded where others had failed. Through a relative of Duffey's he had tracked down her new telephone number in Texas. He told Duffey that he was interested in her experiences in Saline County and that he had already interviewed Linda Ives. Duffey talked to Hillyer, but she, too, sensed that he was obsessed. He asked her to let him interview her on tape. She declined. The next thing she knew, he was at her door. Hillyer reported the recent news that the FBI was now investigating the Henry-and-Ives deaths. Since the video would be reporting on the travesty in Saline County, Duffey decided to lend some limited support. She told Hillyer that she would read a short, prepared statement about her experience with the drug task force and that Hillyer could not use even that until she knew what its context would be and specifically gave her permission. Duffey felt the need to be cautious. Talented as Hillyer obviously was, it was clear that he hated Bill Clinton. The next day, when Hillyer returned and set up his camera, Duffey read a general statement: Arkansas had some dirty politics. There was a lot of official corruption. As the corruption surrounding Harmon had become evident, she had sought help from several sources, all without success. Hillyer left and Duffey forgot about him.

Months later, in March 1994, she received a package in the mail from an address in California. Opening it, she found a videotape entitled *Circle of Power.* This was the result of John Hillyer's work, his personal crusade against President Bill Clinton. When released nationally later in the year, as *The Clin-*

ton Chronicles, it was promoted widely on conservative talk radio and by fundamentalist Christian ministers, including Rev. Jerry Falwell. It sold tens of thousands of copies.[8] Reviled by Clinton supporters, it was largely scorned by the mainstream press, as editors who took the time to view it recoiled from its many extravagant and unsupported claims. At the time that Duffey received the tape, however, its remarkable public life had not yet begun. It was being distributed only to those involved in its making and to all the members of Congress. After dinner, Duffey and her husband slipped the tape into their VCR and sat together to watch.

Against a background of ominous music, the video announced that "most Americans are not aware of the extent of Bill Clinton's criminal background. . . . " The narrator alluded to Clinton's "absolute control over the political, legal, and judicial systems of Arkansas," and suggested that, as president, he was now assuming the same "absolute control" over those systems in the federal government. With Clinton's election, the narrator warned, "the hijacking of America was under way." Duffey had expected the tape to be critical of Clinton, but she had never expected this. She was shocked by the virulence of the diatribe.

The Duffeys watched as the video traced a winding course through Arkansas and its recent history. Much of what they heard was new to them, particularly allegations of cocaine being smuggled by airplanes into Mena, a small town in western Arkansas; of money-laundering through a state lending agency; and of cocaine use by friends of the governor and by the governor himself. They had no way of knowing how much—if any—of what they were hearing was true. But they listened with particular attention when the narrator moved on to matters relating to Saline County. "Clinton had integrated a number of corrupt cops, judges, and politicians into high-level positions to ensure the continued success of the drug-smuggling and money-laundering operation," the narrator intoned. "All was going well until a fateful night in the fall of 1987."

Linda Ives, whom Duffey had not seen since she walked out of the elevator with Dan Harmon, appeared on the screen. "There seems to be a small airstrip in the area," Linda said, looking into the camera. Duffey was amazed. "There have been sightings of airplanes flying very low, with lights off, in the area." Jean had no idea Linda had heard of the planes. The narrator then came back with an account of the ordeal the boys' families had suffered with Dr. Malak. So far as the Duffeys knew, this portion of the tale was accurate. Then there was Linda again, saying how, in trying to deal with Malak, she and Larry and the Henrys had "met with resistance from all fronts: local law enforcement, the state crime lab—everybody we turned to."

The video next explored the impact that one of Malak's rulings had on

Clinton's mother. Linda was shown saying, "I do know that there were some damages settled out of court and Virginia Kelley was forced into retirement." From there the story moved into the string of unsolved murders that had plagued Saline County since the deaths on the tracks. And it told of how Jean Duffey, the former head of the local drug task force, had been "forced into hiding." To Duffey's surprise, the tape Hillyer had shot of her reading her statement was aired during this sequence, though the narrator's voice-over obscured her words and a big black circle obscured her face. She was miffed at the liberties Hillyer had taken, though she had to concede that he had not significantly violated his promise.

Then it was back to Linda Ives. "There aren't any words in the English language that can describe how it makes you feel as a parent to see what our officials are capable of doing."

The tape then wound its way out from Saline County, back to the broader allegations of drug running and money laundering, and to a discussion of Clinton's promiscuity. As it concluded, again with warnings and ominous background music, Jean Duffey found herself puzzling over the significance of something that was not on the tape. In everything Linda Ives had said, she had never once mentioned Dan Harmon. Yet he had been her hero. For years Linda Ives had credited Harmon for his help on the case in every public statement she made. Yet there had been no mention of Harmon here.

Jean turned to her husband. "Duff, she knows. Linda Ives knows about Dan Harmon."

FOURTEEN

BARRY SEAL AND MENA

EARLY 1994

When the videotape arrived in Linda's mail, she could tell from the cover that it was an unabashed attack on Clinton. That came as no surprise. Hillyer and Matrisciana had never disguised their intent to gather stories unfavorable to the president. Linda knew they planned to distribute the tape to Congress. She regarded it as a form of artillery, a weapon to be used in a political battle—a campaign against the president that held little interest for her. As she carried the tape into the family room, she imagined that, whatever was on it, it could hardly have much effect on her life. Her battle was what it had always been: to find out who killed her son. Her focus was local. All Linda wondered, as she slipped the tape into the VCR, was how Matrisciana and Hillyer had managed to set her narrow complaint against Clinton, for his unwillingness to fire Malak, into their general attack. She clicked the remote and quickly found out.

UGLY ACCUSATIONS

The Clinton Chronicles wasted no time on niceties. As the narrator spoke of the "hijacking of America," a pronouncement flashed on the screen claiming that "all information presented in this program is documented and true." From that dire beginning, the tape spun an ugly, elaborate drama about cocaine, money, and murder, a drama in which Clinton, portrayed as power-driven and amoral, was the essential, central character. Linda watched with some surprise as a story she had never heard—and one she was not sure she believed—unfolded before her eyes.

It focused primarily on two things: an obscure state lending agency known as the Arkansas Development Finance Authority, or ADFA, which the video claimed had been a front for laundering drug money; and a small town in the mountains of western Arkansas called Mena, the airport of which was said to have been the command post of "one of the biggest drug-smuggling operations in the United States." According to the video, ADFA had served as "the center of Bill Clinton's political machine," while the drug running at Mena had all occurred under Clinton's "approving eye." The gist of the documentary was that during the 1980s, as much as $100 million a month in cocaine had been flown into the airport at Mena and that much of that money had been laundered through ADFA, a bonding agency Governor Clinton had created to help small businesses get started. Several Clinton associates were portrayed as playing central roles in this scheme. Webb Hubbell, one of Hillary Clinton's partners at the Rose Law Firm, was also reported to have ties to Mena through a business owned by his father-in-law, a business that, though already well established, had received the first loan arranged by ADFA.[1] Even Clinton's brother, Roger, was tied in to the seedy saga. Much of the video's story was told by Larry Nichols, a former ADFA employee who had unsuccessfully sued Clinton after being fired from his post. In a tone of righteous indignation, Nichols claimed, "Bill Clinton not only was part of a system that was laundering millions of cocaine dollars, but he was signing off on it."

The accusations were immense. They left Linda confounded. She could not fathom how her story was supposed to fit into this outlandish plot. But the narrative took a sadly familiar turn when she saw herself on the screen. What Linda heard herself saying was no different from what she had said for years. But now, as she watched the video, she saw her story cast as the dramatic, emotional centerpiece in a tale of almost preposterous intrigue. She did not know how to assess all that had come before—the allegations about money laundering at ADFA or Clinton's purported involvement in drug running at Mena—but she was relieved to find that the part relating her experiences was accurate.

From its account of the boys' murders, which the narrator explained were believed to have been drug related, the story widened back to Mena and to reports of how investigations into the drug smuggling there had repeatedly been "shut down." To explain why Larry Nichols was fired from ADFA in 1988, and why, as Nichols himself said in the video, "to this day, some people in Arkansas think I'm an evil person," the video turned to Jim Johnson, a former member of the Arkansas Supreme Court and a once prominent segregationist. Johnson offered his observation that Nichols's fall had been Clinton's doing. As Johnson explained the situation, "Clinton's spin doctors attacked the messenger rather than answer the charges Nichols had made." The video concluded by describing the president as "a draft-dodging womanizer" and "a pathological liar."

Linda was no fan of Bill Clinton's. But that was solely because of her Malak experience. She was put off by the video's obsession with Clinton's "womanizing." Sex was a nonissue to her. Compared to who killed her son and who covered it up, any affairs Clinton might have had were irrelevant. She could hardly believe the video's suggestion that the deaths of Kevin and Don were linked to a giant cocaine conspiracy that had somehow involved the governor. The filmmakers had essentially gotten her story right, but she had no background from which to assess the rest of the video's allegations. To her, they sounded preposterous.

In many respects, they were. After the public release of *The Clinton Chronicles* in mid-1994, Linda watched as the video was condemned, ridiculed, or totally dismissed by most of the nation's news outlets. Although its makers boasted that their contentions were "documented and true," several important factual errors were quickly identified. Yet that and the fact that it was shunned by the mainstream media did not seem to dampen interest in the tape. In fact, it seemed to fan viewer interest, particularly among conservatives. The videotape took on a life of its own. It became a star feature on right-wing talk-radio shows and spawned a thousand sermons on corruption and immorality. By October 1994, Pat Matrisciana, who had marketed the video for $19.95 through his Citizens for Honest Government, said that at least one hundred thousand copies had been sold.

Newspapers in Arkansas and elsewhere scorned *The Clinton Chronicles,* but in light of the national attention the video was attracting, they could not ignore it. The *Arkansas Democrat-Gazette,* a generally conservative newspaper which had refused to endorse Clinton for president, reviewed the production's inaccuracies. FANCIFUL VIDEO ATTACKS CLINTON, a headline read. TAPE'S KEY ACCUSATIONS HAVE FAMILIAR, IF HOLLOW, RING.

The article highlighted a number of errors:

- The video charged that all of Clinton's campaign records had been destroyed. In fact, all were intact and available at the office of the Arkansas secretary of state.

- The video claimed that Webb Hubbell, Hillary Clinton's law partner, had drafted the legislation that created ADFA and that a $2.85 million loan made to Hubbell's father-in-law, Seth Ward, had never been repaid. ADFA officials said that Hubbell had had no part in the agency's creation, and that the loan to his father-in-law—for $2.75 million—was repaid in 1989.[2]

- The video claimed that "ADFA was created to launder $100 million a month in drug money coming into Mena." But ADFA officials derided that contention, pointing out that if the agency had laundered that much money for even one year, the total would have come to $1.2 billion. In the agency's nine-year existence, officials said, it had granted only $1.7 billion in loans.

The list went on and on, weakening the production's credibility with every paragraph. As for the cocaine busts in the 1980s of Governor Clinton's half brother, Roger, and his bond-dealer friend, Dan Lasater, the *Democrat-Gazette* reminded its readers of what many already knew. The video claimed that Lasater had gone "to jail with Roger Clinton for less than eight months." The facts were that Roger was sentenced to two years in prison on cocaine charges in January 1985. He was released fifteen months later, in April 1986. Lasater was sent to prison in January 1987 and served less than a year in a federal penitentiary. After reading the *Democrat-Gazette*'s review, the kindest conclusion a reader could draw was that the "reporting" in *The Clinton Chronicles* had been sloppy from beginning to end. Harsher assessments were that the video was a scurrilous and slanderous attack.

As Linda watched the savaging of Matrisciana and Hillyer's videotape, she could only remind herself of what she personally knew to be true: that the part of the tape in which she figured had been accurate. For all the criticism the production received, no errors were reported in its account of events relating to Saline County. No part of her story was challenged in the press. It was hard for her to believe that Matrisciana and Hillyer had concocted their story about Mena and ADFA entirely out of thin air. Their allegations were outrageous, but Linda knew that outrageous things happened and that sometimes they touched the most ordinary of lives—lives like her own. If the video had gone too far in some respects, maybe its critics had gone too far in others, by dismissing it entirely.

Now that she had seen *The Clinton Chronicles*, a disturbing statement from years ago began knocking around her head. It was something Richard Garrett had said shortly after the shocking murder of Keith McKaskle. That would have been five years ago, in 1988. Linda went to her files to look it up. It had been on the program *Unsolved Mysteries*, when the host, Robert Stack, had asked Garrett for his own opinion about Kevin's and Don's deaths. "Saline County and the central Arkansas area are overrun at this time with drug trafficking," Garrett had said, "and it's drug trafficking at a high level that extends to other states and other counties." The statement had been perplexing.

It would be up to her, Linda decided, to satisfy herself as to which elements of the tape were true and which were not. If any part of the tape's premise was valid—if Kevin's and Don's deaths were in any way linked to a cocaine operation larger than she could have imagined—that was something she needed to know. Slowly, painstakingly, in the months that followed the video's release, Linda familiarized herself with a part of her state's recent history that she had largely ignored, preoccupied as she had been with the battles she had been waging since Kevin's death.

BACK TO 1982

Linda focused on the production's main theories. Was it possible that Kevin and Don had died over a load of cocaine that had been shipped from Central America to Mena, and then to a drop site at tracks near Alexander? And if that was true, could it be that Roger Clinton and Dan Lasater, both of whom had been convicted of distributing cocaine, had connections to that larger operation? She had long suspected that Steed, some Benton police, and perhaps some Saline or Pulaski county officials had been involved in the local drug business, but now, for the first time, she wondered if state officials were also involved. Was it possible that this little-known state agency, ADFA, had been used to launder cash? She knew that many people found the video's allegations offensive. But her story was offensive, too, and she knew that it was true. For the first time since Kevin and Don had died, Linda began to wonder if the key to understanding their deaths might lie, not in Saline County, but beyond.

Over the next several months Linda reconstructed for her own information, all that she had missed in the reporting during the 1980s and early 1990s about ADFA, about the trials of Roger Clinton and Dan Lasater, and about the airport at the little town of Mena. Instead of driving to Little Rock to read through the files at state police headquarters, she went to the public library and read back issues of the state's daily papers, beginning in the early 1980s. What she found was that the actual history disclosed a more intriguing picture than the coarsely drawn scenario presented in the *Chronicles*. It was a picture that, in the months ahead, would change dramatically her perception of what factors may have come to bear on the case of Kevin and Don.

Digging back into the newspaper files, Linda learned that the story, in effect, had begun in 1982, when Kevin and Don were only fifth graders. Virginia Kelley was fighting to save her career after the death of Susan Deer. Bill Clinton was staging his first big comeback after being defeated in 1980 for his second two-year term as governor. Whether anyone in Arkansas politics knew it at the time or not, that was also the year that a pilot named Adler Berriman Seal decided to move his business from Louisiana to Arkansas. Barry Seal's business was cocaine.

Seal flew out of Louisiana's lowlands into the hills of southern Arkansas, then west over Arkansas's Ouachita Mountains toward the Oklahoma border. He headed his plane toward Rich Mountain, the second highest point in Arkansas. Rising to an elevation of more than twenty-six hundred feet, Rich Mountain had snared more than a few pilots on flights between Dallas and St. Louis, but it posed no threat to Seal. A pilot since he was a teenager in Baton Rouge, he had gone to work for TWA at age thirty-three as one of the youngest pilots in airline history. When he'd discovered he could earn more money hauling cocaine for a Colombian cartel, Seal had established a large and illicit air-cargo enterprise. He flew many of the runs himself. After years of flying drugs out of the jungles of Central America and outrunning authorities in the United States, Rich Mountain was scarcely a hazard to Seal. He landed a few miles south of it, at a small airfield on the edge of Mena, a quiet city of fifty-two hundred that existed mostly on manufacturing.

For years Seal had headquartered his smuggling operation in Baton Rouge, but by 1982 the Louisiana State Police were breathing down his neck. A move was in order, and, for reasons that have never been explained, Seal decided he would be safer in Arkansas. He landed his plane at Mena's Intermountain Regional Airport, maneuvering it so deftly that workers at the airport were surprised, when the door of the cockpit opened, to see a fat man stepping out.

Police in Louisiana had become more familiar than they wanted to be with the Fat Man, as Seal, who weighed almost three hundred pounds, called himself. For six years Louisiana state police had been watching him fly in and out of Baton Rouge on what they believed were smuggling runs. But catching him with the goods had proven difficult. Seal was a smart and elusive quarry. On top of that, the investigators in Louisiana had learned that he had powerful connections in the federal government, connections that may have been the reason Seal had been able to avoid detection.

Jack Crittendon was a sergeant with the Louisiana State Police while Seal was still operating in the state. Crittendon later recalled how one day he and a lieutenant had called Seal on the phone and asked to talk with him at a Baton Rouge steak house.[3] "We were working close with the DEA in Baton Rouge," Crittendon said. "We were aware that they were going to arrest him soon on a quaaludes charge, so we went to him and we said, 'Look, we're in behind you.' We told him we'd like for him to turn around and cooperate with us and with the DEA and with the U.S. attorney in Baton Rouge.

"We were looking across the table at him. Now, the man had a mind for business. With his mind he could have been the head of a Fortune 500 company. It just so happened that his business was smuggling. We told him we wanted the cartel. He said he'd have to give it some thought. But mainly what he said, and what struck both of us as strange, was that he'd have to talk to his people. That's what he said: 'I'll have to talk to my people.' "

Crittendon and the lieutenant could not figure it out. "At that point Barry had more resources than the Louisiana State Police. He was the boss of his own operation. And he was going to have to talk to his people? We knew he wasn't going to the Ochoas, the leaders of his cartel in Colombia, and ask if they minded if he went ahead and informed on them. And we knew he wasn't going to talk it over with the people working for him. That would have destroyed the organization. So who were these people he was going to have to talk to?"

The two policemen could only conclude that Seal was referring "to somebody he was already working for." They had no idea who that was, but not long after that conversation, Seal called them back with his answer. He said he would not become an informant. At that point, Crittendon recalled, "we said, 'That's fine with us, but wherever you go, they're going to be after you.' And, in fact, it was shortly after that, he turned up in Mena, Arkansas."

Within weeks of that conversation, Seal began moving his fleet of airplanes and helicopters to Mena. Investigators never were able to ascertain exactly how many aircraft he controlled, but by early 1982 they knew that he had shifted his base of operations to Arkansas. They knew because, though Seal made it a point to work from pay phones, calls to his pager were being monitored. As a result of that intelligence, Seal's watchers in the Louisiana State Police contacted A. L. Hadaway, the sheriff of rural Polk County, Arkansas, and notified him that the smuggler was setting up his headquarters in a hangar at the Mena airport.

The FBI also contacted Sheriff Hadaway and asked him to monitor the smuggler's activities. For some time, the FBI, DEA, and other agencies had been tracking Seal's activities as part of an investigation into international cocaine smuggling, code-named "Coinroll." Hadaway checked on Seal as he could and made inquiries about Rich Mountain Aviation. Over the course of the next several months, he learned that Rich Mountain had installed "drop doors" in the bottom of several of Seal's planes. Such modifications are supposed to be reported to the FAA, because they weaken a plane's structure, but the alterations of Seal's planes were not reported. Seal also had nine aircraft rigged with sophisticated electronic equipment, at a cost of $750,000. The bill was paid in cash.[4] By the autumn of 1982, it was clear that Seal had completed his move to Mena.

Meanwhile, the IRS was watching him, too. The smuggler had been at Mena for less than a year when William C. Duncan, an investigator for the U.S. Treasury Department, received a call from Asa Hutchinson, the U.S. attorney for the Western Judicial District of Arkansas. Hutchinson invited the IRS agent to a meeting in his office in Fort Smith, a city north of Mena on

Arkansas's border with Oklahoma. With Hutchinson when Duncan arrived was a DEA agent by the name of Jim Stepp. Hutchinson and Stepp told Duncan that U.S. Customs officials had been watching Seal, and that, as part of a coordinated effort, they wanted Duncan to look for evidence of money laundering in the businesses and banks around Mena.

According to Duncan it was not long before he found sizable cash deposits, the hallmark of laundered money. The process was simple. Rich Mountain Aviation was obtaining cashier's checks in amounts just under ten thousand dollars at a variety of financial institutions in Mena and surrounding towns. The limited size of the deposits avoided the need to file a Currency Transaction Report, a form required by the IRS for amounts over ten thousand dollars. The requirement for CTRs, as they are called, was put into place specifically as a means of foiling attempts to launder large bundles of cash. Duncan reported to his superiors that in November 1982, the owner of Rich Mountain Aviation had taken a suitcase full of cash to an officer of one of Mena's banks. According to statements Duncan took from the tellers, the bank officer went down the teller line handing out stacks of bills, each totaling slightly less than ten thousand dollars, and got nearly seventy thousand dollars worth of cashier's checks in return. The checks were made out to a construction company in Houston, Texas, which then built a new hangar for Seal at the airport.[5]

While Duncan was building his case, the Arkansas State Police were developing an interest in Seal, too. Russell Welch, a state police investigator who lived in Mena, was assigned to keep an eye on the airport. Over time, Welch, a meticulous record keeper, familiarized himself with the array of aircraft that began appearing at the field. During the next several months, with the help of his counterparts in Louisiana, Welch began to understand the scale of the transportation system Seal had brought to Arkansas. Mena was only its hub. Seal himself would later testify that his empire included a Lear jet, as well as helicopters, surplus military cargo planes, and several single- and twin-engine planes. He also had at his disposal two ships with sophisticated navigational and communications equipment—one of which boasted a helipad—and numerous cars and vans. Seal claimed that he employed more than sixty people whose activities he coordinated through state-of-the-art electronics. His communications equipment featured ultrahigh-frequency radios with scramblers, pocket-sized encoders for telephones, and high-frequency satellite communications devices like those used on air force B-52s. For navigation his pilots had night-vision goggles and other devices, which Seal once described as being of the same range and quality as those used on nuclear submarines.[6] As Welch began to learn, this was no penny-ante operation.

By contrast, the investigators were working with little more than their skills and a pair of binoculars. Sheriff Hadaway was limited in how much time he could spend monitoring the activities of an international cocaine smuggler, but the case seemed in capable hands. Duncan, with the IRS, and Welch, with the Arkansas State Police, were pouring hundreds of hours into the effort, Welch checking phone records and the tail numbers of planes to track Seal the smuggler; and Duncan examining banking transactions to gather evidence of money laundering. The two learned a lot about Seal, but what they mostly learned was that he was no ordinary drug runner.

Seal had entered the army young and, according to several sources, worked for Special Forces. Out of the army in 1972, he joined Trans World Airlines. But in July of that year, while he was supposed to be on sick leave from TWA, he was arrested at a New Orleans airport as he prepared to take off for Cuba in a DC-3 laden with fourteen thousand pounds of C-4 plastic explosives. Awaiting the shipment in Cuba were opponents of President Fidel Castro who had been trained by the CIA. Seal was charged in federal court but later acquitted because of "government misconduct" in the case. A U.S. attorney familiar with the peculiar acquittal said that the federal reluctance to prosecute may have been an "indication" that the attempted flight to Cuba had been a government operation.[7]

The episode cost Seal his job with TWA. He then turned his talents to full-time smuggling, a career that paid well. As Seal himself would later testify, he entered the drug world because it was exciting—"so simple, so lucrative," as he put it—and because "the money involved was incredible." From the early 1970s until 1980, Seal's cargo was mainly marijuana. In 1980 he switched to the lighter, much more valuable cocaine. At that time cocaine brought into the United States sold for between twenty thousand dollars and fifty thousand dollars a pound. By his own account, Seal averaged about ten smuggling flights a year, over a period of ten years, carrying from six hundred to twelve hundred pounds of the drug each trip. Seal boasted that one of his planes had made eighty-five successful drug flights and that none of his flights had ever been intercepted by U.S. authorities.[8]

Seal was once apprehended in Honduras. He remained jailed there for seven months before he managed his release, reportedly by bribing a Honduran judge. According to Seal's account, it was after that experience, as he was leaving Honduras on a commercial airliner, that he found himself seated next to another drug trafficker, who would introduce him to the overlords of Colombia's powerful Medellín cartel. Seal later claimed that with his aviation and business skills, he became, in effect, the cartel's vice president for transportation.

He offered this explanation of how his operation worked. One of his planes would take off just after dark from somewhere near Baton Rouge. As it approached the U.S. border at the Gulf of Mexico, it would fly low to avoid radar. Once across the gulf, the pilot would traverse the Yucatán Peninsula and continue south, hugging the eastern coastline of Central America until he reached Colombia, where officials had already been bribed to ignore the violation of their airspace, with payments of up to twenty-five thousand dollars a flight. The plane would land at a jungle airstrip in north central Colombia. Cocaine would be loaded and the plane would be refueled. In less than an hour it would be back in the air, headed for the United States. This time, crossing the Gulf, the heavy plane would drop so low that its belly would almost skim the waves. As the aircraft neared the Louisiana coast, it would quickly ascend, trying to mimic the appearance on radar of a helicopter rising from an offshore oil rig. In case the ruse failed, Seal had spotters waiting on the ground, watching for the plane with binoculars to see if it had been followed. If all was clear—and it generally was—the pilot would fly to a prearranged drop zone and discharge the cargo by parachute. The crew of a helicopter stationed nearby would then move in for the pickup. The empty plane would return to its home base. The helicopter delivered the payload to other Seal employees who were waiting in vehicles. From there the cocaine would be taken by land to middlemen for repackaging and further distribution.

It looked to Welch and Duncan like Seal must have police on his payroll—and not just in Colombia. He was getting away with too much and he had been for too long. At the same time, they also knew that there were other investigators, like themselves, who wanted Seal brought to justice. It looked like a tug-of-war, but even as it was being played out, events were unfolding in Washington that would give Seal's protectors a hefty advantage.

SEAL GOES TO WASHINGTON

In the summer of 1982, at about the same time Seal was moving to Arkansas, CIA director William Casey set in motion a plan called "Black Eagle," a scheme based in the office of Vice President George Bush, to provide arms to Nicaragua's Contra rebels, the "freedom fighters" supported by President Reagan. The man in charge of Black Eagle was Donald Gregg, a former CIA officer who later would become Bush's chief of security. Welch and Duncan, like the rest of the country, knew nothing of Black Eagle or the role Barry Seal allegedly would play in it. In Arkansas, Duncan and Welch pursued their investigations, gleaning what they could about Seal's activities. Seal, unperturbed by the surveillance, moved into the new hangar at Rich Mountain Aviation.

The hangar was not the only new construction. At the end of 1982, the owner of Rich Mountain Aviation bought 109 acres of land farther back in the mountains, near the tiny town of Nella, where he began clearing for a two-thousand-foot airstrip. When Welch asked him what he was up to, Hampton said the strip was to be a private one. He said he was planning to build a house on the land someday and wanted to have the airstrip in first. After its construction, a state game warden reported that residents living around Nella had complained about the heavy air traffic at the strip. Nella was extremely isolated. In the mid-1980s, most houses did not have phone service and some lacked electricity.

Nor was that the only strange activity that followed Seal's arrival. At about the same time the new airstrip was built, Sheriff James Carmack of nearby Montgomery County reported receiving "numerous reports of people in camouflage, with weapons, practicing river crossings and that sort of thing." Carmack said a hunter had shown him a cache of six "military-type" weapons, including an M1 carbine and Mini-14 carbines, all painted in camouflage and hidden in a roadside culvert. Residents speculated that the armed men were members of paramilitary or survivalist groups. But Carmack, who had recently retired from the army, doubted that explanation because of reported descriptions of the soldiers' coloring. "If I had my pick," he told Welch and Duncan, "it was either Afghan soldiers training there or some of the Nicaraguan Contras."

Duncan and Welch were baffled. They focused on the drugs and the money. They had begun to suspect that they might be tangling with an operation out of their league. They knew from Louisiana that Seal had boasted of CIA connections, and they worried that, after working to develop their case, it might be pulled out from beneath them by some other branch of government. They raised the concern with Hutchinson, the U.S. attorney at Fort Smith, but he assured them that if Seal could be shown to have broken the law, he would be prosecuted like anyone else.

Reassured, the investigators told Hutchinson that they hoped to get indictments soon. What Welch needed to charge Seal with drug smuggling was evidence that Seal was not dropping all of his cargo over the pine forests of the South, but bringing some of it with him when he landed at Mena. The year after Seal arrived, that evidence began to accumulate. In March and April 1983, an informant at the airport reported the arrival of two loads of drugs. Soon after that, another informant reported that a man from Ohio who had done avionics work on some of Seal's planes had arrived at Mena carrying two duffel bags of cocaine. DEA agents were reporting similar intelligence. In a 1983 memo to the Arkansas State Police, one DEA agent noted, "Seal is believed to utilize the Mena airport for transferring cocaine smuggled into the United States." Another report that year noted that the New Orleans FBI had told the Arkansas FBI that around Thanksgiving, Seal would be in Mena "either to deliver cocaine or to pay for their last load."

While Welch and Duncan marveled at the range of Seal's activities, particularly in light of how many federal agents seemed to know about them, there were indications that the smuggler's luck was running out. In the spring of 1983 a federal grand jury in Fort Lauderdale, Florida, indicted Seal on charges of smuggling Quaaludes and laundering money, the charges the Louisiana police had been expecting. Seal posted bond of a quarter of a million dollars. Duncan and Welch continued to watch him. As far as they could tell, despite the pending charges and the multiple investigations, Seal remained free on bond and conducted business as usual throughout 1983.

SOME UNUSUAL CONNECTIONS

By 1994, when Linda began her research into Mena, all of this had been reported, though only in random spurts. There had been no cohesive structure, no organization to the story. No wonder it had been hard to absorb. It had drifted into public awareness pieces at a time, and even the newspapers that attempted to report its bits and pieces never seemed to know what to make of them. The idea that, in the midst of a national "war on drugs," a cocaine smuggler on the scale of Barry Seal might have been allowed to import cocaine into the United States unchecked—for years—first in Louisiana and then in Arkansas, was almost too much to believe. Yet as Linda read on and on, she found that no one had disputed the growing suspicion. To the contrary, as new evidence developed, it was constantly confirmed.

The discovery was an eerie one. Since Kevin and Don had died, Linda had come to see their murders at the center of what was becoming to her a widening disillusionment. From a point of simply trusting authorities, she had moved to mistrust of the local sheriff, then to mistrust of the medical examiner and the state police, and finally to mistrust of federal authorities, after U.S. Attorney Banks absolved Harmon and dismissed the allegations against him. At the same time, she had questioned herself at every step. Why would the sheriff . . . ? Why would Malak . . . ? Why would the state police or the U.S. attorney foil this investigation? But the fact was that they had. Now, as Linda read about Barry Seal, she felt the chill of a possible answer. Seal, the flagrant cocaine smuggler, ran his operation in Mena, Arkansas, but he had friends in Washington, D.C.

That Seal had some influential connections had become obvious as early as February 1984, after he was convicted at his trial in Fort Lauderdale and sentenced to ten years. Faced with prison for the first time in his life, Seal was suddenly willing to make the bargain he had rejected when it had been offered to him by the Louisiana State Police. He asked to become an informant in exchange for a suspended sentence. But federal prosecutors in Fort

Lauderdale were not interested. With his options narrowing, Seal called on what appeared to have been some old but substantial connections. According to his own later testimony, a month after his conviction in March 1984, Seal flew his Lear jet to Washington, D.C. There he met with two members of a drug task force headed by Vice President Bush. The meeting paid off for him. Someone put him in touch with DEA officials in Miami, and they, unlike the federal prosecutors at his trial, were willing to negotiate. Days later, Seal signed an agreement to cooperate with the U.S. government and to become an informant for the DEA's Group Seven in Miami. That same month, DEA and FBI agents had a meeting about Seal in Hot Springs, Arkansas. What they decided at that meeting has never been revealed.[9]

Welch and Duncan, who were monitoring Seal in Arkansas, were not told of the change in his status. Contrary to law enforcement courtesy and convention, the DEA sent no notification that Seal was now working as a federal informant. Meanwhile, Welch and Duncan noticed no change in his activities. He remained out of prison, flying into and out of Mena, his fleet and his operation intact.

The world would have been a different place, Linda thought, as she sat in the library rewinding spool after spool of microfilm, if the people of Arkansas had known what Barry Seal was up to at Mena—and how little was being done to stop him. For her, those years in the early 1980s had been a blur of happy activities. But cocaine had been in the news, and heavily so in Saline County. Now that she thought of it, cocaine had been at the heart of the Saline Memorial Hospital scandal. That had been in 1984—the same year that Seal flew to Washington to arrange his freedom with the vice president's drug task force.

THE HOSPITAL

Linda revisited the hospital scandal. The *Benton Courier* published its first reports of it in March 1984, when E. F. Black, the hospital's longtime administrator, abruptly resigned. Linda remembered that Black had been convicted of defrauding the hospital. Now she learned that there had been more.

Black and four other men had formed a partnership to buy and resell a piece of property that was under consideration as the site of a proposed hospital. Black's lake house had been used for parties where Black and his partners courted investors.[10] According to state police reports, the main entertainment at the parties had been prostitution and cocaine. On top of that, a state police investigation had found a hidden videotape camera in a closet, where it had been set up with a view of the bedroom.

Looking back, Linda now read how Harmon had handled the hospital case. Parts of it struck her as very familiar, especially Harmon's talk. Within days of his appointment as assistant special prosecutor, Harmon had stood in front of the courthouse telling reporters that the hospital investigation "just gets bigger and bigger." Evidence would be brought before a county grand jury, but with so much involved in the case, he said, it was "going to be hard to know where to stop."

It stopped in September 1984. After asking all the hospital's directors to resign, the grand jury indicted Black and six other defendants. Of the eighty-five charges filed against the defendants, five were for bribery; all the rest were for theft. Although the grand jury found that hospital funds had been used to pay prostitutes and "to buy cocaine for parties," no one was indicted for drugs or solicitation.

The outcome disgusted at least one grand juror who later complained that the six months she'd spent on it had been a waste of time. "Danny pretty much ran it all," juror Norma Gilland said. "We heard testimony about how they always had plenty of drugs, but we never found out where it came from because Danny didn't try. He didn't ask about the cocaine. He told us what charges could be brought, and against whom, and what class of charge they could be. Everybody wanted to throw the book at them, but Danny told us this was all we could do."[11]

As Linda looked back on that investigation, she had many questions. Like his train-deaths grand jury, Harmon's hospital grand jury had ended with more questions than answers. Who had supplied the cocaine at the parties? Why had no one been charged? Why had Harmon been appointed special prosecutor? Had the videotapes actually been destroyed? And was any of this connected to Mena?

At the very least, Linda reflected as she put away the papers, Saline County and Mena had one thing in common: certain crimes involving cocaine were for some reason not being prosecuted. Linda knew that she might never find the answers she was seeking. But by God, she would try. She turned her attention back to Mena and to Seal, whose international cocaine import business had continued uninterrupted throughout the hospital scandal.

SEAL'S DEALS

Although he could not have known it at the time, Seal was getting himself entangled in what would later be recognized as a scandal of incalculably larger proportions than any surrounding some little county hospital. To avoid prison, the smuggler had made a deal with U.S. authorities, and now they were demanding that he fulfill his part of that bargain. Flying, which in his career had always been risky, suddenly became hazardous. In 1984 the United States had two consuming interests in Central America: the region was supplying tons of cocaine, which U.S. politicians wanted stopped; and a civil war was raging in Nicaragua, pitting the Contra guerrillas, whom President Reagan supported as "freedom fighters," against the Sandinista government, which Reagan viewed as dangerously leftist.

In Barry Seal some U.S. officials saw a juncture of the two interests: drugs and ideology. Seal's access to the region for the former made him a pawn in the politics of the latter. His own covert interests were now melded to the covert interests of Washington.

In December 1981, at almost the same time that Seal decided to move to Arkansas, President Reagan authorized the CIA to undertake a program of support for the Contras. But Congress was divided on the wisdom of that decision. In 1984, as the Reagan administration was vainly seeking ways to increase funding for the Contras, it enacted the Boland amendments to limit covert activity in the region. One of the amendments specifically barred the CIA and the DIA, the Defense Intelligence Agency, as well as any "entity engaged in intelligence activities," from assisting the Contra rebels. Reagan and some of his advisors, including marine Lt. Col. Oliver North, of the National Security Council, hoped that if public opinion could be turned against the Sandinistas by showing them engaged in drug trafficking, the Boland amendments might be repealed. That was where Barry Seal—the new informant—came in.

On June 24, 1984, Seal flew his personal cargo plane, a military surplus Fairchild C-123 which he affectionately called the Fat Lady, to an air force base in Ohio where CIA personnel installed a hidden camera behind the bulkhead of the plane's cargo bay. He then flew to Nicaragua. "It's a large aircraft," he later testified. "It has a wingspan about the size of a C-5. You can drive a tank in it. It's camouflaged in color, a huge airplane." Although the camera reportedly malfunctioned, he returned to the United States and landed at Homestead Air Force Base near Miami, with a payload of cocaine and a set of blurry photographs. The photographs were supposed to be the real prize. Seal told his handlers that the photographs showed Pablo Escobar-Gaviria, a top-ranking member of the Medellín cartel, standing on the airstrip with Sandinista officials as cocaine was loaded into Seal's plane. The quality of the pictures was so poor, however, that Seal's statement was the only evidence linking the Sandinista official to the drugs.

Even so, within a month, the photos were leaked to the media as evidence of Sandinista complicity in the drug trade. On July 17 some of them appeared in the *Washington Times,* accompanied by an article quoting unnamed U.S. government sources as saying that highly placed Nicaraguan officials had "actively participated in the drug-smuggling operation." The attempt to portray the Sandinistas as drug lords was complete. But the ploy ultimately proved less than successful.[12] The Boland amendments were not repealed. For Seal, the trip's consequences were disastrous. He later told friends that the release of the photos, which he had not expected, put his life in jeopardy. They revealed to his drug contacts in Nicaragua his new relationship with the U.S. government.

THE ROGER CLINTON STORY

Arkansas's papers were not reporting much of this in 1984. One of the stories they were reporting, Linda realized as she read back in the files, was the indictment of Roger Clinton, the governor's younger half brother, for distributing cocaine. Roger Clinton lived in Hot Springs, and so it fell to Asa Hutchinson, the U.S. Attorney for the western district, to announce his federal indictment. The next day a distressed Governor Clinton read a brief prepared statement to the press. "My brother has apparently become involved with drugs, a curse which has reached epidemic proportions and has plagued the lives of millions of families in our nation, including many in our state." He left the microphone without taking questions. Col. Tommy Goodwin, the head of the state police, told reporters that when he notified the governor that Roger might be arrested, Clinton had instructed him to handle the case as any other.

But as Linda pieced together the story, she found what seemed to be anomalies. Travis Bunn, a Hot Springs undercover policeman, had tape-recorded evidence of Roger selling cocaine. Bunn believed that Roger was part of a larger operation and intended, in investigative parlance, to "nab him, roll him over, and go on up the line." But when an Arkansas State Police officer who was assigned to the Hot Springs area notified his superiors of the intended bust, state police officials took over the investigation.[13] Bunn said that when that happened, after almost a year of developing the case, he turned to another officer who had been investigating Roger Clinton and announced, "We've been screwed."

From that point on, the investigation of Roger Clinton became, in Bunn's words, "just a damage-control operation." After the state police turned the case over to federal authorities, Bunn was never called to testify before the federal grand jury that investigated the governor's brother, nor was he called to testify at Roger's trial, despite his familiarity with the case. Bunn, a former military intelligence officer and member of the military intelligence hall of fame, came away from the experience with contempt for the state police. "The only reason this case got as far as it did is that they knew I had Roger already," he said. "I had him before they ever got into it. And that was something they couldn't undo."

Roger Clinton served thirteen months of a two-year federal sentence. But the fallout from his arrest did not end there. Over the course of the next two years, following one of the most convoluted investigations in Arkansas history, the arrest of Roger Clinton for cocaine would be followed by the arrest, also for cocaine, of Roger Clinton's employer, Dan Lasater, a wealthy bond dealer and former horse breeder.

It was hard for Linda to sort out the story, though, over time, the investigation of Roger Clinton and Dan Lasater had provided some interesting insights into their relationship. Clearly Lasater had been Roger Clinton's friend. Once, after the younger Clinton had gotten into trouble for using cocaine, the bond dealer had offered him a chance to recover at an estate he owned in Florida. Another time, when Roger was desperate to pay off an eight-thousand-dollar cocaine debt, Lasater had loaned him the money. And Roger Clinton was not the only member of the family with ties to Lasater. The bond trader was one of Bill Clinton's largest financial supporters in his campaigns for governor. And Virginia Kelley, who leased a box next to his at Oaklawn, was also Lasater's friend.

While Bunn saw Roger Clinton's arrest as little more than "a damage-control operation," others took it as a sign that drug laws were being fairly enforced. Even as citizens felt sympathetic to the governor and his family for the painful situation, the arrest of someone so close to the state's highest official reassured many that no one was beyond the law. It was an impression that U.S. Attorney Asa Hutchinson reinforced. At a speech to a Lions Club meeting in the state's western district, Hutchinson said that he and other officials were working aggressively to change the state's image "as a haven for drug traffickers"—traffickers who he said were "sneaking drugs into Arkansas directly from Mexico, South America, and Florida." While he said most of the narcotics arriving in Arkansas were distributed out of state, Hutchinson also told the group that "a big portion" was being sold wholesale to dealers working in Arkansas. To Linda, the acknowledgement by a U.S. attorney in the mid-1980s that Arkansas was "a haven" for international drug traffickers echoed the remark Garrett had made after the killings began in Saline County. It now seemed to her that in the years leading up to Kevin's and Don's deaths, many law enforcement officials were aware that an international drug ring with a national distribution network was operating out of Arkansas—and that, as Hutchinson had noted, "a big portion" of its business was being conducted in the state.[14]

Talk was one thing, but arrests were another. Despite the U.S. attorney's tough-sounding speech about cracking down on traffickers, Barry Seal, who some investigators were beginning to think was the nation's biggest drug trafficker at the time, continued to operate with apparent impunity from an airport a few miles from Hutchinson's office. Seal knew that while some law enforcement authorities were out to get him, others were committed to making sure that he was never put on the spot. In November 1984, when a reporter in Louisiana told Seal that authorities there were planning to indict him, the pilot scoffed.

"If they indict me," Seal said, "it means that I go to court. It means that then I get to tell my side of the story. All of this and much, much more that you're now hearing from me will be put out in the public eye. The Justice Department is not going to tolerate this. There's no way they can indict me."

As it turned out, Seal was wrong—in part. Louisiana did indict him, but his case never went to trial. He pleaded guilty and worked out an agreement that let him stay out of prison.

Linda fumed. Why had no one—not in Florida, nor Louisiana, nor Arkansas—slammed this man into jail?

RUSSELL WELCH AND BILL DUNCAN

By 1985, Welch of the state police and Duncan of the IRS were wondering the same thing. After months of investigation they had taken their evidence against Seal to Hutchinson to be presented to a federal grand jury. The evidence included testimony from a variety of sources that Seal was, in Duncan's words, "doing some work for the United States government" in Central America and "smuggling on the return trips for himself"; that aircraft were being illegally modified for drug drops and having their identification numbers changed; and that more than a quarter million dollars in cash had been laundered through the banks in tiny Mena alone. Welch and Duncan supplied Hutchinson with a list of some twenty witnesses they wanted called, a list that included Barry Seal and people involved with Rich Mountain Aviation.

The two investigators had every reason to expect that Hutchinson would act on their recommendations. He always had in the past. But in this case, to their surprise, Hutchinson did not fully oblige. Instead, he subpoenaed only three of the twenty witnesses the investigators had recommended, and after the three testified, Duncan later reported, two emerged from the jury room furious. One of the witnesses, a secretary at Rich Mountain Aviation, had given Duncan sworn statements about money laundering at the company, transcripts of which Duncan had provided to Hutchinson. But when the woman left the jury room, she complained to Duncan that Hutchinson had asked her nothing about the crime. As Duncan later testified, "She basically said that she was allowed to give her name, address, position, and not much else." The other angry witness was a local banker who had conducted a search of his bank's records and, in Duncan's words, "provided a significant amount of evidence relating to the money-laundering operation." He, too, emerged from the jury room soon after having gone in, complaining "that he was not allowed to provide the evidence that he wanted to provide to the grand jury."

Duncan considered what was happening highly irregular. He later testified in a deposition that the grand jury foreman and other members of the panel had "specifically asked to hear the money-laundering evidence—specifically asked that I be subpoenaed—and they were not allowed to have me subpoenaed. She said the whole grand jury was frustrated." The frustration felt by the investigators and the grand jurors was compounded by the fact that now, not only Hutchinson, but a new U.S. attorney, also seemed to be going nowhere with the investigation. Hutchinson had resigned as U.S. attorney in October 1985 to make what turned out to be an unsuccessful bid for the U.S. Senate. He was replaced in the office by his assistant, J. Michael Fitzhugh.

Duncan testified at his deposition that the difficulties he and Welch had experienced under Hutchinson intensified under Fitzhugh. At one point Duncan stated in his deposition that the grand jury foreman "indicated that Mr. Fitzhugh explained to them that I was in Washington at the time and unavailable as a witness, which was not the truth." Duncan's superior at the IRS, his chief of criminal investigation, made several trips to Fort Smith to complain in person to the U.S. attorney, but the trips were to no avail. The witness statements gathered by Duncan and Welch were never presented to the grand jury, and no one was indicted. In 1991, as Duncan was being deposed about the U.S. attorneys' handling of the case, he was asked what conclusions he and his superior had drawn. He answered matter-of-factly. "There was a cover-up."

The officials taking Duncan's deposition were Arkansas attorney general Winston Bryant and Arkansas congressman Bill Alexander. They asked, "Are you stating now under oath that you believe that the investigation in and around the Mena airport of money laundering was covered up by the U.S. attorney in Arkansas?"

Duncan replied again, "It was covered up."

"I had a very good working relationship with all the assistant United States attorneys and with the U.S. Attorney's Office for the Western Judicial District—never any problems," he explained. "The office was open to me, and I visited with them every time I was in Fort Smith. And we couldn't understand why there was this different attitude. I had found Asa Hutchinson to be a very aggressive U.S. attorney in connection with my cases; then, all of a sudden, with respect to Mena, it was just like the information was going in, but nothing was happening over a long period of time. But just like with the twenty witnesses and the complaints, I didn't know what to make of that.

"Alarms were going off. And as soon as Mr. Fitzhugh got involved, he was more aggressive in not allowing the subpoenas and in interfering in the investigative process. He was reluctant to have the state police around, even though they were an integral part of the investigation. For instance, when the money-laundering specialist was up from Miami, Mr. Fitzhugh left Mr. Welch in the hall all day, until late in the afternoon, and refused to allow him to come in. We were astonished that we couldn't get subpoenas. We were astonished that Barry Seal was never brought to the grand jury, because he was on the subpoena list for a long time. And there were just a lot of investigative developments that made no sense to us."

Asked to elaborate, Duncan continued, "One of the most revealing things was that we had discussed specifically with Asa Hutchinson the rumors about National Security [Administration] involvement in the Mena operations. And Mr. Hutchinson told me personally that he had checked with a variety of law enforcement agencies and people in Miami, and that Barry Seal would be prosecuted for any crimes in Arkansas. So we were comfortable that there was not going to be National Security interference." Another "very strange thing," he said, was that "we were dealing with allegations of narcotics smuggling, massive amounts of money laundering. And it was my perception that the Drug Enforcement Administration would have been very actively involved at that stage, especially along with the Arkansas State Police. But DEA was conspicuously absent during most of that time. The FBI appeared on the scene intermittently. Usually when Russell and I were going to conduct some credible interviews, Tom Ross, from the Hot Springs FBI office, would suddenly appear on the scene. He would make some trips to Baton Rouge with us. U.S. Customs was conspicuously absent also. It was primarily just Russell Welch and myself."

Linda noted a pattern in what she was reading now that made her sick to her stomach. Just as Detective Bunn had been perplexed that he had not been called to testify before the federal grand jury investigating Roger Clinton, and Jean Duffey had found it strange that she had not been called to present her agents' findings before the federal grand jury investigating Saline County, here were Welch and Duncan reporting that they also had been troubled by the fact that they had not been called to testify before the federal grand jury on Mena. Until now, Duncan said in his 1991 deposition, "every grand jury case that was ever presented where I conducted the investigation, I was the law enforcement officer who summarized the evidence before the grand jury."

Duncan suspected that, despite Hutchinson's earlier assurances that the case would be pursued like any other, he and Welch were dealing with interference from a higher level than Hutchinson's office. One day not long after news of the grand jurors' frustrations had been leaked to the local media, the two investigators received what sounded like confirmation of their suspicion. Two Fort Smith men, an architect and a draftsman, called them to report that a friend of theirs, an assistant U.S. attorney in Hutchinson's office, had mentioned to them over coffee that orders had come from Miami to "shut down" the Mena investigations. It was secondhand information but interesting nonetheless. This was months before the investigators were to learn of Seal's deal with the DEA.

While Welch and Duncan were struggling to get Seal and his associates indicted, Seal's helicopters continued to operate from their hangars. But if the Justice Department was not reining in Seal, other forces were beginning to. On February 20, 1985, Emile Camp, Seal's chief pilot, was expected to fly in to Mena but never arrived. Officials at Rich Mountain Aviation reported Camp's Piper Seneca missing, prompting a two-day search. On February 23 Seal and his brother Ben, who had joined the search in two of their helicopters, found the wreck of Camp's plane on Fourche Mountain, ten miles north of Mena. Camp was dead inside. The National Transportation Safety Board blamed the crash on pilot error, and Freddy Hampton, the owner of Rich Mountain Aviation, commented that Camp thought he was a better pilot than he was. But others at the airport were skeptical. Many, including Sheriff Hadaway, considered Camp to be as proficient in the air as Seal. "He could find this airport at night and land without lights," Hadaway told a reporter. "I've seen him do it."[15]

The loss of Camp was a blow to Seal's organization. Soon there would be others. As part of his deal to become an informant, Seal was now appearing as a witness at trials all over the country, testifying on behalf of the federal government in cases against other smugglers. His testimony was often startling. In one trial he estimated that before becoming a DEA informant, his income from smuggling had been between $60 million and $100 million—and that it had not dropped off after he began cooperating with the DEA. In another, Seal stunned the courtroom by testifying that his gross income for the seventeen-month period from March 1984 to August 1985—the very time when Welch and Duncan were trying to bring evidence against him before the federal grand jury, and *after* his deal with federal prosecutors in Miami—had been three quarters of a million dollars. Questioned as to the source of that income, Seal testified that $575,000 of it, which the DEA had allowed him to keep, had come from a single cocaine shipment. Pressed further, he said that he was working for the CIA and the DEA, and that he had imported fifteen hundred pounds of cocaine since going to work for the DEA.[16]

For Seal, such inexplicable juxtapositions of cooperation and criminality were not new.[17] And they would continue. In October 1985, with his smuggling operation still going strong, Seal again flew to Washington, D.C., this time to appear as a guest before President Reagan's Commission on Organized Crime.[18] Seal's cooperation with federal authorities appeared to be paying off. His testimony helped bring federal indictments against eleven men, among them Pablo Escobar, Carlos Lehder, and Jorge Ochoa Vasques, who together were believed to control about 80 percent of all the cocaine emanating from Colombia. In addition, Seal's testimony in Las Vegas helped federal officials there convict nine men in a major narcotics smuggling and distribution ring. In December 1985 a federal judge in Florida reduced Seal's sentence to six months of probation.

But Seal's problems were far from over. As a result of testimony about his income, the IRS was after him for payment of some $29 million dollars the agency claimed he owed in back taxes. According to his former secretary, Seal was "highly tense and nervous" about the widening tax case. But he had other reasons to worry, as well.

While Seal's sentence had been reduced to a few months' probation, federal judge Frank Polozola of Baton Rouge had dictated certain conditions. The terms bothered Seal. Polozola had ordered Seal to spend each night of his probation at the local Salvation Army Community Treatment Center, checking in and out on a schedule. This was at a time when it was well known that the Medellín cartel had placed a $1 million bounty on Seal's life, the result of the Reagan administration's release of the clandestine CIA photos taken from the back of his plane. It was even known that two members of the cartel were in the courtroom when Judge Polozola issued the order, along with the added stipulation that Seal would be barred from carrying a firearm or employing a bodyguard who did. Seal felt, as he told a friend, set up like a clay pigeon.

That was the state of affairs for Seal shortly after Christmas 1985, when he agreed to meet with Welch and Duncan. The two drove to Baton Rouge where they interviewed him in a hotel. Duncan recalled the meeting as frank. "He basically admitted that he had been a smuggler," Duncan testified. "He said he had told the people at Rich Mountain Aviation that they were guilty of money laundering and should be prepared to plead guilty to it." Seal was subpoenaed to testify against his alleged associates in Arkansas on January 22, 1986, in federal court at Hot Springs. To the disappointment of Welch and Duncan, he did not appear. And soon after, it became clear that he never would.

Less than one month later, on February 19, 1986, six weeks after his meeting with Duncan and Welch and almost a year to the day after the crash that had killed his chief pilot, Emile Camp, Seal pulled his white Cadillac Fleetwood into the parking lot of the Salvation Army treatment center at the time he had been ordered to report. He stepped out into a hail of machine-gun fire. Seal died on the spot, almost instantly, from six .45-caliber bullets that ripped into his chest, neck, and head. At the time of his death, he was scheduled to be a key witness in the trial of Jorge Ochoa Vasques.

Upon news of Seal's death, a DEA spokesman sounded stunned. "There was a contract out on him and everyone knew it. He was to have been a crucial witness in the biggest case in DEA history."[19] Others, however, were not surprised. A longtime friend and a former smuggler from Louisiana, went so far as to say that Seal had been "set up" for the kill. He and others speculated that Seal had been positioned to be killed because he knew too much about illegal U.S. government operations. Whatever the case, Seal's flying days were over. Months after he was buried in a sky-blue casket, three Colombians, convicted of first-degree murder in his death, were sentenced to life in prison.

Funny, Linda thought. Seal's murderers seemed to be the only people connected to him ever to have gone to prison.

THE LOUISIANA ATTORNEY GENERAL COMPLAINS

Incredulity over the handling of Seal's probation was widespread, but nowhere better expressed than by William J. Guste, Jr., the Louisiana attorney general. Two weeks after Seal's murder, Guste wrote a searing letter to U.S. Attorney General Edwin Meese, in which he formally requested that the Justice Department "undertake a complete investigation with respect to the government's relationship to and handling of informant Adler B. 'Barry' Seal." Guste noted that Seal "was probably one of the biggest drug smugglers ever brought before a court in the history of our country. By his own admission, he had flown over 100 flights, each bringing in between 600 and 1,200 pounds of cocaine, and was never intercepted by a government agency. At a wholesale average of $50,000 a pound, he had smuggled between $3 billion and $5 billion of drugs into the United States. His smuggling brought dope to thousands whose lives have been adversely affected by it. He had brought enough cocaine into this country to give a 'high' to almost one hundred million users. And he earned between $60 million and $100 million by criminal activity."

Outraged, Guste continued: "I, for one, was shocked when I learned of his death. In October, as chairman of the Subcommittee on Narcotics and Drug Interdiction of the President's Commission on Organized Crime, I had presided over a seminar at which Barry Seal testified. His purpose there was to inform the commission and top United States officials of the methods and equipment used by drug smugglers.[20] I give this information to establish that he was a heinous criminal. At the same time, for his own purposes, he made himself an extremely valuable witness and informant in the country's fight against illegal drugs. He had cooperated with the government in testifying before federal grand juries, and was scheduled to be a key witness in the government's case against Jorge Ochoa Vasques."

Guste went on to suggest that Seal's murder called for "an in-depth but rapid investigation into a number of areas." Guste asked:

- "Why was such an important witness not given protection whether he wanted it or not? Barry Seal refused to go into the Federal Witness Protection Program. But he could have been imprisoned in some town in America under an assumed identity. Instead, he was given sentences in cases against him in Florida and in Louisiana that permitted him to live in a halfway house in Baton Rouge and required him to report daily to the Salvation Army there. Why did the government permit this after it was made aware of the fact that Ochoa investigators had been following Seal and that these investigators were actually in court at the time his sentence was announced? Prior to his death, Seal said that having to report to the Salvation Army every day at the same time made him a 'clay pigeon.' He virtually predicted his assassination.
- "After he was sentenced to 10 years, why was Seal given a reduction of sentence under Rule 35 in the Florida cases and set free prior to his completing his agreed upon task, which was to testify against the Jorge Ochoa cartel?
- "Despite the enormity of his crimes, he actually served three or four months in jail and a month in a halfway house. Why?
- "During the time that Seal was cooperating with the DEA and the Justice Department and acting as an informant, how was he supervised, regulated, and controlled? Was it done according to the DEA Agents' Manual for dealing with informants?
- "Was Seal allowed to travel extensively in the company of potential violators without surveillance?
- "Was Seal allowed to work in an undercover capacity in Arkansas and Louisiana without notification to Louisiana and Arkansas officials?
- "How were the contraband drugs he brought into the United States while cooperating with the DEA regulated and controlled?
- "Was Seal's drug smuggling organization allowed to remain intact during and after the time of his cooperation with the government? If so, why?
- "Was he permitted to keep hundreds of thousands of dollars which he made while working for the DEA by actually smuggling drugs into the United States? How was such money accounted for?

- "What effort was made under the RICO Statute to recover the profits and equipment Seal had acquired from illegal smuggling?
- "What was the nature of the cooperation between the state and federal law enforcement agencies in Louisiana and those in Florida? The transcript of the testimony in connection with the Rule 35 hearing before Judge Roettger in Florida has been held *in camera*. Now that Seal is dead, cannot this transcript be made public?

"All of these questions, and others that will undoubtedly develop, cry for investigation. And law enforcement agencies and the public have a right to know the answers. I trust this request will receive a positive response."

Eventually there was word from Washington relating to Seal, but it was not what Guste had sought.[21] Two weeks after the Louisiana attorney general wrote his letter to Meese, President Reagan went on television and again presented Seal's pictures as evidence that the Sandinista government was running drugs. "I know that every American parent concerned about the drug problem will be outraged to learn that top Nicaraguan government officials are deeply involved in drug trafficking," he declared in an appeal for Contra aid. "This picture, secretly taken at a military airfield outside Managua, shows Frederico Vaughan, a top aide to one of the nine commandants who rule Nicaragua, loading an aircraft with illegal narcotics bound for the U.S."[22]

But officials in Louisiana were not buying the federal sanctimony. A month after Reagan's televised speech, two Louisiana state police investigators wrote an angry letter of their own to the Drug Enforcement Administration. They blamed the agency for failing to protect Seal from the Medellín cartel and charged that the DEA had allowed Seal to pose as a drug smuggler undercover while continuing to operate his lucrative—and highly illegal—business as a real smuggler at the same time.

So much duplicity, Linda thought. How far does it extend? Could others in Arkansas also have received such elaborate concessions?

FIFTEEN

INCURIOUS IN ARKANSAS

STILL EARLY 1994

Reading about Seal, Linda was reminded that the darkness she had been fighting took on many guises. It had been operating in her state for years on a larger scale than she could have imagined. Few had recognized it. The story felt too familiar. If there were elements of the Seal investigation that made "no sense," as Duncan had said repeatedly, she had experienced investigations like that, as well. U.S. attorneys shutting down cases? She had encountered that. And pleading with authorities for explanations, as the Louisiana attorney general had done? She had spent seven years doing that. She had met with only heartbreaking indifference. Linda did not know if Seal's activities at Mena were related to Kevin's and Don's deaths. But they had three things in common: cocaine, Arkansas, and airplanes. Now she had a few questions of her own. Questions that Guste had not raised.

"NOTHING WE CAN TALK ABOUT"

Where was Bill Clinton in all this? Why, if one of the biggest cocaine traffickers in U.S. history had settled in *his* state, had the governor of Arkansas said nothing—especially after his own brother had gotten tangled up in what Clinton had called this "curse which has reached epidemic proportions"? After Seal's death, what had happened to all his money—and his airplanes and other equipment? And why had Meese and his Department of Justice never put a stop to Barry Seal?

Linda was surprised, as she went back over the record, at how much had come to light about Barry Seal and Mena. But critical questions, like Guste's, had not been answered. Why, she wondered, after Seal's death, had it taken an official from Louisiana to complain about the official treatment of Seal, while in Arkansas, where he had operated for the past four years, no state or federal official, other than Welch and Duncan, had uttered a peep?

In her mind she saw the same dark tarp that had been pulled over Kevin's and Don's bodies and pulled over corruption in Saline County, now covering Seal's operation. Crimes simply disappeared beneath it. Silence held the tarp in place—a silence built of secrecy and official denial. Linda had experienced that in Saline County, and now she could see how it had worked at Mena. Outright contradictions were a common occurrence. At the same time a DEA spokesman in New Orleans acknowledged that yes, federal officials had known that Seal used the Mena airport, Don Whitehead, the special agent in charge of the FBI's Little Rock office, told reporters that his Bureau had no reason to investigate the airport. In fact, records would later indicate that the FBI had kept a file on the Mena airport for years. Similarly, despite Duncan's efforts to bring indictments for money laundering in the Mena case, the public affairs officer for the IRS in Washington would announce, "The IRS has nothing open there that we can talk about."[1]

THE DAN LASATER STORY

The hands-off approach to Seal by federal agencies was especially perplexing since, at the same time that the Mena investigation seemed stalled, federal investigators in Arkansas were directing a significant amount of attention toward Dan Lasater, the bond dealer who had employed Roger Clinton. In October 1986, eight months after Seal's murder, Lasater was indicted for distributing cocaine at parties. From where she stood now, Linda thought the world in that year before Kevin's death looked upside down. The entire situation was crazy. While turning their backs on Seal and his massive cocaine operation, federal officials in Arkansas were—what? Focusing their investigative energies on a wealthy recreational user? Nothing about the two cases made sense. But Linda had learned long ago that when things did not make sense on the surface, it was only because the reasons—the parts of the puzzle that would make the picture snap together—were hidden.

On the day that Lasater appeared for sentencing on a plea of guilty to distributing cocaine, the judge made a point of describing how far the millionaire had fallen. Having started out poor in Arkansas, Lasater had worked at a McDonald's in Indiana as a teenager; started his own restaurant chain in his twenties; sold it at age twenty-nine for $1.7 million; sold his next venture, a string of steak houses, for $25 million; became one of the leading winners in the world of thoroughbred horse racing; and, when he'd gotten into the Little

Rock bond business, made another fortune there. By 1986 when he was indicted, Lasater had bought another restaurant, acquired condominiums in Hot Springs, and was entertaining the nation's rich and famous at his most spectacular purchase since the racehorses, the seventeen-thousand acre New Mexico ski resort known as Angel Fire.

Lasater maintained his office in Little Rock, Arkansas's political and financial center, but he considered Hot Springs his second home, with its racetrack, night life, and hustle. He moved through the city like a king, because when it came to the city's passion for horse racing, Lasater was a king. In the late 1970s, while Lasater's stable was setting national records, he had enjoyed unparalleled status at Oaklawn as the leading winner for seven straight years. A major celebrity at the Arkansas track, he rubbed shoulders with other celebrities, including the flamboyant Virginia Kelley, one of Oaklawn's most ardent fans. It was Kelley who introduced her son Roger to Lasater.[2]

After Lasater's indictment, Governor Bill Clinton acknowledged that Lasater had been a "political ally." A son and daughter of Clinton's campaign treasurer, whom Clinton had appointed to the state board that regulates horse racing, had both gone to work for Lasater's bond house in the months leading up to his indictment. Patsy Thomasson, Lasater's executive vice president, had been another close associate of Clinton. As a former chair of the powerful State Highway Commission, where she was the first woman to hold a seat, Thomasson was both a key player in state Democratic politics and Lasater's right-hand administrator. After the 1992 election, she went to Washington, where she was placed in charge of office administration at the Clinton White House.[3]

Clinton's political opponents questioned the connection between Lasater's bond house, Collins Locke & Lasater, and the Arkansas Development Finance Authority, or ADFA, the agency Clinton had started to help fund business start-ups. Critics pointed out that the young company had underwritten fourteen of the agency's bond issues entirely or in part, earning some $649 million from the transactions. Clinton argued that other bond houses had gotten comparable amounts of the agency's business, and that he was only interested in seeing it spread around. Still, it proved embarrassing for the governor when the news surfaced after Lasater's indictment that one of the bond issues his company had underwritten was for a new radio system for the Arkansas State Police—and that the deal had been struck while Lasater was being investigated by both the state police and the FBI.

In fact, that investigation had been rife with anomalies. Linda learned, going over the files, that on at least twenty occasions confidential informants had given police statements that alleged that Lasater used and distributed cocaine: at parties at Angel Fire, on his corporate jet, in his Little Rock office, and at friends' homes in Little Rock and Hot Springs. Yet, despite aborted money-laundering investigations at Angel Fire and at Lasater's bond business, and despite questions about the source of the "lavish" amounts of cocaine that showed up at his parties, the indictments handed down by the federal grand jury in October 1986 were remarkably narrow in scope. Lasater and nine other people, including Lasater's business partners, stood accused of "distributing" thousands of dollars worth of cocaine, but the U.S. attorneys stressed that the men had not actually sold it. Rather, the indictment said, they had distributed the drug freely at "social occasions" without receiving "monetary remuneration."

Reporters and others who were familiar with how much powder cocaine was being consumed socially in Little Rock were bewildered by the prosecution of Lasater and his cronies, especially when it was emphasized that the men had given the drug away and their supplier was never identified.

Lasater served six months in a federal penitentiary for distribution of cocaine.[4] Upon release, he cashed in one of the benefits of having been "a political ally" of the governor. In 1990, a week after Clinton's reelection as the state's chief executive, Clinton granted Lasater a highly unusual partial pardon, restoring his right to bear arms and thus to continue hunting in the state. The pardon went largely unnoticed by the state's news media.

On the surface, it again appeared that a prominent Arkansan had been punished for breaking the law. But among law enforcement officers, several questions about the case lingered. The pardon was one.

Another subject of speculation that raised eyebrows about Lasater was a series of trades that was executed by Lasater's bond business on behalf of a Kentucky man who denied knowledge of how millions of dollars in trades had turned up in his account during 1985 and 1986. It was unclear what these trades represented since the confirmation slips reported only transactions conducted on paper, and these were apparently electronic. Nonetheless, investigators noted with interest that the voluminous activity in the account ended abruptly in February 1986, the month Barry Seal was killed.

There were other disturbing aspects of the Lasater investigation. The fact that Lasater's company had underwritten the bonds for the state police radio system at a time when he and his partners were under investigation by that agency was ironic enough. But it also turned out that Lasater had been conducting business with Mike Mahone, the officer who was assigned to investigate his finances.

As Linda read, she shook her head in outrage. Although Lasater's connection with cocaine was under federal investigation, both in Arkansas and at his Angel Fire resort in New Mexico, several police officials complained that his finances had barely been examined. Only later did the public learn, in one brief article that ran almost as a footnote to the Lasater prosecution, that

Mahone was himself under investigation by both the FBI and the state police internal affairs unit for alleged obstruction of justice.[5]

Lasater's own unsworn statement about Investigator Mahone, in his plea bargain with the U.S. attorney, was never made public. But when a source who knew of Linda's interest sent her a copy of the FBI interview, she found its allegations maddening.[6] Lasater alleged that he had flown Mahone to Angel Fire as his guest, that he had helped Mahone sell his house, and that he had arranged for Mahone to receive a twenty-five-thousand-dollar loan. In turn, Lasater claimed that Mahone had shown him reports and state police documents relating to the investigation. He said Mahone also had offered him advice on how to "protect" himself from further disclosures.

Details of the Mahone investigation were kept quiet and he was never charged with a crime. However, immediately after Lasater's indictment, Col. Tommy Goodwin placed Mahone on administrative leave, where he remained for two years on full salary, until the state police commission quietly reinstated him. At that point Mahone resigned. With no official finding of wrongdoing, he retained his full state police retirement benefits.[7]

Linda thought back to her first meeting with Colonel Goodwin. Kevin and Don were killed in August of '87, ten months after Lasater's indictment. She had met Goodwin in '88. That was during the two-year period when Goodwin was allowing Mahone to remain on administrative leave, not working but drawing his state police salary. For Linda, the question was obvious: Had police assisted the subjects of other investigations—perhaps the suspects in the deaths of Kevin and Don—as Lasater claimed Mahone had assisted him?

Her distress intensified as she read on. Another remarkable allegation by Lasater when questioned by the FBI was his claim that at the height of the state and federal investigations into his own drug use and financial affairs, he had invited several of his law enforcement friends to fly on his private planes, first to a World Series game in St. Louis, and later to a University of Arkansas football game in Jackson, Mississippi. Among the guests on both flights were a state representative, an administrative assistant to Colonel Goodwin, and three narcotics investigators from the Pulaski County Sheriff's Office.

THE CIA AT MENA

Three months before Lasater's indictment, in July of 1986, a sheriff in a west Arkansas county near Mena said that "a very respectable" citizen had reported seeing soldiers—about twenty or thirty of them—wading across the Ouachita River. The man said he had spotted the soldiers in the vicinity of Nella, the remote mountain town where Freddie Hampton had installed his mysterious dirt airstrip. It was hard to tell what was going on. Seal was dead, but the FBI now admitted that it was conducting "an ongoing cocaine trafficking investigation" in the area. Meanwhile, George Proctor, the current U.S. attorney in Little Rock, praised the level of coordination between law enforcement agencies in the Lasater investigation. To Welch and Duncan—and to Linda as she read it—Proctor's statement was laughable.

By now, Welch and Duncan were thoroughly stymied. It looked as though the mystery of what Seal had begun at Mena—and what seemed to be continuing after his death—would never be exposed. But at the moment when the mystery looked most intractable, a soldier in the jungles of Nicaragua aimed his rifle and shot a piece of the puzzle out of the sky. The shot echoed through the halls of Washington and reverberated through the hills around Mena.

On October 6, 1986, less than three weeks before Lasater's indictment and seven months after Seal's assassination, a Sandinista gunner shot down the Fat Lady, the C-123 that had been Seal's personal aircraft. Killed in the crash were the pilot, his copilot (an Air Force Academy graduate from Arkansas), and a Nicaraguan radio operator. Another member of the crew, Eugene Hasenfus, the forty-five-year-old cargo officer, parachuted to safety. When taken prisoner by the Sandinistas, Hasenfus, a former marine, reported that he was working under contract for the CIA and that the plane had been carrying ten thousand pounds of ammunition, uniforms, and medicine for the Contras. Telephone records taken from the plane showed frequent calls to CIA safe houses in El Salvador, supporting Hasenfus's claim.

Hasenfus told his captors that he worked for "Max Gomez," who was the "CIA's overseer." In the months that followed, Max Gomez was revealed to be the alias of a retired CIA officer whom Oliver North had recruited to coordinate the Contra resupply operation. His real name was Felix Rodriguez, and he was a friend and former colleague of Donald Gregg, the national security advisor to Vice President George Bush. Documents found in the Fat Lady's wreckage identified the plane as now owned by Corporate Air Services, a Pennsylvania company whose proprietor—once the veil of several dummy corporations had been lifted—was Richard Secord, a retired air force major general, former deputy assistant secretary of defense, and current partner of Albert Hakim, an Iranian-born businessman who was helping to finance North's resupply effort. If Seal had had CIA connections, it now appeared that his plane had continued them. And if Seal had had uncommon access to Vice President George Bush, a former head of the CIA, it appeared that the smuggler's strategic position as head of a covert air transportation system crucial to the Contra resupply effort might have been part of the reason why.

When news of the shoot-down reached Washington, CIA and State

Department officials falsely denied knowledge of Gomez and of the Contra resupply operation. The following month, however, a Lebanese periodical, *Al Shiraa,* published an article that revealed that the United States had sold arms to Iran—and the Iran-Contra scandal was off and running. As a result of the Fat Lady's crash, elements of North's clandestine Contra resupply operation came to light, along with information about Vice President Bush's involvement in it. As an article in the *Washington Post Magazine* later said of Bush, "He knew—in fact, his was the first office in the White House to learn—a former CIA op named Eugene Hasenfus was shot down while flying aid to the Contras. He knew Hasenfus was not the only demi-spook running around on this secret, air-borne, aid-the-Contras operation."[8]

INVESTIGATIONS THWARTED

In 1994, as Linda educated herself on these events, she noticed that all of the reports about the suspicious activities at Mena had been written after the downing of Seal's plane. None of his activities, apparently, had been known to reporters while he was alive. Since the grand jury was conducted in secret and no indictments were ever brought, what few reports had circulated about strange activities at Mena's airport had been impossible to confirm. It was easier for the state's major media to dismiss the reports for what they were: unsubstantiated rumors. One group was more aggressive than the reporters had been, however. A cluster of students at the University of Arkansas at Fayetteville, which lies north of Fort Smith and Mena, led by a handful of Vietnam veterans, became known as the Arkansas Committee, and over the course of the next few years, it would be responsible for bringing to light much of the dark history surrounding Mena.

As Linda read through the newspapers from that era, she could not help but notice that the earliest reports on Mena had appeared in December 1987, almost two years after Seal's murder and barely four months after her son's. Appropriately, the reports had come from Fort Smith. Theresa Dickie, of KFSM-TV, presented filmed interviews with people who had been involved in the Mena investigation. In one segment, Terry Capehart, a Pope County deputy sheriff, described how he had monitored aircraft on which the identification numbers had been altered. "I saw with my own eyes planes where the N-number was changed." In another Dickie interview, a former secretary at Rich Mountain Aviation claimed she had been told to deposit large sums of cash in amounts of less than ten thousand dollars to avoid having to file Currency Transaction Reports. After the third installment in her series on Mena, Dickie complained to other reporters that she had been instructed to prepare no more reports on the subjest. "There will be no more calls to Mena, Arkansas," Dickie said she was told, "or you will be out of a job."

Near the time of Dickie's reports, Rodney Bowers, a reporter for the *Arkansas Gazette*'s Fort Smith bureau, wrote that a congressional investigator had arrived in western Arkansas to conduct interviews about alleged criminal activities at Mena's Intermountain Regional Airport. "We're looking at various things pertaining to drugs and guns," Bowers quoted the unnamed investigator as saying. Bowers wrote, "The investigator is assigned to the House Subcommittee on Crime. Local, state, and federal agencies are investigating a drug smuggling ring that allegedly was run by convicted smuggler Adler Berriman Seal of Baton Rouge. Sources said Seal, who became a federal informant and began working with the Drug Enforcement Administration in March 1984, used the Mena airport as a base of operations from early 1981 until his death on February 19, 1986, and possibly was involved in running guns to the Nicaraguan Contras." The article quoted investigators as having said that "Seal's involvement with the government has complicated their efforts to have prosecuted those people involved in Seal's pre-1984 activities at the airport."

A report carried by the Associated Press at the end of 1987 noted that the unnamed Washington investigator had spoken to former Polk County Sheriff Hadaway about whether he knew anything relating to a DEA official in Miami who was involved in the Seal case. "He went all the way from asking about smuggling drugs to asking about smuggling weapons," the former sheriff said. Hadaway was quoted as saying that if activities at the airport were part of a government operation, "I wish they would tell us. If it is, they owe us an apology and I owe some people at the airport an apology." Adding to the mystery, an unidentified member of the House subcommittee was quoted as having told reporters, "There was apparently a problem with people like Seal, who worked for the government and, from all appearances, worked for himself also."

By itself, Seal's story was almost too complex to be unraveled. But combined with the even more complex Iran-Contra saga, it became a black hole that most editors dared not look into. Seal was dead. Arkansas editors saw Iran-Contra as a Washington story. National papers saw Mena as a local story. Iran-Contra was receding into the past, and a thousand other stories demanded attention. But stories connecting Iran-Contra to Arkansas kept popping up. And Linda wondered if, embedded in them, were further links to Saline County.

In 1988, about the time that the Iveses and the Henrys were confronting Dr. Malak, Larry Nichols, a longtime Contra supporter, went to work for ADFA. In March 1988, seven months after the deaths on the tracks, Nichols filed what seemed to be a routine request for the governor's office to issue three honorary parchments known as Arkansas Traveler certificates. These certificates, presented as a gesture of goodwill to visiting dignitaries, foreign guests, and exchange students, have no legal significance, though they bear the governor's signature. Ordinarily they attract little attention. But years later, when Nichols's request was discovered, the names of the visitors he had sought to honor added to the intrigue surrounding Mena. The men were Mario Calero and Adolpho Calero, two brothers from Miami, and Maj. Gen. John K. Singlaub of Phoenix. The discovery raised questions that have never been answered: What had brought Adolpho Calero, the leader of the Nicaraguan Democratic Force or FDN, the largest and most active group of Contras, and Singlaub, one of the Contras' most prominent supporters, to Arkansas? And why, when members of the Arkansas Committee first sought information about the certificates, did Clinton's office deny any knowledge of them? According to citizens interested in Mena, the governor's office reported finding records that the certificates had been issued only after the Arkansas Committee released photocopies of them to the press.

For years after Seal's arrival at Mena, Welch and Duncan kept a low public profile. But by 1988, reports of the investigators' frustration with the U.S. attorneys' handling of the Mena case were making the papers. "The investigation has been before grand juries for two and a half years," the *Arkansas Democrat* reported in April 1988, "without any indictments being returned." Chris Curtis, of Little Rock's CBS affiliate, KTHV, reported that after unsuccessful attempts to get information about Mena from federal officials, he sought help from one of Arkansas's congressmen, Rep. Bill Alexander. The *Arkansas Gazette* subsequently reported that Representative Alexander, a Democrat, had asked the General Accounting Office to investigate possible links between Oliver North, the Mena airport, drug sales, and Panamanian general Manuel Antonio Noriega.

Suspicion about Mena was building. The worst suspicion—that Contra supporters were using drug pilots to carry their cargo of guns and ammunition south, while allowing them to bring cocaine into the United States on return flights, and possibly taking a cut on the proceeds to fund their covert operation—was hard to believe for its sheer repugnance. By the spring of 1988, U.S. Senator John Kerry, a Democrat from Massachusetts, had the Senate Foreign Relations Subcommittee on Narcotics and Terrorism, which he chaired, investigate that possibility. Specifically, the committee was investigating allegations that profits from drug sales had been used to finance the Nicaraguan rebels. Of particular interest to Arkansans who were only now beginning to learn about Seal was a comment by the lawyer for Kerry's subcommittee who said that the investigation would deal with "allegations of narcotics trafficking related to [Oliver North's] air operation."

Even with the advantage of hindsight, it was hard for Linda to reconstruct that story. There were so many stray pieces, all seeming to point to Mena, but not enough of them to form a clear picture. Shortly after Seal's death, for instance, the Christic Institute, a liberal Washington, D.C., law and public policy center, filed a lawsuit alleging that for at least the past twenty-five years, a "secret team" of former military and intelligence officers had been engaged in an international criminal conspiracy—a conspiracy involving drug smuggling, gun running, and money laundering—with the support of some U.S. officials. As it turned out, several of the defendants named in the lawsuit were the same ones named in the emerging Iran-Contra scandal. The suit alleged that proceeds from the sale of cocaine by the Colombian drug cartel were used to buy guns, which were then flown to Nicaragua.

Mena figured in the lawsuit. In a pretrial deposition, Eugene Wheaton, a former military criminal investigator, alleged that Seal had used Rich Mountain Aviation and the airstrip at Nella as his base for smuggling guns and drugs, and that political pressure had been used to block the Mena investigation. Michael Tolliver, a convicted smuggler, said in a deposition that Seal had recruited him in July 1985 "for some interesting work," after which Tolliver said he was paid seventy-five thousand dollars a flight to deliver arms to the Contra rebels. Tolliver testified that everyone knew Seal was working for federal officials, running military supplies to Central America and allowed to "sort of be an entrepreneur . . . on the way back." Another jailed pilot, Gary Betzner, told the *Wall Street Journal* in 1987 that he had run into Seal at Illopango Air Base in El Salvador, the headquarters for North's resupply operation.

The Christic Institute's lawsuit was never tried. In June 1988 a federal judge dismissed the case, finding that the plaintiffs had failed to prove their contentions.

A few weeks later, Sheriff Hadaway, a former president of the Arkansas Sheriffs Association, resigned as sheriff of Polk County, ending twenty years in law enforcement. He said disillusionment over the Barry Seal episode had in part prompted his decision. It looked to him, Hadaway said, as though Seal had "performed any services the United States government asked him to do as long as he was paid and was not sent to jail." It was a situation the sheriff could not abide. As he told the *Arkansas Gazette,* "I can arrest an old hillbilly out here with a pound of marijuana and a local judge and jury would send him to the penitentiary, but a guy like Seal flies in and out with hundreds of pounds of cocaine and he stays free."

In August 1988, exactly one year after Kevin and Don were murdered, the Reagan White House ordered the CIA, the Defense Intelligence Agency, and the National Security Agency to refuse to turn over information sought by the General Accounting Office for its investigation into Mena. Arkansas congressman Bill Alexander, who had requested the investigation, complained, "There are a lot of people dead set against telling people what their government is doing." Looking at the date of that story, Linda realized with a start that at the same time she was beginning her quest to unravel the drug-tinged mystery of what had happened to Kevin and Don, a U.S. congressman was trying to unravel the drug-saturated mystery at Mena. Linda took no comfort from the fact that they had both been stymied in their quest. The question in both instances was why. In her own case she felt that she had arrived at a part of the answer: Certain people in law enforcement—government officials—had been involved in the dealing of drugs. And now it looked like that was the story at Mena, as well.

In both cases, political considerations had diverted investigations and caused cases like Harmon's and Seal's to go unprosecuted, even while official rhetoric was coming down harder and harder on drugs. As far back as the week before Seal's death, Lt. Bob Thomasson of the Louisiana State Police, one of the investigators most familiar with the smuggler, had expressed that frustration in a memo. "It is the belief of this writer, that when the vice president made fashionable the interdiction of drugs and prioritized in the government rumor mills the establishment of a link between the Sandinista government in Nicaragua and drug trafficking, the rule books of many government agencies were thrown away in deference to making a case."[9]

Whether for money or political purposes or both, Linda thought, the result in her case, as at Mena, had been the perversion of justice.

"DOWNPLAY AND DE-EMPHASIZE"

Now, as Linda brought herself up to speed on the events that had paralleled her own personal struggles, she was able to see her county's problems in the context of a bigger picture. A national tug-of-war was being waged over the release of information about Mena, and the side favoring secrecy was winning. She learned, for example, that in 1989, while Saline County was coping with the additional unsolved murders of Keith Coney, Keith McKaskle, Gregory Collins, and Jeff Rhodes, and the disappearance of Boonie Bearden, a public affairs officer for the U.S. Customs Service in New Orleans acknowledged to reporters that his agency was among those conducting an investigation into activities at Mena. "The Customs Service is aware that the area has been used as a servicing point for narcotics smugglers out of South America," he said, "and it is a continuing investigation."

Right, Linda thought. This was seven years after Duncan had been brought in on the case, and he had been told at that first meeting that U.S. Customs already was watching Seal. If Customs was so aware of and interested in the investigation, where had its agents been all those years when Duncan and Welch reported almost no involvement by the agency at all? As Linda knew too well by now, a lot of crime, complicity, indifference, and inaction could be hidden behind the word "investigation."

Others had reached the same conclusion. In 1989 Joe Hardegree, the prosecuting attorney for Polk County, issued a written statement explaining why there had been no prosecutions of any of the participants in the alleged drug running or money laundering at Mena. "I have good reason to believe that all federal law enforcement agencies from the Justice Department down through the FBI to the DEA all received encouragement to downplay and de-emphasize any investigation or prosecution that might expose Seal's activities and the National Security Council's involvement in them.

"It was in this framework that the federal grand juries and law enforcement authorities in Arkansas apparently stopped in their serious deliberations or investigations concerning Barry Seal's activities and all of the surrounding circumstances." Hardegree added, "The really unfortunate aspect of this whole matter is the apparent fact that the federal investigation of drug traffic in connection with the Mena airport came to be intricately involved with international politics and more particularly with the private wars conducted by the Reagan White House in Washington. I believe that the activities of Mr. Seal came to be so valuable to the Reagan White House and so sensitive that no information concerning Seal's activities could be released to the public. The ultimate result was that not only Seal but all of his confederates and all of those who worked with or assisted him in illicit drug traffic were protected by the government."

Even jaded as Linda had become, that was a stunning statement. Here was the prosecuting attorney for the district that served Mena saying that he believed that "not only Seal but *all of his confederates* and *all of those who worked with or assisted him* in illicit drug traffic *were protected by the government*." Seal's business was an international one. He was suspected of contacts with organized crime. It seemed likely, especially in light of former U.S. Attorney Asa Hutchinson's remark, that a "large portion" of Seal's business was in Arkansas. Was it possible that Seal had business contacts in Saline and Pulaski counties, and that the pilots seen flying over the tracks at Alexander—low enough perhaps to have been dropping bundles of cocaine—had been part of Seal's organization? It seemed to Linda not only possible, but likely. If that was the case, was it also possible, even likely, that officials had attempted to "downplay and de-emphasize" crimes associated with the cocaine network because, as Prosecutor Hardegree suggested, certain persons connected to those crimes had "worked with or assisted Seal"?

It was an incredible idea, she realized. But she also understood that it was no more incredible than the reality she had before her: two federal investigations—one into murder and cocaine in Saline County and the other into cocaine and money laundering at Mena—had inexplicably ended without any indictments.

BILL DUNCAN

In 1989 Bill Duncan ended his seventeen-year career with the IRS. Like Sheriff Hadaway, he had lost his appetite for law enforcement after witnessing his government's handling of Seal. But it was what he had witnessed in committee rooms in Washington, D.C., where Seal's case was being investigated, that led Duncan to turn in his badge.

The beginning of the end for him came in late December 1987, four months after Kevin's and Don's deaths and almost two years after Barry Seal's. Hayden Gregory, the chief counsel for the House Judiciary Subcommittee on Crime, contacted Duncan and told him that the committee was trying to figure out why no one had been indicted in connection with the Mena investigations. Duncan flew to Washington to testify. But before he appeared, officials at the IRS assigned two agency attorneys to help him prepare what he would say.[10] This was not unusual. Agents were routinely advised by so-called disclosure litigation attorneys on how to avoid revealing secret tax return or grand jury information, as is required by law, while testifying before Congress. But to Duncan's amazement, the IRS gave him instructions that he believed "would have caused me to withhold information from Congress and to also perjure myself."

Duncan said the lawyers were concerned about how he planned to answer if members of the committee asked him why he thought the investigation at Mena had gone nowhere. Duncan told them that he intended to mention the possibility that orders to back away from the case had come from the highest level of the Justice Department. This was not idle speculation. Duncan intended to tell the committee that a confidential informant who worked as a secretary at Rich Mountain Aviation—and who was the daughter of a high-ranking Colombian official—had told his co-investigator, Russell Welch, "that Attorney General Edwin Meese had received a several-hundred-thousand-dollar bribe from Barry Seal directly." Duncan told the lawyers he could not corroborate the allegation, but that the exact figure the informant had reported was $450,000. In light of the informant's position and background and the unusual treatment Seal and his operation had received from federal authorities, Duncan had taken the allegation seriously.

But when he outlined what he intended to say to the IRS, "they told me to tell the Subcommittee on Crime that I had no information about that." In addition, he recalled, one of the lawyers "told me not to offer any opinions, even if specifically asked for my opinion by the Subcommittee on Crime. They told me not to volunteer any information. Basically, they did not want me saying anything that would reflect badly on the U.S. Attorney's Office in the Western Judicial District of Arkansas." Duncan refused. He felt that to do as he was being asked would be to take part in what he considered to be an already full-blown cover-up.

"It made no sense for me not to give full and complete testimony," he explained. "We had conducted textbook investigations of all the individuals at Mena; there were a variety of legal issues involved, which I had always had them in the loop on. We had proceeded very soundly. There was nothing for us to be ashamed of. The investigations were thorough, to the extent that we could conduct the investigation without subpoenas. And I would have thought that the Internal Revenue Service would have wanted a complete disclosure to Congress about the problems that we encountered. But quite the opposite was true. They obviously did not want any negative testimony coming from me concerning the U.S. Attorney's Office.[11]

"At one point," he continued, "when we were arguing about the Meese allegation, [the lawyer] told me that she had discussed my frustrations with the personal assistant to the commissioner of Internal Revenue, who was Larry Gibbs at the time—and the personal assistant's name was Bryan Sloan—and that Bryan Sloan had told her, 'Bill is just going to have to get the big picture.' "

That was it for Duncan. He gave the testimony he had been warned against giving and shortly thereafter resigned. He felt that he had gotten "the big picture," and he wanted no part of it.

CLINTON VAGUE ON MENA

Back in Arkansas at this time, Jean Duffey was developing her Saline County Drug Task Force, and the lack of indictments in the Mena investigation was turning into an issue in the race for the state's attorney general. In 1990 Asa Hutchinson, the former U.S. attorney who had overseen the Mena investigation from 1982 through most of 1985, was running as the Republican candidate for attorney general against the incumbant, Winston Bryant. Bryant printed campaign flyers accusing his opponent of failing to pursue the case. Hutchinson sued Bryant for libel, arguing that the investigation was "still developing" when he had resigned the office. Hutchinson lost the election.

Arkansans were beginning to realize that something peculiar had happened at Mena. But few could have said what that was. At the same time, the story of Barry Seal was working its way into the national consciousness. In late 1990, HBO began filming *Doublecrossed,* a movie based on Seal's life. Dennis Hopper starred as Seal, and Robert Carradine played a DEA agent. But even with Seal dead—and moving into the realm of legend—the real-life story of what he had brought to Mena reeled on. In May 1991, the same month that U.S. Attorney Banks ended the grand jury without issuing any indictments relating to Saline County, Attorney General Bryant sent petitions to Lawrence Walsh, the special prosecutor for the Iran-Contra investigation. Bryant said that the petitions bore "the signatures of more than 1,000 citizens, mostly Arkansans, who are calling for an investigation" into the activities of Barry Seal. "Their specific concern," Bryant wrote, "as well as my own, is to learn why no one was prosecuted in Arkansas despite a mountain of evidence that Seal was using Arkansas as his principal staging area during the years 1982 through 1985. The people of Arkansas need, and deserve, a final and full accounting of this matter, and it is our hope that the Office of Independent Council can provide one."

Bryant's action touched off a flurry of supportive editorials from newspapers around the state, the one in the *Gazette* being typical. Its headline read, LET'S GET TO THE BOTTOM OF IT. But federal barriers went up as fast as the demands for disclosure poured in. In May 1991, in response to requests submitted three years earlier by Bryant and the state's two daily newspapers, the FBI responded that it had located "60 documents totaling 208 pages" relating to its investigations at Mena. However, the letter noted, those files could not be released because the FBI's investigation into Mena remained open.[12] As a result, the *Gazette* reported, Seal's activities at Mena "remain shrouded in mystery."

In July 1991, at about the time that federal officials in Little Rock prepared to arrest Dan Harmon for not filing his tax returns, Duncan, who by now had taken a job as the chief Medicaid fraud investigator in Attorney General Bryant's office, again flew to Washington, D.C. This time he testified before the House Government Operations Subcommittee on Commerce, Consumer, and Monetary Affairs. Asked again what had happened at Mena, Duncan offered this explanation: "The evidence details a bizarre mixture of drug smuggling, gun running, money laundering, and covert operations by Barry Seal, his associates, and both employees and contract operatives of the United States intelligence services. The testimony reveals a scheme whereby massive amounts of cocaine were smuggled into the state of Arkansas and profits were partially used to fund covert operations."

Attorney General Bryant and Representative Alexander kept up the drumbeat for disclosure. In September they flew to Washington to deliver evidence to Walsh's staff that Bryant said linked the CIA to drug running and gun smuggling at Mena. "There is absolutely, positively an Iran-Contra connection with Mena, Arkansas, without a doubt," Representative Alexander said after the pair delivered boxes of documents. "And we have produced several witnesses who make that connection." As for the investigation, the congressman said, "The feds dropped the ball and covered it up. I have never seen a whitewash job like what has been executed in this case. It is unbelievable to me that such crimes can be gotten away with in this country. But so far they've done it." Noting that on the day before their arrival, Walsh had dropped efforts to pursue criminal charges against North, Representative Alexander added, "The fact remains that there has been a conspiracy of the grandest magnitude that so far has not been prosecuted, and law-abiding citizens in our country, I think, stand on the side of discovery and prosecution of crimes that have been committed."

In light of such serious allegations from prominent state officials, a few reporters turned their attention to Governor Clinton, who had made almost no public comment about Mena in the decade since Seal's arrival. Clinton, as governor, was titular head of the state police, and Colonel Goodwin, noting that the investigation at Mena had been the longest and most expensive in his agency's history, said that he had kept the governor apprised.[13] The summer of 1991 was a busy time for the governor. While Attorney General Bryant and Representative Alexander were pressing Walsh to include Mena in his Iran-Contra investigation, Dr. Malak was resigning as medical examiner, and Governor Clinton was on the verge of announcing his candidacy for president. Nonetheless, two reporters for the *Arkansas Democrat* managed to extract a few words from the governor on the question of what he knew about Mena.[14] They wrote: "Gov. Bill Clinton broke his silence on the issue Tuesday, saying 'a very vigorous state police investigation' that began 'when the very first evidence of illegal activity came to light' raised questions of links between the airport, the federal Drug Enforcement Administration, and the CIA."

The report continued, quoting Clinton: "When the investigation was completed, the deputy prosecutor for that region, Charles Black, very much wanted to proceed." Clinton said he had authorized financial help for a grand jury investigation but that "nothing ever came of that." During a subsequent federal grand jury investigation, Clinton continued, "our state police investigator was not called to testify until very late in the proceedings," at which point he was asked a "limited range of questions. Then, three or four years ago, we shipped off our entire investigative file to a congressional committee," a subcommittee of the House Judiciary Committee. "That was the last I heard about it," Clinton said.

Within days, Charles Black, the Pope County prosecutor, publicly disputed the governor's recollection regarding his offer of financial help. Black said it was true that he had personally delivered a letter to Clinton containing a request for funding, so that a local grand jury could investigate. "To the best of my recollection," Black said, "Governor Clinton's verbal response was to the effect that he would have someone check on the availability of financial aid and get word to me." Black said the governor's office never followed up on that offer. "Quite frankly, even if I had been made aware that twenty-five thousand dollars was available, that specific amount would have been tantamount to trying to extinguish a raging forest fire by spitting on it. That characterization is due to the interstate and international ramifications of the illegal activities disclosed in the mammoth investigative file compiled by Russell Welch and Bill Duncan, among others." When members of the Arkansas Committee asked the governor's office to release records relating to Prosecutor Black's request, members reported that officials there told them they had been "unable to find any records."

The governor's minimalistic, almost casual, and curiously incurious reaction to what a local prosecutor, his own state police, the Louisiana state police, at least one federal investigator, two attorneys general, and a handful of U.S. congressmen now believed had been a massive, international drug operation with headquarters in Arkansas reminded Linda of how Bill Clinton had stood quietly apart for so long from the furor surrounding Malak. By now she understood the power of distance, the power of inaction. By doing nothing and saying little, Linda reflected, whether about Malak or the airport at Mena, Clinton had been able to avoid the appearance of responsibility, and no one had asked him the questions that, to her, would have seemed so obvious:

Governor, weren't you outraged? Did you ever question the U.S. attorneys about why they weren't pursuing the case? Did you never demand an explanation from Washington as to what was going on in your own state? Did none of this mean anything to you?

"HIGH-LEVEL, BI-PARTISAN CABAL"

With a few exceptions, the national media seemed equally incurious. As Clinton's campaign for president progressed, *Unclassified,* the newspaper of the Association of National Security Alumni, noted in early 1992, "Mena figured in so many of the activities associated with Iran-Contra—not to speak of other covert actions—that its almost complete lack of mention in the national media has always been puzzling. Even after Arkansas Gov. Bill Clinton emerged as a leading Democratic presidential candidate, Mena and the guns, drugs, and Contra stories associated with it were apparently of no interest. The question is, why?"

The paper added, however, that thanks to the efforts of the Arkansas Committee, Representative Alexander, and Attorney General Bryant, the almost mind-boggling scope of the story was starting to emerge. "Alexander Cockburn has written four dynamite accounts in *The Nation*, Debra Robinson has supplied a fine piece for *In These Times,* veteran White House correspondent Sarah McClendon has taken up the cudgels in her widely circulated newsletter, and *Time* has launched a major investigation, which may or may not get printed. However, to date, Clinton, despite his other troubles, is not being asked to talk about how a large-scale covert activity could be conducted in his state, with allegations of drug and gun running and money laundering, without his knowledge and/or cooperation."[15]

In fact, *Time* did publish a story, but only about a tangential aspect of the Mena case, to which it concluded there was little substance.[16] McClendon, on the other hand, wrote flatly, "There is ample evidence that Bush, Clinton, [Senator David] Pryor [D-AR], [Senator Dale] Bumpers [D-AR], [Rep. John Paul] Hammerschmidt [R-AR], various U.S. attorneys, Arkansas state officials, and Arkansas financial institutions knew plenty about the illegal activities at Mena but permitted these to proceed."[17]

The article in *Unclassified* posed a serious question, one that had been gradually forming in Linda's mind the closer her review drew to the present. It was in many ways the most chilling thought she had had since Kevin's death. During Clinton's presidential campaign, the media had been quick to report the allegations that Gennifer Flowers had had an affair with Clinton. They had questioned him about his experience with marijuana, and delved into the circumstances surrounding his Vietnam-era draft deferral. But questions about Seal's remarkable staying power in Arkansas were never brought up. It seemed incredible that, in the heat of his presidential campaign, Vice President Bush would not have used the information—which was known by that time—that Clinton had allowed an international drug smuggler to operate in his state unhindered for the better part of four years. And it seemed equally incredible that Clinton would not have used the information—also known—that Bush had apparently had some fairly close associations with Seal. The publication *Unclassified* expressed what Linda had begun to think:

"In its paranoid moments (more frequent than usual in presidential election years)," the editors wrote, "*Unclassified* is half-persuaded that there is some high-level, bi-partisan cabal conspiring to keep Mena from being fully exposed. In other, possibly saner periods, *Unclassified* suspects that the leadership (if that is the word) of both major parties has decided mutually to put

Iran-Contra and all that pertains to it into an Orwellian memory hole, and the major media have agreed to go along."

"An Orwellian memory hole . . . "The phrase expressed exactly the sense that Linda had had ever since her ordeal started: that there were things the public had learned on some level but did not want to let itself remember. There were topics too frightening to examine. Issues too big to be confronted. By now, even Sheriff Hadaway had withdrawn to his own version of a memory hole. As Clinton's campaign headed toward the Democratic National Convention, the former Polk County sheriff told members of the Arkansas Committee that all that had happened at Mena was "a long-since dead issue," one he no longer cared to discuss. "The grand juries that took testimony about this incident did not return any indictments and the general public in the community where it occurred did not and do not give a damn about what occurred," the embittered lawman said. "I resigned and retired primarily because of the injustice in the federal system, and I have spent the last several years forgetting that all this ever occurred."

Linda could understand how the people Hadaway described felt. There had been a time when she, too, found it comfortable to believe that corruption was far away or in the past, or that it was somebody else's problem. That had changed since Kevin's death. By now she had experienced enough to sympathize with Hadaway, as well. Almost worse than enduring misdeeds was the nightmare of confronting mass denial. Dan Harmon had been elected prosecuting attorney. Bill Clinton had won the White House. On the surface, life continued as normal. But for Linda and for people like Hadaway, Jean Duffey, Russell Welch, and Bill Duncan, there was no more life as normal. They had seen beneath the surface. They had lifted too much of the tarp.

SIXTEEN

THE FBI ENTERS THE CASE

JANUARY 1994–DECEMBER 1994

Linda was unscrambling the pieces of the Mena story. It would become a very long chore, one to which she would devote hundreds of hours in the months to come. But in the meantime, another question closer to home demanded her attention. At the end of 1993 the FBI had taken over the train-deaths case. Agents were attempting to place the teenage boy who said he had been at the tracks in protective custody. They told Brown that the story the boy told matched information they already had.

"EVIDENCE OF CONCEALMENT"

Within days of the FBI's abrupt decision, Dan Harmon stopped by the house to visit Larry and Linda. Almost two years had passed since the couple had talked with him. He said he wanted to hire a forensic specialist to reexamine the boys' deaths, using money seized by his drug task force, and that it bothered him that the deaths remained unsolved. Linda listened politely, responding that, of course, she and Larry still hoped the killer or killers would be found. As soon as Harmon left, she made notes of the conversation. Such record keeping was a protective measure she had adopted in the past year or so; it was something she wished she had begun after her very first meeting with Steed. But then she had not imagined the need for such caution; now it was all that made sense. Recalling Harmon's visit, Linda wrote, "He said he wanted to see what we thought about the idea. If we had any better ideas, he wanted us to tell him what they are." She had offered no suggestions.

And then there was the knife. Shortly after Detective Brown had begun investigating the case, he had received a visit from a woman who'd identified herself as the girlfriend of a small-time Saline County drug dealer whom Harmon had sent to prison. She'd explained to Brown that she thought he was the first investigator she could trust. She'd told him that her former boyfriend knew who killed the boys. Then she'd handed Brown a long, narrow knife that looked like a bayonet. The woman said her boyfriend had told her it was the actual murder weapon. Removing the knife from its leather sheath, Detective Brown noticed what he thought might be flecks of blood.

The knife posed a problem for Brown. He wanted to have it tested, but the sheriff's office lacked such facilities, and after all that had transpired in the case, he was not certain he could trust any testing conducted at the state crime lab. Brown took the knife to the Little Rock Police Department, which had a small lab of its own. As 1993 was drawing to a close, Brown received a written report from a department technician. It said that "a bayonet, military type" had been tested "for blood, hairs, and fibers," with a "positive reaction." But LRPD officials, who had no jurisdiction in the case, ordered the knife returned to Brown. When agents for the FBI took over the case, Brown surrendered the knife to them.

Linda was not happy about this newest involvement of the FBI. Suspicious of the decision by U.S. Attorney Banks to disband the investigation into corruption in Saline County, she worried that just when it looked like Detective Brown might be developing some leads in the case, the FBI, for some reason, would move to bury it.

By the end of February Linda could contain her misgivings no longer. She called the FBI's office in Little Rock and spoke with Administrative Special Agent Al Finch. He told her that the FBI was just an assisting agency in the investigation and that if she wanted any information about the case, she should contact the Saline County sheriff. Linda blew up. She told him she knew that the FBI had instructed Brown to turn over his work on the case. Finch tried to calm her down. As she wrote later in notes of that conversation, "Finch then told me that if I would sit back and let them do their job, the case would be solved by the end of the year." The remark had been meant to soothe her, and at one point in her life, six or seven years earlier, it might have. But by now Linda was long past easy placation. "I don't have the luxury of sitting back and letting other people do their jobs!" Later, more calmly, she observed in her notes, "This was not a pleasant conversation."

The following day, Finch called Linda back and told her that he thought she might have misunderstood what he had said the day before. "I told him," she wrote, "that I hadn't misunderstood anything and that I hoped he had not misunderstood me. I might have to sit back and watch another investigation of my son's murder be shut down, but I would not sit quietly this time. He again told me that the case would be solved by the end of the year."

AGENT PHYLLIS COURNAN

It was not an auspicious beginning. But within days, the FBI's involvement took what appeared to be a more positive turn. In early March, Larry and Linda received a phone call from an Agent Phyllis Cournan, who explained that she had been placed in charge of the investigation into the deaths of Kevin and Don. Then she said something that almost dumbfounded Linda. Cournan said federal officials had been reviewing the circumstances under which former U.S. Attorney Chuck Banks had shut down Govar's 1990 investigation. Banks, a Republican, had left office as the U.S. attorney in Little Rock in March 1993. In the last year of George Bush's presidential administration, Banks had been named as a candidate for federal judge, but the Senate had not voted on the nomination and the possibility had become moot when Clinton won. Linda felt encouraged that someone was at least examining the way Govar's investigation had ended.

At Cournan's request, Govar transferred several large file boxes marked SCI, for "Saline County Investigation," from the U.S. attorney's office to the FBI. In the past, federal investigators had stayed out of the train-deaths case, explaining that no evidence had surfaced that the murders rose to the level of federal crimes. But much had happened since those early days. Now, as Govar later explained, as a result of the earlier investigation, "we thought we might develop evidence of a racketeering case that we could prosecute federally, or violations of the federal drug kingpin statute, that would show that the train deaths had been part of those enterprises."

Govar warned Cournan that getting witnesses to talk in Saline County might prove difficult. During his own investigation, in 1990 and 1991, several witnesses had testified about dealing drugs in Harmon's presence and of being advised by Harmon when police were getting close. Since that investigation—and particularly since the leak of his memos to Banks—Govar had watched Harmon prosecute several of the witnesses who had provided information against him. As far as Govar was concerned, the prosecutions were Harmon's way of warning other drug dealers in the district who might consider testifying against him in the future. "What other conclusion could you draw," Govar asked, "except that he intended to retaliate and make an example of them, so that other people would keep their mouths shut? The whole situation was a constant pattern of intimidation. It made other people who might want to come forward very reluctant, once they saw what happened to those who did."

Cournan wanted to get the boys' clothes tested by the FBI lab and went to retrieve them from the Arkansas Crime Laboratory. "After she arrived there," Govar related, "I got a very strange call from the evidence custodian at the state police. He said that he had the clothes and that he could give them to us, but that he would have to have a subpoena.

"That was very unusual. In all the years I had been a U.S. attorney, that had never happened. But at any rate, we issued the subpoena and found that the clothes of the victims had never been submitted for forensic examination, where they could have been checked for body fluids, hair, and tissue samples. I had Agent Cournan send them to the FBI Crime Lab for a complete forensic and DNA analysis."[1]

Once the clothes were on their way to be tested, Cournan tried to contact Jean Duffey through Duffey's brother, David Keesee. When Duffey refused to return the calls, Cournan asked Keesee to tell Duffey what she had recently told Larry and Linda: that Justice Department officials were examining the handling of Govar's investigation. When Jean's brother relayed that message, Duffey thought, Well, maybe this is more serious. She picked up the phone and called Cournan. "Is it true?" Duffey asked. "Yes," Cournan replied.[2]

"What can I do?" Duffey asked.

"Help me," Cournan replied. "Fill me in. Help me understand what has been going on."

During the months that followed, Cournan and Duffey spent hours on the phone discussing Saline County's turbulent recent history. For a time, Cournan became intensely interested in James Callaway, the used-car dealer who was in prison for his role in the gambling-house killing, as well as for selling drugs. Duffey told Cournan she doubted that Callaway had been much of a player. "I've been down that trail, Phyllis. I don't think it goes anywhere. I think Callaway's got connections. But overall, I don't think he was much more than a patsy for Dan Harmon." The two discussed what Duffey's undercover task force had learned and the allegations contained in Govar's leaked memos. Cournan revealed little, either about the case or of a personal nature, but over time she let Duffey know that she was engaged to be married to a member of the Secret Service.

Like Duffey, Linda had been encouraged by Cournan's interest in the case. For her and Larry both, some hope and trust in the FBI had been restored. In addition, Linda liked Cournan personally. Soon after their initial phone contact, the agent had come to meet Larry and Linda at their home. She was thirty-nine, petite, and athletic. Before being assigned to the case, her job had been to administer physical fitness tests to other agents. She asked Larry and Linda if they would come to the FBI office in Little Rock for a more formal interview.

They went a few days later and sat in a room with a large interior window with a pane of darkened glass. Cournan asked questions, and as Linda later recalled, "We just kind of laid everything out about what we thought about everybody." Linda explained her growing suspicions of Dan Harmon. At one point Cournan excused herself and stepped out of the room. Larry turned to Linda and, indicating the darkened glass, asked in a whisper if she thought they were being videotaped. Linda replied in a normal voice that she expected they were. "Quiet," he said, "they'll hear you."

"They probably will," she answered. "But what do we care who hears?"

Buoyed by Cournan's investigation, Linda continued her work with Parents of Murdered Children, traveling around the state on speaking engagements. Attorney General Winston Bryant was frequently a guest at the same engagements. By this time Linda had learned something about Bryant's demands a few years earlier for explanations about the crimes at Mena, but so far, the two had never discussed Barry Seal or the mysteries surrounding him. All Linda knew was that lately, when reporters asked Bryant about Mena, he seemed to shy away from the subject. His curiosity appeared to have vanished since Clinton had been elected president. That was surprising to Linda. Didn't Bryant see Clinton in the White House as an advantage? Couldn't Clinton order Justice Department officials to explain, once and for all, what had happened with Seal at Mena? After all, Seal had operated from his own state. And if, as Clinton had said, the whole matter had been under federal control—well, who was now in a better position to demand explanations from federal officials? Mysteries could have been cleared up, speculation laid to rest. If even a fraction of the suspicions were true, the public had been cruelly betrayed; a housecleaning was in order; bureaucratic heads should roll. A change of administrations would have been the perfect time to do that. But Clinton had made no move to illuminate this dark chapter in his state's history. And now Bryant had ceased his clamoring. Linda made a mental note. The next time she and Bryant were together, she would ask him why.

The opportunity arrived soon enough. Bryant and Linda, along with one of his aides, were in a car traveling to a speaking engagement when someone mentioned something about Mena. "That reminds me, Winston," Linda said. "I've been wanting to ask you about that."

What happened next came as a surprise. As Linda later recalled, "Winston went off like a rocket. I'd never seen him like that. It was out of character from everything I'd come to know of him. I'd never seen him get so riled over anything, let alone an innocent question. His voice was raised. He became agitated, very irritated, and to put it mildly, he went off on a tirade. He was talking about how all these people had tried to say these things about Mena, and they wouldn't let it die, and that there had been nothing there, but that if something had been there, the statute of limitations on it had run out. He went on like that for about ten minutes.[3]

"When he finally wound down, I said, 'Winston, let me tell you something. I'm one of those people who are out there who are not going to let it die. I don't care if the statute of limitations has run out, people should know what their officials did—all their officials, including you.' Well, with that the conversation died. We rode a long way in total silence."

"THERE CAN BE NO CONCLUSION"

Linda understood by now that political change can change a politician. To her, whatever had happened at Mena had been criminal. It may have verged on being treasonous, if agents of the U.S. government had been giving "aid and comfort" to drug dealers while this country was engaged in a "war" on drugs. At the very least, lives had been devastated by the drugs Seal and his cohorts had imported for years, with the apparent knowledge and acquiescence of several federal agencies. To Linda, this was hardly the sort of matter that should evaporate in the minds of politicians just because some statute of limitations had expired.

She had read the testimony of Jack Blum, an investigator for Senator Kerry of Massachusetts, that the Contras were moving drugs "not by the pound, not by the bag, but by the ton, by the cargo planeload."[4] And she was aware of the well-founded suspicion that some of the planes Blum referred to were part of the fleet controlled by Seal. She had also read the conclusions of Kerry's subcommittee, as reported in December 1988, barely four months after Kevin and Don were killed. "It is clear," the report had said, "that individuals who provided the support for the Contras were involved in drug trafficking. . . . "

What struck Linda as odd was that none of the evidence linking Seal to Mena and to Oliver North's Contra supply operation had been refuted by federal authorities. Instead, the evidence that the government had ignored cocaine trafficking on an almost imponderable scale had itself been largely ignored. Events that were never supposed to come to light in the first place were being allowed by official inaction to drift into the mists of history, where it was hoped they would be forgotten. But unlike Bryant, Linda was not inclined to forget. Mena might still hold critical clues about what had happened to her son, as well as why all investigations that might have solved the case had been quashed without explanation. The allegations surrounding Mena were so serious, so profound in their implications, that they "cried out" to be investigated, as Bryant himself had once said, until not one question remained. How many other mothers had watched their children die in crimes related to cocaine? Where was justice for them? To Linda, the question of how that cocaine had been reaching communities like her own was not one to be brushed off, especially when, to quote Bryant again, "a mountain of evidence" suggested not only drug running on a massive scale, but government involvement in it. Despite what Bryant was saying now, Linda reminded herself that there was no statute of limitations on murder.

A few people agreed. She liked what the columnist Molly Ivins had had to say about George Bush's decision to pardon figures involved in the Iran-Contra affair. Scorning the pardons as "enough to gag a maggot," Ivins observed, "Iran-Contra included literally the setting up and financing of a secret government, to carry out policies made in secret, without the advice, consent, or knowledge of the people or their elected representatives. It included a consistent policy of lying both to the people and to their representatives. In no way did those who set out on this folly . . . observe their oath to protect the Constitution, nor were they troubled by the several laws they broke with a sense of self-righteous superiority."[5]

But Ivins was in the minority. As time passed, interest in Mena waned, even as interest in another Arkansas enterprise flared. By the time Larry and Linda had their first meeting with Agent Phyllis Cournan, Robert Fiske, Jr., had been appointed as a special prosecutor to investigate a small Arkansas land deal known as Whitewater. Linda and Larry could never see what the Whitewater fuss was about. Compared to what had transpired at Mena, the suspicions about Whitewater seemed minor and petty. The only explanation they could imagine for the focus on Whitewater, coupled with the complete disregard of Mena, was that, while Clinton might have had some explaining to do about Mena, Republicans had a lot more.

The following June, the *CBS Evening News* briefly broke away from its Whitewater coverage to broadcast an interview with Charles Black, the prosecutor from Polk County, Arkansas, who had asked for Clinton's help in funding a local grand jury to investigate Mena. Black reiterated his recollection that Clinton had assured him that he would "get a man on it and get back" to Black, but that the promised follow-up had not come. When CBS asked the White House for comment, spokesman John Podesta said that twenty-five thousand dollars had been offered. "The governor took whatever action was available to him," Podesta told CBS. "The failing in this case rests with the Republican Justice Department."

Linda scowled as she watched the broadcast. No, she thought, there is only one Justice Department. It is not Republican or Democrat. And if it was involved in the crimes that have been alleged, that needs to be acknowledged.

Fortunately for Linda, one newspaper shared her view. On June 29, 1994, a few weeks after the CBS report, the *Wall Street Journal* ran an article by Micah Morrison entitled "Mysterious Mena." The piece outlined the saga of Barry Seal, the unsuccessful efforts of Duncan and Welch to get subpoenas issued, the connection to Iran-Contra that surfaced when Seal's plane was shot down in Nicaragua, and the attempts by Arkansas congressman Bill Alexander and Arkansas attorney general Winston Bryant to persuade Iran-Contra special prosecutor Lawrence Walsh to include Mena in his probe.

That article was followed a few months later by another one about Lasater, this in the *Albuquerque Journal*, which had an interest in Lasater because he owned New Mexico's popular Angel Fire resort. The paper quoted a former Arkansas state trooper, J. N. "Doc" DeLaughter, as saying that he believed the 1986 narcotics investigation of Lasater had been shut down for political reasons. DeLaughter told the paper that he and another state police investigator who worked on the Lasater case were excluded when then U.S. attorney George Proctor and federal agents interviewed Lasater and others, including Roger Clinton. According to the news report, DeLaughter said he had been given the unusual order to make only oral reports on his findings in the Lasater case and to make them only to Colonel Goodwin.

Lt. Larry Gleghorn, DeLaughter's supervisor at the time, corroborated part of DeLaughter's account. Gleghorn told the paper that he, too, had been angry about being excluded during federal interviews of Lasater. And he said that "no copies were made" in the Lasater investigation. "Anything anyone ever did in this investigation went to Little Rock, and none of it ever came back to us," Gleghorn said.[6]

Beyond a few bursts of such reporting, the media showed little interest in the events linking cocaine to politics during the 1980s and early 1990s in Arkansas. Official intransigence was no doubt part of the reason, it being hard to report such a story without access to investigative records. Clinton placed blame for what happened at Mena on "the Republican Justice Department," yet even after Clinton's election, officials in the Democratic Justice Department were still not talking. The FBI denied access to its records, contending that the case was still open. The DEA was no more forthcoming. In August 1994 the agent in charge of the DEA's office in Little Rock told a reporter for the *Arkansas Times* that after all the years of investigations at Mena, "no conclusion was determined." Asked what he meant by that, he elaborated, "Sometimes that is the conclusion: that there can be no conclusion."[7]

POSSIBILITY OF A NEW VIDEO

In contrast to the rest of the nation, Pat Matrisciana, who had produced *The Clinton Chronicles,* remained obsessed with the Arkansas stories. Early in the summer of 1994 he called Jean Duffey from his office in California and asked what it would take for her to cooperate in a new video that dealt specifically with Saline County. Duffey could hardly imagine what could persuade her, but she agreed to meet Matrisciana in Little Rock. She still made infrequent trips to Arkansas to visit relatives, but since Harmon still had warrants out for her arrest, the visits were brief and cautious. As she explained to Matrisciana when they met for lunch, "I'm still ducking quietly in and out of the state, and I keep a very low profile when I'm here."

He told her that he was outraged by her story—the fact that a former deputy prosecutor now feared returning to her home state—and wanted to film it. She outlined her complaints about the quality and tone of *The Clinton Chronicles.* Chiefly, she told him, the production had strung together serious but unsupported allegations; she thought that the emphasis on Clinton's womanizing "went way too far"; she mistrusted videographer John Hillyer's hatred of Bill Clinton; and she would have nothing to do with Larry Nichols, Clinton's chief accuser in *The Clinton Chronicles.* "He's pompous and arrogant and I feel he has a personal agenda," Duffey said, "and most important, he's been discredited. I won't align myself with him and I don't want to have any part of his 'get Bill Clinton' campaign."

Genially Matrisciana persisted. "What can I do to get you to tell your story?" Duffey answered that she wanted to see the story presented the way a prosecutor would present a case to a jury—with witnesses, evidence, and documentation—so that by the end, the jury could make up its own mind about what had gone on in Saline County. And on top of that, she added, "I would have to have final approval of the script."

"Okay," Matrisciana agreed. He told Duffey that he had recently hired Nancy Kurrack, an Emmy-winning producer from Chicago.[8] "Just meet her," Matrisciana urged. He promised to fly Kurrack to Houston to meet Duffey within a few weeks. "And then," he added excitedly, "you and Linda Ives will have to meet."

After their lunch, Matrisciana took Duffey to an office where another meeting had been arranged so that those familiar with the case could compare notes. There she met John Brown, the Saline County sheriff's investigator who had been working on the Henry-and-Ives case; Brown's wife, Karen, in whose office they were meeting; and Brown's boss, Sheriff Judy Pridgen. Duffey had known Pridgen only in passing when Duffey was deputy prosecutor and Pridgen an officer with the Benton Police Department. Duffey also knew that Pridgen and FBI agent Cournan had been talking since Cournan entered the case, and that the agent respected the sheriff.

The group talked for about an hour about the significance of the location at which the boys' bodies were found. Brown told of the police files he had found in which people in the area around the tracks had reported low-flying planes at night. He also related a conversation he had had with a pilot living in Texas. He said the man admitted to having been a drug pilot and that, because of that, he wanted to be identified in Brown's reports by an alias.[9] "Joe Evans"—not to be confused with Seal's mechanic, also named Joe Evans—said he had flown drugs to points near the Saline-Pulaski county line, precisely where the boys were killed.

"That's it, then," Duffey exclaimed. "This whole, massive cover-up is because the drugs were Mena drugs!" Brown felt that the Mena drugs were connected to Saline County, but not necessarily to the Henry-and-Ives murders. "John," Duffey insisted, "put it all together. The shutdown of federal grand juries. The smuggling going on at Mena. And now a pilot saying that he personally dropped cocaine on the tracks by the county line . . . " To Duffey, the connection seemed obvious. But Sheriff Pridgen was also reluctant to make the leap from drugs and failed investigations in Saline County to drugs and failed investigations at Mena. She felt that the drugs must have come in on trains. Duffey objected. "I've never been able to get that to wash," she told Pridgen. "I think that the train theory was perpetuated to distract all of us from thinking about planes."

NANCY KURRACK

Matrisciana sent Nancy Kurrack to Texas to meet Duffey as he had promised. And as Matrisciana had predicted, Duffey liked the seriousness with which Kurrack approached her work. The women talked for hours, Duffey once again acquainting an incredulous listener with the strange history of Saline County. As they talked it became evident to both of them that the story could not be told without the involvement of Linda Ives. Kurrack picked up the phone and called her.

Linda listened as Kurrack explained their idea. "I've got to tell you right now," Linda interjected, "I won't have anything to do with it if Larry Nichols is involved."

"That's the same thing Jean told me," Kurrack laughed. Linda went on to identify some of the same complaints with *The Clinton Chronicles* that Duffey had listed for Matrisciana. "I'm very concerned with accuracy," Linda said. Kurrack assured Linda that accuracy in this new video was what she wanted, too. A week later, Kurrack, Duffey, and Linda met at a Little Rock office.

Linda liked Kurrack immediately. What reservations she had had about participating in another Matrisciana production, Kurrack quickly dispelled. She made it clear that she was a journalist and intended to stick to journalistic standards. That was all Linda wanted to hear. Since the month after Kevin's and

Don's deaths, Linda had relied on journalists to keep her story alive—until the case could be solved. Government had failed, and its failures had been reported every step of the way. To the extent that the story was known, ordinary citizens were appalled. She had to believe that eventually, if attention could be maintained and more of the story revealed, some power of public outrage might force an explanation. Linda agreed to participate.

Excited as she was about meeting Kurrack, what Linda would remember most from that day was her first encounter with Duffey. The two became instant friends. Physically, they could hardly have been more different—plump Linda and lanky Jean—but they understood each other as no one else could. Like two battle-scarred veterans, they left the meeting to discuss in private what they had endured.

Unlike most veterans, however, they did not enjoy the luxury of reflecting on a war that was finally over. As they met, comparing notes of the past half dozen years, the deaths of Kevin and Don were as unsolved as they had been on the morning the bodies were found. Harmon held sway as prosecutor, and Duffey remained a fugitive. And in the halls of power, in Washington as well as in Arkansas, the crimes of Mena were being dismissed as a shadow from a prior administration. It was a disheartening landscape, but now that they had met, Linda and Jean took heart from each other. Several times in the next few months, Duffey sneaked back into the Seventh Judicial District to visit her parents and Linda. Jean understood that accountability and a decent investigation were all Linda wanted. She was determined to help her get it.

The two promptly exchanged their files. Linda sat up many nights reading Jean's diaries from the year before her task force was shut down. Here was another woman's experience with many of the same situations that had touched Linda over the past few years. According to one 1990 entry in Jean's diary, for example, Bob Govar had mentioned that two years earlier he had received a call from the CIA, reporting a threat on Garrett's life. That would have put the call in 1988, at the height of the grand jury inquiry Garrett and Harmon were conducting into Kevin's and Don's deaths—and near the start of the string of murders. Linda knew at the time that someone had shot out the windshield of Garrett's car, but she had never heard of a call from the CIA relating to threats on Garrett. When Linda and Larry had expressed their concern to Garrett over the car incident, he had minimized the event, attributing it to a domestic dispute. Linda remembered that even then, the explanation had not rung true. Now she was learning that Jean Duffey also harbored doubts about the occurrence. Even in 1990, when Govar told Jean about the threat, the story had made no sense. Why would someone from the CIA, of all places, even have known about a threat against a deputy prosecuting attorney in some podunk Arkansas county? There had been no answer then, and now, against the backdrop of what Linda knew about Barry Seal, the question was even more intriguing.

Another amazing discovery for Linda in Jean's papers was Scott Lewellen's notes. Linda never had any idea that after the shutdown of Duffey's drug task force, Lewellen, on his own, had spent several weeks questioning people about the murders of Kevin and Don. Linda pored over Lewellen's notes, particularly the report of his interview with Curtis Henry. Here, for the first time, she learned about Curtis's suspicion that planes had been dropping drugs at the site on the tracks where the boys were killed.

For the first time since Linda's disillusionment with Harmon, she felt that she had an ally—and a highly informed ally, at that. As a result of Duffey's experience as a prosecuting attorney, her contact with Deputy U.S. Attorney Govar, and her position as head of the district's drug task force, she was familiar with both the district's law enforcement and seamy underside. The women kept each other's fax machines humming. They reminded each other of episodes they had forgotten. They made time lines, compared notes, and relayed some of what they discovered to Agent Cournan. They also kept in touch with Nancy Kurrack, who was at work on the new video.

The production, still in the talking stages, had already hit a snag. Kurrack, Duffey, and Linda all agreed that to tell the story of drugs in Saline County in relation to the story of drugs at Mena, they would need the help of Duncan and Welch, the investigators most familiar with Seal's operation in Arkansas. The problem was that Duncan and Welch wanted nothing to do with the production. Earlier they had agreed to be interviewed for *The Clinton Chronicles* in the belief that it would be an unbiased, journalistic effort. Instead, as Duncan later put it, the video "was a bunch of crap." Duncan politely told Kurrack, "I would not have done that interview if I'd known how it was going to be used." Worse, he said, he felt that the wide dissemination of *The Clinton Chronicles* had undermined years of serious effort to expose what had actually happened at Mena, because the video's slant was so blatant, and its truths were intermingled with inaccuracies.[10]

Kurrack tried to assure Duncan that her video would be nothing like that. She begged him and Welch to meet with Jean, Linda, and herself. Reluctantly the two men agreed. In the fall of 1994 the five met at the lodge at Queen Wilhelmena State Park, on a mountain outside of Mena. Here, together for the first time, were Linda Ives, Jean Duffey, Russell Welch, and Bill Duncan—the state's four most frustrated whistle-blowers. For years, all had been trying to call their government's attention to broad-based, cocaine-related corruption in Saline County and at Mena. And for years they had been ignored, rebuffed, and ridiculed. They did not need to get acquainted.

They knew one another's stories. Welch had retired from the state police in disgust, Duncan had resigned from the IRS, Duffey had fled to Texas, and Linda Ives was still battling, seven years after the fact, to learn not only who had killed her son, but why his murder had remained unsolved. There, amid the mountains that had harbored Barry Seal, they got down to work with Kurrack.

Explaining that she had had no hand in producing *The Clinton Chronicles,* Kurrack promised that her commitment was to reporting only what could be documented. She assured Duncan and Welch that she had editorial control and would not release the segments where they appeared without their explicit consent. As Jean and Linda had been persuaded by Kurrack's sincerity, so were Duncan and Welch. But they told her they would have to sleep on the matter.

The next morning, Linda, Jean, and Kurrack met in the lodge's restaurant. Welch arrived and said that he would participate, but it was a while before Duncan showed up. When the quiet ex–Treasury agent finally walked in, he apologized, explaining that he had gotten up early and gone to the Mena airport, where he had been praying since dawn over his decision. To the relief of all at the table, Duncan said he would participate, too.

FAITH IN THE FBI

Linda had learned from Cournan that Kevin's and Don's clothes had finally been sent to the FBI crime lab for analysis, along with the bayonet that had been given to John Brown. She understood from Cournan that due to a backlog at the lab, the reports might not come back for months. In the meantime, Linda and Cournan kept in touch by phone every two or three weeks. Linda urged Cournan to include some of the other drug-related killings, particularly Keith McKaskle's, in her investigation, but Cournan insisted that she had to limit her investigation to the deaths on the tracks. To Linda, that looked like tunnel vision, an almost naive approach to what she had come to regard as a complex situation. "Sometimes," she told the agent, "you need to broaden your view. In order to understand one thing, you need to look at others." But Cournan was adamant.

The agent insisted that Kevin's and Don's deaths might never be solved if she allowed herself to be distracted. "This thing has so many tentacles and arms," she told Linda, "you could go off in a million directions." Duffey supported Cournan's approach. "The one thing I do understand is that if she tries to connect this with Mena, it will never go anywhere," Jean told Linda. "It's local folks who killed Kevin and Don. Let her focus on that." Once, however, to Linda's relief, Cournan did report that a number of "offshoot investigations" had arisen from information she had uncovered.

Linda felt comfortable with Cournan, whom she regarded as "ethical and very by-the-book." Because of that, Linda dared not press Cournan for information, no matter how much she yearned for news. When she talked to Cournan, Linda kept her questions general. Typically she would ask, "How are things going?" Gradually Cournan let Linda know about some aspects of the investigation. One time she said, "We're looking for Caucasian hairs." At another point Cournan told Linda that she had subpoenaed hair, blood, and fingerprint samples from a Saline county sheriff's deputy. Yet whenever Linda asked Cournan whether any word had come back on the clothes, Cournan told her no. But she added that that was just as well, because as long as no findings came back that would limit the scope of her search, she could continue to issue subpoenas and cast a broader net.

HIGHWAY SIGNS

The year 1994 had been a strange one. Appropriately, it ended on a strange note. In December a friend of Larry's who worked on the railroad called him. "You won't believe what I saw on the interstate while we were driving through Kansas City, Missouri." The man, who lived in Arkansas, said that as he approached a highway overpass, he saw a sign painted on it that said: BILL CLINTON KNOWS WHO KILLED KEVIN IVES. He said he nearly had a wreck.

Linda and Larry tried to imagine what it could be about. They had no relatives—no friends—in Kansas City, and they certainly had never blamed Clinton for the deaths. They speculated that whoever had written the sign may have seen *The Clinton Chronicles* and jumped to an angry conclusion. But that explanation sounded lame. Why would anyone in Kansas City bother about a seven-year-old murder in Arkansas?

A few weeks later, on December 29, Linda received another strange call. In her work with Parents of Murdered Children, she had helped compile a book of families' reminiscences about the children they had lost. Kevin, of course, was in it. The second call was from a member of that organization. The woman said that her brother-in-law, a truck driver who was visiting for the holidays, had been browsing through the book when he came to the photo of Kevin Ives. Pointing to it, the man told his sister-in-law that while passing through Springfield, Missouri, recently, he had seen a sign on an overpass that read: BILL CLINTON KNOWS WHO KILLED KEVIN IVES.

Linda would never find out any more about who had put up the signs or why. But jarring as such stories were, she knew they were meaningless. An honest investigation was all that mattered and, at last, seemed that was under way. She had faith in Phyllis Cournan.

But 1994 closed with no arrests. The FBI's prophecy of the previous February—that if Linda would just "let the FBI do its job," the case would be solved by the end of the year—had not materialized.

SEVENTEEN

STOLEN FROM THE EVIDENCE LOCKER

1995

Since the day Kevin died, Linda had kept an inner balance between hope and caution. Too many times she had let herself believe that something proper would be done in Kevin's case, only to have to pick up the pieces after that expectation was dashed. She had reacted guardedly when first told that the FBI had become interested in the case. But word that federal officials were reviewing at the decision to "exonerate" Harmon over Govar's objections had nudged her toward a bit more hope. As she had gotten to know Phyllis Cournan, her confidence had grown.

DAN HARMON'S DESCENT

There was even reason to hope that Harmon, the apparently invulnerable prosecutor, was about to be discovered for the threat he was. The year 1994 had ended with the allegation that he assaulted his current wife, Holly DuVall.

After twenty-two months of marriage, the two were now estranged, Dan having filed for divorce in October. The violence of their breakup was chronicled in police reports, which were picked up by the papers. According to police incident reports, on December 29 Holly DuVall Harmon drove to the apartment where she was living and found her estranged husband inside. He told her he was conducting a search. After that, Holly drove to the Benton Police Department and two officers accompanied her back to her home. They wrote: "Dan was gone, but the place was trashed; credit cards cut up, photos cut up, clothes thrown about the room, etc." Establishing that Dan Harmon was no longer on the premises, the police left.

The next morning, Holly was back at the police station, crying. This time the officers noted that she had "a large puffy bump on the left side of her head, redness and bruises on the side of her neck, a scraped left elbow, and mud on her right pants leg." Holly told them that Dan had returned to the apartment at approximately 8:00 A.M., and that when she opened the door to let him in, "he assaulted her by striking her with his hands and feet, he choked her, and told her he was going to kill her. . . . She stated she screamed, but he told her all her neighbors were gone, so go ahead and scream."

Holly told the police that the attack was interrupted by a workman passing by. This time the officers advised her to seek medical attention and to stay with friends or relatives outside of Saline County. Although Arkansas law would have allowed them to arrest Harmon based on his wife's injuries, he was not arrested and the police told her that because of his position, a special prosecutor would have to be appointed.

Even though Linda had not had contact with Harmon for years, she, along with others in the district, knew of at least some of his personal problems. They had been reported in the papers. There was the pending divorce from Holly, his fourth wife, an attractive blond woman half his age. His finances were in a shambles. Recently, for the second time in his life, he had filed for bankruptcy, listing assets of $22,670 against debts of $126,383. And allegations of drugs and violence had once again emerged.

On January 2, according to Benton police reports, officers were responding to a call from Holly's sister, who had reported being harassed by Harmon, when the officers passed Harmon on the side of the road and he flagged them down himself. Harmon told the officers that he had arranged for Holly to be committed to a Little Rock psychiatric hospital "for having suicidal tendencies," but that he could not find her. He believed her sister was hiding her. The police proceeded to the sister's house. There, the sister told them "that she was asleep when she was suddenly awakened by someone banging violently on her front door. . . . She could see Harmon banging on the door and hear him yelling. She stated she refused to answer the front door because she is very frightened of Harmon. . . . " Later that afternoon, police accompanied members of Holly's family to Dan's apartment to discuss his recent behavior. "Harmon opened the door, inviting all the parties into the residence," the report of that meeting noted. "As officers and family entered, Dan began raising his voice, with general indignities being blurted out intermittently." A session followed in which Holly's relatives confronted the prosecutor about her injuries. When one asked Harmon if he had in fact held a gun to Holly's head, Harmon, the report said, blurted out: "Do you know why? Because she made a goddamn drug run to Texas! The prosecutor added, "And those police reports are lies."[1]

The next episode involving the couple centered on a major Saline County drug dealer by the name of Shelton Corley. Harmon's drug task force had first arrested Corley more than a year earlier, in October 1993, two months before Dan and Holly were married. In that arrest, court records showed that an informant wearing a body microphone had gone to Corley's house to buy an eight ball—an eighth of an ounce—of methamphetamine for $250. After the informant arrived at the house, a woman living with Corley received a phone call. She hung up, yelling a warning that the house had been "bugged." Everyone fled. But the warning had come too late. Corley was caught. He was prosecuted, convicted, and placed on probation. The following summer, he was arrested again, this time for growing marijuana. By Thanksgiving Corley was still free on the marijuana charge and living in a trailer when sheriff's deputies, acting on a tip, confronted him once again, this time with a search warrant. During the search of Corley's house, police confiscated several items, including twenty-five firearms, some marijuana, thirty-one used syringes, more than seventy thousand dollars in cash, a fifteen-thousand-dollar certificate of deposit, and, according to the deputies' report, "one photograph of Holly Harmon." The photo had been taken at Corley's house.

Harmon watchers speculated that that search, which had taken place on November 23, may have prompted the prosecutor's subsequent attack on Holly. Two weeks after the search of Corley's house, Holly reported to police that Dan had broken into her apartment, "then jerked the phone plug off the wall and took a 9mm Smith and Wesson pistol out of her purse . . . " According to the police report, "The suspect Harmon then began yelling for the victim Harmon to come out of hiding, saying that she was a 'dead motherfucker' and a 'dead whore.' " Later that day, he threatened to burn down her apartment. An officer wrote, "I went to the apartment and spoke to Dan. Dan would not come outside, stating, 'Fuck you and fuck her, too.' I advised him why I was there and he assured me he would not burn down the apartment or hurt himself. . . . "

Reporter Rodney Bowers of the *Arkansas Democrat-Gazette* covered the stories most closely. Bowers had been one of the first journalists in the state to report on the clandestine activities at Mena. Now, living in central Arkansas, he was heading the paper's Benton bureau. Bowers infuriated Harmon by scrutinizing Holly Harmon's police reports and, as time passed, asking why Dan had not been charged with assault. When Bowers put the question to Benton police chief Rick Elmendorf, mentioning the prosecutor's admission, as cited in a police report that he had held a gun to his estranged wife's head, Elmendorf answered, "We didn't have a warrant."[2] Elmendorf explained that arrest warrants were issued by judges, generally at the request of the prosecuting attorney's office. In this case, no prosecutor had forwarded such a request.

When Bowers asked if officers would have arrested anyone else under similar circumstances, Elmendorf replied, "More than likely."[3]

Linda could hardly believe that Elmendorf had made the statement with a straight face. Of course the prosecutor's office had not requested a warrant! Harmon was the prosecutor. What amazed her was that even though weeks had passed since the alleged assaults on Holly, no special prosecutor had been assigned—and no one was complaining. To the contrary, when Bowers asked Ray Baxter, head of the Saline County Democratic party, about Harmon's violent behavior, Baxter said, "What he does in his personal life isn't any business of the state Democratic party." The opinion apparently was widely shared. In January 1995, with the news reports about Harmon still fresh, several community leaders publicly lent their support to an effort Harmon was heading to establish a local drug-rehab facility. Lib Carlisle, a Saline County real-estate dealer and the head of the state Democratic party,[4] was present to applaud the project, as were Judge Cole and about a dozen other prominent citizens. Without a hint of irony, Harmon told the crowd that part of the rehab facility would be a shelter for battered women and abused children.

This is what Linda had learned to live with. She lived in a county and in a state, it seemed, where the obvious had been so long subverted that the absurd supplanted sense. Malak could mangle ruling after ruling and receive nothing but high-level support. Harmon could travel to Indiana to testify on behalf of a drug dealer he said he had never met, and no one would demand an explanation. Evidence of Barry Seal's drug operation at Mena could mount without contradiction, and no one in power seemed interested.[5] Why would she be surprised that Dan Harmon could simultaneously be investigated by the police for battering his wife and congratulated by Judge Cole and others for his efforts on behalf of battered women?

It looked to Linda as if power at many levels had learned it could mock the truth, and that if it stuck to its story long enough, it could controvert common sense. Linda did not know what to call this kind of arrogance. She had encountered it for the first time when Sheriff Steed's deputies insisted to the train crew that the tarp they had reported seeing had never actually existed, that it had been an optical illusion. Now, in the same way, the county's political powers were ignoring the alleged attacks on Holly Harmon, treating them as an illusion, and extolling their friend Dan Harmon as a man who built shelters for battered women. There was a kind of madness in it, but then there had been madness in it all along.

Linda could only hope that an image so glaringly at odds with reality would eventually fall apart, and in fact, within four days of Harmon's announcement about the shelter for battered women, another crack appeared in his facade. This time it was his third ex-wife, Teresa, who called police claiming that he had come to her house, hit and kicked her, and threatened to kill her if she called the police. A friend who said she had witnessed the assault told Bowers of the *Democrat-Gazette* that Harmon threatened her, as well. When Bowers contacted Teresa, she told him, "Danny really is a nice guy, but he's sick." Explaining that he had beaten her throughout their marriage, and beaten the wife before her, Teresa added, "He needs help." But she said she would not be filing charges. "I'm afraid he'll set me up and I'll lose my kid," Teresa told Bowers. "He has that kind of power." The friend who witnessed the attack agreed that tangling with Harmon was probably unwise. "I have no reason to get him on my bad side," she said. "If everybody will leave it alone, it will go away."

Linda could sympathize. But she also knew better than to believe that violence ignored would ever "go away." In a letter to the *Benton Courier*, she wrote: "Just as he has done in the past with previous wives, Dan Harmon beats, batters, and threatens his present wife, Holly, and just as they have done in the past, Rick Elmendorf and others help him hide his crimes." She complained, "The *Benton Courier* should be running editorials on this matter. The citizens and every official in Saline County should be demanding Dan Harmon's and Rick Elmendorf's resignations. Instead, they simply look the other way."

Later, when Bowers interviewed Linda about the letter, he asked her about the prosecutor's ability to hold the affection of voters even after being investigated by a grand jury, attacking women, and not filing his taxes. "That's the sad thing," Linda said. "He could have been anything he wanted to be, done anything he wanted to do. He is an absolutely masterful attorney and prosecutor. I've seen none better. But he's manipulative. That's what makes him what he is. He's a masterful manipulator."

Unchecked by any authority, Harmon crowed. A week after the alleged attack on Teresa, he bragged to the *Arkansas Times,* "I believe in treating people fairly, and under my definition, that's pretty tough. Our Seventh Judicial District has the longest sentences and the highest conviction rate of any drug task force in the state." When asked about his temper, he flared, "Sure I have a temper. I'm a dinosaur among a society of sheep. I believe in standing up for what I believe and I believe in telling everybody else to go to hell."

By the end of February, his cockiness appeared justified. Rather than arresting him, Elmendorf gave the police file on Harmon's alleged assaults to Sam Ed Gibson, Benton's city attorney, requesting an opinion as to what should happen next. A month later, Elmendorf reported that Gibson had found "no basis" to charge Harmon with anything. The file on the prosecutor was closed.[6]

Linda and Jean tried to dissect why Harmon seemed to be getting away with so much. He was a winning politician, of course, someone the Democratic party did not want to censure. And Republicans in Saline County were relatively few and far between. He was the prosecutor who presented the police department's cases, so there might be a natural reluctance there to, in effect, bite the hand that took its cases to court. But they also suspected that Dan had something else up his sleeve, some card that he pulled out whenever he was about to be called to account. They believed a good explanation must exist for why Dan was allowed to get away with all he did. Whatever that explanation was, it was one of the most carefully guarded secrets in the county.

By summer, it looked like all had been neatly forgotten. The problem for those who wanted to keep it that way was Harmon. Questions kept arising about his handling of certain drug cases—and he kept talking with his fists. There were questions, for instance, about Roger Ward, the accused drug-runner and would-be traveling companion of Holly Harmon. Although Ward had pleaded guilty to five felonies the previous year, a check of the files disclosed that the prosecutor's office had never completed the paperwork to have him sent to prison. County officials acknowledged that, despite Ward's alleged involvement with Holly, Harmon had remained active in Ward's case.

Such a conflict of interest might have been unacceptable in other jurisdictions. But in Saline County, as Linda reflected, it was business as usual. And so, it seemed, was Harmon's temper. In September the press reported that a former drug dealer who was recently paroled from the state penitentiary claimed that Harmon had come to his house and threatened to kill him "if he found out that his wife [Holly] had been there." The man told investigators that when he opened the door, Harmon attacked him, seriously biting the man's thumb in the process. Though another man at the house confirmed the account, the victim, who had been prosecuted by Harmon in the first place, opted not to press charges.[7]

Linda shook her head. So this was what it had come to: the bankrupt district prosecutor biting a parolee, while convicted drug defendants were going free. Retaliation and intimidation had become a way of life. Those who had reason to fear Harmon knew that he could—and would—use his official power against them.

"JOE EVANS"

The situation might have been unbearable for Linda, except for Agent Cournan's repeated assurances that the FBI's investigation was going well. By now, a report on Kevin's and Don's clothes had come back from the FBI lab. Linda did not know at the time, but Cournan had told Govar that analysis had revealed semen on the back of one of the boys' pants. There was also some other material on the clothing from which technicians thought they could extract DNA.[8] Cournan and Govar discussed the possibility of taking blood tests and tissue samples from some of the suspects in the case.

At the same time, Govar's attentions were being drawn elsewhere. As an outgrowth of Cournan's investigation, the FBI was following up on information that out-of-state motorists passing through Saline County were being stopped on Interstate 30 by members of Harmon's drug task force. Informants told federal agents that drivers found carrying drugs were being threatened with prosecution unless they surrendered cash, and often their vehicles. In addition, there were reports that Roger Walls, the head of Harmon's drug task force, was spending larger sums of money than his annual income would seem to support. With the help of the FBI, Govar launched what he would come to call his "second Saline County investigation." Harmon was again at its center. And again Govar quietly began calling witnesses.

While all this was going on, Jean tracked down the retired pilot now living in Wichita Falls, Texas, who went by the alias "Joe Evans." She considered the contact a long shot, but being in Texas, it was something she could do. He told her an astonishing story. Evans said that he had been a pilot for hire, working for anyone who would pay, and that some of the jobs he had flown had been for the CIA—hence his insistence on the alias. He said he was paid for these jobs with checks drawn on the U.S. Treasury. Duffey asked him about Mena. Evans said that he had worked for what he knew to be a drug operation that was based there, and that one of his jobs had been to fly duffel bags—not of drugs, but of cash—to a drop site in Saline County that his employers designated as A-12. He said a pilot flying at night would locate the site by heading north of Benton along the railroad tracks in the direction of Little Rock. Interstate 30 would be on the left. After coming over a small rise in the topography—Bryant Hill—the pilot would see the lights from a large institution on the right. At that point he was to drop down and pass over a set of railroad lights that hung across the tracks. Once he passed the lights, he was to slow down almost to stall speed, count to ten, then push his cargo out of the passenger door. Evans said he had done this on several occasions. During the summer of 1987, Evans said, word had passed through the organization that one of the drops to A-12, drop number forty-six, had not been retrieved by its intended recipients but apparently had been stolen before they could get to it. The people Evans said he worked for were furious about the missing money. And they were alarmed at having lost the transponder that was placed in the bag so it could be located. Evans said there was some concern that the instrument might link the flight to Mena. The flights had continued, he said, but with the ground team on heightened alert. Evans said that in August, after drop fifty to the area, he and the other pilots learned that two boys had been killed at the site by the group waiting to make the pickup.

It was a fascinating tale, but Jean was skeptical. Linda, when she heard of it, was even more skeptical. "Jean, I've been to that stretch of the tracks a dozen times. There are no lights like he describes there." The women dismissed Evans and his story. But toward the end of 1994, sheriff's detective John Brown, who had also spoken with Evans, mentioned the story to Linda once when Larry happened to be in the room. Linda dismissed it, pointing out that there were no such lights over the tracks.

"Wait a minute," said Larry. "They don't sit like that now. But back then they did." He explained that at the time when Kevin and Don were murdered, there was an array of signal lights just to the south of Shobe Road. Called bridge signals, they were arranged on a platform that spanned the tracks, supported by metal posts on either side. The railroad had removed them in the late 1980s because of the maintenance needed to paint so much metal. The structures were torn down and replaced with simpler lights to the side of the tracks, known as pole signals. There was a moment of stunned silence as Larry's remarks sank in. Suddenly Evans's scenario sounded plausible. From the point where Larry said that the lights had once stood to where Kevin's and Don's bodies were found was a distance of about one mile.

Jean reported the information to Cournan. She warned the agent that she did not know how much credibility Evans should be accorded. But, she added, here were some very specific details that had never been described before and that would seem hard for anyone to fabricate, given that the lights Evans said he had relied on had long since been removed. As Cournan continued her investigation and the months passed, the question about the mysterious Joe Evans was one of a growing number that Linda hoped Cournan was pursuing. But she never asked Cournan about him, and Cournan never mentioned Evans herself.

Knowing that Cournan was talking to both of them, Linda and Jean felt free to discuss her information with each other and with their husbands. They disclosed it to no one else. Though Linda tried not to press Cournan in her conversations, she harbored a thousand questions. What of the Saline County drug dealer whose bayonet had been submitted to the FBI lab for testing? Cournan would not discuss the results of the lab tests. Nor would she discuss some information that had been relayed to Linda by Brown: that semen had been discovered on the back of the underwear worn by Don Henry. What did the FBI make of that? Were genetic samples being compared? Who was the FBI questioning? Had anyone *ever* interviewed the two drug dealers whose names had kept popping up?

DRUGS, GUNS, AND MONEY LAUNDERING

Trusting the investigation to Cournan, Linda turned her attention to creating the script for the new video. The story that she, Jean, and Nancy Kurrack wanted to present was complicated and far-reaching—a lot to tell in a sixty-minute production. In March 1995 Linda and Jean flew to California where they sat around Nancy's kitchen table and attempted to simplify the tale. But as they talked, they encountered another problem. Linda and Jean were convinced that the reason no investigation into the boys' deaths had succeeded was that the crimes were related to Mena, where an alliance between state and federal officials had ensured that no investigations would succeed.

Kurrack wanted proof. She insisted that the women support their suspicions with documentation. Linda and Jean protested. How can we offer documentation, they demanded, when even Bill Duncan and Russell Welch could not get the U.S. attorney to issue subpoenas for *their* investigation? How could Linda and Jean prove a link between the two cases when nothing about the investigations into either one had proceeded along normal lines? How could they do anything other than present a reasonable suspicion when, in both cases, state and federal officials appeared to be actively avoiding the issue? How, in short, could they prove that A led to B led to C, when B was being kept unknown?

Kurrack sympathized. She could understand the women's need for closure and why they would grasp at that possibility as the only one that made sense. But she wanted to film a documentary. That meant to her that what went into the script had to be supported. Lack of government cooperation—or even governmental obstruction—could not be an excuse. She wanted no unsupported leaps in the story.[9]

Linda and Jean finally agreed. Yet, they could not shake the question: why had so many investigations backed away from these two murders? "There's got to be a reason someone's protecting Harmon and his thugs," Linda said. "I admit that the major piece of evidence—the reports of airplanes over the tracks—is not very tangible. But still, something made Kevin and Don important. We know what happened in Saline County. All we can do is tell the story." By the time Linda and Jean left California, they had helped outline a script. In a few months Kurrack and Hillyer would fly to Arkansas to shoot footage for the documentary.

Other media, meanwhile, were becoming curious about what had happened at Mena. During the summer of 1995 the *Arkansas Times* reported that a crew for a British TV newsmagazine had spent a week in the west Arkansas town filming a segment about its airport. Linda knew that the interest in Britain had probably been piqued by reports in the *London Sunday Telegraph* by

Ambrose Evans-Pritchard, the paper's Washington correspondent. Among other things, Evans-Pritchard reported that Seal had been "working for the Defense Intelligence Agency (DIA) all along, answering to a top-secret outfit in Fort Meade, Maryland, known as the U.S. Army Operations Group." Several other conservative publications picked up the story, as well, some of them reporting that Kenneth Starr, the new special prosecutor in the Whitewater investigation, was also looking into questions concerning Mena.

The most sensational of the Mena articles appeared in the *American Spectator,* in a July 1995 article by R. Emmett Tyrrell, the magazine's editor. Tyrrell quoted an Arkansas state trooper by the name of L. D. Brown, who claimed that in the mid-1980s, while assigned to Governor Clinton's security detail, he had personally witnessed Barry Seal's drug-running operation. Brown said that he had applied for a job with the CIA, with the governor's encouragement, and that while waiting to learn if he had gotten the job, he had been contacted by Seal. Brown, a former narcotics officer, said he flew aboard Seal's C-123 on two flights to Central America—flights during which he was shown both the plane's cargo of M16 rifles for the Contras, and afterward, packets of cocaine, for which he said the guns had been exchanged. Brown told Tyrrell he'd severed his nascent association with the CIA in disgust and reported the incident to Clinton, but that the governor had not reacted with the outrage Brown had expected. Instead, Brown said, Clinton had casually dismissed his concern with the comment, "That's Lasater's deal."

POLITICS AS USUAL

By the mid-1990s, a handful of print reporters in Arkansas and across the nation had also developed a serious interest in Mena. Their reports circulated among a growing network of concerned citizens. These included members of the Arkansas Committee, a few lawyers and investigators, and people like Jean Duffey and Linda Ives, whose lives had been touched by the mystery. Faced with the high level of government secrecy about Mena, many of these people collected and shared documents on their own, in an effort to piece together what was known about Seal's activities. Some were sent documents by anonymous sources working at various agencies.

The FBI interrogation of Lasater, in which he reported his entertainment of law enforcement officials and the alleged help from the state police investigator assigned to review his finances, was one such document. Another that made its way into Linda's hands was a memorandum titled "Mena, Arkansas, and Narcotics," which was sent from the FBI office in Hot Springs to the office in Little Rock on February 5, 1986, exactly two weeks before Seal's murder. It reported that the U.S. Attorneys, on January 17, 1986, "advised that he was withholding presentation of captioned matter to the federal grand jury. . . . He advised that he will not utilize Seal as a government prosecution witness in view of his lack of credibility in other mitigating circumstances. . . . " Linda found the memo remarkable, citing Seal's "lack of credibility" as a reason for not calling him before the grand jury seated in Fort Smith. Yet, as Linda and others were well aware, by the time the memo was written, federal prosecutors in other jurisdictions had been relying on Seal's testimony for more than a year in drug cases around the country.

Scattered reports about the airport drifted into the national media, but no publication took a more active interest in the story than the *Wall Street Journal.* In September 1995, in the aftermath of L. D. Brown's allegation in the *American Spectator* suggesting that Clinton had known about Seal's activities, the *Journal* called for a thorough investigation of Mena, one that would seek out the truth, regardless of the political fallout. Noting what it called "the short-circuiting" that had occurred in "nine separate state and federal probes into Mena," the paper insisted that what happened there still "cries out" for investigation. And "if some chips fall on the Republican side," the editors wrote, "so be it. Important questions need to be answered."

To Linda, the editorial was one of the first from the national media that made nonpartisan sense. As Kenneth Starr's Whitewater investigation dominated the news in Arkansas, she marveled that so much money and effort were being poured into suspected financial misdealing, while allegations of wholesale drug running and money laundering in the state had been completely brushed aside. She did not care about the politics of whoever had killed Kevin and Don, nor did she care about the political affiliations behind the drug trafficking at Mena—except to the extent that they may have been used to cover up the crimes. As a mother and as an American, she wanted explanations, the politics be damned.

But explanations she had never gotten, and she would not get them now. Cournan had grown quiet. After Brown leveled his allegations in the *American Spectator,* Asa Hutchinson, who was now chairman of the state Republican party, sent a letter to the chairman of the House Judiciary Committee seeking yet another congressional inquiry into alleged money-laundering activities at Mena. Linda laughed. It had been Hutchinson, after all, who, as U.S. attorney, had declined to issue the subpoenas requested by Duncan and Welch.

But Hutchinson was not the only politician who seemed to have done an about-face about Mena. When a reporter for the *Arkansas Times* sought Attorney General Bryant's comment on Hutchinson's request for a congressional inquiry, Bryant, the onetime advocate of total disclosure, dismissed the entire idea. "It's too late to bother with it. That's basically my position. An investigation might furnish some answers to some questions that have been raised, but here's the problem with an investigation: One, the statute of limitations has long since run [out] on criminal as well as civil liability. Two, most of the important players are now deceased. I'm speaking specifically about Barry Seal. And three, Mena occurred during a Republican administration, and it was really an international problem, and the federal government was the one that, in my opinion, had the ultimate responsibility at Mena and failed to do anything. The problem is that the entire episode happened on the Republicans' watch."

It's a game to them, Linda thought. It's politics. First Hutchinson, the Republican, blunts the investigation, and then he calls for one. First Bryant, the Democrat, demands an investigation, and then he says it's "too late to bother." Was there no one in any elected position willing to get to the bottom of this? As always, when Linda felt almost overcome by disgust, she tried to direct her energies where they might accomplish something. Fortunately, there was the video.

By late summer the planning for the video was complete and Hillyer was back in town, filming. He recorded interviews with investigators Duncan and Welch, and with Sharline Wilson, now at the women's unit of the state penitentiary. But in August the project suddenly screeched to a halt. Kurrack's mother died, and after the funeral, Matrisciana contacted Linda and reported that Kurrack would not be able to continue with the project because she was needed at home in Chicago to help her ailing father.

MESSAGE AT THE GRAVE

It was August 23 again, 1995, the eighth anniversary of Kevin's death. Linda was back at the cemetery. She had a lot to tell Kevin—about Cournan's investigation, the video, and the ongoing battle to get information about Mena. But as she approached his grave, something caught her eye—something in the grass. Drawing closer, she was able to make out what appeared to be two small plastic toys. She picked them up. The first was a plastic badge, with the word POLICE emblazoned across it. The other was a play target—the type often seen at a police shooting range—bearing the outlined image of a man.

Linda sat shaking at the graveside. Even here, she thought, there is no peace, no rest from this horrible crime. She'd come here to be alone for a few minutes with her memories of Kevin, but now, even at the cemetery, she found she had to be braced. Other people did not have police badges and toy shooting targets left on their loved ones' graves. There was peace at other graves. But not here. And peace would never settle here, she knew, so long as Kevin's murder and Don's continued to be covered up. Feeling far from tranquil, Linda cleaned up around Kevin's grave as she always did. And as she always did, she silently renewed her pledge to him that she would not give up seeking answers. When she walked out of the cemetery, she carried the police toys with her.

The next day she called Cournan to tell her about the badge and the target. The agent agreed: they appeared to be a message.

Linda hung up the receiver slowly, feeling a familiar dread. She recalled a conversation that Jean had recently reported having had with Cournan. Jean said Cournan had mentioned that Floyd Hays, an FBI agent who worked in Hot Springs, had been assigned to assist her on the case. Jean had reacted with surprise. She knew that Hays and Agent Tom Ross had been assigned to investigate Mena. She also knew that Duncan had testified that the agents' role in the Mena case had been limited and somewhat unclear. Besides, Jean thought, Hot Springs and Mena were in the feds' western district of Arkansas. It seemed unusual to her that Hays would be assigned to assist in an investigation being conducted out of Little Rock. Jean became suspicious.

"Phyllis," she said, "they're getting ready to shut you down."

Cournan scoffed. "Who has the power to shut down the FBI?"

"Who indeed?" Jean responded.

In the weeks that followed, Jean and Linda heard little from Cournan. Linda tried to dismiss Jean's concern. Cournan had gone too far with this investigation, she tried to assure herself, for it to be halted now. Since the visit to Kevin's grave, and her subsequent call to Cournan, Linda had fallen back into a familiar mode, reminding herself not to worry. Yes, the agent seemed more distant. But then Linda calmed herself remembering that there was probably a very reasonable explanation for Cournan's apparent detachment. Now married, Cournan was about to have a baby. In fact, she had mentioned on the phone with Linda that her maternity leave would begin the next day.

"INTO THE BEAR'S CAVE"

As fall gave way to winter, investigators for the IRS and the FBI in Little Rock deepened their probe of Harmon's use of his district's drug task force. Govar, at the U.S. Attorney's Office, subpoenaed records. Besides Harmon, the heat was on Roger Walls, whom Harmon had installed to replace Duffey. After years of investigating Harmon, Govar was closing in again.

In November, satisfied with the investigation's progress, he decided to take some time to go deer hunting with friends. When the men had gathered at their camp, in pine woods about ninety minutes south of Little Rock, they had a few drinks and Govar called home to check in. It was a call he would later wish he had skipped. He was told that his office wanted him to come back, that a problem had arisen and that he was needed in court the next morning. Annoyed, Govar started drinking coffee and preparing for the drive back. He told his friends that he would get dinner on the way home. He left the camp, winding his Toyota 4-Runner through the woods, then pulled onto Highway 167. The road passed through Grant County, which was part of Harmon's district.

In Sheridan, the county seat, Govar stopped at Catherine's Restaurant, the biggest diner in the town of barely three thousand residents. The unsuspecting federal prosecutor did not realize that Roger Walls, the subject of his current investigation, was also in the room. Govar had never met Walls, never seen a picture of the man. He knew that IRS and FBI accountants had become intrigued by a number of Walls's purchases—and were scrutinizing them closely. But Govar had not been intimate with the details. He did not realize that Catherine's Restaurant and its adjoining motel had been the most suspicious of all of Walls's purchases.

Govar ate a big dinner, paid for it, and left. About a half mile down the two-lane highway he saw a state police car on the right side on the road, parked behind another car. It looked like the trooper was issuing a citation. Govar veered slightly to the left to pass. Immediately the state police car pulled out, lights flashing. Govar pulled off the road. The trooper said he was stopping Govar because he had crossed the center line. He asked if Govar had been drinking. Govar acknowledged that he had. The officer administered a field sobriety test. Govar failed, with a reading of .16, considerably over the state level for legal intoxication of .10. The trooper arrested Govar. Later that night he was released into the custody of a friend.

The next day Govar reported to his boss, Paula Casey, the current U.S. attorney. Govar understood the implications of his arrest: he would be disqualified immediately from the Harmon-and-Walls investigation. The U.S. attorney's office could not risk any suspicion that his actions in the case might be motivated by retaliation. Govar pleaded guilty to a charge of driving under the influence. He was fined, and had his license suspended.

Govar's removal from the Saline County investigation could hardly have come at a more remarkable time. After nearly a decade of investigating Harmon, Govar missed being involved in the biggest break in the case.

STOLEN EVIDENCE

The incident again involved Holly DuVall Harmon, who was now living in Hot Springs at a condominium complex. Holly was twenty-seven, Dan was fifty-four. Their divorce would be final at the end of November. In mid-

November, she called the Hot Springs police to report a disturbance at her apartment.

Upon arriving, officers found Holly DuVall upset with a couple of guests and demanding they be removed. To the officers' surprise, the man said he was willing to go, but not before the police searched his car for drugs. He explained that he was afraid Holly might have planted narcotics in the vehicle. Complying, the officers found used syringes and a handgun but no drugs. Because of the syringes, they called a drug dog to the scene. When the animal arrived, it focused on the car's spare tire. Officers deflated the tire, but again, no drugs were found.

The incident might have ended there, except that during the commotion the manager of the complex arrived with a request of his own for the police. He said he was planning to evict DuVall, and before he did, he wanted police to search her apartment. She gave her permission, they complied, and in a duffel bag in a closet, they found what appeared to be four bricks of cocaine.

No one ended up being charged in the incident because the bricks were quickly determined to be fake, comprised of a substance that only resembled cocaine. Again, the incident may have never come to light. But a Hot Springs television reporter had stopped by the complex during the episode. That evening the story of the fake cocaine found in Holly DuVall Harmon's condominium was aired on the evening news. By the next morning, the state's major media were interested. What, they asked, had the prosecutor's estranged wife been doing with bricks of fake cocaine, and how had she gotten them?

The story swept Saline County, where, for many, reports of Harmon's contentious public life and riotous domestic life had become a form of entertainment. Linda read the latest reports with little surprise. Over the past few years she and Larry had talked often about how, of all the people they knew—their neighbors, Larry's co-workers, their friends at church, and those they had met through Parents of Murdered Children—no one operated in such a drug-saturated environment as did their own prosecuting attorney, the popular antidrug crusader, the head of their local drug task force. They had long since stopped believing that he was the white knight he pretended to be. For years Linda had wondered how long Harmon could disassociate himself from drugs by laying the problem at the feet of those around him. Now, as newspapers reported the source of DuVall's fake cocaine, the implications for Harmon grew serious.

The bricks, which were taped in a bundle, bore markings indicating that they had been tested at the Arkansas Crime Laboratory. A chemist there reported that the packet had been part of a drug seizure of twenty bricks sent from Saline County. Twelve of the twenty bricks had contained cocaine that had tested 97 percent pure. Drug task force records showed that the cocaine had been seized on Interstate 30 in Benton on December 14, 1993, from the trunk of a rented car driven by two Houston men. Officers working for the drug task force had made the arrest and seizure. After being tested at the crime lab, the bricks had been returned to Harmon's office, where they were to have been held in the prosecutor's evidence locker for presentation at the men's trials.

But a further check of the records showed that the men had never gone to trial. Harmon had charged them with one count each of possession of cocaine with intent to deliver. Hearing dates were set for the following month, but neither man appeared. Records indicated that both had been released from custody and never brought to trial.

Linda read what was in the news—and read between the lines. Ever since Harmon had assumed control of the drug task force, there had been rumors that he was using it for shakedowns. Now it looked like the rumors were true.

Questions about how DuVall had gotten the fake cocaine packets were dominating the county gossip. How had the packets been removed from the evidence locker? Were other packets missing, as well? What was the condition of other evidence in the D.A.'s safe? Why had the Houston men been allowed to leave the state without facing trial?

As though these very same questions were bothering him, Harmon called for a state police investigation. He had no explanations to offer reporters and he was growing impatient with their questions. Walls defended Harmon, confirming Harmon's assertion that as prosecutor, he had never had a key to the evidence locker. Walls said that only he, as head of the drug task force, and his chief investigator possessed keys, and that he had no idea how the security of the evidence locker had been breached.

Lawyers speculated about what effect the discovery of the violation would have on past and pending trials. It looked to many like a prosecutorial nightmare. A few days after the discovery, Paul Bosson, the prosecuting attorney at Hot Springs, dropped word to reporters at the *Democrat-Gazette* that Harmon may have been in that city when officers recovered some of the stolen drugs. "We got wind that on the night the disturbance call went out, Harmon was in town, in the very next apartment."

It's like something Pogo used to say, "It gets interestinger and interestinger."

THE FBI DETERMINATION

On November 29, ten days after the discovery of the Saline County evidence in Holly DuVall's condominium, Linda and Larry drove to Little Rock to meet with Agent Cournan. Also attending the meeting was Agent William

Temple, the second-in-command at the Little Rock FBI office. Linda had had almost no contact with Cournan since the anniversary of Kevin's death when she'd reported finding the police toys at the cemetery. Finally she had called to request a meeting to learn where the investigation stood. When the four had assembled in Temple's office, they were joined by another man, who was introduced as a bureau lawyer.

Temple began, "I think I know why you're here, but why don't you go ahead and tell me anyway." To Linda he seemed arrogant, almost flip.

She replied, "We want to know the status of the case." Referring to her notes, she read aloud Agent Finch's comment in February 1994, that if she would just sit back and let the FBI do its job, the case would be solved by the end of the year. Looking up, she told the agents, "Well, it's the end of 1995."

Temple's response almost knocked Linda out of her chair. He told her and Larry that the FBI had not been able to find any evidence pointing to murder.

"There is no evidence," he said.

Linda stared at him in amazement.

Temple added, "It might be time for you to consider that a crime was not committed."

Larry was quiet. Linda could feel herself begin to shake. For nearly two years, Cournan had been telling her and Jean Duffey that the investigation was going well. Now, with Cournan at his side, Temple was telling them this. Not only was the investigation over, but she and Larry were hearing Temple tell them the same thing they had been told, first by the Saline County Sheriff's Office, then by Fahmy Malak: no crime had been committed. Eight years had passed since the exhumations and Dr. Burton's autopsies and the grand jury that had ruled the deaths murders—and now this. Linda sat in the FBI office scarcely able to breathe. She realized that when she cried it was usually because she was angry. She was furiously angry now—and she was crying—and she could not find a Kleenex.

Why would the FBI spend nearly two years on a case for which not a shred of evidence existed? She did not believe what Temple, and now Cournan, were telling her. She knew that Cournan had invested hundreds of hours in the investigation. She recognized the difficulties inherent in making a case in murders that were now more than eight years old. She would not have been surprised if Temple and Cournan had told them, "Mr. and Mrs. Ives, we've worked this case hard for two years now. We've done everything we know to do. We've got some good ideas of what we think happened, but we don't have enough to go to court." She and Larry had braced themselves for that. *That's all they would have had to do and I would be sitting here with my mouth shut,* Linda thought. Instead, this: Temple telling them, on behalf of the

FBI, that it might be time for them to consider that a crime had not been committed!

Linda fired questions at them. Had the Justice Department been looking at Chuck Banks and the way he'd shut down the Harmon investigation, as Cournan had said? Temple responded that he had never heard such a thing. Turning to the Bureau attorney, Temple asked, "Do you know anything about that?" The lawyer shook his head. "I think I would have heard that if it had happened." Linda looked at Cournan. She wanted to ask, "Were you lying or are they?" She wanted to ask Cournan why she had told Jean that Floyd Hays had been brought in to assist on the case more than a year into the investigation if there had been no evidence. There were dozens of questions she wanted to blast in Cournan's direction, but Linda's respect for the agent stopped her. Cournan had worked hard on the case. Maybe there was an explanation. Maybe there was something that she could not say in this meeting, here with Temple—something that she might explain to her and Larry later. Linda opted not to put Cournan on the spot.

Instead, she asked about the teenage witness, the boy whom the FBI had tried to place in protective custody. Cournan told them that while he had heard voices that he thought he recognized, he had not seen anything. Linda said, "That's not what he told me."

Cournan repeated that there was no evidence, there were no suspects.

Linda asked about the clothes. The agents said they had been unable to extract DNA because the clothes had not been properly stored.

She said, "What about the knife?" Cournan said that it was clean. "That knife had blood on it," Linda said. "You know it did. The Little Rock police intelligence unit even generated a report on it. I've seen it. They didn't know if it was animal or human, but they said it was blood."

Cournan answered evenly, "Little Rock intelligence never issued a report. The knife was clean. It had nothing but rust on it."

"That is a lie. That is a lie," Linda said. Throwing her pencil on the table, she rose and grabbed her purse. "I don't have to listen to this bullshit." She told Larry she had to leave. He said he would follow in a few minutes. He had a few more questions to ask.

In a rest room outside the office, Linda finally found a tissue. She rummaged through her purse and swallowed a tranquilizer. Resting her cheek against the room's cool tile, she tried to compose herself. But Temple's words kept pounding in her head: *It might be time for you to consider that a crime has not been committed.* This was madness—cunning and treacherous. Had all that she and Larry endured for the past eight years been for nothing? Could everything that had happened, every investigation they had fought for, every bit of information that had surfaced, be whisked away just like that? Here again was the optical illusion, the suggestion that they set aside the evidence of their senses. A crime had not been committed! Linda wanted to scream. What had the FBI been investigating for the past two years if there had never been a crime?

EIGHTEEN

"JUST A NUTCASE"

JANUARY–MAY 1996

The days following the meeting with FBI agent Temple were dark for Linda, darker than any had been since Kevin's death. Larry tried to soften the blow. He reminded her that Temple had said only that they should accept the *possibility* that a crime had not been committed. To Larry, that made some difference. To Linda, it was splitting hairs. What mattered was that after devoting two years to the case, the FBI had shut it down. In their desire for a fair investigation, she and Larry were no better off than they had been the day after the boys were killed. Their hopes were exhausted.

By now Linda understood how differently she and Larry coped. Larry had been as disappointed as she with all the failed investigations, but he had never been as angry. And in the absence of any hard evidence, he refused to speculate.

"I'm a realist," he told her. "That's one place where you and I differ. I look at things the way they are, and you kind of form your own picture. You form your own opinion." Sometimes, he told her, he thought she formed those opinions too quickly.

THE LETDOWN

It was an old debate for them. As far as Linda was concerned, there was a reason no evidence had surfaced. There was a reason to believe that law enforcement officials had been involved in the crime and in its cover-up. It now appeared that federal agents had been involved in other cocaine-related crimes in Arkansas, and in their cover-ups, as well. When officials fail to fulfill their investigative or prosecutorial duties, citizens can do nothing but hypothesize. Denied a fair investigation, she and Larry had been left to wonder, just as

Duncan and Welch had been left to wonder about Mena. The FBI had taken Linda and Larry's good faith and twisted it, just as Govar's and Duffey's investigation of Harmon had been plowed under and just as the investigation of Mena had gone nowhere. She could not understand how Larry could continue to trust in any of it.

"I don't believe I can force the triumph of good over evil," she told him one evening, as the shock of the meeting with Temple subsided. "And believe me, I don't have any illusions about which side is going to win. But I'm not going to just lie down and let them roll over me." There was a fatalism in her view that was new. But despite it, the old resolve had returned. It had been nice to live with some hope, but if that was not going to lead anywhere, she welcomed the return of her anger. At least she could trust it. And there was Jean to count on, as well—Jean, who felt as betrayed as she.

"I'll tell you what we're going to do," Jean told Linda on the phone. "We're going to keep this thing alive, and the way we're going to do that is by dusting off our video and getting it into production." Completing the video they had begun with Nancy Kurrack—keeping "this thing" alive—was all they could see to do.

The women foresaw problems from their association with Matrisciana and his *Clinton Chronicles.* But Matrisciana had taken an interest in their battle with Saline County officials when the rest of the media had not. He had been willing to help them tell their story and had given them control of the script. If no civil authority, either in Arkansas or in the nation, was willing to push for justice, Linda and Jean resolved to tell that story. They would take their allies where they could find them. If Matrisciana was to be their vehicle, they were glad to have his help.

Another ally closer to home turned to another medium. Jean's brother, Mark Keesee, established a Web site where he began posting information about the case. It was a vast undertaking, one to which Mark would devote countless hours. Already reports were spreading around the Internet relating to Kevin and Don, Saline County and Mena, and many of them were either laced with error or absolutely false. Mark wanted his site to be accurate, a place where Linda and Jean could present their evidence. Within weeks, he established "idmedia.com"—the "id" for Ives and Duffey—and began posting records from the past eight years.

RAIDING THE COURTHOUSES

The saga in Saline County continued to unfold as quickly as Mark could post the news on the Internet. Two days after the discovery of the fake cocaine at Holly DuVall's condominium—packets that the crime lab reported originally had contained one hundred thousand dollars worth of cocaine—federal officials reported that Holly had apparently stumbled into an unrelated sting operation. Agents monitoring an informant's phone calls picked up a call placed by DuVall from a phone traced to Harmon's apartment. Federal and state agents reportedly heard Holly arrange to buy some methamphetamine, then recorded her meeting with the informant and arrested her immediately afterward. Dan Harmon insisted that he was not present at his apartment when his ex-wife made the call. But the situation was worsening for Harmon. First, evidence stolen from the safe was found in his ex-wife's possession. Now officials had records that his phone had been used to arrange a drug buy. Facing mounting pressure, Harmon relinquished the part of his prosecutor's duties that placed him in charge of the district's drug task force. But he angrily made it clear he would not step down as prosecutor. Sheriff Pridgen was appointed to take over as head of the drug task force.

Linda read the news to Jean that state officials were considering withdrawing funding for the district's drug task force.[1] She knew that Jean would feel some vindication. Linda related how Judge Cole had not answered reporters' questions about his order to destroy the evidence in the case of the two men from Texas, even though it had not gone to trial. In phone calls over the next several days, Linda passed on to Jean more of what Rodney Bowers had reported based on his examination of courthouse records. Besides the unprosecuted case of the Texas men, Bowers found several other drug-related cases in which district officials either had released defendants without scheduling trials or had failed to issue warrants when defendants had not appeared for court.[2] Bowers reported that records on two other drug-related cases were missing from the courthouse entirely.

A few days after those reports began, a half dozen FBI agents pulled into the parking lot of the Saline County circuit clerk's office. They walked to the front door and posted a sign that read CLOSED FOR INVENTORY.[3] As reporters and courthouse staff watched from outside, the agents downloaded computer files and hauled out boxes of records to a waiting U-Haul truck and a Chevrolet Suburban. Two blocks down the street, another dozen or so federal and state officials swarmed into Harmon's office. The prosecutor, who had come to his office wearing jeans and a gray pullover knit shirt, appeared agitated but not surprised. He told reporters that he had been notified in advance that the agents planned to confiscate his files, but he was indignant at the way the confiscation was being carried out. Comparing the agents' methods to those of the KGB, he complained bitterly that the FBI had "leaked" word of their plan and described the event as a "raid." When reporters questioned Harmon about DuVall's call to the informant from his apartment, the cocaine packets taken from his evidence locker, and the Texas men who had been allowed to leave the state without prosecution, Harmon snapped, "Why don't y'all get a job? I've got freedom. Get away from me."

Linda was almost as indignant as Harmon—but for different reasons, of course. What kind of "raid" is it, she asked Jean on the phone, when the subject is notified in advance? Harmon always seemed to get special treatment. In her most cynical moments Linda wondered if the records had been removed, not for purposes of investigation, but to prevent further scrutiny by Bowers—and perhaps more embarrassing disclosures. What if it was all a ruse?

Whatever was going on, it continued. The week after their raid, federal agents expanded their seizure and executed similar search warrants at the courthouses in the district's other two counties.

As the latest Saline County probe expanded, the ongoing investigation of Roger Walls, Duffey's replacement, also came to light. Bowers reported that agents were questioning how, within a single year's time, Walls had been able to amass almost $500,000 in bank loans—part of it for the purchase of Catherine's Restaurant—on an annual salary of $34,200. Payments on the loans reportedly exceeded $24,000 a year. When asked about his debts, Walls admitted that he had no income besides his salary and revenues from the restaurant and an adjacent motel, for which he was also indebted. Still, he contended that investigators had examined his finances and found nothing wrong. He insisted that he would remain as the drug task force's director.

Linda found the reports on Walls's finances almost more interesting than the missing drugs. During their married life, she and Larry had bought a house and financed a car or two. They knew what it was like to ask the bank for a loan. Linda knew that she and Larry earned more than $34,200. But she could not imagine any bank in Benton allowing them, in the course of just one year, to rack up almost a half million dollars in loans, as banks had been willing to do for Walls. Linda suspected that what she was seeing was the money side of drugs, the business behind the trade—an aspect almost never glimpsed. She had long assumed that business interests in the district were supporting the local drug trade and keeping certain corrupt officials, including Harmon and Walls, in power. She figured it was the same at Mena; money called the shots. Since she had begun to pay attention to the business of cocaine, she had grown used to reading about the arrests of low-level users and dealers, but she never read about the investors, the behind-the-scenes profiteers in this dangerous high-stakes black market. If agents were investigating Walls's financial condition, Linda wondered if the investigation could be—or would be—confined to only him and Harmon.

At the moment it looked like the two were the only targets of the probe.

Bowers reported that federal agents were building a racketeering case against "certain officials" in the Seventh Judicial District, and that indictments were expected soon. As he put it, federal investigators had been looking into the assets seized by the drug task force and that the numbers were "not adding up." Harmon responded by calling the federal agents "thugs." He scoffed, insisting he had nothing to hide and that he was "not that goddamn stupid" as to have kept incriminating evidence in his office. In almost the same furious breath, he announced that he would be running for reelection.

OUT OF HIDING

To Linda and Jean, Harmon was projecting. After all, who was really the thug? And whose agents were like the KGB? The worse the stories grew, the more Jean realized that Harmon's mounting disgrace would have to change some perceptions of her. She, her agents, and their informants had gathered evidence long ago that Harmon was involved in drug activities. After Banks cleared him, Harmon had been able to use his office to intimidate other witnesses and to send Jean into hiding. Now Jean decided to come out of hiding. For the first time since she had fled Arkansas five years earlier, she agreed to be interviewed by the *Arkansas Times*. She told of the instruction she had been given when she became director of the drug task force: that she was not to use her agents to investigate public officials. And she recounted how, within weeks of the task force's organization, they had begun coming in off the streets with information linking public officials, including Harmon, to drugs. "It all happened very quickly," she told the paper. "It was amazing."[4]

Moreover, she said, the problems with record tampering that federal officials were now investigating had been called to their attention years ago. "We ran across situations where certain case files didn't reconcile with the arrest records. There were instances where weapons, vehicles, drugs, and money had been confiscated, but the records didn't line up with the final court orders on the disposition of those items." Duffey explained how she had channeled all the information she and her officers had developed to Govar at the U.S. Attorney's Office and how, once Harmon had launched his own grand jury, U.S. Attorney Chuck Banks had advised her to tell Harmon all she knew.

Recalling "the bludgeoning" she had taken from Harmon in the media, Jean reflected, "They could have just sat still and quietly let me go away on Dec. 31 [1990], as I'd said from the beginning I planned to do. But we were building cases, so I had to be discredited. Everything we did had to be discredited. And it was."

Now it looked like Harmon and his choice to replace her, Roger Walls, were the ones who were being discredited. "I'm talking now," Jean told the

Times, "because I think it's getting pretty obvious to the public that there are elected officials in the Seventh Judicial District who are involved in drugs. I hope the public will start asking questions as to why the last federal investigation was shut down—especially when the feds have known about illegal activities in this district for years."

Harmon responded with familiar derision. "Ms. Duffey is insane," he told the *Times* for an article that was published with Duffey's interview. "Ms. Duffey is like most animal activists. She's a nut." As to the earlier federal investigation, he insisted, "If there had been anything there, Chuck Banks would have pursued it. Everybody's corrupt, according to her, from the mailman on down. These are the same things she's raised before. She's certifiable."

After that interview, Pat Lynch, a Little Rock talk-show host known for his liberal views, invited Jean on his show.[5] She recounted recent developments in the county, including Agent Temple's remark to Linda and Larry Ives that, in the deaths of their son and Don Henry, "a crime may not have been committed." As far as she and Linda were concerned, Jean said on the air, a crime most certainly had been committed, and the FBI was now part of its denial.

The comment elicited a quick response from I. C. Smith, the special agent in charge of the FBI's Little Rock office. Smith told the *Benton Courier* that he believed Duffey was mistaken in her conclusion about any "cover-up," though he acknowledged that his office did believe that "some doubt" remained "as to the causes of death" in the case of the boys on the tracks. He denied that the investigation had been closed, but said that the Bureau instead was wrestling with "the very real problem of determining whether federal jurisdiction would apply."[6]

Linda was incensed. On top of everything else the FBI had done, she felt Smith was now calling her a liar. Smith had publicly voiced two opinions about the case. One echoed Dr. Fahmy Malak's ruling that the deaths may have been suicides or accidents. "Something terrible happened out there on the tracks," he once told a reporter. "Was it murder? I don't know."[7] He had also pointed out that most murders do not meet the criteria that would establish them as federal crimes. If law enforcement officers had been involved, acting "under color of law," the case would have warranted federal investigation as a civil rights crime. But, despite the lengthy investigations of official corruption in Saline County, Smith had never suggested that the FBI suspected police involvement. He had never publicly explained the FBI's interest in the case. To Linda, Smith's ambivalence was but another maddening example of the way logic had been trampled in this case. Either the FBI believed it had jurisdiction or it did not. If public officials were implicated in the murders, there would be no doubt that federal jurisdiction applied. On the other hand, if no one suspected official involvement, why had the FBI spent two years investigating the case?

Linda called the *Courier* and informed the paper of what Smith had *not* said: that for almost two years an FBI agent had reported to her and to Jean Duffey that progress was being made in the case. She said she found Smith's statements insulting and unbelievable. Another paper in the district agreed. "Whether or not a crime actually occurred," an editorial in the *Malvern Daily Record* read, "the case certainly *appears* to have been conveniently swept under the rug by local officials, the FBI, and the U.S. attorney's office. . . . " Recalling how quickly the FBI had acted on the Oklahoma City bombing case, the paper's editor added, "We're not asking a whole lot of the FBI. Just catch the crooks, if there are any. If there aren't, then close the case and tell us why."[8]

THE ABDUCTION

By now, questions about the deaths on the tracks and the many murders that had followed were not the only ones hanging over the district. Questions about Harmon were mounting by the day. In February 1996 state officials acknowledged that Harmon had not been reporting his drug-fund accounts. A few weeks later, in March, Holly DuVall appeared in federal court in Little Rock, accompanied by her ex-husband, to plead guilty to a charge of possession of methamphetamine. She left the courtroom facing a possible prison sentence of up to one year and a one-hundred-thousand-dollar fine. Two weeks later, Harmon surprised voters in the district by announcing that, come January, he would relinquish his post of prosecutor—a job that he had held for a total of ten years. He touted his record for prosecution of child-abuse cases and noted that, during his years as prosecutor, his office had never lost a murder case. "I feel I have accomplished all I set out to do as a prosecutor. There's very little left for me to do there." And then he dropped the other shoe. Instead of running for reelection, he announced, he would run for sheriff of Saline County.

Again Linda was on the phone to Jean. It was a relief to be able to laugh. "Can you believe it?" Linda sputtered. In running for sheriff, Harmon would be opposing the incumbent, Sheriff Judy Pridgen. John Brown, who had resigned as Pridgen's deputy, was also running against her, as was another candidate. Linda told Jean that the *Benton Courier* was reporting Harmon's candidacy without so much as a mention of the controversies surrounding him—the alleged beatings of his former wives, the drug cases that had gone unprosecuted, Holly's alleged call to a meth dealer from his apartment, or the current investigation into cocaine missing from the evidence locker. As though none of that were going on, the paper was merely reporting that while under

Harmon's direction, the drug task force had been "third in the state in the number of arrests, and the amount of property seized and forfeited, and number-one in the length of sentences assessed drug dealers." Sure, the women laughed. He really cracked down on his competitors. For years Linda and Jean had wondered about the paper's indifference to Harmon's behavior. And here it was again, more blatantly than ever. "If this is the way everyone in this county thinks," Linda told Jean more soberly, "Danny'll be our new sheriff."

But if Harmon had supporters who were trying to save him from himself, he was also on a course of self-destruction that was veering beyond their efforts. According to news accounts, on March 30 Sheriff Pridgen reported that at about 3:00 A.M. she had been awakened by a call from one of her deputies informing her that Holly DuVall's father, Wilson DuVall, had called the sheriff's office to report that Harmon had abducted his daughter. Fearing a political conflict of interest because Harmon was now her political opponent, Pridgen told the deputy to notify the state police. This is what reporters were able to piece together, based on police reports from the people involved:

The incident had begun the day before, at a Piggly Wiggly grocery store in Hot Springs, where Holly had taken a job. Harmon came into the store, yelled at her, and during the disturbance that ensued, shoved her and the store's manager, who had tried to come to her aid. When local police were called, they charged Harmon with two counts of misdemeanor battery. Later that night, when Holly got into her Chevrolet Blazer for the thirty-minute drive back to Benton, she saw Harmon following behind her in a blue Buick sedan. She told police he followed closely, driving erratically, repeatedly forcing her off the road. Reaching Benton at about 2:30 A.M., she drove to her parents' home. Harmon followed her into the driveway, ramming the back end of the Blazer. DuVall said he then pulled her out of her car and forced her into his. This was confirmed by DuVall's father, who said he heard the crash in the driveway and went to the window, from which he saw Harmon "drag" Holly from her car. Holly DuVall said Harmon then took her on a wild drive through the three counties in the judicial district, "yelling and screaming" for much of the time, at speeds approaching one hundred miles per hour. When Harmon drove into Malvern, DuVall said, he tried to persuade her to go to a motel. When she refused, he drove her back to his home in Benton. There, she said, he calmed down and told her that she could drive the Buick home.

At about eight-thirty the following morning, an officer with the Benton Police Department cited Harmon for running a stop sign. The officer was not aware of the alleged abduction and Harmon was not arrested. Later it was learned, however, that when the officer called in Harmon's license and registration, he had been informed that the prosecutor was driving on a suspended license and that there was an outstanding warrant for his arrest, the result of his failure to appear in court in another county on a traffic ticket he had received there.

In the meantime, DuVall and her father had gone to the sheriff's office, where both had given statements. Checking the Buick, deputies found the left front parking light broken. The car, which bore dealer's plates, did not even belong to Harmon. A few days earlier, he had told the owner of a local used-car lot that he was thinking of buying it, and the dealer had let him take it to "try it out."

While the DuValls were still at the sheriff's office giving their statements, Harmon arrived in a mood that deputies later described as "real belligerent." They arrested him, charged him with kidnapping, terroristic threatening, and aggravated assault, and put him in the jail. Within hours, with Harmon still behind bars, Judge Cole was telling reporters that because Harmon was innocent until proven guilty, he could continue to serve as the district's prosecutor while preparations for his trial proceeded. Conceding that "as long as he's in jail, he's going to have a difficult time," Cole authorized Harmon's release on a twenty-thousand-dollar personal recognizance bond. That done, the judge withdrew from the case, saying that he would ask the state Supreme Court to appoint a special judge and a special prosecutor.

Linda suspected she was seeing a couple of dramas playing out. One was the familiar one of perpetual support for Harmon from powers within the community. The other was Harmon's own: his increasing drive to self-destruct, a drive that was beginning to make supporting him difficult, even for his most ardent backers. Harmon's behavior, which had never been moderate, was escalating—becoming more violent and erratic. It remained volatile even while he was in jail. When Judge Cole authorized a signature bond, Harmon refused to sign. He accused Pridgen of arresting him for political reasons, to keep him from campaigning against her. He told reporters that he was going on a hunger strike in order to force authorities to grant him "his day in court." Pridgen questioned whether anyone—herself included—could speed up Harmon's trial when there was no prosecuting attorney to pursue it, and Judge Cole, along with the district's other judges, had withdrawn from the case.

THE VIDEO

Linda and Jean had stayed involved in the production of the new video, and in March, 1996, *Obstruction of Justice* was released without fanfare. There was no public showing in Saline County or anywhere else in Arkansas. Instead, the video was distributed mostly through the conservative outlets that had first become interested in Saline County through *The Clinton Chronicles*. But this video was no *Clinton Chronicles*. Linda and Jean were proud of it. They had been involved in it since the beginning. This time, when the completed video arrived in the mail, they expected nothing in it to come as a surprise.

The tape opened with the date Linda and Larry would never forget—August 23, 1987—printed in stark white on an all-black screen. The first scene was of the railroad tracks where Kevin's and Don's bodies had been found. A narrator, explaining that they had been run over by the train, continued, "Little did anyone know at the time that these two friends had unwittingly stumbled into an underworld of drug smuggling and government corruption. . . . " Linda, in a pink sweater, seated in her home, was shown saying that she believed law enforcement officers had killed the boys and that a cover-up of the murders had begun immediately. Thereafter she appeared intermittently on the video, summarizing the story of the past eight years as the events had appeared to her. Much of the story was told with the help of archival film from Little Rock television news. Clip after clip showed local TV reports detailing Malak's ruling, the mounting pressures against him, and Clinton's support of him. There was also archival film of Dr. Joycelyn Elders, whom Clinton had since appointed to be U.S. surgeon general. In one clip Elders told a Little Rock TV crew, "Based on the facts I have, I really feel that Arkansas owes Dr. Malak a great debt and a real apology."

Linda was then on the screen, commenting: "It didn't matter what Malak did. . . . Clinton defended him." The story recounted the grand jury investigation led by Garrett and Harmon, and the number of witnesses and informants who had died or disappeared. The narrator explained that authorities "suddenly found themselves in the awkward position of having to try and convince the public that the deaths of these key witnesses, coming at a crucial point in the investigation, were merely a coincidence."

Linda added, "The people whose testimony might have solved this case years ago have systematically been eliminated. There apparently was a great deal of fear that these people could implicate very powerful players." A television news clip of the grand jury's conclusion included the voice of Judge Cole as he advised the jurors that he was ordering that their final report be kept secret. "I know that because you could not repeat in the report much of the testimony that you heard and evidence that you received, that you are somewhat frustrated, and that's understandable. . . . " Then there was film of the grand jury foreman, Carl Allen, complaining about the secrecy. "In the final analysis, I know that the grand jury hated to give it up because I think the public needs to know about the seriousness of the drug problem here in Saline County, and maybe the surrounding counties." But news clips showed Harmon and Garrett taking a different view. As the grand jury investigation into who had killed the boys ended, Garrett acknowledged on film, "We certainly don't have any suspects at this point in time." Harmon glossed over the jury's concerns, choosing, as had Judge Cole, to compliment the disgruntled jurors. "Whatever comes out of it, if someone's charged or not charged—the grand jury did a fine job."

Swiftly the video switched to the story of Jean Duffey and public corruption—particularly as it concerned Harmon. The video outlined how Govar's memos naming Harmon as a suspect had been leaked to the media and how, at about the same time, Duffey's drug task force had been shut down.

The video showed inmate Sharline Wilson, one of Duffey's former informants, in footage shot at the Women's Unit of the Arkansas Department of Correction, where she had been sentenced to thirty years after being prosecuted by Harmon on a second-offense drug charge. Describing the testimony she had offered before Govar's federal grand jury, Wilson said on-camera, "I was asked quite in depth about the drug trafficking that went on with Dan Harmon. . . . I was assured by the U.S. Attorney's Office that my name, that my testimony, that my statement—that the people that were on that witness list—would never, ever be revealed. Well, ha-ha. You know, someone in the U.S. Attorney's Office had given Mr. Harmon a list of the effective witnesses. You know, that don't give you a very good feeling. I'm scared of these people. I'm very scared of them."

After a series of TV news clips of Banks's public announcement clearing Harmon, the video moved to John Brown, the former Saline County detective. It was Brown who made the link on the video between drug corruption in Saline County and drug corruption at Mena. He said the first indication he had "that Mena might tie in to the deaths of these two kids" had come when Russell Welch, the Arkansas State Police investigator at Mena, gave him an audiotape of a statement made by a confidential informant in a federal prison. The informant alleged that the boys were killed because the drug activity they had discovered was connected to the drug enterprise headquartered at Mena. The video explained briefly what was known about Barry Seal and his use of airplanes to distribute cocaine. Brown told of reports he had found in the Saline County Sheriff's files dating back to 1987 and 1988, of residents living near where the boys' bodies were found "complaining of planes flying over the tracks at approximately one hundred feet above ground level, with their lights off at night." The video suggested that officials had both ignored the drug activity at Mena and interfered with the investigation of the deaths of the boys on the tracks.

Linda explained that when investigations repeatedly failed, especially when they had never followed standard practices in the first place, it was hard not to be suspicious. For her, the common denominators of cocaine, airplanes, and stifled investigations at Mena and in Saline County were too strong to overlook. She believed the situations were linked. "When the Mena connection was made in my mind, and I looked back on everything that had happened," she said, looking into the camera, "I knew it was the only thing that had ever made sense to me."

The video concluded with the recent news about Harmon: the complaints of domestic violence, the packets of fake cocaine found in DuVall's condominium, the discovery that the packets had been removed from the prosecutor's evidence locker, the confiscation of the drug task force's files, and the unconfirmed reports that federal investigators had been developing a racketeering case against Harmon and others in the district. "However, after years of seeing investigations go nowhere," the narrator intoned, echoing Linda's and Jean's assessment, "a weary public remains skeptical." Citing Agent Temple's recent observation that in the case of the deaths on the tracks, "a crime may not have been committed," the video ended with footage of Linda in the empty courtroom where, almost nine years earlier, the Saline County Grand Jury had ruled that Kevin's and Don's deaths had been murders. Somberly Linda expressed her belief that "what is happening here in Arkansas is only a small sample of what is happening nationwide.

"This is not a political issue with me," she said. "We were never a political family. Our lives revolved around the ball field and going to the lake and all the things that a family does—until the Arkansas political machine reached into our lives and destroyed the tranquillity that we had. And I want the American people to know that we have to stand up against this kind of corruption. We have to hold our officials accountable and make them work for us instead of against us."

Larry's reaction to the production was divided. He applauded Linda for having kept the questions about Kevin's death before the public. This was another part of that effort. He could see how much of their difficult tale had been compressed into a clear presentation. But Larry disapproved of some of the conclusions Linda and Jean had drawn. "If you can't prove it beyond a shadow of a doubt," he told his wife, "maybe you shouldn't say it. I've seen how rumors get started on the railroad," he said. "Somebody says something, and where there was an 'if' before, this time it's a 'sure.' When you get a lot of people involved, sometimes things can change. Things get bigger and more stuff gets added to it. You can get consumed by that kind of stuff unless you just stand back."

For her part, Linda admired her husband's gentleness and respected his desire to "just stand back." She was grateful that he was as tolerant as he was slow to judge, that he was not one of those men who think their way is the only way. There had been times when she had been upset with him because she did not think he was as angry as he should have been. And he had been upset with her about some things she had said in public that he thought would have been better left unsaid. But long ago they had worked out this part of their relationship. They learned not to expect each other to be something they were not. Linda gave Larry the peace he wanted, not involving him in her efforts. And he let her do her work. But he did make one demand. The cost of Linda's long-distance phone calls was hovering around $350 a month. "I work as much as I can," he told her. "If you're going to talk that much, I think you should pay for it yourself." Linda agreed and found a job where she could work three days a week as a medical records clerk.

THE RADIO TALK-SHOW CIRCUIT

The phone in Linda's kitchen rang constantly in the months after the video's release. Linda and Jean became popular guests on radio talk shows around the country. From a chair at her kitchen table, Linda answered questions about the past decade's events in Saline County for listeners from New York to California. A few hosts, such as Lynch in Little Rock, could be described as politically liberal. Most were unabashedly conservative. Although Linda found most of them gracious and generally well informed about the video, she quickly grew to dislike doing the interviews. They were not like the media contacts to which she had become accustomed. While these interviews were to talk about the case, they were also to promote the video, and instead of the focus being primarily on Kevin and Don, the hosts' main interest was on President Bill Clinton. Linda and Jean developed a standard response to the inevitable Clinton questions. "We think that people in his administration interfered with the investigation, but we're not interested in criticizing Mr. Clinton. Our focus is on the local level, on finding and prosecuting the people who murdered Kevin and Don."

They explained that at this point the only justice they could envision would be through a civil rights lawsuit.[9] But litigation would be costly. To help with the anticipated expenses, Linda and Jean established a "Civil Justice Fund," to which Matrisciana agreed to contribute part of the price of every video sold. Even so, Linda grew to hate doing the radio shows. "I feel like this poor little mother who's trying to hawk a video. I feel like everybody thinks I'm looking for sympathy." She wanted people to understand it was not sympathy she was seeking. She was looking for justice.

Despite Linda's distaste for the radio shows, she and Jean continued to do them through the summer. Linda would recount the story up to the part where Jean's drug task force was formed, then Jean would tell about Govar and the federal grand jury. Then they both would tell what they knew about the FBI investigation, mentioning Agent Cournan by name. The decision to do that had not been an easy one. And it led to one of the biggest disagreements

Linda and Larry would have. They both felt that Cournan had worked diligently on their case. But now Linda and Jean were relating Cournan's statement to them that the Justice Department had been looking into Banks's conduct in Govar's grand jury investigation—something that, until now, the two women had not revealed. Larry thought that in doing so they were betraying Cournan. Linda argued that it was the FBI who had broken faith, and as a result, all bets were off. She argued that she and Jean had nothing to offer—no way to tell their story—except by putting forth the truth of their own experiences. "I like Phyllis as much as you do," she told Larry, "but Phyllis made her choice. If I have to choose between loyalty to Phyllis or loyalty to Kevin, my allegiance is with Kevin."

The decision carried immediate consequences. An FBI agent contacted Jean's brother David, who had been the first to hear from Cournan. The agent questioned him about what Cournan had said. The Bureau also sent an agent from Washington, D.C., to Houston to question Jean at her home. Oddly, even though Linda was the third person to whom Cournan had made the remark about the purported review of Banks's conduct, no FBI agents questioned her. Jean and Linda were sorry to see Cournan exposed to internal scrutiny because of what they were saying, but they were not sorry enough to stop. This, they thought, was just one more example of the FBI in action: While Harmon, whom the FBI had been investigating for years, remained in office, they were pouncing on Cournan, one of the few investigators Linda and Jean had encountered who had tried to do her job.

"NOT SO CROOKED AS CRACKED"

In early April 1996, two days after deputies confined Dan Harmon to the Saline County Jail, he complained of back pain. They moved him to Saline Memorial Hospital. Doctors there attributed his pain to dehydration resulting from his hunger strike. "They figured they could arrest me on nothing, then let the case drag out until after the election, if it ever comes to trial at all," he told reporters from his hospital bed. "They've bitten off a chunk of me. Now let's see if they can chew it."

Linda wondered if there was a warning hidden in his words. For years Harmon had been allowed to operate with an impunity that would have been denied anyone else. The question always had been, why? Linda and Jean suspected that Harmon used information as a weapon, perhaps blackmailing influential people. Maybe it was information relating to drugs that had come to him through his grand juries. Or maybe it went back as far as the hospital grand jury, where sex and videotapes of prominent people had been alleged but never confirmed.

The state Supreme Court appointed Circuit Judge Hamilton Singleton of Camden, in southwest Arkansas, as special judge in Harmon's case. Singleton, in turn, appointed Paul Bosson, the prosecutor from Hot Springs, to serve as the special prosecutor. Harmon, who had begun eating again in the hospital, told the *Benton Courier* that DuVall had fabricated the story against him. He told the paper that, though he loved his former wife, when she was under the influence of drugs, "she gets real resentful, irritable, irresponsible, she's just totally different." Six days after his arrest, Harmon agreed to sign the bond authorized by Cole. He was released from the hospital and, within days, began his campaign for sheriff.

In mid-April, at a traditional outdoor debate for the candidates, Harmon shared the platform with Pridgen and the two other challengers. When it came Harmon's turn to speak, he verbally attacked Sheriff Pridgen for having attended meetings of the League of Women Voters, contending that the League members got together to "downgrade men." In an appeal for higher standards, he said, "I was born and raised here. I know the problems. Primarily I want to return the sheriff's office to its proper role—promoting harmony and trying to get along with the other law enforcement agencies." When Pridgen took the podium, she did not deride the prosecutor, who had recently been in her jail, nor mock his call for higher standards. Instead, she acknowledged her membership in the League of Women Voters. "I go to meetings," she said. "We don't talk about men." A Republican opponent, nonetheless, huffed that Pridgen was expecting a free ride in the campaign. "She thinks just because she's a woman, she can walk away with it. She has to work for it just like the rest of us."

Linda and Jean had never indulged in a discussion of misogyny as a possible explanation for some of their experiences. Both women had enjoyed long, comfortable marriages to men who respected and encouraged them. They tended not to think in terms of sexism. They regarded Harmon as a bully who, until his arrest by Pridgen, had been supported by a vast enabling system of the district's good ol' boys.

It was a system, however, whose power they may have underestimated. After Harmon's arrest, a reporter for the *Arkansas Times* conducted a casual noontime interview at Pinky's Restaurant on Interstate 30. The reporter questioned eight Benton professionals about "Danny" and his problems. The men spoke of Harmon affectionately, as though he were a kid brother whose escapades, while essentially harmless, were always landing him in trouble. But when the talk turned to Jean Duffey, the discussion's tenor changed. "She's crazy," one man said, echoing Harmon's assessment. Another said "eccentric," and his companions at the table agreed. The reaction to Linda Ives was even stronger. "Mrs. Ives cracked up," one man said authoritatively. "She's a profoundly disturbed woman. She's got it in her mind that Dan Harmon was there on the tracks that night watching those boys be murdered. He worked with her and tried to explain that there just was not any evidence. The FBI tried to explain that to her, too. But she won't listen." Some men voiced the opinion that the boys probably had not been murdered, as others nodded in agreement. "Malak may not have been right about the marijuana," one man commented, but, he added, "I think we've given too much credence to this Dr. Burton. The guy's kind of sleazy himself." Another man chimed in dismissively, "This whole thing's been fanned by these fruitcake nuts." Another diner suggested, "Mrs. Ives has held on to her grief too long." Knowingly he added, "You have to wonder why—whether there was some guilt in that relationship with her son."[10]

Harmon's reputation for domestic abuse, his untimely payment of income taxes, and the allegations linking him to drug traffickers had all been overlooked in the county for years. And they were still being overlooked. Meanwhile, among at least one group of noontime regulars, Harmon's critics—Linda Ives and Jean Duffey—were dismissed as crazy women or worse. If the men at the table noticed any pattern of special treatment for Harmon, none mentioned it. Even now, as Harmon stood charged with three felonies and two misdemeanors in connection with the abduction of Holly, and as he was being investigated about the stolen cocaine evidence, the wink and the nod continued. In mid-April 1996 Paul Bosson, the special prosecutor from Hot Springs, filed a motion for Harmon to have a psychiatric evaluation. "There is reason to believe," Bosson's motion read, "that the behavior of the defendant calls into question his fitness to proceed due to mental disease or defect."

To Linda it looked like someone wanted badly not to bring Harmon to trial. Reporters were equally astonished. They questioned Bosson about the rarity of a prosecutor filing a motion to protect the defendant. It was a point Bosson acknowledged. "Usually such a request comes from the other side," he admitted. "But it isn't too unusual. We've done it here before." Harmon's lawyer, by contrast, called the motion "very unusual," and Harmon himself objected.[11] Noting that Bosson's request was "a defense motion, not a prosecutor's motion," Harmon angrily insisted, "A prosecuting attorney does not have the right to force anyone to enter a plea based on mental defect or disease."

It was a bizarre situation. It reminded Linda of Harmon's trip to Indiana with former sheriff Larry Davis to speak on behalf of an accused drug dealer they said they had never met. But the roles seemed to be reversed. To Linda and Jean, these latest activities looked like an effort to help Harmon, even if he did not want the help. In the days that followed, Bosson's actions seemed to further indicate a reticence to prosecute Harmon. First, he announced that he was dropping the kidnapping charge based on statements DuVall had made. "If she isn't willing to proceed," he said, "we could be just spinning our wheels." By the beginning of May, with the primary elections drawing near, Bosson still had not decided if he would file additional charges against Harmon. When questioned, he blamed a still incomplete investigation by the state police and reported that the case could not possibly be wrapped up until after the May 21 primaries. Bosson insisted that politics had played no part in his decision.

But, whether it was intended to or not, the delay did not help Harmon. The district's confidence in Danny finally ran out. On May 21, 1996, voters handed him the worst defeat of his career. Pridgen easily won renomination as the Democratic candidate. Linda and Jean had doubted this day would ever come. What they had believed about Harmon, it now seemed, the district also thought. At the same time, they knew better than to think that Harmon's defeat at the polls meant justice would now be done. The drug business in the county, and probably in the state, was too big for that to happen. But at least Harmon had lost control of the district's drug task force. Now he would not be sheriff. And come the end of the year, he would no longer be prosecutor. It was a victory of negatives. Linda and Jean were satisfied nonetheless.

No one expected Dan Harmon to slide quietly from public view. Still, no one was prepared for his next display. On the morning after the election, during a heavy rain, the switchboards at the Saline County Sheriff's Office and at the Arkansas State Police Headquarters began to light up with calls from drivers going to work along Interstate 30. Dozens of them picked up their cell phones and reported that Dan Harmon was standing in the rain on the side of the freeway. In one hand he held a sign from his defunct sheriff's campaign. The other hand he shook in a clenched fist at passing motorists. By the time police arrived, he was gone. But the incident, which was widely reported, bolstered the spreading belief that, as one supporter put it, Harmon was "not so much crooked as cracked."

Or maybe he was high on drugs. But no one mentioned that.

NINETEEN

PREFERENTIAL TREATMENT

JUNE–DECEMBER 1996

Five years had passed since the *Arkansas Times* published its article "Out of Control in Saline County," discrediting Duffey and offering an almost affectionate portrayal of Harmon. Harmon had been prosecutor throughout that time and, until his replacement was sworn in, he still held the office. Eight days after the highway incident, Rodney Bowers, the reporter for the *Democrat-Gazette,* went to Harmon's office to inquire about the drug task force's status. When Bowers asked Harmon if he could speak with him, Harmon lunged, shoved him into the foyer of an adjoining courtroom, pushed him to the floor, and pummeled him about the face and on the head as Bowers yelled for help. Several of Harmon's employees rushed into the room. A couple of them pulled Harmon off Bowers, while Harmon kept trying to kick the reporter. When Bowers got up and struggled to a nearby pay phone to call police, Harmon broke free from his restrainers, tackled the reporter again, knocked him down, and slammed his head into a bench. Once again the prosecutor had to be restrained.

"EVERYONE ADVISED THEY SAW NOTHING"

Saline County deputies arrived quickly at the scene and began to question witnesses. "Everyone there advised they saw nothing," the deputies reported. Bowers told the deputies that he had been afraid to fight back for fear that Harmon would send him to prison if he struck a blow. "It's a heck of a feeling having the prosecuting attorney on you, hitting you, and you thinking he can send you to prison if you do anything about it." During the second part of the assault, while Bowers was trying to reach the phone, he said he had heard one woman scream for help and another yell, "Dan, it's not Holly! It's not Holly!"

A deputy took Bowers to a local clinic where he received medical treatment for cuts to his head, face, hip, chest, and ribs. While Bowers was at the clinic, Harmon burst into the sheriff's office. Deputies had to look at him twice. It was Harmon, all right, but hairless. In the hour since the attack on Bowers, Harmon had rushed into a barber shop and had his head shaved bald. According to deputies, the unfamiliar-looking prosecutor ran to the jail door, kicked at it, and yelled, "I just beat the shit out of Bowers, that reporter for the *Democrat,* and I'm here to do my time." When Sheriff Pridgen appeared, Harmon lunged at her. It took four deputies to restrain him. The jailer, James Richard Friend, was injured in the scuffle which was captured on closed-circuit video. "Harmon moved toward the exit door and Friend stepped in front of him," the deputies' report of the incident said. "Harmon pushed Friend; then a confrontation began, in which the suspect Harmon elbowed Friend in the groin and stomped Friend's right foot. Friend had had surgery on the foot the day before and this incident caused the foot to bleed." Judge Cole signed a warrant for Harmon to be arrested on charges of battery of the officers. On the warrant the judge entered the notation that Harmon had volunteered to undergo a physical and mental evaluation.

The *Democrat-Gazette,* which had not editorialized about Harmon's alleged attacks on women, was now indignant. "This is deplorable," Griffin Smith, Jr., the paper's executive editor, fumed. "Rodney Bowers is a good reporter trying to do his job. Neither he nor any other citizen ought to be in danger of violent physical assault from a public official. . . . "

Harmon gloated. "Rodney Bowers has lied about me for three solid years," he told the *Benton Courier* from his room at the Hot Springs County Medical Center's psychiatric unit. When the article ran, it was accompanied by a police mug shot of Harmon wearing a mustache but no other hair. He explained that his shaved head was a symbol, a protest against the mistreatment he had received from the media. "I had told Bowers repeatedly I will not talk to him because he is a liar," Harmon said. "I told him not to come around me, not to get in my face, that I had nothing to say to him." On the morning of the attack, Harmon said, "I'm walking in the door as this guy's walking out, and . . . the guy gets right in my face. He looks like a drug addict, to me, and that's what I thought he was. I thought he was a druggie." In the end, Harmon announced that Bowers had been "lucky." "It could have been a lot worse, if some people hadn't pulled me off him."

Bosson still had not filed charges in the incident involving DuVall. Questioned about Harmon's latest rampage, he was reduced to stating the obvious.

"Dan Harmon is a violent person who is unable to control his temper." Bosson said he would file a complaint of misconduct against Harmon with the state Supreme Court's Committee on Professional Conduct, an action that could lead to the removal of Harmon's license to practice law. In the weeks that followed, John Brown, who was now the chief of police at Alexander, editors at the *Arkansas Democrat-Gazette,* and the police chief at Malvern, one of the cities in Harmon's district, all filed similar complaints. "This is just a nutcase," Bosson said. "It's just a shame. The bad part about it is, this is a total disgrace to every prosecutor in the United States and also to every lawyer." Harmon had attacked Bowers while out of jail on bond from his earlier arrest. Nonetheless, at the same time Bosson was describing the prosecutor as violent and out of control, he once again allowed him to be released from custody, this time on a twenty-five-hundred-dollar bond.

Out of the psychiatric hospital and out of jail, Harmon held a press conference a few days later in the courtroom where he had attacked Bowers. He told reporters that he had been diagnosed as suffering from "an adjustment disorder" or difficulty in controlling his temper. As for Bosson, he said, "Personally, I like having an idiot for a prosecutor." Complaining that he was tired of being "tried, convicted, executed, and generally maligned by the press," he told the media that he wanted to be left alone. Noting that he still had seven months left in office, he said, "I want only to incarcerate as many illicit drug dealers as possible between now and January first." Asked if he would consider resigning, in light of the charges against him, Harmon shot back, "Hell, no."

THE *WALL STREET JOURNAL*

While the drama surrounding Harmon played out in Saline County, and while Kenneth Starr, the special prosecutor in the Whitewater case, expanded his dragnet investigation in Arkansas, the editors at the *Democrat-Gazette* engaged in a little drama of their own with the editors of the *Wall Street Journal.* The Arkansas editors were particularly offended by Micah Morrison's characterization of Arkansas as a backwoods beset by conspiracies. Linda knew Morrison by now. He had interviewed her at length about her experiences in Saline County. In light of the ongoing mysteries at Mena, parts of which the *Democrat-Gazette* had reported, and the kid-glove treatment accorded to Harmon, even after he had attacked one of the paper's own reporters, Linda was a little surprised by the Arkansas newspaper's reaction.

The *Democrat-Gazette* took exception to Morrison's charge that the Arkansas press was being "controlled by financial interests closely tied to the political establishment . . . " And it was quick to point out a few of Morrison's factual gaffes.[1] But what really seemed to rile Paul Greenberg, the *Democrat-*

Gazette's conservative editorial page editor, were what Greenberg called the *Journal*'s "ever more baroque suspicions" concerning conspiracies in Arkansas. Even John Brummett, the paper's most liberal writer, who considered the *Wall Street Journal* "probably the best newspaper in the world," decried its editorial page as being "out of its mind."

On April 18 the *Journal* upped the ante with a lengthy article by Morrison entitled "The Lonely Crusade of Linda Ives." It began:

"Linda Ives appears to be a simple housewife . . . but her tale is one of the most Byzantine in all Arkansas, involving the murder of her son and his friend, allegations of air-dropped drugs connected to the Mena, Arkansas, airport, a series of aborted investigations, and, she believes, cover-ups by local, state, and federal investigators." From there, Morrison compactly outlined the story of Kevin's and Don's deaths, through the botched county investigation; through Malak's marijuana ruling and the bungled state investigations; through Duffey and the aborted federal investigation into corruption in Saline County; through former Arkansas State Police officer L. D. Brown's allegations that Clinton seemed to know about drug running at Mena, through the recent and unfruitful FBI investigation into the deaths of the boys on the tracks; and through the winding saga of Dan Harmon, from his role as antidrug crusader, to a suspect in Govar's probe, to his status at the time of the article as a defendant charged with violent felonies and as a suspect in a new federal investigation into racketeering. Most of the events outlined in his article had been reported first, over the course of almost a decade, in the pages of the *Democrat-Gazette*. What apparently infuriated that paper's editors was that Morrison was now linking these events by pointing out their common denominators of drugs and failed investigations.

The *Democrat-Gazette* responded with a scathing editorial entitled "The Arkansas X-Files and the Decline of an Old Friend." In it, the editors derided Morrison's conclusions. "There is apparently no old story, discredited piece of gossip, or wild rumor that the *Journal* won't take seriously so long as its subject is Arkansas," they fumed. "What used to be an aberration on its part has become an addiction; the conspiracy theories now come so fast and thick that some days they threaten to swallow up the rest of the page. . . . "

Referring to the article on Linda Ives, the paper complained: "This time Mr. Morrison rounds up a couple of million of the usual suspects and throws them together in hopes that something will come out of this sweep-the-kitchen stew of names, suspicions, and general wackiness. The ingredients include, but are not limited to: the Mena drug investigation, the late Virginia Kelley's career as a nurse, Fahmy Malak's tragicomic tenure as medical examiner, and Dan Harmon's tragicomic tenure as prosecuting attorney of the Seventh Judicial District."

Morrison, the piece concluded, "takes the deaths of two young men, a poorly performed autopsy, politics, confusion, a hot-dog prosecutor, and a mother still grieving for her son, and comes up with: 'The case started nine years ago, when Bill Clinton was governor of Arkansas. Today, with Mr. Clinton in the White House, it is still rattling through the state, with one of the principal figures making bizarre headlines in the local press as recently as the last few weeks. Above all, the "train deaths" case opens a window into the seamy world of Arkansas drugs.' "

"What would the *Journal* come up with next?" the Arkansas paper demanded. Then, derisively, it answered its own question: " 'Arkansas and JFK.' Why not?"

To Linda, it looked like the *Democrat-Gazette* had aimed its barrage at Morrison's willingness to question the irregularities that had surrounded Kevin's and Don's deaths, as well as Mena, and Harmon's tenure in office. She wondered if the editors had simply become inured to the outrages the paper itself had reported. She could not understand the paper's snide description of what it called Morrison's "recipe for a good story." According to the *Democrat-Gazette,* that included starting with an "all-star cast," finding "a way to connect each name to the other," and always remembering "that lack of information translates into withholding evidence and/or obstruction of justice."

To Linda, that "lack of information" the paper cited should have been an embarrassment—a call to arms. Here were at least two grossly mishandled murders, a huge and well-documented drug operation, and a violent prosecuting attorney whom no one seemed willing to censure—and instead of demanding to know why each of those situations had been allowed to occur and then to persist, the editors at the *Democrat-Gazette* chastized the *Journal* and Micah Morrison for having the nerve to notice that all the events were connected by drugs.

THE DEAL

On June 13, three weeks after the attack on Bowers, Bosson charged Harmon with five felonies and one misdemeanor, the total from his recent confrontations. The charges included two felony counts of second-degree battery resulting from the attacks on the deputies and one felony count each of terroristic threatening, aggravated assault, and false imprisonment for the abduction of Holly DuVall, as well as misdemeanor charges relating to the attacks on Bowers and the manager of the Piggy Wiggly store. If convicted on all counts, Harmon faced a maximum sentence of thirty years in prison.

This was a first. But Linda and Jean were wary. Everything they knew about this district told them that Harmon would never face prosecution. Saddened by their cynicism, they settled back to watch. After years of Harmon's abuses, a few voices now called for his resignation. The *Arkansas Democrat-Gazette*'s was among them. Calling Harmon "the Disgrace of the 7th Judicial District," the paper suggested, "Dan Harmon needs help—before he hurts others. And the people of Saline County deserve a prosecuting attorney who doesn't skirt the law or take it into his own hands." As to those Harmon employees who were reluctant to report what they had seen of their boss beating Bowers, the editors reflected: "What a climate of collaboration, or maybe just animal fear, must pervade the Saline County Courthouse if not a single person would step forward at once to bear witness to what happened there." The *Benton Courier* did not comment.

Within days, Linda and Jean's cynicism was confirmed. A week after charging Harmon, Bosson accepted a plea bargain in which all five of the felony counts against him were dropped or reduced to misdemeanors. In exchange for releasing Harmon from all felony charges, Bosson accepted an agreement that Harmon would simply leave office as prosecuting attorney four months ahead of schedule, on September 1 instead of on January 1. Bosson said that his objective in accepting the deal had been to get Harmon to resign. He refused to explain why, if that had been the case, he was allowing Harmon to remain in office until September 1, a date still more than two months away.

To Linda and Jean, the deal looked like another raw example of politicians protecting their own. No judge or lawyer in the district called for Harmon's immediate ouster. And no paper called his plea agreement a disgrace. Bowers was no longer allowed to report on Harmon, having become, as a result of Harmon's attack, a subject of his own story. To Linda and Jean, Bowers's removal left a significant void in the coverage. No one demanded to know why Bosson had not prosecuted Harmon. This was not a case, after all, where evidence or witnesses were lacking. Two of the victims of Harmon's assaults were deputies. His attack on them in the jail was recorded on videotape. Wilson DuVall was a witness to the abduction of his daughter. There was evidence of the broken signal light on the car. It looked to Jean, a former prosecutor herself, like the case against Harmon was an almost certain win—if a prosecutor had wanted to win. Instead, Bosson had bargained. Why? And for what? That Harmon would resign as prosecutor a few months sooner than he would be leaving office anyway?

Bosson's statement about wanting to remove Harmon from office was a laugh. Though Bosson insisted that Harmon had not received preferential treatment, Linda and Jean knew that if he had prosecuted Harmon and won a conviction on even one of the five felony charges, Harmon would have been disqualified from practicing law. His days as a prosecutor would have been over. Bosson could have removed him from office that way. But he had chosen not to. Linda and Jean thought that it looked like the plea bargain had been struck entirely in Harmon's favor.

Wilson DuVall took a similar view. He complained bitterly that his family had not been informed of the plea agreement until after it was signed. Sheriff Pridgen also took a dim view of the deal. With Harmon facing no jail time, she voiced her continuing concern for the safety of some of his victims. As if to confirm the sheriff's fear, on the day after the plea agreement was signed, Harmon's third ex-wife, Teresa, called the Benton police to report that Dan, who had come to pick up their son, had once again become violent. She told police he had choked her and struck her on the head. "He's a crazy man," she told reporters. Vowing to leave town, she added, "I'm not going to wait around until he kills me."

After that attack, a few more people, including Pridgen, called for Harmon's immediate removal from office. Reporting on the growing chorus of complaints, the *Courier* noted, "Perhaps the loudest and most vigorous call for Harmon to step down came from the team of Linda Ives and Jean Duffey," both of whom, the paper said, had been "very outspoken in their opposition to Harmon and other public officials in the county." Linda spoke out again now. "I don't think there is any doubt in this wide world that he received preferential treatment," she told the Benton paper. "There are never any consequences to his actions."[2]

Finally, disgust took its toll. On the Fourth of July 1996, the *Courier* reported that "without much explanation and sounding a bit battle weary," Harmon announced that he would resign, effective July 10.[3]

DRUG CASES "THROUGH THE CRACKS"

At last, unbelievably and despite the efforts of those who had tried to help him, Dan Harmon was out of office. Richard Garrett took over as acting prosecuting attorney. Seven months had passed since the confiscation of the prosecutor's files, and so far not one indictment had been handed down. When reporters asked U.S. Attorney Paula Casey when the investigation might be concluded, she responded—in what struck Linda as an understatement—that sometimes FBI investigations get "hard to predict."

Twelve weeks after Harmon left office, James Steed collapsed and died. His death was ruled a heart attack.[4] Linda's mistrust of Steed had never wavered. Now, suddenly, Harmon was out of office and Steed was dead at age fifty-one. As she read his obituary, she noted that Rick Elmendorf, Steed's former chief deputy, had served as one of his pallbearers. Another pallbearer was Robert Shepherd, the former sheriff from the district, whom Clinton had appointed to be the state's drug czar.

In the months after Harmon's departure as prosecutor, Linda reduced her radio appearances, then stopped them altogether. She and Larry began to talk about buying property in the mountains on the western edge of Saline County and of building a new house. But such dreams were in the distance. In the meantime, the extent of the corruption Linda and Jean had been fighting was gradually coming to light.

It was learned that shortly after Christmas 1995, at about the time that Harmon's drug task force was coming under investigation, two men from Sheridan, Arkansas, had been stopped by a state police trooper on a traffic violation. The trooper had searched their truck and found nearly three pounds of methamphetamine, three loaded handguns, a bag of marijuana, and open containers of whiskey and beer. He had arrested the men, and the state police had turned the case over to federal authorities. The move had infuriated Harmon, who was still in office at the time. Calling the tactic "inexcusable," he had railed, "I strongly object to this type of undermining of local law enforcement. All I know is that these men are drug dealers and I want them in jail."

Now, in 1996, the rest of that story was emerging. A check of the county records, which federal agents had returned to the courthouse, revealed that Harmon's office had charged one of the Sheridan men on three previous occasions: once for being caught with marijuana, a handgun, and a set of scales in his car; a second time for allegedly selling "a quantity of methamphetamine"; and a third time for allegedly trying to kidnap his nephew. But Harmon had brought none of the cases to trial. [5]

For Linda, another case that would never be prosecuted struck even closer to home. It concerned a dead teenage boy, an alleged drug user whom Harmon had failed to prosecute, and his family's failed efforts to obtain justice in the case.[6] When the stepfather called the prosecutor's office, demanding to know how the person charged with manslaughter in the boy's death had escaped prosecution, he was told, "Well, I guess he fell through the cracks." "That," the stepfather commented, "was no consolation to us."

Linda's heart went out to the family. The episode reminded her once again of how tragedies were compounded when justice was not served. It was not merely a matter of some bad guys getting off. Or even of public officials profiteering from crime. It was a matter of human grief. Every day Harmon had remained in office after someone could have removed him, she thought, the misery had been compounded.

"NO RECORDS" ON MENA

But the mess left behind in Harmon's office was hardly the stuff of news. In Arkansas in 1996, all stories were eclipsed by Kenneth Starr's unpopular

Whitewater investigation of suspected white-collar crimes. Linda and Jean were not particularly interested in the examinations of the Clintons' business dealings, and they were even less interested in the allegations of sexual improprieties. Unless Starr was looking into what had transpired at Mena—which it now appeared he was not—they considered his investigation a sham, a political probe that would not go near the most delicate question of Clinton's governorship, because inevitably such a probe would touch Republicans, as well.

A few inquiries, however, did question what had gone on at Mena. During 1996, investigators for the House Banking and Financial Services Committee continued their visits to Arkansas, where they said they were looking into allegations that state agencies had laundered money from Barry Seal's operation. A spokesman for Jim Leach of Iowa, the committee's Republican chairman, explained that because "there's been a lot said about Mena," Leach wanted to "find out what the truth is and put it out to the public."

Charles Black, the former deputy prosecutor at Mena, told reporters that he had told Leach's investigators in a sworn deposition that he had seen enough evidence of money laundering at Mena that he himself could have gotten convictions. He said he could not understand why the evidence had never been presented to a grand jury. "To me," Black told a Fort Smith radio station, "that is a more interesting question than the fact [that the money laundering] took place in the first place. It's like the cover-up of the crime is often more interesting than the crime."

Even after being interviewed, however, Black, a Democrat, added that he did not expect anything to come from the congressional investigators' work. In comments that Linda thought sounded as jaded as some she and Jean had exchanged, Black said, "Based on what I have heard, if they do get to the bottom of the matter and do a full investigation . . . the results will damage as many Republicans as Democrats. And for that reason, my cynical belief is that there is a lack of motivation in either party to fully and properly investigate it."[7]

A mistrust of government as a result of Mena cropped up in other places, too. In July 1996, the month Harmon resigned as prosecutor, a columnist in the *Arkansas Times* noted that a year earlier she had submitted a request to the FBI, under the federal Freedom of Information and Privacy Act, for any records in its files relating to drug smuggling, money laundering, and gun running at Mena. The writer reported that J. Kevin O'Brien, chief of the agency's Freedom of Information and Privacy Acts Section, had recently responded: "A search of the indices to our central records system files at FBI Headquarters revealed no record responsive to your FOIPA request."

The columnist impolitely wrote that she did not believe O'Brien. She pointed out that she had in her possession a 1986 memo regarding Mena from

FBI special agent Tom Ross of Hot Springs, in which he stated that he had reviewed "the extensive investigation conducted in this matter." Besides that, she said, she had a letter that O'Brien himself had written in 1991 to Arkansas attorney general Winston Bryant, who at that time had also asked to see the FBI's files regarding Mena. In that letter O'Brien had notified to the Arkansas attorney general that his agency had located "60 documents totaling 208 pages" concerning Mena. But, O'Brien had added, "all 60 documents concern an FBI investigative matter which remains pending in our New Orleans Division. Therefore, all 208 pages are denied in their entirety. . . . " Now O'Brien was saying that a search of the agency's files had turned up "no records" relating to Mena. "Either O'Brien is flat-out lying," the *Times* columnist wrote, "or the records have been destroyed."[8]

That same month, the *San Jose Mercury News* published an explosive series of articles by its staff writer Gary Webb, reporting that during the mid-1980s, at about the same time Seal was operating, a San Francisco Bay area drug ring sold tons of cocaine to Los Angeles street gangs and funneled profits to Contra groups affiliated with the CIA. According to Webb, the CIA had thwarted repeated attempts to prosecute the ring's kingpin, possibly to cover up ties between the traffickers and Contra leaders. The articles did not say explicitly that the spy agency knew about the drug deals, but their suggestion that the CIA had been involved in them triggered a national outcry, particularly among African-Americans.

To Linda and Jean the furor was interesting, to say the least. The anger and sense of betrayal that residents of crack-infested L.A. neighborhoods were voicing directly echoed their own. For the first time since Linda and Jean had considered the possibility that crimes in their community might be related to government-sanctioned drug running at Mena, another group of citizens in another part of the country was now considering a remarkably similar possibility.

The *Mercury News* later backed away from Webb's most serious implications, those impugning the CIA, after the *New York Times,* the *Washington Post,* and the *Los Angeles Times* all ran lengthy investigative pieces of their own that disputed major points in the *Mercury News* account. All found, as the *Washington Post* reported, that "the available information does not support the conclusion that the CIA-backed Contras—or Nicaraguans in general—played a major role in the emergence of crack across the United States." Jerry Ceppos, executive editor of the *Mercury News,* admitted that the paper "did not have proof" that top CIA officials knew the Contras were getting money from the L.A. drug connection.

To Linda, however, the situation reflected the same Catch-22 that she and Larry had so often debated. She believed, as the *Post* had put it, that "the available information does not support the conclusion" that anyone connected to the CIA had had anything to do with bringing cocaine into the United States. On the other hand, at least so far as Mena was concerned, she knew that, as Arkansas attorney general Winston Bryant had once said, "a mountain of evidence" existed that cried out for investigation. The CIA was an ultrasecret organization. "Available information" about its activities was scarce even when those activities were legal.

As far as Linda was concerned, legitimate questions about the CIA and cocaine would linger until government officials offered full explanations about Barry Seal's activities in Arkansas, and, apparently, similar activities elsewhere. But there was little reason to expect such disclosure. Crucial information remained unavailable. The FBI denied the very existence of records relating to Mena. Nor were reporters the only ones who were finding it hard to get information. As Jack Blum, a Senate investigator looking into possible links between the CIA and cocaine, told Webb, "The Justice Department flipped out to prevent us from getting access to people, records—anything that would help us find out about it."

Blum was no gumshoe reporter. As chief investigator for Senator John Kerry's two-year probe of CIA connections with Contra drug smugglers, he knew how resistant certain agencies were to release information. In October 1996 Blum testified before the Senate that, while the Kerry committee found no evidence that the CIA had targeted African-Americans for drug sales, its investigation had been repeatedly stymied by William Weld, who was then an assistant U.S. attorney general.

"When we got into this area, we confronted an absolute stone wall," Blum told the Senate hearing. "Bill Weld, who was then the head of the criminal division, put a very serious block on any effort we made to get information. There were stalls; there were refusals to talk to us, refusals to turn over data. An assistant U.S. attorney who gave us information was reprimanded and disciplined, even though it had nothing to do with the case in a confidential way. . . . We had a series of situations where Justice Department people were told that if they told us anything about what was going on, they would be subject to very severe discipline."[9]

Besides the difficulty he had had getting information from the Justice Department, Blum testified, "We ran into another procedure which was extremely troubling. There was a system for stopping customs inspections of inbound and outbound aircraft from Miami and from other airports in Florida. People would call the customs office and say, stand down, flights are going out, flights are coming in. . . . That I found to be terribly troubling, and it's a matter that you all should be looking at very carefully."

Finally, when Kerry asked Blum to describe his investigators' encounters with officials at the Justice Department, Blum replied, "They would tell U.S.

attorneys, systematically, 'You can't talk to them. Don't give them paper. Don't cooperate. Don't let them have access to people who you have in your control.' And we had a very tough time finding things out."

Linda knew exactly how Blum felt. She figured that on Capitol Hill, as surely as in her own backyard, the term "available information" meant little. She reminded herself that it was significant that, even as the editors of the *San Jose Mercury News* were distancing themselves from Webb's reports, they did not dispute his contention that government agencies had hindered the paper's investigation: Freedom of Information requests to the CIA and DEA had been denied, and a request to the FBI had been ignored.

As Linda turned her calendar to November 1996, she realized that she was not as alone as she had felt at the beginning of the year, after that shocking meeting with Agent Temple at the FBI office in Little Rock. It was true that politics still held the winning hand. Politics had kept Harmon from facing trial. Politics continued to protect the unseen financial interests that backed the drug trade—local, state, and national. And politics continued to subvert any hope of a full investigation into what had transpired at Mena—or on the tracks when Kevin and Don were killed. Yet, through the diligence of a few honest investigators and the digging of a few reporters, some changes had come about, some nastiness had been exposed. Voters in the Seventh Judicial District, finally having had enough, had defeated Harmon at the polls. Even the dark question of whether federal agents had fostered connections to cocaine traffickers was beginning to attract some national attention. Respected newspapers, both liberal and conservative, were mentioning the CIA and cocaine in the same sentence, and they were beginning to notice the secrecy government agencies were maintaining around those topics.

Then something else quite improbable happened. In November 1996 Leach's congressional committee released a declassified summary of a report from the CIA inspector general's office about that agency's activities at Mena. Not surprisingly, the CIA insisted that, after reviewing about forty thousand pages of materials and interviewing more than forty people, it had come up with no evidence that any of its personnel had been involved in "money laundering, narcotics trafficking, arms smuggling, or other illegal activities at or around Mena." But the report did acknowledge that during the 1980s, the CIA had been at Mena. For two weeks, the report said, the CIA had run a "joint classified training operation with another federal agency at Mena Intermountain Airport."

Nor were those the only revelations. The inspector general's office also acknowledged:

- that the CIA had used Mena for "routine aviation-related services" on equipment the agency owned;
- that L. D. Brown, the state trooper who claimed to have flown out of Mena with Seal on a CIA-related flight, had indeed been a candidate for CIA employment in 1984, when Brown said the flight occurred;
- and that CIA personnel had had "limited contact" with Seal, during "a DEA sting operation" in which the CIA had installed cameras in Seal's plane, although the report claimed that there was "no evidence" that the CIA knew Seal's "true identity" at the time.

Despite the disclosure's limits and the elaborate disclaimers that accompanied it, Linda found it a remarkable admission. She considered it amazing that ordinary citizens, all working against secretive officials and agencies, had been able to uncover and report as much as they had about Mena—and about the CIA's presence there. She felt a strengthening of the resolve that had been wounded in the visit with Temple.

TWENTY

SUSPICIONS CONFIRMED

1997

In November 1996, just a few days before the CIA acknowledged its presence at Mena, Linda received a startling—and disturbing—call from a New York reporter visiting Little Rock. Philip Weiss, a freelance magazine journalist, told her that he had been asked to prepare an article for the *New York Times Magazine* about people who hated Clinton. Linda protested that she had never considered herself a Clinton hater. When interviewed on radio, she had always tried to make it clear that she was not interested in bashing the president, only in getting to the bottom of her son's murder. Why had Weiss called her?

"NUTCASE MATERIAL"

Weiss explained that Mark Fabiani, a White House associate counsel, had provided him with a set of newspaper clippings about people who opposed the president. Among the items was a story about "the boys on the tracks." Weiss said that some of the stories in the White House file alleged that the president had been involved in an array of murderous conspiracies. Some were obviously "ridiculous," he said, while others seemed "weird and a little crazy." But the story about Linda Ives had intrigued him. Later he would explain, "I asked someone friendly to the administration about the boys on the tracks case and they knew nothing about it. They pooh-poohed it. I think they expressed some vague sympathy to Linda Ives. They weren't dismissive of her, they were dismissive of the case. They said there is this mother who is very aggrieved, but her case has no connection to the administration. That's what I heard."[1]

Linda was angry and suspicious. "In other words," she told Weiss, "you're going to do a story about all of the Clinton bashers, and you want to include me." She knew nothing about Weiss. She told him that she did not want to be included in any article about either conspiracy theorists or Clinton-haters. In fact, she did not hate Clinton. She felt that she was being set up. What was most disconcerting was the idea that Fabiani, a White House lawyer, or anyone connected to the president, had been passing out packets of press clippings about citizens who they thought opposed the president. Linda could not believe she had been included in such a thing. Her next thought was to call Micah Morrison, the reporter and editorial page writer for the *Wall Street Journal* who had written about her earlier in the year. Linda liked Morrison and trusted him. "Micah, who the hell is Phil Weiss?"

Morrison praised Weiss's reputation as a journalist. "Why do you want to know?"

"He's doing a story on Clinton haters, and Mark Fabiani at the White House sicced him on me."

Linda told Morrison about the packet of press clippings Weiss said Fabiani had given him. Included in the packet was the article Morrison had written about her. Morrison was as surprised as Linda. Bemused, she asked him, "What would the White House care about me?"

After talking to Morrison, Linda called Weiss back. "Frankly," she told him, "I don't think I belong in your story." But, she said, she knew he would write it anyway, with or without her cooperation. So she would talk to him, though she admitted she was nervous. "All I ask is that you be fair and factual. And if you're not," she warned, "God will never let you sleep again."

Meanwhile, intrigued by Linda's call, Morrison made a few of his own. They resulted in an article that appeared in the *Wall Street Journal* on Jan. 6, 1997, in which Morrison broke the news that the White House was distributing to selected reporters packets of news clips detailing what it called "conspiracy theories and innuendo." Included in the packet was a White House document that purported to explain how these "theories and innuendo" often gained currency in the mainstream press. According to the White House report, Morrison wrote on the *Journal*'s editorial page, "Bill Clinton's Whitewater problems are due to a 'media food chain' through which conservative philanthropist Richard Sciafe engineers a 'media frenzy. . . .' "

Morrison paraphrased the report's scenario: "Mr. Sciafe's funding of the Western Journalism Center and publication of the *Pittsburgh Tribune-Review* introduces 'conspiracy theories and innuendo,' which are then picked up by the likes of the *American Spectator* magazine and London's *Sunday Telegraph*. From there they enter the 'right-of-center mainstream media,' such as the *Washington Times* and this editorial page. Then Congress looks into the matter and the story now has the legitimacy to be covered by the remainder of the

American mainstream press as a 'real' story. . . . " Morrison quoted Lanny Davis, the new White House special counsel, as saying that the report, titled "Communication Stream of Conspiracy Commerce," had been created "in response to press inquiries and provided to journalists who asked."

"Writers with a pro–White House history have recently been asking questions about the *Wall Street Journal*'s coverage of Arkansas housewife Linda Ives, whose crusade for answers to the unsolved deaths of her son Kevin and his friend Don Henry was detailed here April 18," Morrison wrote. "Indeed, this editorial page first learned of the 'conspiracy report' from Philip Weiss, a writer on assignment for the *New York Times Magazine,* who cheerfully acknowledged that he had discussed the Ives case with White House officials and had been given a report on 'the conspiracy feeding frenzy.' "[2]

Three days later, Morrison's discovery became the main topic of discussion at a White House press briefing led by presidential press secretary Mike McCurry. By then, reporters had learned that the Democratic National Committee had had a hand in the report. Minutes into McCurry's briefing, a reporter asked, "Mike, this three-hundred-page report that Fabiani and the DNC put together—what was the purpose of it? Why would the White House waste its time putting together this 'media food chain' theory?"

"It's not a waste of time," McCurry replied. "We were really responding to requests. This is a document we gave Wolf [Blitzer] of CNN, back in 1995, so you've had it for about over a year now." A ripple of laughter passed through the room because, as was later pointed out, few of the reporters present had ever heard of the report, and even Blitzer said he had never seen it. Unfazed, McCurry continued. "About every news organization in this room, in fact, we've provided these materials," he said, "because we wanted to refute some of the very aggressive charges being made fallaciously against the president, most often on the Internet, coming from a variety of kind of crazy, right-wing sources. Now, what you're talking about is, in fact, a two-and-a-half-page cover sheet attached to about three-hundred–plus pages of information, most of them news clips written by news organizations represented in this room, and also that the DNC research staff prepared and passed out at press conferences that most of your news organizations attended."

Another reporter asked, "Let me see if I can clear something up. Does this purport to show a conspiracy on the part of the news media?"

"No, absolutely not," McCurry said. "It purports to show that the conspiracy theorists who are very active on the subject of Whitewater and other subjects very often plant their stories, plant their information in various places, and then we kind of give you a theory of how things get picked up and translated and moved through what we call 'the media food chain'. . . . A good example of this: the *Wall Street* editorial page carries a column that mentions this deep, dark, secret, 330-page report that then gets picked up by the *Washington Times* and written and then gets asked here in the press briefing room. So in other words, in this Fellini-like manner, what we are doing right now is proof positive of the kind of cycle that we're talking about."

At one point McCurry explained that the report was an effort by Fabiani "to really help journalists understand that they shouldn't be used by those who are really concocting their own conspiracies and their own theories and then peddling them elsewhere." Piqued by the suggestion that they were being manipulated, the reporters continued to question McCurry. In turn, he tried to describe the scurrilous nature of the clippings provided with the report. Over the next several minutes, McCurry referred to the articles as "some crazy rumor that's now chased itself all the way around in a circle," "a lot of crazy stuff," "a lot of trash," "bad information," "nutcase material," and "political attacks on the president." When asked if the White House had spent taxpayers' money to rate how reporters were covering it, McCurry responded testily, "We're trying to protect reporters, not rate them. We're trying to protect people from getting a bunch of bad stories in their papers."

Linda, whose own had been included in the "bunch of bad stories"—and whose call to Morrison had exposed the packet's existence—was insulted. She was offended to learn that the account of Kevin's and Don's murders had been lumped with articles McCurry dismissed as "trash" and "nutcase material." But mainly, she found what was happening stunning. Her long-running demand for explanations had attracted White House attention.

McCurry's press briefing produced a flurry of articles about the heretofore unknown "stream of conspiracy commerce."[3] The *Washington Post* observed: "What's striking about the document is that it lays down this suspicion-laden theory about how the media works in cold print, under the imprimatur of the White House." The *New York Times* echoed the general amazement, noting, "It does not take the CIA or the FBI to know that the White House does not like everything that is written about it."

But to Linda, it was an editorial in the *Wall Street Journal* that again went to the heart of the matter. "Its silliness aside," that paper commented, "the 'food chain' report has to be seen as the nastiness it is. It's part of a generally successful Clinton effort to provoke criticism of members of the press who are reporting the Clinton scandals. Its implication is that because some rumors are extreme, all of the scandal stories are discredited. . . . In fact, the press has erred relatively seldom in spreading unfounded rumor. Especially so considering that the White House has scarcely been forthcoming with the truth."[4]

Two weeks later, after the furor had died down, Morrison mentioned the document again in an article about the CIA's recently acknowledged activity at Mena. It was the first time Linda realized that stories about Mena had also been included in the "nuts and crazies" material. Recalling that when Clinton was asked about CIA activities at Mena during an October 1994 press conference, the president said that, as governor, he had had "nothing—zero—to do with it," Morrison wrote: "The Clinton White House has gone to great lengths to discredit the Mena story. It figures in the notorious White House conspiracy report and was denounced by former Whitewater damage-control counsel Mark Fabiani as 'the darkest backwater of right-wing conspiracy theories.' "[5]

To Linda, it seemed that Morrison, almost alone in the national media, understood the power of stonewalling, denial, and ridicule in suppressing certain stories. Linda could understand the tactic's effectiveness. She had seen Harmon use it virulently against his nemesis, Jean Duffey. It had been used against Duncan and Welch, the investigators at Mena. It was a powerful technique, and hard to withstand, especially coming from government officials. Linda had absorbed the offenses purely out of loyalty to Kevin. She kept her own focus on what she knew to be true: that however the White House might deride her story, the questions she was raising about corruption in Saline County, about the behavior of state officials, and about covert activities at Mena still had not been addressed. That fact could not be changed by mocking her or her efforts.

"PRIVATE ARGENTINA"

On the last Sunday in February 1997, "The Clinton Haters" was the cover story on the *New York Times Magazine.* A color photo of Linda, taken in her living room beneath a portrait of Kevin and Alicia, ran with the table of contents. Her story appeared in a section of the article titled "Martyrs and Murders, the Body Count." Linda's anxiety rose as she read Weiss's explanation that some of Clinton's haters had begun keeping what they called lists of the "body count." "These lists connect scores of violent deaths to Clinton," he wrote. "They are picked up on talk radio; are in 'reports' like 'Murder in the First Degree,' which was prepared by a group calling itself Wall Street Underground, or get posted on Web sites like the one that was maintained by a Dartmouth graduate student from Idaho named Preston Crow, who is cited in the White House [conspiracy] report. As many as 56 murders have been connected to Clinton and his cronies by the Clinton craziest."[6]

After relating some of those deaths, Weiss continued, "The lists make sad reading, and ridiculous reading, but not entirely, and here one can glimpse how a legitimate question gets spun into a conspiracy. Notable on all the lists are 'the boys on the tracks.' This is the case of two small-town teenagers in Saline County, just outside Little Rock, who were killed late one night in

August 1987. They were clubbed and stabbed and their unconscious bodies were laid on the railroad tracks to be mutilated by a train. Their murders have never been solved. One theory given a lot of credence by those who have looked into the case is that 'the boys on the tracks' had wandered in on a drug drop.

"The medical examiner under Governor Clinton, Fahmy Malak, did a terrible disservice in the matter. He said that the boys' deaths were accidental, that they lay down on the tracks in a marijuana stupor. It took years for the family to undo this ruling." The story went on, "Clinton's own connection to the murders in Saline County is plainly indirect. But he did stand by Malak, even as the *Arkansas Democrat* and a group of enraged citizens called for his dismissal. (Malak left the job for a state health department position in 1991.) Linda Ives, the mother of one of the boys, says: 'My agenda is not Bill Clinton. The only goal I have is arrest and conviction in my son's case.' Still," Weiss wrote, "the deaths of the boys have taken on huge emblematic significance to the far right, people who believe that government regularly covers up brutalities."

To her relief, Linda was not mentioned in the article again, except for a reference to Matrisciana's video, *The Clinton Chronicles.* In this connection, Weiss wrote, "Several people who participated in *The Clinton Chronicles* were upset by it. Linda Ives was disturbed by its anti-Clinton agenda. So was Bill Duncan, now the chief investigator with the Arkansas attorney general's office. As an IRS agent in the late '80s, he began making strong charges about an official cover-up of crimes at Mena. 'I would not have willingly been a part of it had I known where that footage would end up,' he says. 'It was used by people for purely political purposes.' "

Linda still wished that she could have been left out of the article completely. But as long as she had been identified by the White House as a Clinton hater, she was grateful that Weiss had recognized "how a legitimate question," as in her case, "gets spun into a conspiracy." She appreciated his willingness to see beyond the White House spin.

Two months later, Weiss wrote about Linda again, this time in a more personal account that appeared in the *New York Observer.* In a section in which the writer described "poetic moments . . . that crystallize an intelligent person's understanding," he wrote, "My own moment with Bill Clinton came last year in Arkansas, and no document drop, however vast, will alter it. On Nov. 4 [1996], I met a woman named Linda Ives at her home not far from Little Rock." After briefly recounting the boys' murders, Weiss observed, "There is plenty of evidence of political obstruction of justice in the case, obstruction reaching to state officials. At the very least, Gov. Bill Clinton looked the other way. He protected the obstructive; he refused to meet with Linda Ives. So, for almost 10 years, Ms. Ives has lived her own private Argentina a few miles from the capital of Arkansas. . . .

"The night after I met Linda Ives was Election Night. I was in the crowd outside the Old State House building for Mr. Clinton's victory speech. I was squeezed against a barricade near a young redheaded woman. On my other side was a rugged guy in black jeans. We got to talking. The woman said she had known one of the dead boys in Saline County. The man said he knew law enforcement there. That's Arkansas; everyone knows everyone. I asked them for their phone numbers to follow up during a calmer time. The man refused. The girl shook her head.

" 'I don't even need a name,' I said. 'Just a phone number.'

" 'I might as well cut my throat,' the woman said. 'They found one witness to the grand jury in Saline County in the dump, burned beyond recognition.'

" 'For us locals, it's a dangerous situation,' the man said. 'It's still too open. And it will be open forever.'

"Bill Clinton was on stage right then, saying, 'Every child deserves a main chance.'

"That's the best understanding I ever got about Mr. Clinton. For all his bright promise and fine beliefs, he long ago made a deal with a benighted political organization that had thugs among its operatives. If you wonder why people hate him, it's because they recognize that training, they sense those crude values, that ruthlessness and lack of moral center. And they want an old-fashioned accounting."[7]

"BASIC FACTS OF TRUTH, HERE AND THERE"

While the national media reported on the Clinton administration's position that "crazy" conspiracy theories made their way into the mainstream press, newspapers within Arkansas had grown oblivious to the whiff of conspiracy in Saline County. More than a year had passed since police discovered the fake cocaine in Holly DuVall's condominium, and no one had been arrested. I. C. Smith of the FBI continued to say that the investigation was ongoing.

Meanwhile, Harmon, having pleaded guilty to two misdemeanor assault charges and no contest to two others, had returned to private practice. When Bowers asked the special prosecutor about his request to have Harmon disbarred, Bosson reported that the state's Supreme Court Committee on Professional Conduct had taken no action on the matter.

In January 1997, while Washington buzzed about the "conspiracy commerce" report, a federal grand jury in Little Rock indicted Holly DuVall and charged her with two counts of conspiracy to distribute cocaine and methamphetamine. U.S. Attorney Paula Casey said she could face ten years to life in prison and a fine of up to $4 million. To Linda, it looked like DuVall might take the entire rap, while Harmon, unscathed, would get a chance to rebuild his law career.

It seemed that even the mysteries of Mena were being blurred and forgotten. They were attracting some attention on the Internet, but what was passing for information was often garbled beyond recognition. The void that should have been addressed by a proper investigation was now filled with distorted shards of what was known and the flotsam of unfounded rumor. Even Mike Huckabee, the current governor of Arkansas, reflected the state of confusion. During an appearance on C-SPAN in February 1997, he took a call from a Bowling Green, Kentucky, resident who asked if Huckabee was "planning to reopen the case of the two teenagers that committed suicide in Mena, Arkansas."

Huckabee corrected the caller's misunderstanding about the geography of the event, noting "that the caller may be referring to two young men, not in Mena, Arkansas, but in Benton, Arkansas, which is several hundred miles from Mena. It is part of what some have produced on a tape linking the Mena airport activities to the deaths of two young people on the railroad tracks in Benton, Arkansas, just south of Little Rock." But he sidestepped the question about renewing investigations. He claimed that such a move would be "highly unprecedented."

The C-SPAN interviewer asked, "Are you often asked about the whole issue of Mena, Arkansas, and the tapes and the conspiracy?"

"Everywhere I go," Huckabee replied. "I mean, it is a constant question." Then, referring to "certain tapes that have floated out there," the governor, who was also a Baptist minister, continued, "There is enough sort of what I call basic facts of truth here and there, but tying certain things together really takes an imaginative leap. Please understand, I am a conservative Republican who lives in Arkansas and in an extreme minority politically, so I have no one to defend or protect here other than the truth. But the truth is that some of these—of what I call just extraordinary allegations—simply have more to do with imagination than they do with reality. I'm not saying that there were not some serious problems that took place in our state, and Lord knows, I don't want to backpedal or act as if we didn't have some problems. Obviously we have the courts to determine that. But everything that happened in our state is not all connected to some master plan, and I think that is utterly absurd for somebody to make those kinds of conclusions."[8]

Right, Linda thought. We have the courts. But if investigations are thwarted, and prosecutors won't issue subpoenas, and U.S. attorneys won't ask for indictments, the courts won't do us much good. A few years ago, hearing Huckabee's gobbledygook, Linda might have picked up the phone and given someone at his office the benefit of her thoughts. Or she might have fired off a letter. But by now she knew that such gestures were pointless. She knew, even if Huckabee was not revealing it to the C-SPAN audience, that the governor of Arkansas heads the state police. And there is no statute of limitations on murder. Governor Huckabee could order the state police to reinvestigate Saline County's string of unsolved murders at any time. He could also demand an explanation from federal officials as to what had transpired at Mena. He could make those explanations public. He could clear the air. But there had been no indication that Huckabee had ever asked the question. Huckabee the Republican governor did not want to delve into what had gone on at Mena any more than had Clinton, the Democratic governor.

In March 1997, three weeks after Weiss's article on "The Clinton Haters" appeared in the *New York Times Magazine,* a federal judge in Little Rock postponed Holly DuVall's trial. The move led to speculation that Holly had begun cooperating with federal agents. In early April that speculation intensified when Bowers reported that Harmon and some area attorneys were suspects in a federal racketeering case involving the Seventh Judicial District's now defunct drug task force. "Federal agents are said to have looked at the task force as a criminal enterprise that possibly violated the civil rights of several people. Court records show that many people arrested by the task force posted cash bonds and had their property seized, but were never prosecuted or repaid. . . . Sources have said that any indictments returned next week may be the first wave of indictments to be brought against people formerly associated with the drug task force, and others will likely follow."

HARMON'S FEDERAL INDICTMENT

And then the impossible happened. U.S. Attorney Paula Casey did what Chuck Banks had declined to do. She and her assistants lowered the boom on Harmon.

On April 11, 1997, a federal grand jury released a fifteen-count indictment that cast Harmon in a despicable light. It charged that for six years, while acting as prosecuting attorney, he had run his office as a criminal enterprise, demanding money in exchange for dropping charges, stealing drugs from his own evidence locker, and conspiring to sell drugs. Concluding that Harmon had run a crime ring—a racket—from his office, it charged him, along with Roger Walls and a local defense attorney, William Murphy, with violating the federal Racketeering Influenced Corrupt Organizations Act. Besides the RICO charges, Harmon faced two counts of possession with the intent to distribute cocaine, four counts of conspiracy to extort money, two counts of conspiracy to manufacture drugs, one count of witness tampering, and one count of retaliation against a witness. "In reality," the indictment stated, "the defendants operated the 7th Judicial District Prosecuting Attorney's Office as a conduit to obtain monetary benefits to themselves and others, and to participate in and conceal criminal activities."

Walls, who stood accused in many of the crimes with Harmon, also was charged with money laundering. William Murphy was named along with Harmon in two counts of extortion. The indictment painted an ugly picture—one that Linda had no trouble believing. It alleged:

- That Harmon, Walls, and Murphy had participated in at least eleven crimes "to obtain monetary benefits to themselves and others, and to participate in and conceal illegal activities"—crimes that constituted "a pattern of racketeering."
- That on October 21, 1995, Dan Harmon and Holly DuVall broke into the Seventh Judicial District Drug Task Force evidence locker and stole cocaine, part of which they intended to distribute.
- That Harmon and Murphy induced one defendant, Dewayne Littlepage, to pay them one hundred thousand dollars to have charges against him dismissed. While on bond, Littlepage managed to raise—through the sale of drugs—about eighty-eight thousand dollars of the cash Harmon and Murphy demanded.
- That two other Murphy clients, Freddie McCaslin and LaJean O'Brien, paid Harmon, Walls, and Murphy about fifty thousand dollars in exchange for Harmon's dropping narcotics charges against O'Brien and dismissing charges pending against McCaslin.
- That Harmon watched a methamphetamine dealer named Ronnie Joe Knight cook about 118 grams of the drug and accepted half of the batch for himself, with the intention of selling it.
- That Harmon and Walls had supplied the chemicals with which Knight manufactured the meth.
- That Harmon and Walls had extorted fifty-five hundred dollars from a Texas man, Ernesto Varnado, who was arrested in 1992 while passing through Saline County on Interstate 30. According to the indictment, Harmon charged Varnado with possession of a controlled substance with intent to deliver and then released him. The following April, Harmon and Walls, alone and without benefit of an extradition proceeding, traveled to Varnado's home in Fort Worth, took him into custody, and returned him to Arkansas where they threw him into the Saline County jail. After Varnado paid Harmon three thousand dollars, Harmon

released him again. But later, Harmon returned to Fort Worth and demanded that Varnado make another payment or be taken back to jail. Varnado handed over twenty-five hundred dollars. Several times after that, Harmon demanded more money, and when Varnado failed to comply, the prosecutor obtained a warrant for his arrest. After being formally extradited to Arkansas and jailed, Varnado entered into a plea agreement and later was released.

- That Harmon, DuVall, and a third person took half the amount of marijuana found in a car driven by Arturo Valdez, which was stopped on the interstate highway. According to the indictment, the three sold the approximately sixty pounds of marijuana and split the proceeds.
- That Patrick Davis, an Indiana resident, paid Harmon ten thousand dollars to be released from jail. The indictment said that Harmon set the price after Davis was arrested on the highway for possession of marijuana. Two days later, Davis's wife traveled from Indiana to Arkansas and brought the money that Harmon demanded.
- That when Shelton Corley, "who often supplied drugs to Holly DuVall and Dan Harmon," was indicted by a federal grand jury and began to cooperate with the U.S. attorneys, Harmon "convinced him" to stop cooperating by promising to keep him out of the state penitentiary.
- That the prosecutor beat up reporter Rodney Bowers in retaliation for articles he had written that were "routinely reviewed by federal authorities investigating Harmon."

The other four counts in the indictment were against DuVall for failure to report the break-in of the evidence locker; against Walls for money laundering in connection with his purchase of the motel; against the sellers of Walls's motel for allegedly making a false statement to a financial institution; and against Murphy, the lawyer, for bank fraud.[9]

A MATTER OF TIME

Linda was pleased that federal officials had finally made a drug and extortion case against Harmon. She was glad that Walls, who had recently run for the state legislature, had been included in the indictment. Linda had almost choked when she read Walls's campaign message: "We must take the criminal off the street! I believe in making every effort to rehabilitate the criminal or the drug user, but we also have an obligation to the large majority who are law-abiding citizens. There is no alternative!"

Now he and Harmon stood accused of abusing, not only drugs, but their oaths of office. The district's two most prominent drug fighters stood charged as drug racketeers. Maybe now it would become apparent why Kevin's and Don's murders had not been solved. If Harmon was convicted on these RICO charges, it seemed to Linda that the boys' deaths would have to be reviewed in a whole new light.

But all was not what it seemed. One aspect of the twenty-nine page indictment was galling. As Linda read it, she noticed with a sinking heart how carefully it delineated the period of time during which the alleged crimes had occurred. Not one of the charges related to events that occurred before August 1991. And yet, as Govar had believed well before that date, the FBI had documented enough criminal activity by Harmon to have him indicted then. To Linda, the starting date of all the crimes was dismayingly significant. Not one preceded the date on which Banks had announced his "absolution" of Harmon. Just six weeks before the earliest crime outlined in this indictment, Banks had held the press conference at which he'd proclaimed that, despite Govar's investigation, "we found no evidence of any drug-related misconduct by public officials in Saline County." Now, under a new U.S. attorney, Harmon, Walls, and a local lawyer were being charged with running a criminal enterprise whose activities could be traced back to a mere month and a half after those remarks—but no further.

The more Linda considered the indictment, the more disturbing this became. Here were federal officials acknowledging that as far back as 1994 and '95, while Phyllis Cournan was investigating Kevin's and Don's deaths, they were also investigating Harmon in relation to "drug activities." They had Shelton Corley's testimony that he had "regularly" supplied drugs to Harmon and DuVall. Two years ago they had evidence that Harmon had attempted to cover up his crimes by tampering with witnesses. But even then, Harmon had not been indicted. Instead, more than a year after the FBI had developed that information, Special Agent Bill Temple, with that knowledge about Harmon available to him, had sat in his office and told Linda and Larry that in the case of Kevin and Don, for which Harmon had led the grand jury investigation, a federal crime may not have been committed.

Linda thought of all the crimes that had been committed in Saline County that remained unsolved or unprosecuted. She thought about McKaskle and all the dead young men who purportedly had known something about Kevin and Don. She thought about the family of the boy killed in a traffic accident by the alleged drug user—the one whom Harmon had charged with manslaughter and not prosecuted. She thought of all the tragedy the county had endured since 1989, when Govar and Duffey had tried so hard to bring an indictment against Harmon—and of the abuse they had taken for their efforts. Linda still wanted someone to tell her why, in all that time, nothing had been done about Harmon. Cynically she told Jean she believed that the only reason Harmon had been charged now was that the theft of the packets from his evidence locker had accidentally come to light. That event had forced the issue. Harmon had strayed beyond his protectors' effectiveness. The appearance of corruption in the district had become too public for officials to ignore.

The more Linda thought about the indictment, the more other questions raised their heads: Why were others not included? Was this to be the end of it—Harmon, Walls, and one lawyer? By now the Web site Jean's brother, Mark, had founded was attracting national attention, having won recognition by Microsoft as "Best of the Web" in its "Crimes and Criminals" category. As Linda's frustration over the indictment grew, she asked Mark to help her post her misgivings. They poured out in a stream of questions.

- "Are we to believe that Saline County and the Seventh Judicial District has been cleaned up now?
- "Do they expect us to believe Harmon and Walls got away for six years with the kinds of crimes included in the indictments without involvement or protection from other public officials?
- "And when is the media going to wake up and smell the coffee? If it had not been for a lone reporter checking out a "domestic disturbance" call he heard on his scanner while cruising around Hot Springs, are we to believe the feds would have done anything even now?
- "Are the feds doing just enough to save face because the media exposed Harmon's blatant distribution of task force drugs?
- "Do the media realize the part they played in protecting Harmon by crucifying Jean Duffey in 1990? Do the media not realize that the position they take on this matter will either help or hinder justice?"

Three days after the grand jury handed down its indictment, Micah Morrison reported on it in the *Wall Street Journal.* He noted that after the murders of the boys, Linda had conducted "a decade-long campaign over the airwaves and lately the Internet" to call attention to corruption in her county. "She scornfully notes," Morrison wrote, "that the current indictment only goes back to August 1991, two months after U.S. Attorney Banks cleared Mr. Harmon in the earlier probe. 'Are we to believe Dan Harmon was clean in June, but dirty in August?' "[10]

DAN HARMON'S TRIAL

To no one's surprise, Harmon denied all the allegations. He ridiculed them as "pretty fantastic" and "something out of *Alice in Wonderland.*" When reporters asked if he would plead guilty to any of the charges, he demanded, "How are you going to plead guilty to something you didn't do?" Then he grew belligerent. "If they can stick some garbage like this on me, then every American ought to be afraid." Walls also declared his innocence and adopted Harmon's tactic of blaming the enemies he had made as a drug fighter. Mocking the caliber of the government's witnesses, Walls declared, "They can go to the penitentiary and pick up all the people they want to."

When Chief U.S. District Judge Stephen M. Reasoner decided to sever Harmon's case from the rest, Harmon expressed delight at the prospect of his trial. "It takes a lot of courage to stand up to the federal government. I had no idea that our government was this vindictive and this political."

On May 27, 1997, Linda found a seat in the packed courtroom as Harmon's trial began. Jean, who was still teaching in Texas, would not arrive for a few days. Jury selection went swiftly, but Linda watched it with growing concern. To her dismay, nine of the jurors were women, most middle-aged or older. They're a lot like me, she thought, and that worried her. She put herself in their place, remembering her first exposure to Harmon. She recalled how disposed she had been to trust authority, how sincere Danny had seemed, and how much she had wanted to believe him—not that she had been alone in any of that. Larry had trusted Harmon, too, as had voters throughout the district—male and female. Until this last election, they had consistently and overwhelmingly reelected him. Even now, Linda knew that she was surrounded in the courtroom by many Harmon supporters.

In his opening statement to the jury, assistant U.S. attorney Dan Stripling admitted the biggest weakness in his case. "A lot of witnesses" would be called "who've been involved in criminal activities." Several would testify against Harmon in exchange for leniency for themselves. Holly DuVall would be one of them. John M. Steward, the man with whom Harmon allegedly shared the proceeds from the sale of sixty pounds of marijuana, was another. Nonetheless, Stripling promised, the evidence that DuVall, Steward, and others would present against Harmon would be convincing.

It seemed to Linda an inauspicious beginning. Stripling looked to her almost preternaturally mild: gray, soft-spoken, tentative. Harmon's attorney, by contrast, was an aggressive ball of fire. Lea Ellen Fowler was quick, flashy, and bold. "Holly DuVall made a deal with the government to save herself from prison," she told the jurors. "Mr. Harmon's main problem was he married Miss DuVall, and Miss DuVall was a troubled young woman with a serious drug problem."[11] Linda recognized the strategy. It was the same defense Harmon always used: his critics were crooks, his wives abused drugs, and the feds were out to get him.

The next day, Steward took the stand. He testified that Harmon "had the opportunity to get some marijuana and wondered if I might be able to sell it. I said I probably could." Steward said he and DuVall sold the marijuana and split their profits with Harmon.

On the third day, DuVall was sworn in. In a calm voice she described herself as a drug addict. She said she had helped her husband, a fellow addict, conceal his habit. "I would go out to purchase some drugs. He couldn't do it. He was the prosecuting attorney. I lied, basically, for several years to protect him. He was an elected official. I wasn't going to tell anyone he was using."

DuVall testified that she first saw Harmon use methamphetamine in 1992 when the two were living together and that she later saw him use both marijuana and cocaine. Under questioning by Stripling, she described how she and Harmon had together stolen cocaine from the evidence locker. DuVall said they entered Harmon's office, climbed into the attic, and then walked along support beams until they reached a corner of the building over the evidence locker. There, she said, she reached her arm through a small open section of the ceiling and removed a sack of evidence from a shelf. "He opened up the sack and he couldn't believe it. It was several bricks of cocaine. We went home and opened a brick and started using." DuVall said that when Harmon became concerned that the evidence might be missed because of the quantity they had taken, they had made fake bricks out of white modeling clay, to replace the stolen ones. But they had never gotten around to putting them back in the locker. Harmon had grown complacent—or smug. "He said this was an old case, that it would never come to trial."

Harmon's attorney vigorously challenged DuVall's credibility and attacked her motive for testifying. "So," Fowler demanded on cross-examination, "when you were faced with imminent jail time, you decided if you had to go, you wouldn't go alone, or you would find a way so you wouldn't have to go at all?" DuVall replied steadily that she did not see why she should be the only one to go to prison.

In other testimony, Martha Littlepage, the wife of Dewayne Littlepage, a drug dealer whom Harmon had sent to prison, said that she had witnessed her husband meet with Harmon and Walls and deliver money in a plastic bag. When asked why she had not reported the bribe, Littlepage responded, "I was afraid of Dan Harmon because he had given Dewayne fifty-six years. I saw how he ran his court. . . . I thought Mr. Harmon controlled most of the counties of the state."

On Friday, the trial's fourth day, Tina Davis recalled how she had received a phone call at her home in Indiana from her then husband, Patrick Davis, who had been jailed in Saline County. She said Patrick directed her to get ten thousand dollars, drive to Arkansas, and bring it to Harmon. After collecting the money in five-, ten-, and twenty-dollar bills from relatives and friends, she made the trip to Arkansas and found her way to the prosecutor's office in Benton.

"I went into his office with him, and he closed the door. He told me there had been a problem and Patrick wasn't getting out of jail. Dan Harmon said Patrick had tried to make a weapon the previous night or sometime before. Later he changed the story and said Patrick had tried to commit suicide." Davis said Harmon told her she would have to raise more money. When she responded that she could not get any more, she testified, "Dan said, 'Well, if you can't come up with more money, then the only other way to get him out of jail is to spend the night with me.' "

Davis said that even as he was talking, Harmon was using drugs. "He reached into a drawer in his desk and pulled out a tray with cocaine on it," she told the court. "He did a line of cocaine in his nose." Ultimately, Davis said, Harmon accepted the ten thousand dollars. He then demanded that she and her husband sign papers indicating that the money had been found on them during the drug bust and constituted a legitimate forfeiture. That document, which was also signed by Harmon and Walls, was introduced as an exhibit. Later, Davis said, she asked Harmon when she and her husband would have to return to Arkansas for court. "He told me we wouldn't receive any paperwork and not to ever come back, not to even drive through the state of Arkansas."

Another prosecution witness, Jack Wooten, testified that Harmon was involved in the manufacture of methamphetamine. Wooten, a convicted drug dealer, said Harmon sat with Ronnie Joe Knight while Knight made methamphetamine and that afterward Harmon had taken two grams of the drug home with him. "Dan Harmon would supply the chemicals to manufacture methamphetamine, and if Ronnie and I would stay in Saline or Hot Spring counties, he would let us know if anything was going to come down."

Fowler attacked Wooten's credibility, as she had that of the other drug dealers who testified for the prosecution. Linda studied the jury. She imagined that they might be thinking the same things she once would have thought: that when drug dealers testified against an aggressive prosecutor, you had to "consider the source," as Harmon himself had told her. When Jean Duffey arrived, Linda expressed her apprehension about the jury and Stripling's low-key prosecution. Fowler, on the other hand, was relentless. She never missed a chance to point out that almost everyone who testified against Harmon had been given a deal in exchange.

By the end of the session on Friday, Linda's nerves were on edge. She walked outside the federal building and saw television cameras lined up and reporters waiting to interview Harmon. She waited nearby to listen. Harmon came out crowing about how the trial was going. When the interviews were over, he spotted Linda and smirked. "Well, hello, Mrs. Ives." As she explained to Larry later that night, the remark set her off "like a rocket."

The next week, it was Fowler's turn. Harmon had maintained an air of confidence that verged on indifference. He kept a hardcover book on the defense table—the writings of Mark Twain—which he read during lulls in the trial. Sometimes during breaks, he leaned back in his chair and rested his feet on the table. But there was nothing lackadaisical about Fowler's defense. She called a string of character witnesses, all of whom portrayed Harmon as a well-dressed, well-mannered man who had never fit the profile of someone who abused methamphetamines. Henry Efird, a former agent with Harmon's drug task force, commented, "Mr. Harmon has always been a very law-abiding citizen." Then, breaking into tears, he continued, "It is really hard to see people of this caliber accusing a man who is so good."

Harmon's most prestigious character witness was Robert Shepherd, the former sheriff of Grant County, friend of Sheriff Steed, and Clinton's state drug czar. In one respect, Linda thought, it was ironic to see the man who had been the state's top antidrug official testify on behalf of an accused drug dealer. But in truth, Linda and Jean were not surprised.

Then came a real surprise. Curtis Henry took the stand as a defense witness. Linda had not seen him for almost seven years, not since he and Marvelle had moved to southern Arkansas. Linda knew that Curtis had long believed in and supported Harmon. But Curtis had eschewed publicity—he never wanted to speak out about the case—so Linda was surprised to see him now. Curtis told of Harmon's attempts "to help find whoever murdered" his son.

On Wednesday another defense witness, former sheriff Larry Davis, took the stand. Davis, who had become a drug task force officer since resigning his role as sheriff, testified that he did not know of Harmon ever having done anything illegal. Stripling knew better. He knew that Davis had harbored suspicions. Under cross-examination, Stripling got Davis to acknowledge that while he was sheriff, he had, in fact, had "several visits" with an assistant U.S. attorney, "taking things to him and then talking to him about the activities in which Mr. Harmon was engaged." Linda and Jean were enthralled. They knew that, though Stripling did not say so, he was well aware that those meetings between Davis and Banks in 1989 were what had prompted Govar's investigation.

Fowler quickly objected. She and Stripling approached the bench. To Linda and Jean, the situation was tantalizing. What would Stripling do? To question Davis about that earlier investigation and the "things" and "activities" he had talked about with Banks would raise questions that verged on an area that seemed to be off-limits. Linda and Jean were betting that Stripling would not go there. And they were right. He returned to the podium and announced, "I have decided not to pursue this line of questioning." Linda slumped, disgusted. Jean leaned over and whispered, "He was about to tread on forbidden ground." Later, when reporters questioned Davis about his 1989 meetings with the U.S. attorney, Davis refused to answer, advising reporters to put their questions to Banks. [12]

Finally, Fowler called Harmon to the stand. A ripple of excitement passed through the courtroom. Linda and Jean braced. Both had seen Harmon sway even hard-looking juries, and this jury did not look hard. Today, though, his usual swagger was gone. He looked humble, almost boyish. When he responded to Fowler's questions, his voice was so soft that jurors strained to hear. Fowler asked him to speak up. Under her gentle guidance, he recounted a childhood of poverty, a stint in the army, and how he had worked his way through college. Linda eyed the jury. Some of the women nodded sympathetically. One appeared close to tears. When Fowler asked about Holly DuVall, Harmon's voice faltered and then faded. Finally he broke into tears as he described his former wife's addiction. He professed his continuing love for Holly, despite the fact that she had changed from a "wonderful woman" into a "hostile," "combative," and "drug-dependent" person. He denied her allegations that the two had broken into the evidence locker together. He expressed his disappointment at her weakness for drugs and his contempt for characters who dealt them. "Number one, I was scared for her safety," he said, his voice breaking. "Number two, she had no business, being my wife, being associated with those people." The page-one headline in the *Democrat-Gazette* the next morning read: HARMON WEEPS FOR ADDICTED EX-WIFE, DENIES ALL.

Harmon returned to the stand again the next day and denied that he had ever received "one dime" as a bribe. He charged that the witnesses against him were lying. He also vouched for his codefendants. "Roger Walls is as honest and straight a person as I've ever met in my life. Roger would not ever be involved with drugs. Roger hated drugs."

But the rebuttal testimony contradicted the defense's picture of Harmon as a gentleman who upheld the law. DuVall, called back to the stand, testified that he frequently struck her with his fists, often in front of his children. Asked how often he had hit her, she answered, "I couldn't even give you a number. It went on for several years. . . . A lot of times he would choke me. It wouldn't leave a mark."

Patricia Vaughn, a girlfriend who testified that she had lived with Harmon since his divorce from DuVall, said that he had introduced her to methamphetamines. "We smoked it. We used the needle . . . sometimes ten or twelve times a day."

Then it was over. After eight days of testimony, the attorneys made their closing arguments and the case was sent to the jury. Linda and Jean awaited the verdict with little hope of a conviction. Jean went so far as to predict on the Web site that "Harmon is going to walk."

THE VERDICT

The jury deliberated all day Tuesday, and it looked like a second day would pass without a verdict, as well. Steve Barnes, a local columnist and television commentator, later described the afternoon. "Dan Harmon was waiting in a little room with his sister and his lawyer and having trouble being still. His sort-of silvery hair had long since grown back from the day, some time ago, when he had gone nuts and had his head shaved [after] beating up a few people in Benton. He'd already beat one federal investigation and would soon beat, after a fashion, a state probe, surrendering his office in exchange for guilty pleas to charges reduced from felonies."

As the afternoon wore on, Barnes reflected on the trial's implications. "It's the uniformed patrolman that comes to mind when we think of the criminal justice system," he wrote. "We don't often remember that at the top of the pyramid are the district prosecutors. A cop is conspicuous for his or her uniform and serious sidearm. But the real power is the prosecutor's: deciding which cases to take to court, and when, and in what fashion; which is to say, who is prosecuted and who is not, and often for what level of offense. The street cops and the detectives, the sheriffs and the troopers—they answer to the prosecutor. There is a limit, however extensive, to the damage any single crooked cop can inflict against justice. But a gone-bad prosecutor, whose domain can encompass several counties and a dozen police agencies, is a nightmare. . . . "

To Linda, Barnes hit the nail on the head. Over the course of the past several years, she had become frighteningly aware of the power a prosecutor wields. She had seen it up close with Harmon, in the control he exercised over grand juries—and over who got prosecuted or protected. She had seen it at Mena, in the refusal by federal prosecutors there to issue subpoenas. She had seen it with Banks, when a probe that could have curtailed Harmon's rule years earlier ended without explanation. Ironically, even now, elsewhere in this same courthouse, a federal grand jury was hearing evidence in a case that Special Prosecutor Kenneth Starr was trying to bring against President Bill Clinton. Many of Starr's critics, including Clinton, were crying foul—that Starr's prosecution was purely political. True or not, Linda thought, the accusations underlined the point: in what they did and did not do, prosecutors who misused their office were in a unique position to undermine justice and make life hell.

She glanced again at the prosecutor on trial. Harmon sat in the courtroom, feet up on the defense table, reading *One Flew Over the Cuckoo's Nest.* She glanced at the jury box—still empty. She began to worry that the jury might be hung. But just before 4:00 P.M., a current buzzed through the courthouse. A verdict had been reached.

Linda took a seat with a clear view of the defendant. Harmon leaned back in his chair at the defense table, still looking cool and cocky. The jury's foreman passed the verdict to Judge Reasoner.

The judge looked at it and began to read. On the first count, the most serious one, charging Harmon with racketeering by using his office to get drugs and money, Reasoner announced, "Guilty."

Linda drew in her breath. Harmon showed no emotion. The judge quickly read through the other counts. Linda scribbled the verdicts. After years of waiting and after a draining, two-week trial, the reading of the verdicts was almost anticlimactic. By the time the bailiff ordered, "All rise," and the judge stepped down from the bench, Harmon stood convicted of five of the eleven charges against him: one count of racketeering, three counts of extortion, and one count of possessing marijuana with the intent to distribute.

Harmon looked dazed. He was no longer the district's powerful prosecutor. He was a convicted felon facing prison.

As the jurors filed silently from the box, Linda watched them with new respect. She had underestimated them. They were ordinary people like her, all right, and like her, when finally confronted with the evidence, they had seen through Harmon's lies. She wanted to thank them personally, though she did not. After a decade of counting on elected officials to uphold their official duties, Linda had finally gotten to see some justice. A federal investigation had turned up evidence. A federal prosecutor had presented it to a jury. And a panel of ordinary citizens, exercising the common sense that had been missing for years, had taken Harmon out of commission.

Their verdict would not clean up Saline County—not by a long shot. But at least part of the protective cloak around Harmon had finally been stripped away. Linda felt unexpectedly buoyed. This time, Harmon's attempt at a cover-up had failed. At last, part of the tarp had been lifted.

RENEWAL

Harmon's conviction came just ten weeks before the tenth anniversary of Kevin's and Don's deaths. On August 23, 1997, Linda returned to the cemetery. Had Kevin lived, he would now have been twenty-seven years old. He might have been married. He might have had children. She shook away the thought. To her, Kevin was still young and happy-go-lucky, as he had been the last time she saw him. She could almost hear his laugh.

Busying herself at the grave, she let her mind wander, expressing, as people will do with the dead, some of her thoughts to Kevin. This battle was not over, she told him. Harmon's conviction had exposed a fraction of the corruption in the district, but only that. She would never believe that Harmon had been able to accomplish what he had—and for so long—without raising the suspicions of other lawyers, other business leaders, other officials. If I could figure out what he was up to, she reflected, as she tidied around the grave, and if Jean Duffey could figure it out, and if Govar had felt the evidence, even seven years ago, was strong enough to get indictments, what had his colleagues been thinking as they watched Harmon all these years? What had Shepherd, the state's former drug czar, been thinking as he watched the maneuverings in Saline County? What had Banks been thinking when he pronounced Govar's evidence against Harmon mere "rumor and innuendo"? What had the attorney general, Winston Bryant, been thinking after Harmon's conviction for not paying taxes, when he spoke on Harmon's behalf before the Committee on Professional Conduct? And what had Bosson, the special prosecutor, been thinking when he let Harmon plead out of five felony charges in exchange for nothing more than a hastened departure from office?

Linda shook her head. Maybe they assumed we'd give up, she told Kevin. Maybe they thought we'd accept whatever they told us. They relied on our trust. Harmon's conviction had shone a light on the misuse of authority in the district and on the complicity that had let it keep going. Only a sliver of the abuse had been illuminated. But the light was important nonetheless.

She wished that she could tell Kevin that everything was clear now, that whatever he and Don had encountered that night ten years ago had finally been fully exposed. But no. What she could tell him was that a few of Saline County's dark secrets had been revealed, and so had some at Mena. Just as Harmon had been convicted, confirming local suspicions about his activities, the CIA had finally admitted what others had long suspected: that it had been involved both with Seal and in operations at Mena. Those were the victories of these past ten years. She sighed. The failure was that much in her own county and at Mena still remained shrouded in darkness.

The secrecy raised other questions Linda wished she could tell Kevin had been answered. If I had been the governor when Seal was here, I would not have been uninterested, she murmured, smoothing the late summer grass. I would not have accepted for a week, let alone for years, any brush-off from federal officials. And if I had been elected president, I would have moved heaven and earth to get to the bottom of the contradictions between a national war on drugs and the evidence of what was happening at Mena.

Yet here we are, she whispered to Kevin, eleven years after Seal's assassination, and the questions that the attorney general of Louisiana posed immediately after his death still have not been answered. Thinking about it, Linda had the same suspicion concerning Mena that she had about Kevin's and Don's murders: that officials hoped that if they could hold out long enough, issue enough denials, suppress enough information, and ridicule those seeking answers, the mysteries would be forgotten. People like her would go away.

She drew in a deep breath. But that won't happen, she vowed to her son. Retracing for the millionth time what she knew and did not know, Linda felt certain that Kevin's death was connected to Mena. Both investigations had been peculiar from the start. And they had stayed that way. For some reason, state and federal officials did not want either of them examined.

In the end, she thought, her ordeal of the past decade arose from a series of thwarted prosecutions. For whatever reason, federal prosecutors in Fort Smith had never prosecuted anyone for what happened at Mena. For whatever reason, federal prosecutors in Little Rock had only indicted Harmon on charges that followed the date of the press conference when Banks had publicly cleared him. For whatever reason, Banks had chosen to ignore almost four years' worth of investigation by state and federal officials and declare the allegations against Harmon mere rumor and innuendo. And for whatever reason, Harmon, the district's hero, had chosen to misuse the grand jury that was called to investigate the deaths of Kevin and Don. How much would her life have been different, she thought, how much pain would have been avoided, if certain prosecutors had done their jobs.

All Linda knew was this: Kevin and Don had been murdered. Others who were said to have knowledge of their deaths had been murdered, too. The prosecutor who had handled the grand jury investigation had been involved in the local drug business. He'd had powerful friends in state government, a proven willingness to use extortion, and kid-glove treatment from other officials who'd kept him in office for years. Meanwhile, at the time Kevin and Don were killed, one of the biggest cocaine-smuggling organizations identified in U.S. history was operating, unimpeded, in Arkansas with the knowledge of state and federal officials. It had clear and disturbing ties to federal agencies. Seal and his organization were protected, too.

Yet none of that seemed enough to prompt deeper investigations. It was as though Saline County, Arkansas, and the nation all were being told what the deputies had told the train crew on the night the boys were killed: that no crime had been committed, and that what looked like a cover to hide the crime was an illusion—not existing at all.

"They won't get away with it, Kevin," Linda said out loud. For a moment she felt again the crushing weight of his death. She had not been able to keep him alive, but she could keep alive the questions that lingered about his murder, and she would—until every last one of them was answered.

"They won't get away with it," she whispered again. Saying it, she felt the old resolve flood back. She straightened and looked at her watch. It was time to leave, time to return to the living world. But she paused a moment longer. There was something more she wanted to tell him.

"Kevin," she confided, "a lot is happening. We're not alone in this anymore. We're not the only ones asking questions."

A smile crossed her face as she felt the familiar flicker of hope. Part of her wanted to trust it. Part knew better. She smiled, realizing that none of that mattered. All that mattered was that she could tell Kevin she had not given up.

EPILOGUE

1998

This story is far from over. Dan Harmon's conviction validated Linda's suspicion that the murders of Kevin and Don had occurred in an environment of local corruption. But more information would bolster her belief that the corruption she had battled in Saline County was only part of a larger mosaic.

ON THE COUNTY LEVEL

After his June 1997 conviction, Harmon was placed on supervised release until his sentencing hearing. The judge ordered him to stay home except to attend church or to go to the job he had taken in a Saline County quarry. Four months into his release, Harmon violated the judge's order by leaving Saline County to visit a girlfriend sixty miles away. The girlfriend had testified against Harmon at his trial, describing how he had introduced her to drugs and how the two of them had used drugs together. FBI agents were alerted to Harmon's visit because they had tapped the woman's phone. They recorded the conversation in which Harmon arranged to bring methamphetamine with him when he came.

When Harmon arrived at the woman's apartment, agents confronted him in the parking lot. Harmon ran into a nearby pond and stood there a few minutes, fully clothed, before walking out and surrendering. When agents searched him, they found no methamphetamine, which dissolves in water. They did, however, find a foil wrapper, in which, they charged, the methamphetamine had been carried. Harmon's supervised release was revoked and he was placed in the Pulaski County jail to await a second trial on the new drug charges.

While Harmon sat in jail, Sheridan attorney Bill Murphy, who had been indicted with him and Roger Walls, pleaded guilty to suborning perjury. A week before he was to stand trial, Murphy admitted that he had coerced his wife into lying before a federal grand jury regarding money he had received from a drug dealer. Other charges against Murphy were dropped, and he agreed to surrender his law license.

Roger Walls went on trial in January 1998. The former administrator of the Seventh Judicial District Drug Task Force cried in court when a jury found him guilty of having conspired with Harmon to commit extortion.

In April Harmon was brought back to court to stand trial on four drug charges stemming from the incident at his girlfriend's apartment. In less than a day, Harmon was found guilty of all four counts.

At the end of July 1998, Harmon was sentenced to a total of eleven years in prison for nine convictions on racketeering, extortion, and drug charges.[1] Judge Stephen Reasoner commented at Harmon's first sentencing hearing that "there is just something extraordinary about someone who is a prosecuting attorney misusing the judicial system."

Linda agreed that there was something extraordinary, all right, but it was the lightness of Harmon's sentences. She thought back to the dozens, if not hundreds, of small-time drug dealers Harmon had prosecuted over the years, including several who had informed against him. Harmon's prosecution of Sharline Wilson, for instance, had resulted in a sentence for her of thirty-one years in the state penitentiary for delivering relatively small amounts of marijuana and methamphetamine—the same crimes of which the former prosecutor himself now stood convicted. His sentence was a third of what she had gotten, and Wilson had not had the added crimes of racketeering and extortion to go with it.

Though Linda understood that different rules applied in state and federal courts, she was disturbed that most Arkansas drug criminals, having been investigated by local and state officials and tried in state courts, received typically lengthy sentences in the Arkansas Department of Correction, while others, whose cases passed into federal hands, received sentences that were much lighter and that would be served in federal prisons. Roger Clinton and Dan Lasater both served fewer than fifteen months on their federal drug convictions, and now Harmon faced just eleven years.

What really galled Linda, though, was that beyond the judge's comment that there was "something extraordinary" about "a prosecuting attorney misusing the judicial system," nothing about Harmon's prosecution acknowledged that abuse. Harmon's racketeering conviction stemmed from his having, as the indictment put it, "operated the 7th Judicial District Prosecuting Attorney's Office as a conduit to obtain monetary benefits to themselves and others, and to participate in and conceal criminal activities." He had operated the prosecutor's office as a crime ring—a racket. But the fact that this was a state office that was being so misused—and that the defendant was a state official—was accorded no greater significance at his trial than if Harmon had been any ordinary citizen running a racket from his home. Yet, Linda knew, official corruption—including state corruption—*was* a federal crime. Moreover, U.S. attorneys were supposed to treat all cases involving high-ranking court or law enforcement officials as national priorities.[2] There had been no hint of that happening here.

To Linda, the worst part about Harmon's conviction was not the tragic delay in obtaining it, nor the relative leniency of his sentences. It was that even now, no one in Saline County had ever been charged with official corruption.

Nor, by August 1998 and the eleventh anniversary of Kevin's and Don's deaths, had any more indictments been handed down. The federal investigation into Saline County was over. Harmon began serving his sentences and insisted that he would appeal. The Arkansas Supreme Court's Committee on Professional Conduct, meanwhile, still had not revoked his license to practice law, pending his appeals. The committee reported it had suspended his license, but only for administrative reasons, because he had not met the requirements for continuing legal education nor paid the annual fee. Garrett continued to serve in the district as a deputy prosecutor.

Rick Elmendorf, the Saline County sheriff's chief deputy who investigated the deaths on the tracks and who later became the chief of police for Benton, where he oversaw the investigation into Keith McKaskle's murder, among others, went on to become chief of police at the Arkansas State Capitol. In March of 1999, after Elmendorf had held that post for four years, Arkansas Secretary of State Sharon Priest fired him. No reason was given at first, but it was later reported that Little Rock police had complained to Priest that Elmendorf had misled some of their officers who were attempting to serve a warrant. Elmendorf refused to comment, but a Little Rock Police Department information report listed the episode as "obstruction" of government operations. A spokesman for the Little Rock Police Department said Priest had been contacted about the incident because, "Our officer felt like he was less than honest." Though Elmendorf was fired from his Capitol job, it was not expected that any charges would be filed.[3]

Linda and Jean remained in close contact. And increasingly they kept in contact with supporters who had become aware of their case through the Internet. In updates posted there, Jean and Linda wrote of their continuing hope that mounting public pressure would one day force government disclosure of what agencies knew about Seal and the government's own clandestine activities at Mena. And they reaffirmed their goal of seeing those responsible for the murders of Kevin and Don brought to trial.

ON THE STATE LEVEL

In August 1999, a federal court jury in Little Rock returned a verdict for almost $600,000 in favor of Pulaski County Sheriff officers Jay Campbell and Kirk Lane. The officers sued Pat Matrisciani for libel based on statements implicating them in the murders in the film *Obstruction of Justice*. Matrisciani plans to appeal. While the libel trial was widley reported, the discovery of depositions taken in preparation for an earlier trial are being reported here for the first time.

In 1983 Clinton's mother, Virginia Dwire Kelley, brought a lawsuit against several administrators of Ouachita Memorial Hospital after administrators there informed her, following the death of Susie Deer, that they would no longer use her as a nurse anesthetist. Lawyers for the hospital prepared to launch a vigorous defense, part of which included a two-day deposition of Kelley. For almost fifteen years, the existence of records from that deposition remained unknown, except to its participants, many of whom said, as late as 1997, that they were afraid to discuss the matter because it involved the president's mother. After Kelley's death, a copy of that deposition surfaced. What follow are Kelley's answers to key questions that were put to her concerning the death of Susie Deer and the autopsy by Dr. Makak.4

Q. Explain to me how you can keep your eye on the chart as well as what is going on in the operating room while you are reading a racing form.

A. Very easily. Very easily . . .

Q. Explain to me how you could monitor the appearance of the patient while you were reading the racing form . . .

A. Well, you can walk and chew gum, right? I could do two things at one time . . .

Q. Would it ever be appropriate for a nurse anesthetist to wear loose hanging jewelry during surgical procedures?

A. Oh, yes . . .

Q. Would it ever be appropriate for a nurse anesthetist to clean her shoes during a surgical procedure?

A. I think there, again, if you get blood on your shoes that you are privileged to lean down and wipe it off. . . . Any time I got blood on my shoes, I tried to get it off as soon as possible. It was awfully difficult to remove after it gets dry. . . .

Q. Have you ever put a towel over an EKG monitor during a surgical procedure so that it could not be seen?

A. Yes, I did that one time. I recall that.

Q. Explain the circumstances, please, ma'am.

A. I don't remember the circumstances. It was just some kind of a joke at the time. . . .

Q. Did you ever have any contact with the medical examiner prior to the autopsy report being filed in the Deer case, any communication with him?

A. No.

Q. Do you know or have you heard whether Bill Clinton ever had any contact with the medical examiner?

A. I have no recollection of it.

Q. Do you deny that that occurred?

A. I deny recalling it. . . .

Q. Did you ever have any conversations with Bill Clinton about that?

A. Yes, I did.

Q. All right. What was said in that conversation?

At this point Kelley's lawyers objected and instructed her not to answer based on a claim of attorney-client privilege. After a brief discussion about whether Clinton had in fact represented his mother in the case, the questioning resumed.

Q. Have you ever consulted Bill Clinton as an attorney regarding the subject matter of the autopsy report in the Deer case?

A. Yes, I have.

Q. Did you do that before or after the autopsy report was filed?

A. I don't recall.

Throughout the deposition, Kelley repeatedly denied any recollection of the timing of her discussions with Clinton concerning the Deer case. At other times she reiterated her claim of attorney-client privilege.

Kelley's lawsuit against the hospital and its administrators failed and she never worked as a nurse anesthetist again. Malak's career went on to become marked by more public controversy. Eight years after Kelley's deposition, during Clinton's first campaign for the presidency, reporters for the *Los Angeles Times* asked Clinton about the Deer case and whether he had intervened with Malak on his mother's behalf. Clinton angrily responded, "There has never been any connection between my mother's professional experiences and actions I have taken or not taken as governor of Arkansas, and I resent any implications otherwise. . . . In fact, it was several years after the incident that I became aware, through the media, that the ruling made by Dr. Malak in this case was controversial."

But now, in light of Kelley's sworn statements, Clinton's answer denying "any connection between my mother's professional experiences and actions I have taken or not taken as governor of Arkansas" appeared to Linda oblique. In 1981, when Deer died, and when Kelley admitted consulting Clinton about Malak's autopsy report, her son was not governor of Arkansas. He had served one two-year term at that point, and he had ten years ahead of him to serve. But at the time of Malak's autopsy, he was temporarily out of office, having been defeated for a single two-year term. To Linda, the carefulness of Clinton's wording in that earlier statement echoed the painful exactitude of statements he would make later in his denials of a sexual relationship with "that woman," Monica Lewinsky.

Reporters seeking to research records from Clinton's administration in Arkansas regarding his relationship with Malak and what he knew about Mena found that that was impossible. Arkansas is one of five states that allow governors to keep their official papers out of the public domain.[5] At first Clinton had indicated he would make his official records public. After his defeat for reelection as governor in 1980, he deposited the records from his first two-year term in the archives of the University of Arkansas at Little Rock. They remained there after he regained the office in 1982.

However, when Clinton launched his presidential campaign in 1991, he ordered the records from his first term removed from the university archives. When he left office as governor, they, along with all his office's records from 1982 through 1991—some four thousand boxes in all—were placed in private storage at an undisclosed location. In 1998, even as planning was begun for the Clinton presidential library in Little Rock, it was impossible for anyone without a court order to see records from Clinton's administration as governor.

ON THE FEDERAL LEVEL

Secrecy at the federal level continued to frustrate the efforts of Linda and many others to clarify what had happened at Mena. But indications mounted that many dark suspicions were justified.

In March 1998 the *Washington Post* reported the CIA's admission that it had not "expeditiously" cut off relations with alleged drug traffickers who supported Nicaragua's Contra rebels.[6] The paper quoted CIA inspector general Frederick R. Hitz as having told the House intelligence committee that the CIA was aware of allegations that "dozens of people and a number of companies connected in some fashion to the Contra program" were involved in drug trafficking.

"Let me be frank," Hitz had said. "There are instances where [the] CIA did not, in an expeditious or consistent fashion, cut off relationships with individuals supporting the Contra program who were alleged to have engaged in drug-trafficking activity or take action to resolve the allegations."

According to the *Post,* "Hitz said some of the alleged trafficking involved bringing drugs into the United States. But, he added, investigators 'found no evidence . . . of any conspiracy by CIA or its employees to bring drugs into the United States.' " The report continued, "The inspector general also said that under an agreement in 1982 between then–Attorney General William French Smith and the CIA, agency officers were not required to report allegations of drug trafficking involving non-employees, which was defined as meaning paid and non-paid 'assets [meaning agents], pilots who ferried supplies to the Contras, as well as Contra officials and others.' " The agreement between the Justice Department and the CIA, the paper noted, had "not previously been revealed."

In July the *New York Times* reported that the CIA inspector general had prepared a second report on its internal investigation into possible connections between the Contras and Central American drug traffickers, an investigation prompted by reporter Gary Webb's controversial 1996 series in the *San Jose Mercury News.* "The CIA is much more reluctant to publicly release the complete text of the approximately 500-page second volume than it was of the first," the *New York Times* article reported, "because it deals directly with Contras the CIA did work with."[7]

Senator John Kerry of Massachusetts, who led the 1987 congressional inquiry into allegations of Contra drug connections, was reported to have asked CIA director George Tenet to declassify the report immediately. But that had not happened. Kerry commented, "Some of us in Congress at the time, in 1985, 1986, were calling for a serious investigation of the charges, and CIA officials did not join in that effort. There was a significant amount of stonewalling." Years after Seal's arrival in Arkansas, the stonewalling continued.

Release of another long-promised report about Mena was similarly delayed. In the summer of 1995, the House Committee on Banking and Financial Services, headed by Republican Congressman Jim Leach of Iowa, had begun its own investigation into questionable activities that had occurred during the 1980s at the small Arkansas airport. By the spring of 1990, however, no report had been made public. Committee spokesman David Runkel blamed official foot-dragging. "We spent an enormous amount of time on this issue," Runkel said. "But we have been delayed by getting information out of the executive branch." He said "the greatest delays" had been caused by a lack of cooperation by "the CIA, the Department of Justice, and the Department of Defense."

Getting explanations from the FBI remained as difficult as getting them from the CIA. During preparation of this book, Freedom of Information requests were submitted to the FBI for records relating to the Bureau's investigations both at Mena and into the deaths of Don Henry and Kevin Ives. Federal law requires prompt release of such public records. Although the request was submitted in 1995, by 1999, the FBI still had not complied.[8]

At first the Bureau reported that it had "no records" relating to "drug smuggling, money laundering, and/or gun running" at Mena. Since that response contradicted earlier statements made by the FBI to the Arkansas attorney general and to others, the denial was appealed. The agency assigned the request an appeal number, but took no further action.

The stonewalling continued for another year, until the author sought the assistance of her congressman, Rep. Vic Snyder of Arkansas.[9] He, too, encountered repeated rebuffs from the FBI. Finally, in April of 1998, the FBI notified the author that it had located four hundred pages of documents that "appear to be responsive" to the original request. However, by September, only thirty pages of those documents had been released, and crucial parts of those were blacked out.

The other request for information—the one relating to the FBI's investigation into the murders of Don Henry and Kevin Ives—provoked a similar response. I. C. Smith, the head of the FBI office in Arkansas, refused to allow Agent Phyllis Cournan to be interviewed about the case, or to allow access to the FBI's file, claiming that the case was still under investigation.

On several occasions Smith had stated that he doubted the FBI had jurisdiction in the case because there was no evidence that a federal crime had been committed. Asked if he had changed his position, he answered no. "I'm doing this because it needs to be done," he said, "and to be candid, I'm probably doing it without sound statutory basis." Asked how he could justify investigating a case for which he claimed to lack jurisdiction, keeping it open, and barring access to its records a full ten years after the crime, Smith replied, "Maybe I'm a little bit of an idealist. Sometimes there's things that just should be done." He suggested filing a Freedom of Information request with the agency's headquarters in Washington.

That request, submitted in 1997, sought release of the Ives and Henry records or an explanation as to how the FBI could justify closing records on a case for which it said it did not have jurisdiction. The agency did not address either question. Instead, in a terse, form-letter response issued in January 1998, it said that a search of FBI files for the names "Don Henry" and "Kevin Ives" had turned up "no records."

NOTES

CHAPTER 1. THE TRACKS

[1] Statement by Stephen Shroyer to Arkansas State Police, May 1988.

[2] Statement taken by R. O. Monroe, claims manager for Union Pacific Railroad Co., Sept. 1987.

[3] Statements by Tomlin to Arkansas State Police, May 3, 1988, and to author in Aug. 1996.

[4] Author interview, Aug. 1996.

[5] Interview with Det. Sgt. Charles Carty, Benton P.D., Aug. 1996.

[6] In one of the suicides, a woman in downtown Benton had waited until a train was almost in front of her before stepping nonchalantly onto the tracks. In another case, also in Benton, a man sat down beside the rail as the train approached. As its horn blared, he laid his head on the track.

[7] Interview by Don Birdsong, Arkansas State Police, June 1988.

[8] Author interview, Dec. 1991.

[9] Author interview, Aug. 1996.

[10] Birdsong interview, June 1988.

[11] Ibid.

CHAPTER 2. "SOMETHING'S WRONG"

[1] This chapter based on interviews by the author.

[2] When Kevin was fourteen, he and a friend went to spend a weekend with a relative living in a nearby town. During the visit, they were out walking late at night when a police officer pulled over to question them. He found the boys

carrying a joint. The boys went to court with their fathers, where they were placed on probation. For several months Larry had required Kevin to submit to random urine tests, which he had had examined by the lab at Saline Memorial Hospital. All the tests had come back clean.

CHAPTER 3. "THC INTOXICATION"

[1] Interview with Curtis Henry, Oct. 1996.

[2] *Arkansas Gazette,* Dec. 1988. These allegations were neither officially investigated nor proven.

[3] *Arkansas Times,* June 1990.

[4] Letter from J. T. Francisco, M.D., to Curtis Henry, Oct. 19, 1987.

[5] Francisco confirmed this methodology in an interview with the author, July 1998.

CHAPTER 4. HARMON AND GARRETT

[1] Garriott explained that the records he reviewed contained no reference to mass spectrometry data. He noted, "The term 'cannabinoid' is not a specific scientific term for any one compound, but can be one of a dozen or so components of the marijuana plant, or another dozen or so metabolites of these drugs that are formed in the human body. This is a critical point, since the finding of a particular cannabinoid, such as the major metabolite of delta-9-tetrahydrocannabinol [THC], in the blood or urine may have no relevance to the effects of the marijuana, as it may be present for a period of days to weeks after use of the drug."

[2] The *Benton Courier,* Feb. 17, 1988.

[3] Transcript of the Seventh Judicial District Prosecutor's Hearing, Feb. 18–21, 1988.

CHAPTER 5. EXHUMATIONS AND AUTOPSIES

[1] In 1998, Carol Pate confirmed the account given by Linda Ives of their meeting.

[2] The director of public safety was a former police officer named Tommy Robinson. After being elevated by Clinton to head the Department of Public Safety, Robinson became a highly controversial sheriff of Pulaski County, then served as a member of Congress.

[3] James Lee, spokesman for Attorney General Steve Clark, said the hiring "followed the color of law, if not the law itself." Clark, incidentally, was later convicted of fraud while in office.

[4] State representative Mike Todd of Paragould, who made the request, said Malak's rulings on the manner of death "tend to limit any other investigation" by local authorities. A sheriff's investigator in the case argued that at the time

the gun went off, the boy had been talking with a friend about his plans after graduation. "A kid talking about his future just doesn't commit suicide," the investigator noted in his objection to Malak's ruling. "This boy showed no tendencies of being suicidal. My investigation shows the boy had a happy home life and had no problems at school. It was just an accident."

[5] Some of the best reporting done on Malak, including the interview quoted here, was done by Bob Wells of the *Arkansas Gazette*.

[6] Specifically, the pathologists were to "conduct an independent peer review of the state medical examiner and the Office of Forensic Pathology of the state crime lab." The board voted to hire Dr. David Wiecking, chief medical examiner for the state of Virginia, and Dr. Russell Zumwalt, the assistant medical examiner for New Mexico, to conduct the peer review.

[7] The remark was made by Arkansas state senator Knox Nelson.

CHAPTER 6. A FINDING OF MURDER

[1] Dr. Fahmy Malak's testimony before the Saline County grand jury, May 11, 1988.

[2] Association director Cary Gaines said that fifty-four of Arkansas's seventy-five sheriffs had responded to the survey.

[3] Interview with Lieutenant Jay Campbell, Pulaski County Sheriff's Office, Jan. 1999.

[4] The hospital investigation is documented in Arkansas State Police files. The scandal and the grand jury that resulted were extensively reported in the *Benton Courier* throughout 1984. A subsequent report appeared in the *Houston Chronicle*, Nov. 27, 1985.

[5] Curtis Henry confirmed his refusal before the grand jury to disclose his daughter's whereabouts in an interview on Oct. 4, 1996. Without elaborating on who he thought had killed the boys, Curtis said, "I refused to tell the grand jury where my daughter was. I left the house to go to the grand jury, I told Marvelle that if I didn't come back, to call the TV, because I had no intention of telling the grand jury anything. I mean, if they killed the brother, are they going to let the sister walk?"

[6] No explanation was offered for Holladay's suspension. Arkansas's Freedom of Information Act excludes records contained in the personnel files of public employees.

[7] Statement by Cox to Arkansas State Police Investigator Don Birdsong, Oct. 17, 1988.

CHAPTER 7. KEITH McKASKLE'S MURDER

[1] Author's interview with Cathy Carty (Pearson) published in the *Arkansas Times*, Dec. 1992. This was the last time the former deputy agreed to discuss any

aspect of this story. When contacted again in 1996 and asked about the train-deaths case, Carty, the first person to object to the treatment of the deaths as accidental, said: "Nothing's going to be done, so I'm doing what everyone else around here has done. I've cut that night out of my life."

[2] These quotations are taken from an interview with Shane Smith conducted by investigators Dave Dillinger and Don Birdsong of the Arkansas State Police. The interview was conducted at the Benton Police Department on Nov. 12, 1988.

[3] Carty interview, *Arkansas Times*, Dec. 1991.

CHAPTER 8. DEATH TOLL MOUNTS

[1] William Crawford Horne, who was convicted of the 1982 beating death of David Michel of Little Rock, was sentenced to twenty years in prison. The conviction was later reversed.

[2] As it turned out, Govar ended up winning a conviction in the case in which Zimmerman was to testify. The subject of the investigation, a man Govar described as "a significant drug trafficker who operated on the Saline–Pulaski county line," was sentenced to sixteen and a half years in prison.

[3] Interview with the author, Nov. 1991.

[4] By way of comparison, in 1998, after a decade of dramatic growth, the total number of murders in Saline County was three.

[5] Frank Pilcher of North Little Rock was convicted and sentenced to life in prison for Jeff Rhodes's murder.

[6] Kenneth Kitler, who was at the time of the trial an inmate in the Arkansas Department of Correction, testified that Rick Cotton, Sr., of Alexander, had made the offer.

[7] Scott Sherill, a forensic serologist from the Arkansas Crime Laboratory, testified that many blood samples collected from the scene were not sufficient to make conclusive findings, other than that they were, indeed, blood, or, in some cases, human blood.

[8] Andrew Smith of Little Rock was brought to University Hospital on June 13, 1989, and was declared brain-dead by doctors the next day.

[9] Based on Little Rock Police Department detectives' files, June 20–23, 1989.

CHAPTER 9. THE GOVERNOR'S MOTHER

[1] Author interviews with members of Laura Lee Slayton's family, June 1997.

[2] From *Leading with My Heart,* written with James Morgan, Simon and Schuster, 1994.

[3] *Los Angeles Times,* May 19, 1992.

[4] Dr. William Schulte, as quoted by reporter Joe Nabbefeld in the *Arkansas Gazette,* March 24, 1991.

[5] Ibid.

[6] *Los Angeles Times,* May 19, 1992.

CHAPTER 10. INVESTIGATING OFFICIAL CORRUPTION

[1] Arkansas state police interview by Investigator Don Birdsong, July 14, 1988.

[2] Trooper Lainhart confirmed in an interview with the author that when he requested a copy of his report from the night of the deaths on the tracks, state police records clerks told him it was not in the file.

[3] "Parents Clear Son's Names," by Lane Beauchamp, in the *Kansas City Star,* April 1, 1990.

[4] At the time, Govar served as the U.S. attorney's lead trial lawyer for the Organized Crime Drug Enforcement Task Force, or OCDETF, in Arkansas.

[5] "Saline County Drug Case Stifled, Prosecutor Says," by Doug Thompson, in the *Arkansas Democrat,* Dec. 3, 1988.

[6] As noted in Chapter 9, Govar felt that the indictment of David Zimmerman on a year-old manslaughter charge was nothing more than an attempt to discredit Zimmerman and the testimony he was prepared to offer before the federal grand jury.

[7] Parts of this section are based on interviews with Assistant U.S. attorney Robert J. Govar, in May and Sept. 1997. Former U.S. Attorney Charles E. "Chuck" Banks has refused to discuss the case publicly.

[8] Ibid.

[9] The FBI sought funding for the investigation at a "Group Two" level. Group Two projects are usually considered long-term, they are generally funded for at least six months, and they require approval from the agency's Washington headquarters.

[10] While reading through the state police files, Linda learned that the FBI had offered laboratory assistance. In the file was a letter written in 1988, in the midst of the grand jury investigation, by Judge Cole to the FBI, in which the judge sought the agency's assistance. With that letter was another one from Don K. Pettus, the FBI's special agent in Little Rock. Pettus replied to Cole that he was "very aware" of the investigation into the deaths and that "as a matter of domestic police cooperation" he offered "the full forensic services of the FBI Laboratory and FBI Identification Division in Washington, D.C." to the Arkansas State Police, to help in that agency's investigation of the case. But there were no more letters; there seemed to have been no follow-up. There was nothing in the file to suggest that anyone had accepted the agency's offer.

[11] The memos, both of which were written by Govar to U.S. Attorney Chuck Banks and to two assistant U.S. attorneys, were dated Feb. 13, 1990, and March 29, 1990.

[12] Brightop presented her testimony on May 25, 1990, in a hearing before U.S. Magistrate Henry L. Jones, Jr. Criswell was facing charges relating to a drug deal that had taken place the previous March 8.

[13] The charge of aggravated robbery was in connection with an incident involving a woman who worked at a liquor store on Baseline Road. Callaway allegedly followed the woman to her home and robbed her.

CHAPTER 11. THE SALINE COUNTY UNDERWORLD

[1] Senator Max Howell represented Jacksonville, one of the larger cities in Arkansas, located in northeast Pulaski County. Governor Clinton, in his first term as governor, named Tommy Robinson, a former police officer from Jacksonville, as director of public safety. When the position of medical examiner became vacant, Robinson assumed the authority to approve the promotion of Dr. Fahmy Malak to the post. Although it was later determined that, by law, the Medical Examiner's Commission, and not Robinson, should have hired the new examiner, the lapse was not challenged in court, and Malak remained in office.

[2] Interview conducted by Robert Govar with Woodrow "Woody" May, Feb. 12, 1990.

[3] Interview with Scott Tracy Mattingly by Investigator Robert Gibbs of the Arkansas State Police.

[4] Interview conducted by Govar's task force, Aug. 31, 1989.

[5] Testimony of Cindy Boshears Tucker before the federal grand jury in Little Rock, Sept. 19, 1989.

[6] Statement of Cindy Boshears Tucker, as reported in Govar memos to U.S. Attorney Chuck Banks, Feb. 13 and March 29, 1990.

[7] From internal memos to U.S. Attorney Chuck Banks written by Robert Govar, Feb. 13 and March 29, 1990.

[8] Harmon's statement was reported by Doug Thompson of the *Arkansas Democrat*, June 15, 1990.

[9] Statement of Arkansas State Trooper Jeff Ramsey, as reported in Govar memos.

[10] State officials are required to investigate allegations of child abuse, including those from anonymous sources. Following a short investigation of Duffey, the Arkansas Department of Human Services, Division of Children and Family Services, notified her that social workers following up on the call had found "no credible evidence of abuse or neglect."

CHAPTER 12. NO CORRUPTION FOUND

[1] Interviews with Sharline Wilson, Feb. 9 and March 19, 1996.

[2] *Arkansas Court Bulletin,* Jan. 2, 1991.

[3] Garrett exhibited a similar ambivalence with regard to this book. He agreed twice to be interviewed, but despite repeated requests to set a date, never was interviewed.

[4] Author interview, May 9, 1997.

[5] Govar said the witnesses did not fail the polygraph on questions about which they were to testify before the grand jury, but on other unrelated matters. He argued unsuccessfully to his associates that this was not unusual since many people, especially those who had been involved in illegal activities, had aspects of their lives they wished to keep obscure.

[6] Benton attorney Ray Baxter represented Callaway. Baxter credited the jury's decision in large part to the fact that one of the witnesses who had identified Callaway as having planned the robbery—Callaway's former sister-in-law, Sherry Mullins—had also been quoted in Govar's memos as having alleged that deputy prosecutor Richard Garrett dealt drugs. Baxter introduced that evidence and then discredited Mullins's testimony when she was unable to identify Garrett in court.

[7] *Arkansas Times,* July 1991.

[8] Interview with author, May 1997.

[9] The trial of Ernest Lemons took place in the Garland County Courthouse on Mar. 30, 1991.

[10] Interview by AP reporter Ron Fournier, June 9, 1991.

[11] Harmon's tax trial was later rescheduled for Feb. 1992.

[12] The program, authorized under the Anti–Drug Abuse Act of 1988 and signed into law by President Reagan, allowed for nine U.S. districts to conduct extensive drug testing before trial and after conviction to study the correlation between drug use and conduct. The other districts were in New York, Michigan, Florida, Minnesota, Nevada, North Dakota, and Texas. When the pilot program ended, in spring 1991, Congress told the participating districts that they could continue the practice if they wished. In a related effort, the U.S. Justice Department financed programs in twenty-four cities to conduct routine drug testing in their courts. Among the cities that participated in that program were Milwaukee; Phoenix; Tucson; Portland, Ore.; and Los Angeles. Those programs were modeled after one begun in Washington, D.C., in 1984. It required that every person charged with a crime be tested for drugs before seeing a judge.

[13] Sources identified the staff members as Field Wasson, Clinton's chief legal counsel.

[14] Nine months after Malak's resignation, he was offered a job as chief medical examiner in Guam. However, that offer, which would have paid $160,000 a year, was soon withdrawn. "The cloud of controversy over Malak outweighed any consideration of him for the job," Guam's *Pacific Daily News* quoted Elizabeth Barrett-Anderson, attorney general and head of the search committee, as saying. She added that Malak "seemed to have the background, but he may find himself in a credibility maze while being cross-examined in the courtroom." The paper reported that Malak had stated on his résumé that he held an associate professor's post at the University of Arkansas for Medical Sciences. Malak remained at his $70,000-a-year post at the Arkansas Health Department.

CHAPTER 13. WIDENING THE CONTEXT

[1] The paper also undertook to reexamine Malak's ruling in the death of Susie Deer, the teenager who had died ten years earlier after a rock-throwing incident. The *Democrat-Gazette* sought a professional review of that ruling by sending records from the case to two out-of-state pathologists, Dr. Vincent DiMaio of San Antonio and Dr. Michael A. Graham of St. Louis. Both concurred with Malak's ruling.

[2] The article, titled "The Boys on the Tracks" and written by this author, outlined the motorcycle wreck of Keith Coney in the summer of 1988; the stabbing of Keith McKaskle in November of that year; the shotgun slaying of Greg Collins, who was subpoenaed to appear before the grand jury, in January 1989; the shooting, burning, and dismemberment of Jeff Rhodes the following April, who had told relatives he had information about the boys' deaths; the shooting of Richard Winters in the aborted robbery at the gambling house three months later; and the shotgun death of Jordan Ketelsen, a convicted drug dealer in June 1990. Ketelsen's death was ruled a suicide. No autopsy was performed and Ketelsen's body was cremated. An eighth man connected to the grand jury, Daniel "Boonie" Bearden, is missing and presumed to be dead.

[3] Rep. Bob Fairchild of Fayetteville was the author of legislation to reform the Crime Laboratory Board.

[4] Dixie G. Martin, reporting in the *Arkansas Democrat-Gazette*, June 22, 1992.

[5] Besides Cole, the two judges supporting Harmon were Circuit/Chancery Judge Phillip Shirron and Chancellor Robert Garrett. Attorney Ted Boswell represented Harmon.

[6] The investigation of one such network, with roots in Lexington, Kentucky, is chronicled in *The Bluegrass Conspiracy*, by Sally Denton; Avon, 1990.

[7] Author interview with Pat Matrisciana, Dec., 1997.

[8] Matrisciana reports that the videotape sold close to a half million copies. A check in 1997 of university libraries in central Arkansas and of all public

libraries in the state turned up not a single copy of *The Clinton Chronicles*, despite the production's Arkansas focus and its widespread circulation.

CHAPTER 14. BARRY SEAL AND MENA

[1] Hubbell's father-in-law, Seth Ward, owned Park-on-Meter, a company in Russellville, Arkansas, which, besides making parking meters, was alleged to have made components of chemical and biological weapons used by the Contras, as well as special equipment for C-130 transport planes. These allegations, which have not been proven, and that Ward has denied, were first reported by Alexander Cockburn in his "Beat the Devil" column in *The Nation,* April 6, 1992.

[2] The article, by Carrie Rengers, also reported that the video charged that Hubbell's law firm "was the only firm handling ADFA loans, even though five other firms in the state were more qualified in bond structuring and applications." In fact, Rengers noted, the Rose firm did handle a large number of ADFA's issues, but five other Arkansas law firms, along with several others from outside the state, also had served as bond counsel for the agency, and one of the Arkansas firms did more business with ADFA than Rose.

[3] Author's interview with Crittendon, as reported in the *Arkansas Times,* May 1992.

[4] Although many investigative records pertaining to Seal remain secret, some have come to light and been widely disseminated. The information outlined here is drawn from the investigations of U.S. Treasury agent William C. Duncan and Arkansas State Police investigator Russell T. Welch, and from Seal's own testimony describing his operation.

[5] This and other statements from Duncan are from depositions taken from him under oath as part of a joint investigation by Arkansas attorney general Winston Bryant and U.S. congressman Bill Alexander on June 21, 1991.

[6] Details about Seal's organization are drawn from his 1985 testimony before the President's Commission on Organized Crime and from records of the Louisiana State Police.

[7] The statement, by Richard Gregorie, a former assistant U.S. attorney who later developed Seal as a federal drug informant, was reported in the *Arkansas Democrat,* Dec. 3, 1989.

[8] From Seal's testimony in a 1985 federal drug trial in Las Vegas, Nevada.

[9] Based on a teletype sent from the Little Rock office of the FBI to the Bureau's New Orleans office, which was released by the FBI but heavily redacted.

[10] Real-estate agent Lib Carlisle was the head of the Arkansas Democratic party. In December 1996 he told the author, "I didn't know drugs were involved at all. When we found out there was a problem, we pulled out."

[11] Author interview with Norma Gilland, April 1996.

[12] The country would later learn that during the same month that the photos were released, in July 1984, CIA Director William Casey introduced North to the Contra leaders, reassuring them that support would continuc and that North would be their contact. From then on, North reported directly to Casey and to Robert C. "Bud" McFarlane, Reagan's national security advisor.

[13] Bunn was not a typical city narcotics officer. Retired from a career in military intelligence, he was inducted into the Military Intelligence Corps Hall of Fame at Fort Huachuca, Arizona, in 1992.

[14] As if to confirm Hutchinson's assessment, a few months after his speech to the Lions, two drug traffickers were charged in Little Rock with running what prosecutors called "one of the largest cocaine-trafficking rings ever cracked in the United States." The defense attorney had unsuccessfully offered what seemed the astonishing defense that the men were smuggling under a special dispensation from the U.S. government because, in addition to their drug enterprise, they were spying on Marxist groups in Colombia for the CIA. The defense failed and the men were convicted.

[15] Deandra Seale, Barry Seal's secretary, later testified that on the day of Camp's disappearance, he and Seal were to have traveled in Seal's Lear jet from Baton Rouge to Mena and on to Miami. But when they arrived at the Baton Rouge airport, she said, they found that Seal's jet had been stolen. According to the secretary, Seal sent Camp to Mena in one of his other planes, while he caught a commercial flight to Miami.

[16] Fred Hampton of Rich Mountain Aviation said Seal also told him that he was working for the CIA. "He had probably been coming here for a year or more before we started hearing the stories about him," Hampton told the *Arkansas Gazette* in June 1988. "We approached him about it and he said he wasn't doing anything illegal and, besides, he was working with the CIA. He said that on more than one occasion."

[17] During the summer of 1985, Seal testified against Norman Saunders, the prime minister of the Turks and Caicos Islands, and other officials. Seal had recorded a meeting in which he said Saunders had accepted a bribe to allow the islands to be used as a stopping point for drug planes. Seal himself had used the islands in the early 1980s.

[18] Ironically, only two months earlier, in August, U.S. Attorney General Edwin Meese and DEA chief John C. Lawn had made a much-publicized trip to Arkansas, where they announced the inauguration of a federal crackdown on home-grown marijuana. At a press conference held in Fort Smith, instead of the more typical site of the state's capitol, they vowed that Operation Delta-9, as it was called, would continue until every known patch of marijuana in the nation had been searched out and destroyed.

[19] Rep. Bill Hughes, a Democrat from New Jersey, said after Seal's death that the smuggler had been one of the most significant undercover drug investigators in U.S. history and that a politically motivated leak had cost him his life. "We've never had, in the history of enforcement, an opportunity to reach that level of the cartel," Hughes said. "In addition to that, Barry Seal was dead. That was the net result of the leak to the press. It was a disaster."

[20] Besides Guste, those present at the seminar and questioning Seal in a closed-door session afterward, were Jack Lawn, administrator of the DEA; William Van Raab, commander of U.S. Customs; Admiral James Gracey, commander of the U.S. Coast Guard; Howard B. Gehring, director of the National Narcotics Border Interdiction System; Lt. General R. Dean Tice, director of the Defense Department's Task Force on Drug Enforcement; Paul Gorman, former U.S. Army general and military commander in the Caribbean; and U.S. Congressman Glenn English, D-Oklahoma.

[21] In 1992 Guste completed his last term as Louisiana attorney general. When asked about his letter of six years earlier to Meese, Guste said that the U.S. attorney general had assured him that the investigation he had requested would be conducted. But, Guste added, if such an investigation had been undertaken, the results of it were never revealed. He said, "There was no public explanation ever given."

[22] The *Wall Street Journal* later reported that federal prosecutors said they never were able to confirm the identity of Frederico Vaughan and that the "military airfield" where Reagan said Seal had landed was actually a civilian airfield elsewhere in Central America.

CHAPTER 15. INCURIOUS IN ARKANSAS

[1] The agency spokesman was Paul Nirdlinger.

[2] Roger, a part-time musician, did miscellaneous odd jobs for the bond dealer, including work as a driver, but the relationship also had personal overtones. A few months before Roger's arrest, Lasater had helped the governor's brother out of what Roger described as "deep trouble" by loaning him $8,000 to pay off a cocaine debt. Such largesse was common for Lasater. At one time he reportedly loaned $300,000 in cash to Kentucky's governor John Y. Brown, and on yet another occasion, by his own account, he had loaned $200,000 to Don Walker, the former governor of Illinois.

[3] Clinton's campaign treasurer was L. W. "Bill" Clark of Hot Springs. His daughter Missy A. Clark had worked in the governor's office before going to work for Thomasson in Lasater's organization. According to the *Arkansas Democrat*, Oct. 4, 1986, Lasater hired Clark's son, Lawrence W. Clark IV, as a trainee in August, two months before Lasater's indictment.

[4] After Clinton's election as president, Proctor, who was Chuck Banks's predecessor in the office, went on to become head of the Justice Department's Office of International Affairs.

[5] *Arkansas Democrat,* Nov. 21, 1986.

[6] Interview by FBI special agent Eugene L. Crouch, Oct. 17, 1986.

[7] Author interview with Wayne Jordan, spokesman for the Arkansas State Police, Feb. 1997.

[8] From an article by Richard Ben Cramer, Aug. 16, 1992.

[9] As reported in a three-part series titled "The Barry Seal/Mena Connection," by Michael Haddigan, in the *Arkansas Gazette,* beginning June 26, 1988.

[10] From the 1991 deposition of Duncan by Arkansas attornery general Bryant and U.S. Representative Alexander.

[11] Duncan's boss, N. Paul Whitmore, who was chief of the IRS criminal investigation division in Little Rock at the time, was present during the session and heard the lawyers' advice. He supported Duncan's account. Both men reported that they had taken and passed polygraph examinations regarding the incident.

[12] The Freedom of Information requests had languished unanswered by the FBI for three years. Federal law in effect at the time they were made stipulated that a response be issued within ten days of the requests' submission.

[13] Author interview, Dec. 1991.

[14] Reporters Linda Satter and Larry Rhodes.

[15] *Unclassified,* Feb.–March 1992.

[16] The article by Richard Behar, published Apr. 20, 1992, examined the story of Terry Reed, who has claimed that he was recruited by North to train Contra air crews, partly at Mena. Reed sued *Time* for libel over the article. Reed tells his story in a book he co-wrote with John Cummings titled *Compromised: Clinton, Bush and the CIA,* S.P.I. Books, 1994.

[17] Sarah McClendon's *Washington Report,* March 9, 1992.

CHAPTER 16. THE FBI ENTERS THE CASE

[1] Author interview, May 9, 1997.

[2] Federal officials would not answer questions about the Henry-and-Ives investigation. Accounts of FBI agents' statements are thus necessarily one-sided, as recalled by Linda Ives and Jean Duffey.

[3] In an interview with this author at about the same time, Bryant outlined a similar position. He said that since the statute of limitations had expired on the alleged drug-trafficking and money-laundering crimes, there was little point in discussing them.

[4] The committee's final report, titled "Drugs, Law Enforcement and Foreign Policy," was published in Dec. 1998.

[5] From Ivins's syndicated column for the *Fort Worth Star-Telegram,* Dec. 31, 1992.

[6] *Albuquerque Journal,* Sept. 20, 1994. Gleghorn added that he did not believe that Proctor, who had since moved to a post in the Justice Department's Office of International Affairs, had been "soft-shoeing" the Lasater investigation or that Clinton had attempted to influence it. Nonetheless, the paper quoted unidentified federal agents as complaining that the investigation had not examined Lasater's financial dealings as fully as required.

[7] Interview by the author with Agent William Payne.

[8] Kurrack had produced a daily television talk show called *Among Friends.*

[9] Brown was put in contact with "Joe Evans" by Scott Wheeler, a freelance reporter in Denver who at the time was also doing some work for Matrisciana.

[10] Author interview, Feb. 1998.

CHAPTER 17. STOLEN FROM THE EVIDENCE LOCKER

[1] As reported by the author, Feb. 10, 1995.

[2] In Arkansas, police do not need for the victim of an assault to be willing to press charges.

[3] As reported by Rodney Bowers in the *Arkansas Democrat-Gazette*, Jan. 4, 1995.

[4] In the months preceding the hospital scandal, Carlisle was a member of the group that was working with E. F. Black, the administrator of Saline Memorial Hospital, to acquire an option on the property that was expected to be the site of the planned new hospital.

[5] Sally Denton and Roger Morris wrote a lengthy piece about Seal that was scheduled to run in the *Washington Post* in Jan. 1995. But charging repeated delays by the editors there, the writers pulled the piece from the *Post,* resubmitting it to *Penthouse* magazine, where it was finally published.

[6] Soon after closing the investigation into Harmon, Elmendorf resigned as Benton's police chief to take a job as chief of the security detail that patrols the Arkansas state capitol. When Elmendorf's successor conducted an inventory of the department's evidence locker, he found that approximately $4,000 in cash that had been confiscated in a 1992 drug raid was missing. Harmon promised to have the disappearance investigated.

[7] The former inmate who filed the report was Doyce G. "Bo" Ross of Hot Spring County.

[8] Interview with Govar, March 1998.

[9] Author interview with Kurrack, Feb. 1998.

CHAPTER 18. "JUST A NUTCASE"

[1] Funding for the task force was just under a quarter million dollars per year.

[2] According to Bowers's report, the cases involved men arrested on May 13, 1993, and charged with possession of a pound of cocaine; two Mexican men charged with possessing "more than ten pounds" of marijuana; a man charged on June 30, 1993, with delivery of "a quantity of cocaine"; and another man charged on March 1, 1993, with possessing "more than thirty pounds of marijuana." Only one of the men had posted bond, though all had been released.

[3] The circuit clerk was Jim Crone. Authorities said his office was not a target of the investigation.

[4] *Arkansas Times,* Jan. 5, 1996.

[5] At the time, Lynch served on the national board of the American Civil Liberties Union.

[6] The *Benton Courier,* Jan. 31, 1996.

[7] Author interview, May 1996.

[8] Feb. 5, 1996.

[9] At the time, Linda was not certain what a civil lawsuit might entail or against whom she might bring the action. If enough evidence could be gathered, she hoped to file a wrongful death lawsuit against those who she believed had been involved in the killings and against officials for conspiracy.

[10] Author interview, June 19, 1996.

[11] Harmon was represented in this proceeding by Robert Ginnaven III.

CHAPTER 19. PREFERENTIAL TREATMENT

[1] Morrison had written, for example, that former Arkansas Attorney General Steve Clark had been run out of office for having dared to oppose Bill Clinton, but the fact was that Clark was removed from office after having been convicted of fraud. Morrison also implied that the *Democrat-Gazette* editors were Clinton apologists, when local readers knew that the paper had not even endorsed Clinton for president.

[2] Duffey was once again traveling freely in Arkansas. After Harmon's departure as prosecutor, she had filed a petition in district court seeking that the warrant for her arrest be withdrawn. Barbara Webb, by then the new prosecuting attorney, had not opposed the petition and it had been approved.

[3] After Harmon's resignation on July 10, 1996, the task of appointing a replacement for Harmon fell to Arkansas Governor Jim Guy Tucker, who had himself recently been found guilty in federal court of mail fraud and conspiracy charges arising from the Whitewater investigation. Tucker resigned from the office of governor on July 15, ten days after Harmon surrendered his post as prosecuting attorney.

[4] After his defeat for reelection as sheriff, Steed had gotten a job with the state, assessing jail conditions.

[5] The other man in the car was convicted in 1996, in Judge Cole's court, of possessing methamphetamine with intent to deliver. He was sentenced to life plus thirteen years in prison and fined $65,000.

[6] The defendant was charged with manslaughter, possession of methamphetamine, and possession of drug paraphernalia following a traffic accident in which the boy was killed. The case languished for almost two years, by the end of which Harmon had never brought the case to trial. The victim's mother told the *Democrat-Gazette* that she had called Harmon's office repeatedly in the months after her son's death to urge that the defendant be tried. On each occasion, she said, Harmon or one of his staff had assured her that, though a court date had not yet been set, they would not let the accused get off. After Harmon resigned as prosecutor, the victim's stepfather again called the office to check on the status of the case. This time, he said, a man told him that the case had been dismissed because it had not gone to trial in time.

[7] Interview with radio station KWHN.

[8] Author article, July 5, 1996.

[9] Taken from testimony given on Oct. 23, 1996, in a hearing "on the allegations of CIA ties to Nicaraguan Contra rebels and crack cocaine in American cities" before the U.S. Senate Select Committee on Intelligence, Senator Arlen Specter, chairman.

CHAPTER 20. SUSPICIONS CONFIRMED

[1] Author's interview with Weiss, April 1998.

[2] Weiss confirmed that Morrison's published account of this exchange was "accurate."

[3] McCurry said that, having been commissioned by Fabiani, the report had been written by Christopher Lehane.

[4] "The White House Conspiracy," unsigned editorial, Jan. 13, 1997.

[5] "Mysterious Mena: CIA Discloses, Leach Disposes," Jan. 29, 1997.

[6] According to Weiss, "Thirty-five of those deaths came in one swoop: the crash of the former Commerce Secretary Ron Brown's plane in Croatia last year. Another person on the list is a Resolution Trust Corporation investigator who leapt to his death from an apartment complex in Arlington, Virginia." Also frequently cited on the lists, Weiss wrote, is the unsolved murder of Jerry Parks, a Little Rock private investigator who had provided private security for Clinton's 1992 campaign. Parks was gunned down in Sept. 1993, while driving through a wooded area on the outskirts of Little Rock.

[7] From "Gore Looks Like a Stooge in Those Huang Papers," *New York Observer,* April 28, 1997.

[8] C-SPAN, *Washington Journal,* Feb. 2, 1997.

[9] The final draft of the indictment was filed in U.S. District Court in Little Rock on May 14, 1997.

[10] April 15, 1997.

[11] Parts of the reporting on Harmon's trial are drawn from articles that appeared in the *Arkansas Democrat-Gazette* under the bylines of Linda Friedlieb and Joe Stumpe.

[12] Stripling, the assistant U.S. attorney, interviewed in April 1998, said he did not "have a good recollection" of why the indictment had gone back no further than August 1991. "I'm sure we had statute of limitations problems," he said. He noted that RICO cases can extend back ten years, but added that some of the other crimes had five-year limitations. In general, he said, he did not wish to discuss Harmon's case, out of fear that he would inadvertently disclose information that had been revealed only to the grand jury.

EPILOGUE

[1] Reasoner also ordered Harmon to pay $16,000 in restitution to victims of the two extortion schemes and to pay a $25,000 fine.

[2] 18 U.S.C. 1511, 1951, 1962, and others.

[3] The circumstances surrounding Elmendorf's firing were reported March 25, 1999, in the *Arkansas Democrat-Gazette.*

[4] The depositions for the civil lawsuit, No. 83-6026, filed in U.S. District Court in the western district of Arkansas, were conducted on Sept. 1 and 2, 1983, in Hot Springs.

[5] The others are Iowa, Maryland, Rhode Island, and South Dakota.

[6] "Inspector: CIA Kept Ties with Alleged Traffickers," by Walter Pincus, March 17, 1998.

[7] "CIA Worked with Suspected Drug Traffickers, Report Admits," by James Risen, July 17, 1998.

[8] A Citizen's Guide on Using the Freedom of Information Act and the Privacy Act of 1974 to Request Government Records; First Report by the Committee on Government Reform and Oversight, March 20, 1997.

[9] A similar request for assistance was submitted to Rep. Asa Hutchinson, because of Hutchinson's former role as U.S. attorney for the western district of Arkansas, during part of the time that Mena was under investigation, and because of Hutchinson's outspokenness about the need to curtail drug trafficking. In Jan. 1998 he responded that he had contacted the FBI concerning the request and would "be back in touch" when he heard from the agency. As of Sept. 1998, no more had been heard from him.

INDEX